PORTUGAL

NATIONAL GEOGRAPHIC
TRAVELER

PORTUGAL

by Fiona Dunlop
photography by Tino Soriano

National Geographic
Washington, D.C.

CONTENTS

Pages 2–3: Rock formations of the Ponta da Piedade, south of Lagos, in the Algarve
Opposite: Shops and outdoor cafés line pedestrianized Rua Augusta, in Lisbon's Baixa district.

TRAVELING WITH EYES OPEN

Alert travelers go with a purpose and leave with a benefit. If you travel responsibly, you can help support wildlife conservation, historic preservation, and cultural enrichment in the places you visit. You can enrich your own travel experience as well.

To be a geo-savvy traveler:

- Recognize that your presence has an impact on the places you visit.

- Spend your time and money in ways that sustain local character. (Besides, it's more interesting that way.)

- Value the destination's natural and cultural heritage.

- Respect the local customs and traditions.

- Express appreciation to local people about things you find interesting and unique to the place: its nature and scenery, music and food, historic villages and buildings.

- Vote with your wallet: Support the people who support the place, patronizing businesses that make an effort to celebrate and protect what's special there. Seek out local shops, restaurants, and inns. Use tour operators who love their home—who love taking care of it and showing it off. Avoid businesses that detract from the character of the place.

- Enrich yourself, taking home memories and stories to tell, knowing that you have contributed to the preservation and enhancement of the destination.

That is the type of travel now called geotourism, defined as "tourism that sustains or enhances the geographical character of a place—its environment, culture, aesthetics, heritage, and the well-being of its residents." To learn more about geotourism, visit National Geographic's Center for Sustainable Destinations at *nationalgeographic.com/maps/geotourism.*

PORTUGAL

ABOUT THE AUTHORS & THE PHOTOGRAPHER

Author **Fiona Dunlop's** peripatetic life has led her from her native Australia to an upbringing in London, and subsequent jobs in continental Europe followed by a return to London. During 15 years spent in Paris, she was strongly involved in the arts before concentrating on journalism. Since then, she has written for numerous international magazines and national newspapers. She has spent long research periods in developing countries working on travel guides to India, Indonesia, Singapore and Malaysia, Vietnam, Mexico, Costa Rica, and southern Africa. More recent publications include *In the Asian Style* (on Asian design) and *New Tapas,* an illustrated book on Spain's tapas bar tradition. In between her more exotic travels, Dunlop has regularly visited Spain to write articles and books, including *National Geographic Traveler: Spain.*

Emma Rowley wrote the updates and sidebars for this edition. With a university degree in Spanish and Portuguese, Rowley moved from her native United Kingdom to Portugal and spent nine years working for an Oxford-based travel company, managing trips in rural Spain, Portugal, and the Azores. She has since turned her skills to travel writing, contributing to more than a dozen different guidebooks and related articles.

Born and raised in Barcelona, Spain, **Tino Soriano** divides his work between photojournalism and travel photography. He has received a First Prize from the World Press Photo Foundation as well as awards from UNESCO, Fujifilm, and Fotopres. In addition to Portugal, since 1988 Soriano has photographed in Spain, France, Italy, Sicily, Scotland, and South Africa on assignments for National Geographic. His work has also appeared in *Geo, Merian, Der Spiegel, Paris Match, La Vanguardia, El País,* and other major magazines. Soriano likes to write, and he has published *El Futuro Existe* (a story about children with cancer); *Travel Photography* and *Beats From a Hospital* (both in Spanish); and *Dalí, 1904–2004.* He has also photographed for the following guides in the National Geographic Traveler series: Sicily, Madrid, and Florence & Tuscany.

CHARTING YOUR TRIP

Most travelers to Portugal visit Lisbon, Porto, the Algarve, and possibly Madeira, but you should also explore some of the hinterland, with its dramatic scenery of mountains, cork forests, and rivers; delve into its history and cultural heritage, visiting castles, monasteries, and medieval villages; and sit back to enjoy its gastronomy and fine wines. This destination has become a favorite of visitors from all over the world.

How to Get Around

Portugal's main cities of Lisbon and Porto are best explored on foot, as many sites are within a short distance of one other. Be sure to take comfortable, sturdy shoes, as both cities are hilly, many of their streets cobbled and slippery in wet weather. Where transport is necessary, both cities have efficient metro systems as well as not-to-be-missed historic trams.

For north-south travel within the country, the excellent express train service (Alfa Pendular; see Travelwise p. 235) runs between Porto in the north and Faro in the south, through Coimbra and Lisbon. Other cities are covered by frequently stopping, intercity connections; regional trains meander along some beautifully scenic routes, but can be painfully slow. To reach more remote areas, a rental car is indispensable, giving you the freedom to explore at your own pace. These are best booked online before arrival (see Travelwise pp. 234–235).

Admission Costs

The €–€€€€€ scale used in this guidebook delineates entry fees into attractions in Euros:

€ = Under €5
€€ = €5–€10
€€€ = €10–€20
€€€€ = €20–€30
€€€€€ = Over €30

If You Only Have a Week

Immerse yourself in the bustle of Lisbon life before discovering some of Portugal's other prominent attractions. The suggested itinerary keeps up a brisk pace; for a more relaxed trip simply omit some of the recommendations.

Begin your trip by spending **Days 1** and **2** exploring Lisbon's treasure trove of sites. Hop aboard a tram up to the sprawling Castelo de São Jorge, wander the warren of Alfama streets, and ride the train along the river to

■ **The Marquês de Pombal was responsible for much of Lisbon's orderly appearance.**

Belém, where you'll find a cluster of worthy museums and the magnificent Jerónimos monastery. Don't forget to take a culture break for a coffee and delicious *pastel de nata* (custard tart) in the Pasteis de Belém shop. Next day catch the metro to the Gulbenkian, in the north of the city (São Sebastião metro stop) to see this museum's breathtaking art collection; be sure not to miss its exquisite Lalique display. Walk back down the Avenida da Liberdade to the Baixa and Chiado for a look at the historic shops and experience an evening of fado music at a restaurant in the Bairro Alto.

Day 3, board a train to Sintra, 19 miles (30 km) to the northwest, for a day trip devoted to palaces and gardens. Admire the 16th-century polychrome, Mujédar tiles in the Palácio Nacional de Sintra and catch the bus up to the Pena Palace for the amazing views. If you have time, visit the eccentric Quinta da Regaleira with its mystical well of initiation. End your day by satisfying your sweet tooth with one of Sintra's famed *queijadas* (cheesecakes).

On **Day 4,** pick up a car and drive an hour north to the hill town of Óbidos, walk the ramparts, and pick up a chocolate cup filled with *ginjinha* (cherry liqueur) before continuing north to the monasteries of Alcobaça, 25 miles (40 km) away, and Batalha, 12 miles (20 km) farther, both of which are World Heritage sites. Pause to appreciate the mastery of the detailed stonework. After taking in the grandeur of the monasteries, drive an hour north to spend the night in Coimbra, 55 miles (88 km) from Batalha.

Spend the morning of **Day 5** touring the Universidade de Coimbra, the highlight being without a doubt the ornate baroque library. After lunch, continue north to Porto, 75 miles (120 km) away by car. Stretch your legs in the evening with a walk around the atmospheric city center. From the bottom of the Avenida dos Aliados walk over to Rua Santa Catarina for a coffee at the renowned Café Majestic before strolling back up the hill to the Torre dos Clérigos. The next day, **Day 6,** cross the river to Gaia and visit the port wine lodges, taking time to savor a glass of port on the riverbank. Return to the Ribeira to wander the streets and visit the main sites, especially the church of São

Visitor Information

If possible, find out as much as you can about Portugal before you arrive by checking out some of the following websites: *visitportugal.com, visitlisboa.com, porto turismo.pt,* and *visitalgarve.pt;* or for those with limited mobility, *accessible portugal.com* and *sath.org.*

Once in Portugal, there are many places to pick up tourist information.

If the airport is your point of entry, make use of the information desks usually situated in the arrivals hall: **Lisbon Airport,** tel 218 450 660; **Porto** and **Faro Airport,** tel 289 818 582. Beyond the airports, most towns have a *posto de turismo* (tourist office), where you can find out about local attractions and someone usually speaks English.

Cultural Etiquette

Portugal is still a traditional country where value is placed on good manners, though less so by younger generations. The Portuguese address one another in the formal *você* form of the verb, reserving the informal *tu* for close friends; and they use formal titles such as *senhor, senhora* and *Doutor, Doutora* for university-educated professionals. Dress codes are also more formal; men should not walk around town bare-chested, and modesty is appreciated when visiting churches and other religious buildings.

Francisco with its riotous gilded interior, the Palácio da Bolsa, and the Cathedral.

Day 7, return to Lisbon, located 195 miles (300 km) south, stopping off a little over halfway there at Tomar to see the massive Convento de Cristo, the former headquarters of the Knights Templar, with its mix of architectural styles.

If You Have More Time

If you can spend another week in Portugal, instead of returning to Lisbon via Tomar, set **Day 7** aside for a tour of historic Guimarães and the Douro Valley. Leave Porto and head northeast to Guimarães (35 miles/55 km away) to spend the morning exploring its medieval center and 10th-century castle. After lunch, drive south to Amarante (40 minutes), picking up the N101 to cross the Serra do Marrão; drop down through fabulous terraced vineyards to Mesão Frio; then follow the north bank of the Douro to Pinhão. Treat yourself to a night at the Vintage House (see Travelwise p. 243). Pause frequently during the afternoon to admire the views.

On **Day 8,** travel a couple of hours south to Guarda and the rugged Serra da Estrela mountain range. En route, stop in Viseu to visit the Cathedral with its baroque gilded altarpiece and in Celorico da Beira to see the necropolis of São Gens. Spend the night in Guarda, Portugal's highest town.

Spend **Day 9** exploring the Serra da Estrela before continuing south to the Alentejo. Start by driving south to Belmonte, then west up into the mountains to Caldas de Manteigas (about 90 minutes away). Stretch your legs and try some of the local, tasty mountain cheese, then, back in your car, meander south 20 minutes through the

Best Times to Visit

Portugal is an agreeable year-round destination, with long warm summers stretching from May through September and relatively mild winters in much of the country. Winter runs November to March. The north and the Serra da Estrela region can get snowfall on high ground, while Trás-os-Montes usually experiences the lowest temperatures; however, even the Alentejo can feel bitterly cold when the northern winds blow across the plains. The winter months also bring the highest rainfall, but in the Minho area, showers can occur at any time of year.

The highest summer temperatures occur in the interior of the Alentejo and in the Algarve, where July and August temperatures frequently hit 95°F (35°C). July and August are peak family holiday times at the beach resorts, which pushes prices up, so you may prefer to avoid these months.

Spring and fall are, on the whole, the best times to visit Portugal. Crowds are nonexistent and prices low. Offshore, Madeira offers a year-round temperate climate and attracts many visitors during the winter, especially at New Year's, when a thousand fireworks light up Funchal Bay.

■ Horses and riders alike come looking their best for the annual horse festival in the town of Golegã.

stunning, Zêzere glacial valley to Torre, Portugal's highest point. In the afternoon, travel 102 miles (164 km) south to the fortified hill town of Castelo de Vide.

The morning of **Day 10,** wander the labyrinthine streets and Jewish quarter of Castelo de Vide and walk the impregnable ramparts of the nearby mountaintop village of Marvão. In the afternoon, drive south to Estremoz on rural back roads. The drive takes about two hours, but the journey can be broken for a coffee at the Pousada de Flor da Rosa, formerly the 14th-century headquarters of the Knights of Malta, or for a visit to the Lusitanian horse stud farm of Alter do Chão. This should leave you a couple of hours to explore Estremoz before dark—depending on the time of year. Stay the night in Estremoz, at the palatial Pousada de Rainha Santa Isabel.

On **Day 11,** drive 29 miles (46 km) down the IP2 to Évora and take the day to visit its Roman temple, aqueduct, and churches before watching the world go by from a sidewalk café in the Praça Giraldo. The more active can pre-book a bike tour of the Neolithic remains in the surrounding area.

At the start of **Day 12,** take the N254 south for 50 minutes to Alvito, a town typical of the Alentejo. Continue west, cross-country toward the salt marshes and rice fields of Alcácer do Sal, then on to Comporta and the Tróia Resort at the tip of the peninsula, some two hours away; along the way, note the wealth of birdlife. Stop for a late grilled-fish lunch at any roadside restaurant and take a walk along the pristine Tróia beaches. Sleep at the Tróia Resort or cross to Setúbal on the car ferry and stay at one of the hotels in town. Dedicate **Day 13** to the beach, be it on the Tróia Peninsula or along the magnificent Arrábida coast, west of Setúbal. If on the Arrábida coast, stop for lunch on the sea front in Sesimbra; the fish is superb. Return to Lisbon at the end of the day (50 minutes from Setúbal), and then back home on **Day 14.**

If you've still more time, cap your trip with a long weekend on Madeira island. It's a short flight from Lisbon, and the isle's subtropical climate and amazing scenery are worth it. Plan to visit the botanical gardens, stand on Cabo Girão, and drive the northern corniche; take some sturdy shoes to walk the *levadas*.

HISTORY & CULTURE

■ An ivory Portuguese soldier on
a mission for God and king
■ Opposite: Azulejo tiles depicting
fruit pickers

PORTUGAL TODAY

Clinging to the western edge of Europe, this small country encompasses an unexpectedly broad and seductive spectrum—from stunning, varied landscapes to a multilayered past, majestic monuments, beautiful beaches and islands, top golf courses, succulent regional food, and excellent wines.

Portugal is most definitely not pretentious. Reputedly reserved, the Portuguese are in fact a warm, independent-minded, polyglot people—so all the more excuse to get to know them. Surfers and sunbathers adore the 530-mile-long (850 km) Atlantic coast, which starkly contrasts with the rugged "mountains of the star" (Serra da Estrela), throbbing nightclubs of Lisbon, the medieval hill towns and castles, the stunning terraces of the Douro Valley, the evocative baroque gardens, and the sharp contemporary architecture. Add to this a variety of accommodations, from castles and manor houses to designer hotels, quaint village guesthouses, and

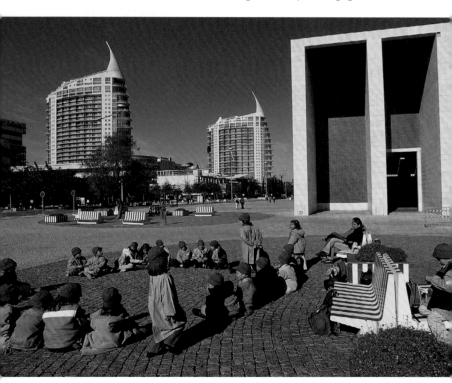

Schoolchildren love Lisbon's Parque das Nações, a high-tech waterfront development.

seaside villas, and you have the makings of a near-perfect holiday destination. Wonderfully unspoiled as of yet, Portugal cannot fail to seduce.

New Portugal

António de Oliveira Salazar's dictatorship (1932–1968) marked a dark period in Portuguese history when social, cultural, and economic life hit an all-time low. Then the 1974 revolution and the 1986 entry into the European Economic Community— now the European Union—brought a radical change in direction and mood, setting off a socioeconomic roll that continues today, despite a still struggling economy. A rigid society frozen in the 19th century was transformed into a dynamic one in harmony with the rest of Europe.

The surge in activity included an ambitious privatization program: More than a hundred state enterprises were sold in a decade. As growth accelerated, European subsidies brought new investment in agriculture and industry.

> **A rigid society frozen in the 19th century was transformed into a dynamic one in harmony with the rest of Europe.**

The modernizing momentum of the 1990s fully realized its impact when Portugal hosted Euro 2004, the European soccer championship and Portugal's biggest ever sporting event. Spectators from all over the world saw a remodeled nation of spanking new architecture, six-lane highways, impressive railways, shining stadiums, and high-rise hotels. Like most of Europe, Portugal was hard hit by the economic crisis of 2008, which left a mark, but the country continues to show encouraging signs of growth; its unemployment rate is currently at a historical low. Despite the ups and downs of the country's modern age, its past has not been lost in the process, as the numerous echoing monasteries, castles, dazzling baroque churches, and beautifully tiled walls testify. Neither has Portugal lost its strong sense of regional identity and traditions, for although only 10 percent of the population still works the land, it remains essentially a rural nation of small-scale towns and villages. Nor is everything perfect, either: Vast areas of countryside still have few roads and definitely improvable road signs, making it easy to get lost, even in this modestly scaled country.

The Lay of the Land

With just under 10 million people inhabiting an area of 35,458 square miles (91,836 sq km), Portugal has one of the lowest overall population densities in Europe, descending to a mere 44 people per square mile (17 people per sq km) in central Alentejo. Lisbon, the capital, lies at the heart of the most densely inhabited region, and its greater urban area is home to nearly 2.8 million, while Porto, the second largest metropolis, leads the north with 1.7 million inhabitants. Outside of these two industrial poles, about one-third of the land is clad in trees, and the rest is given over to either vineyards or farmland.

In the North: The Minho (named for a river that demarcates Portugal's northern border with Spain) and the Trás-os-Montes (meaning "beyond the mountains") areas harbor striking rugged areas where granite-built villages seem trapped in time. On occasion, horses still transport goods and people, and many agricultural

■ A network of 19th-century canals was built in Aveiro to allow shippers access to the sea.

methods should have become obsolete decades ago. Much of the rural population is noticeably elderly, bringing into question the long-term future of these areas. Between the villages are undulating fields blanketed in vineyards, rushing rivers, and the stark granite peaks of Portugal's first national park, Peneda-Gerês. The cities of Porto and Braga have industrial outskirts, but the centuries-old port wine industry takes center stage, especially in the stupendous terraced Douro Valley. Here, too, elegant manors stud the landscape, and medieval castles guard the border with Spain, the archenemy—once reviled and feared. A Portuguese saying, "Neither a good wind nor a good marriage ever comes from Spain," perfectly expresses this sentiment.

Portugal's Center: The enchanting Beiras area radiates from the illustrious and lively university town of Coimbra. The city makes a stimulating launchpad for forays into the rugged hills of the Serra da Estrela, for indulging in spas, or for exploring charming towns such as Aveiro or Viseu.

The Beiras area is often mistakenly overshadowed by more dramatic sites to the north (Porto and the Douro Valley) or to the south, where Portugal's most famous monuments are clustered. The heavy-weight lineup of Alcobaça, Batalha, and Tomar (all World Heritage sites) is in Estremadura, an area heavily crisscrossed by highways and partly industrialized, thus distinctly less rural in spirit. Proximity to Lisbon puts the region on tourist day trips, so do not expect to find yourself alone in Alcobaça's cloisters or beneath the rococo cherubim of Mafra Palace. The coastline, alternating between cliffs and beaches, has highlights such as Peniche and Ericeira, both of which offer some of Europe's best surfing conditions. East of the Estremadura lie the emptier plains of the Ribatejo, a venue for cowboys and occasional bullfights, and the semi-industrialized Tejo Valley, dotted with medieval sites. Cultural interest intensifies again in and around Lisbon, one of Europe's most delightful capitals. Low-key yet sophisticated, brazenly modern and engagingly old-fashioned, Lisbon sprawls over seven hills. Its beautiful site beside the Tejo estuary once connected it more closely with Portugal's overseas possessions than with Europe; the rich cultural mosaic needs several days to explore. A short train ride away is Sintra, a magical hill town of mansions and palaces nestled in forests overlooking the Atlantic. On the coast, dowager resorts like Cascais and Estoril vie with blissfully empty beaches farther north, while the Sado estuary edging the Setúbal Peninsula attracts nature enthusiasts eager to see pink flamingos and dolphins.

East & South: Megaliths, castles of diverse eras, delightful whitewashed villages, swathes of cork oaks, and olive trees characterize the vast plains and rolling hills of the Alentejo. Its warmer climate, cuisine, and village architecture reflect a distinctly Mediterranean character. Traditionally home to *latifúndios* or *herdades* (large-scale estates), the Alentejo has long nurtured radical political movements, unlike the more conservative north. Handicrafts are king here, making it a joy to nose around market towns. The Alentejo coastline boasts unspoiled beaches and dramatic cliffs, in high contrast to the developments of the Algarve in the south, which are meccas for northern European retirees and for charter tourism. The Moors' presence in Portugal was strongest in the Algarve, on a par with neighboring Andalucia in Spain, and is still visible in the humble villages and in the physiognomy of locals. Golf courses are a huge, year-round attraction, and there are a few well-kept secrets, such as the Costa Vicentina, with some of Europe's most beautiful wild beaches.

Farther southwest still, in the Atlantic, the idiosyncratic island of Madeira lies in an archipelago some 440 miles (700 km) off the coast of Morocco. The lush subtropical vegetation, rugged volcanic slopes, and mild climate draw visitors in droves in winter.

Climate

Climatically, Portugal's regions are as different as their landscapes. Although summer brings warm and mainly sunny days to the Minho, the land stays brilliantly green thanks to plentiful rainfall, not shared by its drier, rockier neighbor, Trás-os-Montes. Snow often caps the mountains of the Serra do Gerês and Serra da Estrela (home to continental Portugal's highest peak) in winter, sometimes making roads impassable. Inland Alentejo often sees summer temperatures soar over 104°F (40°C), but coastal areas and the Algarve usually have much milder temperatures. Lisbon enjoys a temperate climate, with most rain falling November through January and temperatures averaging 58°F (14°C) in winter and about 85°F (29°C) in summer. The little rain that falls in the south occurs during the winter.

The Madeira archipelago boasts exceptionally mild temperatures, averaging 72°F (22°C) in summer and 62°F (16°C) in winter, with rainfall mainly concentrated in winter on the more exposed northern side of the islands.

Bullfights

Touradas (bullfights) in Portugal are very low key and restricted mainly to two regions: the Ribatejo, where fighting bulls are bred, and the Algarve, where fights are staged for tourists. The season runs from Easter until October. In the Portuguese tourada, the bull, whose horns are capped, is not killed in the ring. The thrill lies in watching the star bullfighter leap onto a bull to grab its horns while his team attempts to hold it from behind. The most skilled and traditional touradas take place during Santarém's big agricultural fair in June.

Religion & Festivals

Portugal is a deeply devout country, with Roman Catholics constituting an overwhelming majority of its population. Religious orders were banned in 1834. The formal separation of church and state occurred during the First Republic (1910–1926) and was reiterated in the 1976 constitution. Yet church and state remain inextricably linked and churchgoing is very common. The Lisbon area is the least devout, while the north is the most. Portuguese Catholicism distinguishes itself from that of Spain through a more serene and caring face; there is far less anguish and God is perceived as a benevolent, less judgmental figure. Twice a year, some 100,000 pilgrims head to the complex of shrines dedicated to the Virgin Mary at Fátima.

Inevitably such belief brings a highly charged calendar of *festas* (festivals) and *romarias* (pilgrimages)—often a curious mix of worship, processions, and good times. Christmas, though important, does not head the list of major festivals. Carnaval (Mardi Gras), held just before Lent, kicks off the year's big religious celebrations.

> **Portugal is a deeply devout country, with Roman Catholics constituting an overwhelming majority of its population.**

During Easter Week, Braga's torchlit processions rival those of Andalucia in Spain. Outside the main calendar, each region or town celebrates its patron saint with gusto: Lisbon, for example, spends most of the night of June 12 on a delirious roll in honor of St. Anthony, while Porto and Braga celebrate St. John on June 23 and 24.

Some festivals have pagan elements to them. In Trás-os-Montes, December's Festa dos Rapazes (Boys Festival) sees groups of costumed and masked boys (older than 16) cavorting around huge bonfires; they are celebrating the rite of passage into adulthood. Amarante, in the Douro area, observes an ancient fertility rite in which unmarried individuals exchange phallic-shaped cakes and touch the tomb of St. Gonçalo in the hope of a speedy marriage; this takes place the first weekend in June.

Portugal's most gorgeous costumes come out in the Minho—at Viana do Castelo's riotous festival around August 20, at Vila Franca do Lima's Rose Festival in mid-May, and Ponte de Lima's Feiras Novas (New Fairs) in mid-September. Horse lovers should earmark the first two weeks of November and head for Golegã in the Ribatejo to see Portugal's massive annual horse fair with parades, competitions, and occasional bullfights. The Alentejo's busy calendar is filled with hot-blooded festivities often connected with agricultural seasons, food, and wine. Inevitably, the least traditional region is the Algarve, where customs have been diluted by foreign visitors and residents.

Football

Portugal's great sporting passion, shared with most Western European nations, is football. During the soccer season, from September to May, nearly every restaurant has a television set in the corner tuned to the match of the day—local diners being voluble groups of men, though more women are increasingly drawn to the sport. Familiarity with any or all of the main teams, or seeing them in action (see sidebar opposite) is a surefire way to start a conversation. ∎

PORTUGAL: CHAMPIONS AT LAST

Portugal has historically boasted a very respectable soccer team but despite the fact that they've always put first-rate players on the field, they've continually placed only second or third in major tournaments. That changed dramatically on July 10, 2016, when a little-known substitute named Éder scored against host team France to make Portugal champions of Europe at last.

Football, Fado, Fátima

Soccer has been played in Portugal since the 1860s, thanks to the country's maritime trading ties with Britain, whose sailors spread the game worldwide in the Victorian era. Throughout António de Oliveira Salazar's long dictatorship (1932–1968) and up to the Carnation Revolution of 1974 (see pp. 30–31), football was encouraged by the state: Football, fado (see pp. 58–59), and the Catholic cult of Fátima (see p. 139) were seen as distractions from politics.

Portuguese players, led by Cristiano Ronaldo, celebrate their victory over France at Euro 2016.

Always the Bridesmaids ...

Portuguese football arrived on the world stage when Eusebio, a powerful striker born in the former colony of Mozambique, led the country to a 1966 World Cup semifinal. When Portugal won two World Youth Cups in 1989 and 1990, the "golden generation" of players including Luis Figo and Rui Costa were expected to bring success at the senior level. In 2004, an aging Figo led the next golden generation to the final of the European Championship held in Portugal. A nation prepared to party, but underdogs Greece shocked their hosts 1–0 in Lisbon. The baton of expectation was passed to a new generation that included Cristiano Ronaldo, who would carve out an outstanding club career with Manchester United, Real Madrid, and Juventus. It was Ronaldo who finally lifted the country's first senior trophy as Portugal became European champions in Paris in 2016.

EXPERIENCE: Attend a Soccer Game

No visit to Portugal would be complete without experiencing the intensity and spectacle of a professional soccer game, where passions flare and the roar of the crowd can be deafening. Most of the population would swear allegiance to one of the Três Grandes, the three giant clubs: FC Porto, Sporting Clube, or Benfica (the first a team from Porto, the two others from Lisbon). Rivalries are intense, with the league championship usually contested among the three, which regularly compete in the UEFA Champions League too. Benfica were European Champions in 1961 and 1962, while Porto triumphed in 1987 and in 2004, when coached by José Mourinho. For ticket information, contact **FC Porto** (Estádio do Dragão, tel 225 083 352, fcporto.pt), **Sporting Clube** (Estádio José Alvalade, tel 707 204 444, sporting.pt), or **Benfica** (Estádio da Luz, tel 707 200 100, sshop.slbenfica.pe).

HISTORY OF PORTUGAL

More than just textbook history, thousands of years of human endeavor can be seen in Portugal, from Neolithic dolmens to a dazzling network of baroque churches and palaces built on the riches from overseas colonies, to the economic revitalization occurring since a peaceful revolution ended decades of 20th-century dictatorship.

Portugal is one of the oldest nations in Europe. Its borders have remained more or less unchanged for the last 800 years. Before the moment when Afonso Henriques proclaimed himself king of Portucale, in 1139, its history was shared with Spain. Together these two lands saw a succession of invaders and colonizers from northern Europe and from across the Mediterranean, all lured by this peninsula of plenty.

Portugal's Earliest Inhabitants

Although dates in the mists of time are always conjectural, it is certain that humans lived in Portugal up to 30,000 years ago, leaving the rock incisions of Vale do Côa (north of Guarda) as their legacy. Later, about 5,000 to 6,000 years ago, came ritual worship associated with megaliths, of which Portugal claims an astonishing number. Dolmens (stone shelters, probably temples or tombs), cromlechs (stone circles), and menhirs (upright stones) still stand enigmatically from the Minho region to the Alentejo.

 The Romans spearheaded a massive leap forward in infrastructure and government.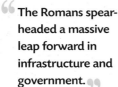

With the inward drift of Celts from the north, settlements took shape as *castros,* fortified hilltop villages of stone and thatch shelters, whose inhabitants were always on the lookout for marauding neighbors. The best example of a castro is Citânia de Briteiros, near Guimarães. During this period, around the ninth century B.C., Phoenicians from the Middle East first moored their boats in the Algarve; they were soon followed by Greeks and Carthaginians. Little remains from this first wave of expatriates other than the introduction of fishing, but life changed radically when the highly structured Romans marched into the south around 200 B.C.

Romans & Other Invaders

Expecting a military pushover, the Romans met a surprising resistance, mainly due to the Lusitani. The major resistance ended in 139 B.C., when the last Lusitani leader was killed, but intermittent warfare continued until 28 B.C. Perhaps out of

admiration, the Romans took the tribe's name for their new province south of the Douro River: Lusitania.

The Romans spearheaded a massive leap forward in infrastructure and government. Olisipo (Lisbon) became the capital in 60 B.C., and other centers developed at Santarém, Évora, Beja, and Braga. By the third century A.D., what is now the Minho was absorbed into the province of Gallaecia (today's Galicia, in Spain). Roads crisscrossed the country, bridges spanned rivers, and *latifúndios* (large-scale estates) became the norm, especially in the Alentejo. The Romans also imported crops: grapevines, figs, almonds, and olives— all of which are still farmed. Major bishoprics were established at Braga and Évora. Altogether, with a network of roads, a legal system, a Mediterranean-style diet, a Latin-based language, and Christianity, the Romans left an indelible mark.

Their empire, however, was in decline and soon dissipated in the face of invaders from the north. In came the Suevi (Swabians), closely followed by the Visigoths. Fractious tribes, they could not repulse the next invaders: the Moors.

Portugal's prehistoric past is on display in the Alentejo, a region rich in megaliths.

The Moors

In 711, the caliphate of Damascus led an army of Arabs and Berbers onto Iberian soil at Tarifa (in Spanish Andalucia). It would take Portugal more than 500 years to throw off these new rulers. Because the Moors never ventured very far north of the Douro River, this region (together with Galicia) remained predominantly Christian and it was here that the *reconquista* (reconquest) was born.

Meanwhile, the Moorish colony of Al-Gharb (meaning "the west," later to become Algarve), initially ruled from Córdoba, lived peacefully and with religious tolerance. Irrigation systems and water mills helped cultivate newly introduced wheat, rice, citrus fruits, and saffron. Mining, too, boosted the economy, supplying craftsmen with copper and silver, and the ceramics industry exploded when the Moors introduced glazed tiles—azulejos.

Little by little, however, the northern Christians were on the move, led by the king of Asturias-Léon. They had recovered Porto by 868, and Coimbra 10 years later. As the reconquista slowly advanced, Córdoba's power fragmented, resulting in numerous small kingdoms or *taifas*. The power vacuum was gradually filled by more fanatical branches of Islam. Over the next two centuries, the fundamentalist Almoravids and Almohads successfully reunited the southern half of the Iberian Peninsula, reestablishing strong government and severe controls. By 1100, the stage was set for a Holy War between Christians and Muslims.

■ **The Moors introduced the art of the glazed tile—azulejo—to Portugal.**

The Emergence of Portucale

At the same time, Portucale (originally the region between the Lima and Douro Rivers) began to emerge, and a sense of national identity took shape thanks to Afonso Henriques, grandson to Alfonso VI, king of Castilla y Léon. Portucale, a county in Alfonso VI's kingdom, was awarded to Afonso Henriques's father in gratitude for his services to the king. When Alfonso VI died, Portucale refused allegiance to the new king. Some years later, Afonso began his quest for power by overthrowing his widowed mother to gain control of Portucale in 1128.

In 1139, a significant victory against the Moors (the Battle of Ourique) gave Afonso the confidence to declare Portucale (Portugal) sovereign and himself king *(dom)*. This was a turning point. Further conquests followed with Santarém and Lisbon both falling into the new king's net, helped by French, English, German, and Flemish crusaders, who washed up on these shores en route to the Holy Land. Afonso Henriques's guilt at using up this precious manpower destined for Jerusalem led him to found the Alcobaça abbey and to donate land to these supporters. The crusaders grew acquisitive, one result being the formidable rise of the powerful Knights Templar, a monastic military order formed at the end of the First Crusade in 1096.

Although Afonso Henriques surrendered some frontier land to the kingdom of Léon, temporarily allied with the Muslims, by the time he died in 1185, almost the entire realm was declared Portuguese. When the Algarve fell to Afonso III in 1249, the reconquista was complete; yet, the kingdom of Castilla disputed Afonso's claim of sovereignty. The 1297 Treaty of Alcañices resolved the matter, formally ceding the Algarve to Portugal's king, Dom Dinis I. By this time the capital had moved from Coimbra to Lisbon.

Dom Dinis & His Legacy

This exceptionally astute and enlightened king, nicknamed "the poet king," embarked on an ambitious program of shoring up his kingdom. By the time Dom Dinis died, in 1325, the country had reached maturity (see sidebar below).

Such progress did not last, however, and Portugal entered an era of stagnation, made worse by the plague that intermittently wreaked havoc over the next century or so. Adding to the troubles were wars with the kingdom of Castilla: Territorial incursions, machinations, alliances, lovers, marriages, and illegitimate sons all played a role. This came to a head in 1385 at the Battle of Aljubarrota when João, the illegitimate son of Pedro I, confronted the Castilians. They were backing Leonor, widow of the former Portuguese king Fernando I, and her daughter Beatriz, who was married to Juan, the king of Castilla. The population was divided over this inheritance issue: The nobles and the church backed the Castilians, while the middle and working classes championed the national candidate, João. Greatly outnumbered by the Castilian army massed against him, João made a vow to build a monastery if he won. Win he did, and his victory led to the magnificent monastery of Batalha, an alliance with England (formalized by the Treaty of Windsor, 1386), an English wife, Philippa of Lancaster, and the uncontested rule of the House of Avis.

House of Avis & the Age of Discoveries

This crucial period in Portuguese history reaped riches from overseas colonies. Philippa of Lancaster proved to be a popular queen, managing to rein in the

Dom Dinis's Accomplishments

During Dom Dinis's reign (1279–1325), more than 50 castles were built along the border, forests were planted, and in 1290 Lisbon University was founded. He also replaced the wealthy, all-powerful Knights Templar with the Order of Christ that was directly under his control, preempting any moves by the power-hungry church. Portuguese became the official language of bureaucracy, as opposed to Latin or Castilian, as well as the vehicle for a flourishing oral culture transmitted by wandering troubadours. Poetry thus blossomed. Dinis also developed the agricultural economy by establishing a network of fairs and markets, encouraging domestic trade and a shift from self-sufficient farming. In 1308, a commercial pact with England laid the foundations for a lengthy—and profitable—alliance. In short, the country flourished under Dom Dinis's rule.

womanizing Dom João I and bear him six children. The third son, Prince Henry, significantly altered his country's fortunes. After capturing the Moroccan stronghold of Ceuta for his father, in 1415, Henry reportedly set up a school of navigation at Sagres, in the Algarve. Henry the Navigator—as he came to be known, surrounding himself with astronomers and shipbuilders—financed numerous expeditions along the African coast. The newly discovered Madeira and Azores archipelagoes both later served as stopovers for Atlantic crossings. It is also surmised that Portuguese explorers reached America in the 1470s, several years before Columbus.

Before his death in 1460, Henry was a trusted adviser to his nephew, Afonso V, who had ascended the throne in 1438. Afonso's reign (until 1481) saw more battles in Morocco and, at home, a strengthening of the power of the *cortes* (court government). Friction with Spain resurfaced and the idealistic yet weak Afonso failed in his military attempt to wrest control of Castilla. His son, João, negotiated peace with Castilla, and on becoming Dom João II (r. 1481–1495) opened the borders to some 60,000 Jews fleeing persecution in Spain.

Meanwhile, out on the high seas, Bartolomeu Dias rounded the Cape of Good Hope in 1488, allowing Portugal to set its sights on the Indian Ocean. By 1494, overseas rivalry with Spain had spiraled to such an extent that the pope stepped in to draw up the Treaty of Tordesillas. It effectively drew a line down the map of the known world to divide it between the two maritime powers: Spain to the west and Portugal to the east. Inadvertently, the line cut through Brazil, so when Pedro Álvares Cabral moored his boats there six years later, this vast territory was signed over to Portugal. It played a major role in Portugal's fortunes for four centuries.

 The Portuguese soon held sway over the entire Indian Ocean and its much prized spice trade, previously in the hands of Arab traders.

Vasco da Gama's discovery of the sea route to India, which he accomplished in 1498 via Mozambique—adding one more African jewel to Portugal's colonial crown—led to untold riches. Ten years later, Afonso de Albuquerque captured the port of Goa, in western India, leading to 450 years of Portuguese rule, and by 1511 his control of Malacca (in Malaysia) gave Portugal a strategic trading center for the East Indies. The Portuguese soon held sway over the entire Indian Ocean and its much prized spice trade, previously in the hands of Arab traders.

When a Spanish expedition led by Portuguese Fernão de Magalhães (Magellan) returned to base in 1522 (minus their captain who had been killed in the Philippines) after circumnavigating the globe, the pride in Portuguese exploration was justifiable. Through immense courage and navigating skill, people from this little seaboard country had

■ **Lisbon's Monument to the Discoveries (1960) commemorates the era of the great discoveries made by Portuguese explorers.**

penetrated regions previously considered inhabited by monsters, proved the world round, and discovered a string of exotic destinations. Henry the Navigator's agile fleet of *caravelas* (inspired by the cargo sailing ships on the Douro), celestial tables, and ocean charts had all paid off richly.

These bountiful new territories changed the face of Portugal. Dom Manuel I (r. 1495–1521) reigned during the period that saw overseas riches transform both Lisbon and the nation, a major expression being the lavish Manueline style of decoration. Manuel dubbed himself Lord of the Conquest, Navigation, and Commerce of India, Ethiopia, Arabia, and Persia. Merchants descended on Lisbon from all over Europe, bringing goods to exchange for gold and ivory from Africa, pungent spices (pepper, cinnamon, cloves) from India and the East Indies, and, by the mid-16th century, silks and porcelain from China. From the New World came strange fruits, vegetables, and other plants—tomatoes, potatoes, corn, tobacco, and cacao. And from the Atlantic itself, off Newfoundland, came *bacalhau,* or cod, a creature that still obsesses the Portuguese palate.

The Portuguese were relatively tolerant of local customs in their newfound territories. Their main concerns were to run their trading stations and zealously impose Catholicism. Mixing freely with local populations, they intermarried, a practice that became common and is still visible in the names and inhabitants of former colonies such as Mozambique, Ceylon (Sri Lanka), and Malacca. Centuries later, many Portuguese natives emigrated to the colonies in search of employment and prosperity. Nevertheless, the Portuguese sorely lacked the middle class needed to build up their overseas territories; the problem eventually proved to be insoluble.

Yet, under the astute Manuel I, Portugal had prospered and made huge advances in social fields, legal systems, and education. The Italian Renaissance had imparted humanistic ideals and a flood of new ideas. This led to a radical reform of the university system, widening the pool of students from the religious orders to include young nobles and bourgeois. The university's increased influence in Lisbon soon posed a threat to the monarchy, provoking Manuel's son, João III, to actually move it to Coimbra, far from the seat of power, and hand over educational guidance to the Jesuits.

End of an Era

Inevitably, the feast of plenty enjoyed from overseas explorations did not last: Overconfidence led to underdevelopment and overstretching; emigration to the new colonies reduced the already small population at home; easy riches led to a loss of skills; and the cost of living rose sharply. In addition, the Portuguese Inquisition targeted Jews in autos-da-fé (public burnings), resulting in a mood of commercial and cultural apathy. When the young king Sebastião I was killed during a bloody crusade in Morocco, in 1578, it was the straw that broke the camel's back.

When Sebastião died he was not alone: Eight thousand men were massacred, including a large section of the nobility. Others were captured, and the national coffers were virtually emptied to pay ransom demands. The country was bankrupt and its golden era well and truly over. By 1580, Portugal was sufficiently on its knees for the Spanish Habsburg king, Felipe II, to walk in and take over as Felipe I of Portugal. Spanish rule lasted 60 years, a period in history that the Portuguese have never forgotten or forgiven.

Spanish Rule

Filipe I, although fresh from Madrid, was the grandson of Manuel I. His fair attitude to his new kingdom helped maintain the independence of the Portuguese parliament and of its empire. He also introduced a more efficient administrative system. But attitudes changed with his son, Filipe II, who, lacking his father's finesse, blatantly exploited Portuguese revenue to finance Spain's battles in the New World. Several years passed before he even visited Portugal after his coronation in 1598. Resentment simmered, throwing up a number of pretenders to the throne. Meanwhile Portuguese overseas possessions were gradually being eroded: The Dutch were on a rampage, carrying off Ceylon (Sri Lanka), Malacca, and parts of Brazil, while the English took Ormuz.

> " **By 1580, Portugal was sufficiently on its knees for the Spanish Habsburg king, Felipe II, to walk in and take over as Filipe I of Portugal.** "

Finally, in 1640, a full-scale revolt took place, sparked by a Spanish recruitment drive in Portugal to help put down an uprising in Catalonia. With French moral support, a group of nationalists drove out the Spanish occupiers from Lisbon and installed a new king on the throne: Dom João IV. This initiated the rule of the House of Bragança, which was to last until the Republic, in 1910.

■ **The staggering baroque interior of Porto's São Francisco church reflects the power and wealth of the Franciscans in the 18th century.**

The House of Bragança

The reborn Portugal got off to a shaky start, unrecognized by most of Europe and hampered by weak leadership. Only the marriage of Catarina de Bragança to the English king Charles II in 1662 managed to forge a serious alliance. After losing several frontier battles, Spain finally recognized Portugal in the 1668 Treaty of Lisbon. In the interim, Portugal had reentered the economic doldrums; having lost the spice trade to the Dutch, it was now losing its sugar and slave markets. A reversal of fortunes came, however, at the turn of the 18th century with the discovery of gold and precious stones in Brazil. Soon a steady stream of riches enabled baroque gilt to unfurl in every palace, church, and monastery in the land.

Dom João V (r. 1706–1750) unashamedly modeled himself on the French Sun King, Louis XIV, and became quite adept at dipping into the public purse. The palace and monastery of Mafra are the most flagrant examples of his disregard for budget. If extravagance was João's second name, his third was libertine, proved by countless children he fathered with nuns. At the same time, trade took off thanks to the efforts of the brilliant though tyrannical prime minister, the Marquês de Pombal. It is no surprise that Pombal's name has outlasted the kings whom he served (João V was succeeded by his spineless son, José I): This farsighted man was responsible for far-reaching reforms.

In 1755, Pombal's talents were severely tested when a massive earthquake hit Lisbon and its surroundings. Some 5,000 people were killed instantly, but the following weeks saw tens of thousands die from disease and famine. Pombal remained clearheaded and ensured that the capital was rebuilt in record time, and intelligently. From then on the marquês instigated massive reforms in taxation, administration, and education; imposed trade barriers and export systems; and abolished the Portuguese slave trade. As his enemies multiplied, though, Pombal became ever more wily and despotic, finally abolishing the Jesuit Order and executing troublemaking nobles. When Dona Maria I took over the throne in 1777, Pombal's days were numbered. She had little respect for his methods and soon had him tried and convicted.

Maria herself, highly religious and mentally unstable, reigned until 1795, when her increasingly erratic behavior prompted her son João to take over, although he was not crowned until her death in 1816. His reign saw yet another momentous period in Portuguese and Spanish history: the Peninsular War.

Teaism

It is no secret that the British like their tea; in fact, they consume more than 176 million pounds yearly. Less known, perhaps, is the fact that it was made popular in England by a Portuguese princess, Catarina de Bragança. Married to King Charles II in 1662, Catarina had grown up in the Portuguese court where drinking *chá* had long been considered the height of fashion among the nobility. On arrival in England, Catarina was dismayed at being offered ale to drink and immediately set about establishing this exotic and expensive beverage as the court's drink of choice.

Peninsular War

Following the French Revolution in 1789 and the rise of power-hungry Napoleon, all Europe was in chaos. In 1801, France threatened to invade Portugal if it did not close its ports to England; since most of Portugal's exports were destined for England, the

■ The 1810 Battle of Buçaco led the allies to victory in the Peninsular War.

Portuguese refused. As a result, France's temporary ally, Spain, invaded Portugal. The peace treaty that ended the so-called War of the Oranges ceded land to Spain and forced the Portuguese to open its ports to the French and pay an indemnity.

Worse followed in 1807, when Gen. Andoche Junot and his French troops marched into Lisbon, although he missed capturing the royal family, who had fled to Brazil on the advice of the British. The royals remained in Rio de Janeiro for the next 14 years. The intervening years saw Portugal ruled by a British governor, Gen. William Carr (later Viscount Beresford), who together with the great tactician, Sir Arthur Wellesley (later Duke of Wellington), finally rid Portugal of its invaders. Successive waves of French attacks were repelled with help from Wellington's ingenious Lines of Torres Vedras before the allies' final victory at the Battle of Buçaco in 1810. Yet again Portugal found itself close to economic ruin, and this was exacerbated by the payoff to Britain for its help, namely the granting of the right to trade directly with Brazil. This concession lost Portugal precious revenue. Beresford was an unpopular, devious governor and the backlash was quick to come. In 1820, a group of Portuguese officers formed a court government and drew up a new constitution inspired by the liberal ideas that had swept Europe.

Civil Turmoil & the Portuguese Republic

João VI was forced to return and 1822 saw not only the independence of Brazil but also João's acceptance of the constitution. One term called for an assembly to be elected every two years by universal male suffrage, while other clauses abolished the privileges of both the nobles and the clergy. João may have signed his name to the document, but his Spanish wife, Carlota, and younger son, Miguel, did not, thus inciting a reactionary movement that simmered for decades. João's death in 1826 resulted in a hornet's nest of maneuvering between the two camps, with the rural population supporting the reactionaries and the big three powers (Spain, France, and Britain) backing the liberals. Pedro, João's eldest son, and Miguel, the youngest, ended up on opposing sides; the Miguelist Wars eventually gave victory and the crown to the liberal-minded Pedro. He ruled until 1834, when his 15-year-old daughter, Dona Maria II, ascended the throne. By then, the revolutionary spirit had abolished religious orders, a significant move in such a fervently religious country.

There followed endless confrontations and even uprisings between nascent political parties, and economic depression prevailed. In 1861, when Maria's son Luís I assumed power, he inherited a modernized infrastructure thanks to Prime Minister Saldanha, but the economy still suffered; emigration soared and the countryside was becoming depopulated. The intellectually inclined Luís nonetheless presided over a peaceful era during which the arts, particularly literature, blossomed. Conservatives and liberals alternated controlling parliament, but growing social discontent took shape as a nationalist republican movement. This came to a head in 1908 in an attempted coup, when Dom Carlos I and his eldest son were assassinated. In 1910, a military coup deposed Dom Manuel II (the younger son), who fled to England. The Portuguese Republic was born.

For the next 16 years, although power was often in the hands of the leftist Democratic Party, there were no fewer than 45 changes of government, accompanied by a general weakening of economic and social structures. Chaos became the keyword as political factions multiplied, unions declared strikes, and the military made sporadic interventions. The republic was on its knees when yet another military coup, in 1926, appointed General Óscar Carmona as president with António de Oliveira Salazar as his finance minister. In six years Salazar graduated to the powerful post of prime minister, a title he did not relinquish for 36 years.

> In 1910, a military coup deposed Dom Manuel II [. . .], who fled to England. The Portuguese Republic was born.

The Salazar Years

It did not take long for Salazar to show his true colors. In 1933, he declared a "New State," modeling himself on Italy's fascist dictator Mussolini. Authoritarian and intent on returning Portugal to its Catholic code after decades of liberal thinking, Salazar repressed any opposition, imposed censorship, and founded a state police organization. These were dark days for Portugal, effectively cutting it off from much of Europe with the exception of the little-loved neighbor, Spain; Salazar actually gave military backing to Gen. Francisco Franco in the Spanish Civil War of 1936–1939. Resistance at home simmered in an underground Communist Party, but it remained powerless.

During World War II, Portugal's loyalties were divided: Traditionally, it should have followed its old ally in foreign affairs, Britain, but politically Salazar's sympathies lay with Hitler. In the end, he played a purely self-interested role, doing business with both sides and profiting royally. Admission to the United Nations came in 1955, but Salazar continued to ignore or repress all warning signs of opposition: One presidential candidate opposed to the dictatorship, Gen. Humberto Delgado, was assassinated by state police in 1965. Salazar's most positive accomplishment came in the sweeping economic reforms which, by the 1950s and '60s, gave Portugal an annual growth rate of 7 to 9 percent.

Meanwhile, Portugal's colonies were being squeezed dry and their populations exploited, while immigrants to the "mother country" found themselves employed as cheap labor. Revolts ensued, usually harshly put down, and wars such as in Angola in 1961 drained manpower and the economy. As the increasingly paranoid Salazar assumed ever more responsibilities, age finally took its toll: In June 1968, at age 79, Salazar suffered an incapacitating stroke when his deck chair collapsed—not the most elegant way to go. Although he clung to life for two more years, the reins of power passed to Marcelo Caetano.

■ António Luís Santos da Costa was elected prime minister in 2015 and re-elected in 2019.

The Rise of Modern Portugal

Ineffective in instigating reform, Caetano was deposed in 1974 in an extraordinarily effortless, bloodless coup—the Carnation Revolution—spearheaded by the MFA (Armed Forces Movement), a group of disillusioned military officers. Anarchy and numerous governments came and went until 1976, when socialist Mário Soares was elected prime minister. In 1986, he became Portugal's first civilian president in 60 years—and a civilian has been president ever since. Also in 1986, Portugal entered the European Union (EU) and a period of boom growth and prosperity followed, funded by European grants. Portugal's profile was raised further in 1998, when it hosted the World Expo, and in 2004 the European Football Championship. The recent global financial crisis caused concerns for the economic future; deep-cutting austerity measures seemed to be slowly pulling Portugal out of its financial troubles. The results of the 2015 elections, later confirmed by the elections in late 2019, brought a left-wing coalition to the government, whose less restrictive socialist policies made it possible to keep the situation under control and even to maintain the previously recorded positive trend. ■

FOOD & DRINK

Much of Portugal's empire was built on its spice trade, and this eastern influence has had a long-lasting impact on the country's cuisine. Portuguese cooks are fearless about spicing things up. It was Vasco da Gama, the first to round the Cape of Good Hope and cross the Indian Ocean, who brought back black pepper and other spices from India, soon followed by nutmeg, mace, and cloves from the Spice Islands.

Thanks to the country's extensive coastline, fresh fish graces many of Portugal's tables.

Piri-piri (Swahili for "pepper-pepper"), a blend of crushed chilies, fragrant herbs, and a dash of lemon, is a legacy that coats countless dishes from Africa to Brazil.

Regional Dishes

Today, regional cuisine thrives in a country that is clearly divided into north, center, and south. In the north and center, in the Minho, Trás-os-Montes, and Beiras areas, an invariable starter is *caldo verde* (cabbage soup), a nourishing mix of potatoes, shredded cabbage, olive oil, and *chouriço* (spicy sausage). Portugal's soup with the strangest name is *sopa de pedra* (stone soup) from the central Ribatejo. Based on a legend, it contains no stones; instead it has beans, smoked sausage, and a mixture of vegetables. *Caldeirada de peixe* (fish stew) is found nearer the coast, together with a variant dish that includes shellfish: *sopa de marisco.*

Portugal can justifiably claim salted cod (*bacalhau*) as its national dish. Possibly less believable is the Portuguese boast of a cod recipe for every day of the year. Pork is another big favorite, with Coimbra claiming the most tender *leitão assado* (roast suckling pig). Virtually nothing is wasted from this animal: The kidneys are pan-fried and finished off with white port, tongues are smoked and made into sausages, and *presunto* (smoked ham) is eaten solo or added to *cozido*, a meat and vegetable stew. Ham and spicy *chouriço* sausages are added to *dobrada*, a Lisbon dish of tripe cooked with haricot beans. In Porto the same dish gains a dash of curry powder.

Another typical countrywide meat is flavorsome kid goat, which is usually roasted *(cabrito assado)*. Duck is incorporated into divine *arroz de pato* (duck rice), a specialty of Braga, while a *feijoada* (a classic bean stew with bacon, meat, tomatoes, onions, and garlic) whets rural appetites throughout the north and center.

Farther south in the Alentejo, *carne de porco à Alentejana* (pork marinated in wine served with clams) is a surprising yet delicious combination. The Alentejo produces the most Mediterranean-style cuisine of Portugal, largely based on olive oil and aromatic herbs. Although once denigrated as basically a peasant cuisine, it is actually rich and varied. The delicious bread and garlic-based *açordas* may be served with prawns or dogfish, lamb stews *(ensopado de borrego)*, or a chilled vegetable gazpacho; other mainstays include chicken pies, smoked sausages, sheep and goat cheeses, pork with coriander, and numerous lamb and game dishes.

The Algarve claims the ubiquitous *cataplana*, a fast-stewed dish of seafood, sometimes with added chopped chicken or pork, cooked in a domed dish similar to that used to make the Moroccan *tajine*; it is yet another innovation from this land of plenty.

Portugal's Sweet Tooth

An outstanding feature of Portuguese cuisine is its vast array of delicately flavored desserts and sweet pastries, whose basic ingredients are egg yolks and sugar. One of the reasons for this is that industrial quantities of egg whites were once used as clarifying agents for red wine, and the surplus yolks were passed on to convents, where nuns concocted cakes for religious festivals. Rivalry added spice to their quality, as each convent sought to attract the favors of patrons. Today there are said to be more than 200 desserts unique to Portugal, the names of some of which—such as *toucinho do ceu* (heaven's lard) or *barriga de freiras* (nun's belly)—still invoke their origins. Most of these delectables are variations of cream or custard tarts, rice or bread puddings, egg-paste pastries, and, in the Algarve, marzipan. The Algarve is the only region where Arab influences are still obvious in fig, honey, or almond pastries.

Local Favorites

Wherever you go in Portugal, you will never be far from great food, but there are several places that any local would tell you are "not to be missed." Try to include some of the following on a visit.

Cherry liqueur *(ginjinha):* A Ginjinha, Largo de São Domingos 8, Lisbon, tel 218 862 449, or out of chocolate cups on Rua Direita, Óbidos. See pp. 148–149.

Custard tarts *(pastéis de Belém):* Antiga Confraria de Belém, Rua de Belém 84–92, Lisbon, tel 213 637 423, pasteisdebelem.pt. See p. 64.

Grilled sardines *(sardinhas grelhadas):* Just

beyond the bridge in Portimão. According to custom, best eaten in months without the letter "r" (May–Aug.). See p. 205.

Piri piri chicken *(frango piri-piri):* Bonjardim, Travessa de Santo Antão 7–11, Lisbon, tel 213 427 424 or Pedro dos Frangos, Rua Bonjardim 223, Porto, tel 222 008 522

Roast suckling pig *(leitão assado):* Pedro dos Leitões, Rua Álvaro Pedro 1, Sernadelo, Mealhada, tel 231 209 950, pedrodos leitoes.com

Salted cod *(bacalhau):* Casa do Bacalhau, Rua do Grilo 54, Lisbon, tel 218 620 000, acasadobacalhau.com

THE ARTS

Portugal's legacy of three-dimensional creativity is something extraordinary. Architecture, sculpture, and the decorative arts are the Portuguese forte, leaving painting to a relative backseat. The nation also excels at literature and music.

Architecture

Portugal's first man-made constructions—dolmens, cromlechs, and menhirs—date from some 6,000 to 5,000 years ago; the most impressive are in the Alentejo region, near Évora. Much later, the Celts erected *castros* (hill towns) of thatched stone huts, usually circular. This rudimentary architecture lasted for hundreds of years until the Romans brought in revolutionary building techniques and vision. Real architecture finally arrived in this far-flung outpost of the Roman Empire, visible today at the temple and baths of Évora, the mosaic-floored villas of Conímbriga, and the extensive foundations at Miróbriga.

> **Some Moorish vestiges survive in churches that were built over the ruins of mosques, and a few archways and the odd tower still stand as well.**

The next major influence came with the Moors, in the eighth century. Yet again, though, Portugal was an imperial afterthought, and the Moors' unrivaled sense of design and decorative detail was never as widespread in Portugal as in neighboring Spain. Little remains in Portugal today since most Moorish structures were demolished during the prolonged *reconquista* (reconquest). Some Moorish vestiges survive in churches that were built over the ruins of mosques, and a few archways and the odd tower still stand as well. Nonetheless, southern Portugal (the Alentejo and the Algarve) has a number of *mourarias* (old Moorish quarters) with webs of narrow lanes resembling North African medinas. Here, too, the patios and tiny windows of whitewashed village houses are clear imports from across the Strait of Gibraltar. One craft technique in particular left an indelible mark: ceramics. Techniques for firing painted tiles (azulejos) were adopted and developed, and they later became a hallmark of Portuguese decorative style (see pp. 70–71).

Romanesque & Gothic: The slow march of the reconquista heralded a new architectural style, the graceful Romanesque imported by French knights and Cistercian monks in the 11th century. Elegant, pure, with generous proportions, and often masterminded by French architects, it never reached the same heights of intricacy in Portugal as in Spain. Granite—Portugal's national stone—was just too hard to work. Yet massive places of worship took shape, becoming important strongholds in the long struggle against the Islamic occupiers. A typical example is Coimbra's lovely old cathedral, completed in 1175, heavily fortified while retaining great simplicity. Many Romanesque elements were later masked by Renaissance, Manueline, and baroque alterations.

■ Festivals rich in tradition and colorful costumes are but one aspect of Portugal's arts.

Close on the heels of this architectural style came the more stylized Gothic look: Pointed arches, rib-vaulted ceilings, and octagonal apses were the norm, while soft limestone was skillfully conjured into figurative and decorative relief. This style emerged in the 12th century, overlapping often with the Romanesque. Central Portugal boasts some superlative Gothic examples, notably the Cistercian monastery of Alcobaça (started in 1178), whose serene, spacious cloister was much imitated. The staggering detail of the abbey of Batalha represents the more complex flamboyant Gothic of the late 14th century. In Lisbon, the western portal of the Jerónimos monastery is a tour de force of craftsmanship of the period.

Hand in hand with religious architecture came sculpture. As cathedrals multiplied, so did funerary art, which reached its apogee, again, at Alcobaça in the beautifully sculpted tombs of the ill-fated lovers Inês de Castro and Dom Pedro. Coimbra, Évora, and Lisbon became prodigious centers for this art form, while Batalha's school was strongly influenced by the Frenchman Master Huguet. French influence also permeated church statuary, which flourished during the Gothic period.

Manueline: Until the reign of Manuel I (r. 1495–1521) there was no specific Portuguese style of art or architecture; most forms and techniques were imported. The horizon changed totally with the evolution of the Manueline style, Portugal's most exuberant artistic expression and a clear reflection of a newfound national confidence. As a new world concept took shape with the first overseas forays, twisted ropes, nautical knots, anchors, shells, coral-like textures, and armillary spheres became the favored symbols used again and again in abbeys, churches, and palaces. Sculptural mastery transformed the arches of simple Romanesque or Gothic cloisters with delicate, lace-like embellishments, while windows and doors were framed in symphonies of intricately carved stone.

In Tomar, the Templar fortress and monastery acquired some exceptional Manueline additions, most notably the chapter house window by Diogo de Arruda. Batalha, too, saw dazzling additions, including the ornately carved doorway to the Capelas

Military Architecture of the Middle Ages

Portugal's military structures evolved in parallel with its abbeys and churches, with simple castles of the 10th century gradually becoming more complex and sophisticated. Dozens were built along the border with Spain, usually incorporated into walled hill towns, during the reign of Dom Dinis I. Keeps became ever higher, culminating in Beja's 138-foot-tall (42 m) structure, while contact with northern Europe and with Asia (via the Moors and the crusaders) brought other features. The Knights Templar made the greatest

contribution, exemplified in the proportions and excesses at Tomar; the Knights' Hospitaller influence was more discreet. Gothic castles of the 14th and 15th centuries saw a French influence in the machicolations and round turrets (as at Santiago do Cacém) as well as the introduction of the barbican, a lower, protective wall outside the main structure. By the late Middle Ages, some fortresses were converted into residences for kings or nobles, and inner comforts appeared in the form of wood paneling and fireplaces.

■ The masterful stone tracery at Batalha creates patterns of light and shadow.

Imperfeitas by Mateus Fernandes. The Jerónimos monastery in Belém showcases some of Portugal's most striking craftsmanship of the time, thanks to the masterful input of Diogo de Boitaca and Spaniard Juan de Castilla. The most integrated and exquisite example of Manueline vision and skill, however, is arguably the Torre de Belém, the work of Francisco de Arruda, brother of Diogo—a confectionery of carved rope, open-work balconies, and battlements shaped like shields. The Palácio Nacional at Sintra also features numerous Manueline details, and copies of its spectacular carved stone window frames can be seen in mansions throughout Portugal.

Renaissance & Baroque: The 16th-century flowering of the Renaissance, with its emphasis on Roman design and proportion and more realistic sculpture, took longer to appear in Portugal and, once again, a foreigner led the way. The prodigious French sculptor Nicolas de Chanterenne left his mark in churches from Coimbra to Lisbon. His countrymen Jean de Rouen and Houdart perfected the art of religious statuary and bas-reliefs. Meanwhile, Portuguese architecture absorbed more classical notes in the work of Miguel de Arruda at Batalha and that of the Spaniard Diego de Torralva, who designed the Grand Cloisters at Tomar.

During the years of Spanish rule and the accompanying Inquisition (1580–1640), architectural style entered a more ponderous period (mannerism), guided by the classicism of Italian architects such as Filippo Terzi. By the end of the 17th century, however, a complete reaction was germinating: the baroque. The word itself derives

■ **The baroque chapel of Nossa Senhora d'Agonia, Viana do Castelo**

from the Portuguese for rough pearl—*barroco*—and it would characterize Portuguese design for more than two centuries. With the Spaniards safely back over the border and gold and precious stones flowing from the mines of Brazil, Portugal experienced a rebirth and a revived sense of buoyancy and optimism. Great swirls of gilded, carved wood careered over interior surfaces, while architecture itself abandoned classical symmetry to embrace fluidity, theatricality, complexity, and ornamentation. Cherubim, foliage, and sinuous lines were carved and gilded *(talha dourada)* to become altarpieces, panels, or frames, while azulejo panels depicting birds, flowers, people, and religious or urban scenes blanketed church and mansion walls.

Although examples abound throughout the country, the north is where baroque soared to delirious heights, notably in Porto's São Francisco church. From 1725 onward, Porto was the base for the most interesting and productive baroque architect, the Tuscan Nicolau Nasoni. He designed numerous elegant

monuments, including the elliptical Igreja dos Clérigos and the beautifully scaled Casa de Mateus. Another creative center developed at Braga, and the glorious staircase of Bom Jesus was a late result. The north also saw a proliferation of baroque gardens, exemplified at Mateus and Braga, and every town boasted a handful of elegant mansions. During the reign of João V (r. 1706–1750), a flood of foreign artists and architects poured into Portugal for well-paid commissions. German Johann Friedrich Ludwig and Hungarian Carlos Mardel created João's palace at Mafra, which ultimately appears more rococo than baroque.

> **Although examples abound throughout the country, the north is where baroque soared to delirious heights, notably in Porto's São Francisco church.**

Pombaline & Neo-Manueline: A new architectural style evolved in the aftermath of the terrible 1755 earthquake: the Pombaline style. With most of Lisbon lying in ruins, Prime Minister Marquês de Pombal masterminded its reconstruction, abandoning the freedom of baroque in favor of more sober neoclassical colonnades and porticoes. The Palácio de Queluz in Sintra, designed by Mateus Vicente de Oliveira, is typical of the style, although its opulent interior is credited to the French architect Jean-Baptiste Robillon. Neoclassicism dominated architecture well into the 19th century, and in Porto it was favored by the influential yet conservative community of English port traders.

Yet the desire for fantasy lay dormant, not lost, and by the mid-19th century the prevailing Romantic ethic ushered in a fashion for the neo-Manueline. Some of the most extreme examples were built in Sintra, where wealthy aristocrats indulged their fantasies. The whimsical Palácio da Pena of Prince Ferdinand of Saxe-Coburg

■ A detail from Nuno Gonçalves's polyptych of the "Adoration of Saint Vincent" (1460–1470) shows the saint with Prince Henry the Navigator on the right.

may be the most stunning creation. The northern equivalent is the extraordinarily lavish palace of Buçaco. Neo-everything became the rage, even extending to neo-Moorish at Lisbon's Rossio train station. By the early 20th century, these revivals merged with the curves and patterns of art nouveau, but they were soon followed by the cleaner, more geometrical forms of art deco, an outstanding example of which is Porto's Casa de Serralves.

20th Century & Beyond: Today, Portugal's uncontested star architect is the Porto-based Álvaro Siza Vieira (b. 1933), following in the footsteps of his teacher, Fernando Távora (1923–2005). Siza's purist approach and concern with site is in harmony with the world's top contemporary architects. His buildings incorporate breathtaking technical feats—for instance, the majestic, swooping roof of the Portuguese Pavilion at Parque das Nações (Lisbon's Expo 98 site). Siza was also responsible for the vast, interlocking exhibition halls of the Serralves Foundation, in Porto, and for the master plan of the Chiado reconstruction following the 1988 fire. The next generation includes Eduardo Souto de Moura (b. 1952), a former collaborator of Siza who designed the Braga stadium in 2003, and João Luís Carrilho da Graça (b. 1952), who designed the strict geometry of the Knowledge Pavilion at Parque das Nações. The youngest wave of architects is spearheaded by Bernardo Rodrigues (b. 1972), Promontório Arquitectos (a group of five archi-tects, founded in 1990), and S'A Arquitectos (a young team working between Lisbon and Barcelona), all of whom work in minimalist mode. Whether the circle returns again to the Portuguese predilection for decorative frenzy remains to be seen, but it is certain that Portugal's architectural style will never be at a standstill.

Painting

Portuguese artistic talent has always leaned more to the three-dimensional than the two. After emerging in the 15th century, local painting was slow to throw off the cloak of foreign (Spanish, French, Italian, and principally Flemish) influence and Portuguese painters never stood out as a specific school or style. Of the notable homegrown individuals, the 15th-century primitive painter Nuno Gonçalves was outstanding. His polyptych of the "Adoration of St. Vincent" is one of the great classics of the period. He was followed in the 16th century by Vasco Fernandes and Gaspar Vaz, both in Viseu, and Jorge Afonso, in Lisbon, who became court painter in 1508. Unusual for the time, a woman excelled in the 17th century: Josefa de Óbidos (1634–1684) dazzled patrons with her warm portraits and still lifes. Her contemporary, Domingos Vieira (1600–1678), produced remarkably compassionate portraits.

During the following century, Domingos António de Sequeira (1768–1837) and Francisco Vieira (1765–1805) both studied in Rome, a sign of the cultural times, and Sequeira contributed greatly to the Ajuda Palace before political turmoil sent him into exile. A hiatus followed, characterized by generally derivative output, while naturalism gradually took over from Romanticism. The towering figure of the late 19th century was Columbano Bordalo Pinheiro (1857–1929), whose brother, Rafael, was the remarkable ceramicist of Caldas da Rainha. He was followed by the short-lived Amadeo de Souza Cardoso (1887–1918), who produced a stream of cubist and expressionist works after joining the bohemian life of Paris's Montparnasse set.

The Salazar regime actively repressed free expression, so mid-20th-century abstract artists got short shrift. Not surprisingly, Maria Helena Vieira da Silva (1908–1992), Portugal's most celebrated abstract artist, lived in Paris. Paula Rego (b. 1935), who lives in London—honored by a solo exhibition at the Tate Museum in 2004—has achieved fame through imaginative figurative work illustrating metaphors and feminist issues. In the 1980s, a new wave of artists, including Julião Sarmento (b. 1948) and Pedro Cabrita Reis

Fashion

In fashion, the name long on everyone's lips is Ana Salazar, who in stature and imagination is the Portuguese Vivienne Westwood. This grande dame of clothing started her career in the 1970s, when she created Lisbon's first postrevolution fashion events. Since she founded her brand in 1978, Ana Salazar has received numerous acknowledgments. She has also opened a boutique in Paris and presented her often controversial collections in Paris and New York. She even designed the uniforms for Portugal's letter carriers. A monograph and a documentary made about her retrace her life and her career path.

With such a radical example to follow, Portuguese fashion remains extreme, with opulence, fantasy, and decadence never far away. Fátima Lopes, José António Tenente, Anabela Baldaque, Dino Alves, Lidija Kolovrat, Alexandra Moura, and Manuel Alves & José Manuel Gonçalves are among the next generation to create waves. The twice-yearly Moda Lisboa, Lisbon Fashion Week, strengthens their impact. In purely industrial terms, fashion is beaten hands down by footwear: The Portuguese shoe industry is number two in Europe (after Italy), churning out more than 100 million pairs annually.

(b. 1956), appeared on the international scene with compelling works that used new mediums and stretched the limits of painting. Since then photography and new technologies have gained the upper hand among younger artists although, as elsewhere, painting is making a comeback.

Design

Portuguese interior design and the decorative arts are as important in the 21st century as in preceding centuries. Lisbon's new waterfront Museum of Art, Architecture, and Technology (MAAT), housed within the 20th-century Tejo Power Station and an ultramodern exhibition wing, showcases contemporary artists, designers, and thinkers. Add to this the didactic role of Lisbon's centrally located Museu do Design e da Moda (MUDE) and you have a healthy panorama.

Among names to watch for is the internationally renowned Joana Vasconcelos who takes everyday objects and transforms them into sculptures and installations, often with feminist or sociopolitical undertones. Objects in ceramic and glass remain at the top of the creative league, but lesser-used materials such as cork (in which the Alentejo region abounds), steel, and plastics are gaining increasing attention, while recycling offers another sometimes humorous direction.

Although post-contemporary design attracts media attention, and is the current rage in hotel interior design, Portuguese classics have not been forgotten. The workshops of Lisbon's Museu de Artes Decorativas play an important role in maintaining complex craft techniques, while more basic handicrafts continue to be the mainstay of some village economies, particularly in the Alentejo and central Portugal.

 Portuguese interior design and the decorative arts are as important in the 21st century as in preceding centuries. 🙽

Music

Fado (see pp. 58–59), the "blues" of Portugal, is the signature national music and has propelled numerous singers onto the international scene, from Amália Rodrigues to Madredeus and, more recently, Kátia Guerreiro and Carminho. Yet there are other forms of music as well, for Portugal's love of song and verse dates back to the troubadours of the 13th century. Political songs *(canção de intervenção),* for example, played an important role in the protests against Portugal's totalitarian regime of 1926–1974, with José Afonso (1929–1987) one of its chief exponents. This new style of urban popular music was notable for its politically and socially engaged lyrics, often written by the singers. Melodies were word born and reinforced the content of the lyrics. The sound reflected a mixture of influences from traditional music, French urban songs of the 1960s, African

■ The Museu Nacional do Azulejo, Lisbon, is located in the former convent of Madre de Deus.

rhythms, and Brazilian popular music. By the late 1970s the revolutionary climate
had subsided and poets, composers, and singers had to redefine their roles. There
soon came a boom in the number of Portuguese rock groups and a local style
emerged.

The last 25 years have been marked by a search for new musical directions parallel
to the "mediatization" and growth of the music-buying public. Arguably the most outstanding sound is that of Madredeus, a quintet of musicians who, from the mid-1980s
onward, developed a unique mix of fado and modern Portuguese folk music.

Jazz has also seen a substantial increase in both musicians and audiences and Susana
Santos (trumpeter, improviser, and composer from Porto) is just one example. Several
transplanted musical traditions—especially from the former African colonies—now
thrive in Lisbon, and foreign styles such as rap and hip-hop have been adapted locally.

Madredeus

Named for the Lisbon convent in which they initially rehearsed (now part of the Museu Nacional do Azulejo), the fado band Madredeus went from strength to strength, led by the haunting voice of their singer, Teresa Salgueiro. The 1987 album *Os Dias da Madredeus* was a watershed in Portuguese music, and Madredeus was soon touring the world, bringing the Portuguese language and echoes of fado to millions. Disagreements between the musicians eventually led to a change in lineup, and in *O Paraiso* (1997) fado was virtually abandoned. Their 2004 album, *Amor Infinito*, and later works bore little relation to the music that so entranced director Wim Wenders while making the 1994 film *Lisbon Story*.

Cesária Évora, from the former colony of Cabo Verde (Cape Verde), has attained international fame with her pulsating style of Cape Verde *morna* (a wistful style of blues). The four accordionists of Danças Ocultas represent an ethno-folk thread that produces a searing sound of pure emotion. Contemporary classical music flourishes, too—Orchestrutopica plays pieces by several young composers—while pop bands such as The Gift and Amor Electro fill concert venues around the country.

Literature

Like music, poetry—especially works of a metaphysical nature—appeals to the Portuguese heart, making it the dominant literary form. As is the case with cinema, Portuguese literature of the 20th century is dominated by a towering yet enigmatic figure: Fernando Pessoa. From a historical perspective, Portugal's equivalent of William Shakespeare is Luís Vaz de Camões (1524–1580); his epic work, *Os Lusíadas (The Lusiads),* celebrated Vasco da Gama's great voyage of discovery to India in 1497. Far from being a figment of Camões's imagination, the story is based on his own experiences while sailing to Goa and traveling in Morocco, and it is rendered in a spirit similar to Homer's *Odyssey.*

Also honored time and again is Almeida Garrett (1799–1854), a poet of the Romantic period who also penned political plays and novels including *Viagens na Minha Terra (Travels in My Homeland).* His contemporary, Alexandre Herculano (1810–1877), was a political activist who spent long periods of exile in England and France; he was also a successful historical novelist. Realism came to Portuguese literature in the works of José Maria Eça de Queirós (1845–1900), whose bestselling novel was *Os Maias (The Maias).*

In the 20th century, Lisbon-based poet Fernando Pessoa (1888–1935) was in full flight. After spending much of his childhood in South Africa, where he became fluent in English, Pessoa started writing poetry in his teens. He led a dreary life as an office translator, but his depressive mind churned with thoughts. He was part of Lisbon's avant-garde movement, founding several literary journals and bringing the tenets of futurism and surrealism to Portugal. Writing under several heteronyms (poet identities), he published widely, yet his genius was only recognized after his premature death from cirrhosis. *O Livro do Desassossego (The Book of Disquiet)* is the collection of his angst-ridden notes and jottings stored in a trunk during his tragic and solitary existence.

José Saramago (1922–2010) was Portugal's most influential writer, having won the Nobel Prize for literature in 1998. His sometimes ponderous work includes plays, poetry, short stories, nonfiction, and novels, blending realism with the fantastical. Saramago's rise to fame came in 1982 with *Memorial do Convento (Memorial of the*

Convent), a lyrical love story set in the convent of Mafra during its 18th-century construction. In 1991, his *O Evangelho Segundo Jesus Cristo (The Gospel According to Jesus Christ)*, which depicted Christ as a typical fallible human being with self-doubts and sexual impulses, scandalized the Portuguese church. The result? Another exiled Portuguese writer—this time to Lanzarote in the Canary Islands.

António Lobo Antunes (b. 1942) has also enjoyed international success. His often dark novels delve deeply into human relationships, incorporate history, and reflect his experience both of war and of clinical psychiatry. Other contemporary names to watch for are Lídia Jorge, José Cardoso Pires, Hélia Correia, and the highly respected philosopher Eduardo Lourenço (b. 1923), whose *Mitologia da Saudade (Mythology of Nostalgia)* is a seminal work.

José Saramago with his wife, Pilar del Río Gonçalves, in 2008.

Cinema

One name dominates Portuguese cinema: Manoel de Oliveira (1908–2015), a celebrated native of Porto. At the time of his death this acknowledged master was the oldest film director in the world, his work spanning the history of film from his first silent movie, in 1928, to his last, in 2012. With astonishing vitality and talent, Oliveira was prodigious in his output, averaging one film a year for the last two decades, and he worked with a host of celebrity actors, from Marcello Mastroianni to Michel Piccoli and Irene Papas. His films are regularly screened at festivals such as Cannes and Venice, the most recent being *Gebo et l'Ombre (Gebo and the Shadow)*, made in 2012, with stars Michael Lonsdale and Jeanne Moreau. Oliveira's fame extends to the United States, where retrospectives of his work have been shown at the Los Angeles

Film Festival (1992), the National Gallery of Art in Washington, D.C. (1993), the San Francisco Film Festival, and the Cleveland Museum of Art (1994).

Another major figure of Portuguese cinema is João César Monteiro (1939–2003). This protagonist of the so-called New Portuguese Cinema in the 1960s only reached cinematographic maturity in the mid-1970s. Monteiro was considered one of Europe's most original directors, making provocative films in which the gritty clashed with the sublime. His last films included *As Bodas de Deus* (1998), *Branca de Neve* (2000), and *Vai e Vem* (2003), which was screened at the 2004 Cannes Film Festival. *A Comédia de Deus* (1995) won him the Jury's Special Prize at the Venice Film Festival.

> **Monteiro was considered one of Europe's most original directors, making provocative films in which the gritty clashed with the sublime.**

Portuguese cinema survives solely thanks to hefty state grants and the input of television channels. With a total population of 10 million, the domestic market is understandably small and Portuguese penetration of the international market is limited. A film is considered a success when it draws an audience of more than 150,000—and very few Portuguese films do. One that did was the hugely successful *Tentação* (1997), directed by Joaquim Leitão (b. 1956). This love story about a priest and a junkie in deepest Portugal features Portugal's biggest star, Joaquim de Almeida. Internationally awarded *Tabu* (2012), by Miguel Gomes, and the highly accoladed *Blood of My Blood* (2011), directed by João Canijo, have undoubtedly been the most successful Portuguese films of recent years. Among the younger generation of directors, Teresa Villaverde (b. 1966) is the most interesting. After beginning her career as an actress in César Monteiro's film *À Flor do Mar* (1986), she surfaced as a director in the 1990s. Her films tend to be angst-ridden stories about adolescents in conflict with society. One of her films, *Três Irmãos* (1994), won Maria de Medeiros the best actress award at the Venice Film Festival.

It is impossible to write about Portuguese cinema without mentioning two highly charged, evocative films about Lisbon by foreign directors. *In the White City* (1983), by Swiss filmmaker Alain Tanner, stars Bruno Ganz and Teresa Madruga in an exploration of alienation and time against a picturesquely decrepit backdrop of the Portuguese capital. And Wim Wenders's *Lisbon Story* (1994) is a masterpiece built on the theme of sound. Filmed around the Alfama, it features the melancholic voices and presence of the band Madredeus and a guest appearance by Manoel de Oliveira. ■

EXPERIENCE: Indulge in Portuguese Cinema

For film aficionados, Portugal offers some great opportunities for viewing national and international arts films. If visiting Porto in late February and early March, a good way to pass an evening or two is to check out **Fantasporto** *(fantasporto.com)*, the country's leading film festival. In addition to showing quality international movies, both commercial and independent, Fantasporto showcases the best of Portuguese films—though beware, if your Portuguese language skills are lacking, it may be worth picking an English-language movie. Either way, Fantasporto is a fantastic way to immerse yourself in Porto's cultural scene, well off the usual tourist trail.

A seductive mix of broad avenues and twisting alleyways,
the old-fashioned and the hip, the past and the present

LISBON

Vintage trams negotiate Lisbon's hills.

LISBON

Stand on the banks of the Tejo River and savor the salty Atlantic air—you will have a clear sense of being on the edge of Europe. Lisbon (Lisboa) is very much that, its character formed more by Portugal's overseas colonies than by European neighbors. Today, its character is sophisticated and liberal, a hub for entrepreneurship and innovation. Humming with visitors, Lisbon's history and culture are being repackaged and rebranded to appeal to the ever more discerning traveler.

Lisbon offers a unique array of cultural attractions, excellent restaurants, atmospheric backstreets, melancholic fado music, efficient public transportation, and plenty of green escapes. The city's riverfront position, too, adds spice to every view, of which there are many from hilltop *miradouros* (viewpoints) and towers. This sense of space is increased by two spectacular bridges: the Ponte 25 de Abril and the 10.7-mile-long (17 km) Ponte Vasco da Gama, a technological feat that disappears over the horizon.

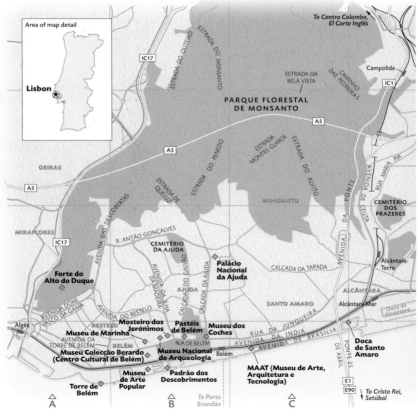

The main districts of interest to visitors are the central Baixa, Chiado, Bairro Alto, and the Alfama. To the west lies Belém, a must-see for its monuments and custard tarts, and heading far east along the Tejo, the family-friendly Parque das Nações. Other places that should not be overlooked include the Museu Calouste Gulbenkian, the Museu Nacional do Azulejo, and the Museu Nacional de Arte Antiga.

Also be sure to explore the vast, wooded Parque Florestal de Monsanto; walk the hand-cobbled, charcoal gray basalt and limestone sidewalks of Chiado and Baixa; and wander the bougainvillea-draped alleys and stairways of the Alfama, Lisbon's oldest district, crowned by the ruins of a Moorish castle. ■

NOT TO BE MISSED:

The city views from Castelo de São Jorge 52–53

Having a morning coffee at the sidewalk café A Brasileira 56

An evening of fado 58–59

Jerónimos Monastery 60–63

Eating *pastéis de Belém* (custard tarts) in Belém 64

The exquisite Torre de Belém 64–65

Admiring the Gulbenkian Museum's stunning artwork 66–68

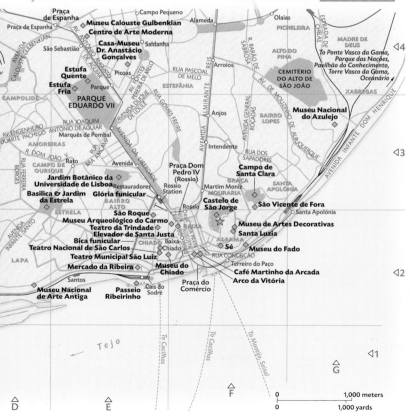

BAIXA & THE DOCKS

Lisbon's commercial heart stretches between two large squares, the Praça Dom Pedro IV, more commonly known as Rossio, and the lovely Praça do Comércio, which opens onto the river. From here it is a natural transition to the central docks, now completely regenerated as one of Lisbon's hottest nocturnal destinations.

■ A view from the Elevador de Santa Justa looks across the Baixa at the Alfama district's Castelo de São Jorge.

Following the 1755 earthquake, which hit the Baixa hardest, the Marquês de Pombal ordered a simple reconstruction to accommodate the artisans based there: a grid layout sliced north-south by the Rua Augusta and streets named after each trade. On the Rua do Ouro (Gold Street) you'll find the 148-foot-tall (45 m) **Elevador de Santa Justa.** This iconic ironwork structure dating from 1902 spirits people up to the Chiado via a walkway at the top; be sure to stop at the top of the tower for fabulous views. Equally delightful is the **Glória funicular,** just north of Rossio station, which takes you up to the Bairro Alto.

Rua Augusta has become a promenading street, its black and white cobbles fronting century-old, traditional stores, banks, cafés, fashion shops, and at the southern end, the **MUDE—Museu do Design e da Moda** *(Rua Augusta 24, tel 218 171 892, mude.pt),* a museum dedicated to design and fashion. Furniture, accessories, and household objects dating from the 1930s onward are exhibited amid exposed concrete, vast modernist countertops, and green and black marble floors.

From here head through the **Arco da Vitória,** a triumphal arch that frames the vast, arcaded

Praça do Comércio. This square, once the site of the royal Palácio da Ribeira, is now home to ministries, Lisbon's Welcome Center, and buzzing outdoor dining. An equestrian statue of Dom José I surveys the scene, while **Café Martinho da Arcada**—once a haunt of the noted 20th-century poet Fernando Pessoa (see p. 44)—offers the perfect spot for a quick *bica* (espresso).

On the eastern side of the square, the **Lisboa Story Centre** *(tel 211 941 027, lisboastorycentre.pt)*, provides visitors with an hour-long history of the city, focusing on the 1755 earthquake and its aftermath.

The Docks

The revitalized docks along the Tejo extend west past Alcântara and east as far as Santa Apolónia (the actual working docks extend farther). Today's occupants of the converted warehouses are no longer importers of exotic goods from Portuguese colonies but hot nightclubs and hip restaurants with a few designer stores thrown in. Traffic can be worse here in the early hours of a Sunday morning than in any midweek rush hour.

The soaring iron-and-glass landmark along this strip is the 1876 **Mercado da Ribeira,** part traditional food market—offering an array of fresh produce, cured meats, and regional cheeses—and part uber-trendy food hall called **Time Out Market,** featuring stalls from some of the city's best known restaurants (see p. 241).

Across the main road is the **Cais do Sodré,** where bus, train, tram, metro, and ferry lines all meet. Trains to Estoril and Cascais leave from here, as does the ferry to Cacilhas. You cannot help but see the statue of Christ, the **Cristo Rei** on the other side of the river. Built in 1959, it towers 360 feet (110 m) above Lisbon

in brazen imitation of the Rio de Janeiro version. If interested, take the elevator to the top of the statue *(Santuário Nacional de Cristo Rei, Almada, tel 212 751 000, cristorei.pt, €)* for fabulous views over the city and south across the Setúbal Peninsula.

Back on the river's right bank, enjoy a breezy riverside stroll and/or some barbecued fish along the **Passeio Ribeirinho** to the west of Cais do Sodré. Beyond Alcântara's maritime terminal is the **Santo Amaro** dock, another urban development that attracts Lisbonites. ∎

Baixa

🗺 49 F2

Visitor Information

✉ Lisboa Welcome Center, Praça do Comércio

☎ 210 312 810

visitlisboa.com

Step Back in Time

At first glance, the Baixa district looks like any other downtown shopping area, but behind many of the 18th-century facades you'll find charming centenary shops. Open since the early 20th century, or even before, and complete with original fixtures, these businesses specialize in everything from hats and gloves to buttons and fine jewels. Don't miss **Confeitaria Nacional** *(Praça da Figueira 18B)*, confectioners since 1829; **Manuel Tavares** *(Rua de Betesga 1A)*, a grocery store established in 1860; the 1886 millinery **Azevedo Rua** *(Praça Dom Pedro IV, 69–73)*; **Retrosaria Bijou** *(Rua da Conceição 91)*, a haberdashery opened in 1922; or the 1925 glove shop **Luvaria Ulisses** *(Rua do Carmo 87A)*.

Mercado da Ribeira

🗺 49 E2

✉ Avenida 24 de Julho

☎ 213 951 274

timeoutmarket.com/ lisboa/conceito

NOTE: Sightseeing boat trips on the **Tejo.** Daily between 10 a.m. and 6 p.m., at 2 or 3 hour intervals, a shuttle-boat connects Praça do Comércio to Belém, with stops in between *(yellowbus-tours.com, €€€€)*.

CASTELO & THE ALFAMA

Lisbon may have been built on seven hills, but its most visible summit monument is without doubt the Castelo de São Jorge. Views from the ramparts of this sprawling castle take in the Chiado and Bairro Alto opposite, the district of Graça behind, and the labyrinthine Alfama below the castle walls. The name Alfama derives from the Arabic Al-Hamma, or hot springs, thanks to the Moors who built this atmospheric quarter of twisting, narrow alleys and stairways.

■ Castelo de São Jorge offers some of the best views across the city and the Tejo River.

Castelo de São Jorge

🅰 49 F2

☎ 218 800 620

💲 €€
Book in advance for bat tour (€€)

🚌 Bus: 737. Tram: 12, 28

castelodesaojorge.pt

Castelo de São Jorge

The classic way to reach the castle is to take the No. 28 tram to Santa Luzia, from where it is a short walk uphill, though swarms of *tuk-tuks* now vie for the trade. The origins of the castle go back to the fifth-century Visigoths and, four centuries later, to the Moors who enlarged it and built walls to surround their *kasbah* (fortress). Further modifications came with Afonso Henriques, Portugal's first king, and until the 16th century it was used as a royal residence. After intermittently functioning as a prison, the castle was completely restored and turned over to the public. It offers a café, gardens, cannon, great views, and—on summer Saturday nights—biologist-led tours to observe the castle's resident colony of five species of bats.

On his return from India in 1499, Vasco da Gama came here for a triumphant royal audience with Manuel I. The site of this meeting, the **Olisipónia,** is now occupied by an innovative multi-media show recounting the city's history. Close by, in the Torre de Ulysses, see an unusual view of the city in the **Periscópio,** an ingenious system of mirrors and screens.

On the southern slope of the castle hill stands a Romanesque **Sé,** or cathedral (Largo da Sé, tel 218 866 752). The sober facade flanked by two towers was built soon after Afonso Henriques took Lisbon from the Moors in the late 12th century. Although greatly damaged in the 1755 earthquake, the Cathedral was successfully restored and today an elegant, vaulted interior leads to Gothic cloisters and a dazzling treasury in the **chapter house** *(closed Mon., €)*. Look for Dom José I's baroque monstrance, an elaborate affair said to incorporate more than 4,000 precious stones. Excavations in the cloisters have revealed Phoenician, Roman, and Arab artifacts.

The Alfama

On the southern side below the castle, the **miradouro de Santa Luzia** overlooks the heart of the Alfama. The exterior walls of the church facing this terrace bear striking azulejo panels that illustrate major events in the city's history. Opposite stands the impressive **Museu de Artes Decorativas.** The decorative arts museum is housed in the 17th-century Azurara mansion. The museum showcases glasswork, silverwork, porcelains, paintings, tapestries, and carpets, all presented according to historic periods in a suitably aristocratic environment. However, the most outstanding rooms are devoted to 17th- and 18th-century furniture, of which many pieces reflect Portugal's fascination for exotic materials and craftsmanship: Take note of the sophisticated portable writing desk from India and the oriental fantasy painted on two lacquered cabinets. A visual feast of azulejos adorn the walls of the main staircase and halls.

Although not strictly part of the Alfama, the white stone monastery of **São Vicente de Fora** *(Largo de São Vicente, tel 218 810 500)* to the northeast is a sight you cannot escape. Built at the turn of the 16th century outside the city walls, its cloister *(closed Mon., €)* walls still retain azulejos telling the fables of La Fontaine.

The huge square behind São Vicente, **Campo de Santa Clara,** hosts the sprawling **Feira da Ladra** (Thieves' Market) every Tuesday and Saturday—a must-see for lovers of antiques and second-hand objects. ∎

Museu de Artes Decorativas

🏛 49 F2
✉ Largo das Portas do Sol 2
☎ 218 814 600
🕐 Closed Tues.
💲 €
🚌 Bus: 737. Tram: 12, 28

fress.pt

Invasion of the Tuk-Tuk

The Portuguese economic crisis has meant that people have had to get creative to make a living. Over the past few years, a new generation of entrepreneurs has injected fresh life into Lisbon: Trendy eateries and bars have sprung up, and dozens of boutique hotels and fashionable hostels have opened. A vast array of quirky tour options are now available including Segways, bikes, and 4x4s. Most notable is the invasion of the *tuk-tuk* (a three-wheeled covered motorcycle), offering anything from quick hop-on, hop-off rides to day-long tours of the city. Ideal for getting up the steep narrow streets of the Alfama, these zippy little vehicles will take you anywhere you want to go. For the sake of local residents and the environment always choose a company that uses electric-powered tuk-tuks *(ecotuktours.com or tejo tourism.pt/en/tuk-tuk)*.

A WALK AROUND THE ALFAMA

Lisbon's oldest quarter, built by the Moors in the 11th century, retains much of its original atmosphere despite, after years of neglect, having undergone a total renovation in order to welcome throngs of tourists. Fading coats of arms bear witness to the Alfama's aristocratic past before the city's fishing community took over.

The backstreets of the Alfama, where Lisbon life can be witnessed and savored

From the Castelo de São Jorge's main entrance on Rua do Chão da Feira, start walking downhill, admiring the tiled facades. As you round the corner, peep inside the 18th-century entrance of the Belmonte patio on your left to see a lovely example. When you reach Largo do Contador-Mor, cross the road to the church of **Santa Luzia ❶**; exterior azulejo panels show Lisbon's appearance, including the Praça do Comércio, before the 1755 earthquake.

Opposite, on the corner of Largo das Portas do Sol, is the **Museu de Artes Decorativas ❷**, well worth a visit (see p. 53). Alternatively, the sidewalk café is a good place to watch the trams go by against a backdrop of the hilltop monastery **São Vicente de Fora** (see p. 53). Just behind Santa Luzia, steps twist downhill into the heart of the Alfama. Follow this convoluted route to a small square. Turn

NOT TO BE MISSED:

- Museu de Artes Decorativas
- Escadinhas de Santo Estêvão
- Museu do Fado

right to Beco da Corvinha and left, down more steps that eventually broaden out at the back of **São Miguel ❸**. Founded in 1150, this church was rebuilt after the earthquake. Orange trees, laundry hung out to dry, potted plants, caged canaries, and private shrines all add to the ambience.

Pass a couple of fado taverns on your right, turn left onto Largo de São Miguel, then right down Rua de São Miguel. Local grocery stores on this typical street signal that the old Alfama has plenty of life in it yet. Turn right at the intersection with Rua da Regueira, then left along the narrow Beco do Carneiro, noting the public washing place. At the end, a staircase leads to the church of **Santo Estêvão ❹** and a terrace viewpoint. Return down the steps to reach a very pretty square. Around the next corner, descend the picturesque **Escadinhas de Santo Estêvão.**

At the bottom of the stairs, turn right onto Rua dos Remédios. On the right, note the lovely Manueline doorway of the 16th- to 18th-century **Ermida de Nossa Senhora dos Remédios,** a sanctuary built for the Alfama fishermen. Inside are baroque azulejos and some 16th-century paintings. This street and its extension, Rua de São Pedro, are the Alfama's busiest shopping streets.

At the Largo do Chafariz de Dentro, the **Museu do Fado ❺** *(tel 218 823 470, museudo fado.pt, closed Mon., €€)* pays homage to the traditional music of Lisbon (see pp. 58–59). Continue along Rua de São Pedro, through the Largo de São Rafael with its ruined Moorish tower, then along Rua São João da Praça. After the church of this name, turn left through a tunnel arch and emerge on the Rua do Cais de Santarém. Turn right to reach the **Casa dos Bicos ❻**, with its unusual diamond-shaped stone projections.

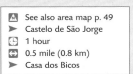

- See also area map p. 49
- ► Castelo de São Jorge
- ⏱ 1 hour
- ↔ 0.5 mile (0.8 km)
- ► Casa dos Bicos

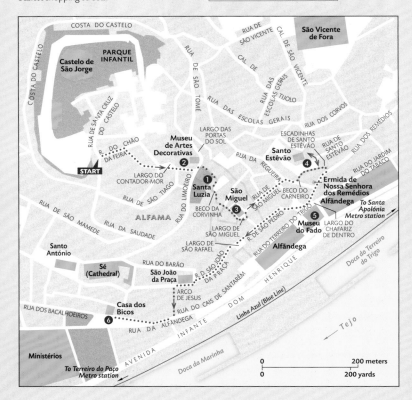

CHIADO & BAIRRO ALTO

Rising to the west of the Baixa is Chiado, which extends into the Bairro Alto. Chiado may be limited in size, but it boasts theaters, art galleries, and museums—including a remarkable archeological museum—as well as wonderful traditional shops. Bairro Alto, on the other hand, is a grid of narrow streets where touristy fado dives and packed restaurants rub shoulders with small, independent fashion stores; in daylight it can seem frayed at the edges.

■ A relic of the 1755 earthquake, this church nave now houses part of the Museu Arqueológico do Carmo.

Once again Lisbonites and tourists alike settle into sidewalk cafés such as the art nouveau institution **A Brasileira** *(Rua Garrett 120, tel 213 469 541),* a favorite of the 20th-century poet Fernando Pessoa (see p. 44), immortalized in bronze outside.

Bairro Alto

Uphill from here is the brick red **Teatro da Trindade** *(Largo da Trindade 7A, tel 213 420 000),* built in 1867 to stage operettas and dance performances. It still hosts theater, musical, and dance performances. Next door, the **Anglo-Portuguese Telephone Company** is a 1920s relic of English commercial activity with window frames painted a classic "post-office green." At the top of this street, the church of **São Roque** is a 16th- to 17th-century design by the architect Filippo Terzi. The 18th-century **Capela de São João Baptista,** a chapel to the left of the altar, is a heavy-duty baroque medley of different stones that was made in Rome and blessed by the pope. A **museum,** to the right of the entrance, displays rich vestments and liturgical objects.

Focusing on scientific, zoological, and botanical studies in the former Portuguese colonies, the

Museu de São Roque

🏛 49 E2

✉ Largo Trindade Coelho

☎ 213 235 444

🕐 Closed Mon. & Tue. a.m.

💲 €

mais.scml.pt/museu-saoroque

When flames shot out of a store on Rua do Carmo in the heart of Lisbon in August 1988, Chiado bore the brunt of the accidental fire—fire engines couldn't get into the narrow streets. Four blocks of this district were reduced to rubble, but intelligent rebuilding, following a master plan by Álvaro Siza Vieira, has restored it to its former self.

Museu Nacional de História Natural e da Ciência and Jardim Botânico *(Rua da Escola Politécnica, tel 213 921 808, closed Mon., €€)*, boasts one of Europe's oldest chemistry laboratories. The highlight here is undoubtedly its 19th-century botanical garden, specializing in trees and shrubs, particularly palms, conifers, and cycads.

Chiado

An inspiring presentation awaits at Chiado's **Museu Arqueológico do Carmo.** A portion of this archaeological museum occupies a 1389 church nave, roofless since the 1755 earthquake. It gives an evocative edge to a display of architectural fragments, all in matching white stone. Inside the chapels at the back is a fascinating collection

---

INSIDER TIP:

Explore Principe Real, the area above the Bairro Alto, buzzing with trendy shops, bars, and restaurants in palatial buildings.

—EMMA ROWLEY
National Geographic contributor

---

put together after the abolition of religious orders in 1834. Note the medieval tomb sculptures of Fernão Sanches (the illegitimate son of Dom Dinis I) and Dom Fernando I, as well as the odd juxtaposition of a library, an Egyptian mummy, two Peruvian mummies, and pre-Hispanic pieces from Central America.

Outside, enjoy a drink at one of the cafés in the pretty square before heading downhill.

At the southern end of Chiado, **Teatro Nacional de São Carlos** *(Rua Serpa Pinto 9, tel 213 253 045, tnsc.pt)* was built in 1793 in a late baroque imitation of Milan's La Scala. Enjoy the opulent decor by catching a ballet, opera, or concert.

EXPERIENCE: Guided Walks by Scholars

Every nook and cranny of Lisbon oozes with history that comes alive for you on a scholar-guided walk. If you'd like to hear about former Phoenician, Moorish, and Roman inhabitants, visit the birthplace of St. Anthony of Padua, and see the site of the Inquisition, then look no further than **Lisbon Explorer** *(tel 213 629 263, lisbon explorer.com)*. The friendly English-speaking guides are entertaining and enthusiastic. The most popular walks last about three hours and cost €150 for the group; they also offer a range of other tours upon request.

One block farther south, the **MNAC—Museu Nacional de Arte Contemporânea do Chiado,** the national museum of contemporary art, displays rotating exhibits of the collection beside major temporary exhibitions. A renovated former monastery, the building has striking, airy spaces perfect for modern art. Don't miss the suspended staircase leading down to the café, terrace, and sculpture garden. Due west of here, along Rua de São Paulo, the **Bica funicular** *(€)* will spirit you back up to Barrio Alto. ∎

Museu Arqueológico do Carmo

- 🗺 49 F2
- ✉ Largo do Carmo
- ☎ 213 478 629
- 🕐 Closed Sun.
- 💲 €
- 🚇 Metro: Baixa-Chiado. Tram: 28

museuarqueologico docarmo.pt

Museu Nacional de Arte Contemporânea do Chiado

- 🗺 49 F2
- ✉ Rua Serpa Pinto 4
- ☎ 213 432 148
- 🕐 Closed Mon.
- 💲 €
- 🚇 Metro: Baixa-Chiado. Bus: 758. Tram: 28

museuarte contemporanea.pt

FADO MUSIC

If there is one sound that is distinctly Portuguese, it is the often melancholic strains of fado (literally "fate"), the local version of the blues. The music originated in early 19th-century Lisbon, more specifically in the dives of the Alfama, drawing on the rhythms of African slave dances, Arab voice medleys, and traditional oral folklore. Recent Lisbon music critic Miguel Francisco Cadete pointed out that its first fans were "pimps, prostitutes, sailors and bandits with knives." Today, however, fado is entrenched in the Lisbon soul.

Generally the untrained voice of the singer is accompanied by two acoustic guitarists, one playing a Spanish guitar, the other a 12-string Portuguese guitar (mandolin-shaped with a flat back). The musicians revel in melodic outpourings of longing, sadness, and fatalism to express the target emotion, *saudade* (yearning). In authentic fado houses you will see improvised musical dialogues between professional and amateur singers. The fado in Coimbra (see sidebar p. 118) has a tradition all of its own: It is sung only by men, the lyrics are more cultured, and the Coimbra guitar gives it a more melodic and solemn sound.

Although its roots are in the lower ranks of society, fado was gradually adopted by the gentry thanks to a scandalous affair in the 1840s between singer Maria Severa and a nobleman, the Conde de Vimioso. From then on *fadistas* performed at aristocratic social gatherings. With the advent of radio, the form took off completely. During the long Salazar years

Take Some Fado Home

Amália Rodrigues: Any of her many "Best of" albums

Mariza: *Fado em Mim* 2001, *Terra* 2008, *Fado Tradicional* 2010

Ana Moura: *Desfado* 2012

Carminho: *Fado* 2009, *Canto* 2014

(1932–1968), fado was initially labeled as harmful to social progress; many singers were banned or forced to become professional and only perform publicly at fado houses. Salazar later embraced fado as the perfect propagandistic tool and it thus became politically tainted, losing its popular appeal. Since the 1990s the music has regained its former status.

Songstresses of Note

Amália Rodrigues (1920–1999), fado's greatest diva, inspired such devotion that her death engendered three days of national

EXPERIENCE: Strum the Portuguese Guitar

Does hearing fado make you want to pick up the Portuguese guitar? It is possible, over the summer months, to take lessons in the instrument with Ricardo Mata *(Rua Augusto Machado 9–1dto, Lisbon, tel 962 238 252, ricardomata.net).* **Mata has been teaching students since 1997 and offers lessons for beginners and up, whether you would like to learn a few basics or polish up some existing skills. Each lesson lasts one hour and packages of four lessons cost around €70–75, depending on the time of day. Lessons can be taken all in one week or spread over two. At other times of the year, Mata is happy to provide tailor-made, private lessons, which can be arranged in advance. See his website for more information.**

Fado musician Mario Pacheco (left) strums a 12-string Portuguese guitar, the *guitarra do fado*.

mourning and a cathartic outpouring of emotion. It seems unlikely that Amália's popularity will ever be surpassed; apart from possessing a gut-wrenching voice and immense beauty, she lived a classic rags-to-riches tale. Her 18th-century town house, chock-a-block with antiques, portraits, and lavish costumes, is a far cry from her teenage years when she sold fruit on the Alcântara docks. The house is now open to the public *(Rua de São Bento 193, Lisbon, tel 213 971 896, closed Mon. & holidays, amaliarodrigues.pt, €€).*

Amália remains an inspiration to fado and popular music artists such as Madredeus (see p. 44), Dulce Pontes, and Mariza—whose confident voice and charismatic stage presence has conquered fans around the world—and more recently to Ana Moura and Carminho. Born in 1984, Carminho is considered one of the most talented fado singers of her generation; her ability to blend traditional and contemporary fado with pop, rock, and jazz, makes her popular with younger listeners. In 2015 she was awarded the Order of Infante Dom Henrique for her services in expanding Portuguese culture around the globe.

BELÉM

Far to the west of the city center is the district of Belém, a must-see for its cluster of major monuments, both ancient and modern. It also plays an important official role in the form of the presidential residence, the Palácio de Belém.

The magnificent Jerónimos monastery and the emblematic, riverside Torre de Belém top the list of amazing sites. In between stand the Centro Cultural de Belém, a cultural powerhouse harboring the innovative Berardo Collection and, on the hill above, the the ornate former royal palace of Ajuda. Between them, several museums cover art, architecture, design, archaeology, marine history, and carriages. Yet Belém is far from being a mere tourist destination: Hordes of Lisbonites descend on this cultural epicenter on weekends and public holidays, partly for the scenic riverside area around the Discoveries monument but equally for Lisbon's most popular pastry shop.

Mosteiro dos Jerónimos

The imposing Jerónimos monastery stands at the back of the monumental Praça do Império, now formal gardens and a vast parking lot. The fabulously ornate facade stonework has been restored to its original, blindingly white state and makes a startling and unexpected sight in this predominantly post-1755 city.

Begun in 1501, this jewel of Manueline style took a century to be completed and, as a result, its architectural and decorative elements span Gothic, Renaissance, and neoclassical forms. Commissioned by Dom Manuel I, the monastery affirmed the political and expansionist power of Portugal at the time, being close to the tidal beach where Vasco da Gama's ships made their triumphant return from India. Financing

■ **Vasco da Gama's magnificent tomb stands beneath the choir gallery of the Jerónimos monastery.**

came from the immense wealth derived from the spices of the Indies, while the gold later flowing from Brazil and Mozambique was destined to be plastered over side chapels and the altar.

Miraculously, the monastery structure was one of the few buildings to survive Lisbon's 1755 earthquake, thanks to its intelligently conceived vaults, although statues tumbled from niches and columns. The unique architectural style won it UNESCO classification as a World Heritage site.

INSIDER TIP:

Snack on sandwiches of fried pork or delicately grilled fresh sardines in the small cafés that line the road to the Jerónimos monastery in Belém.

—JOHNNA RIZZO
National Geographic
magazine editor

On a cultural note, two heroes of Portugal, Vasco da Gama and the poet Luís Vaz de Camões (1524–1580), are entombed at the entrance, beneath the choir gallery. These tombs, together with the tomb of poet Fernando Pessoa (1888–1935) in the cloister and the royal tombs in the chapel (see sidebar above), make the monastery an illustrious resting place.

Once you enter the monastery, you'll find the breathtaking cloister, a Manueline masterpiece,

Jerónimos's Spectacular Manueline Details

Portugal's greatest showcase of Manueline style demands admiration of its details. The brilliantly rendered sculptures of the south portal are the work of the prodigious Spanish artist Juan de Castilla. They are surmounted by a cross of the Knights of Christ and a statue of Prince Henry the Navigator, Manuel I's great-uncle and the man responsible for Portugal's overseas ambitions.

Equally outstanding is the typically Manueline entrance of the west portal, inside the porch, with statues by the prodigious French sculptor Nicolas de Chanterenne. A perfect balance between simplicity and detail is typified by carved rope snaking up columns to the vaulted ceiling. Dom Manuel I's tomb in the main chapel displays a hefty silver tabernacle, and four other royal tombs are held up by marble elephants—further evidence of Portugal's far-reaching explorations.

with arches and slender columns so delicately carved that they look like biscuit-ware porcelain. They were the work of French architect Diogo de Boitaca. Upon his death in 1517, Spaniard Juan de Castilla undertook the upper story, finishing in 1544. Look for the minimalist tomb of Pessoa, whose body was transferred here in 1985. Along with the colorful 18th-century azulejos depicting the life of St. Joseph in the refectory, do not miss the staircase that takes you up to the choir overlooking the church.

Outside, be sure to scan the walls for esoteric symbols carved into the stones; these are the signatures of the stonemasons who worked on the construction.

Mosteiro dos Jerónimos

48 B1
Praça do Império
213 620 034
Closed Mon.
Church free. Monastery €€€

mosteiro jeronimos.gov.pt

NOTE: To get to Belém, take bus 28, 714, 727, 729, or 751; tram 15; or the train (Belém station on the Cascais line).

Two Museums: The 19th-century "modern" wing of the monastery holds an archaeological museum and a maritime museum. The **Museu Nacional de Arqueologia** (*tel 213 620 000, mnarqueologia-ipmuseus.pt, closed Mon., €€*) has some lovely pieces. Look for the second-century Roman statue of Apollo found in the Algarve and granite boars and warriors from the Douro region. The beautiful Bronze Age, Roman, and Celtic jewelry exhibits in the Treasure Room are outstanding. Oddly, one room even holds Egyptian mummies and fiber sandals. The **Museu de Marinha** (*tel 210 977 388, ccm.marinha.pt/pt/museu, €€*) portrays Portugal's maritime prowess through boats and barges, ship models, navigational instruments, naval uniforms,

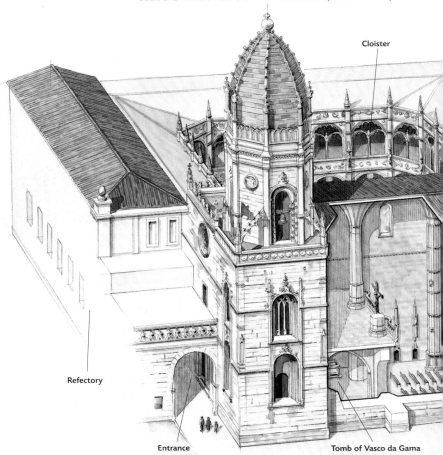

Cloister

Refectory

Entrance

Tomb of Vasco da Gama

and paintings. The most unusual piece in the collection is the seaplane flown in 1922 by Gago Coutinho and Sacadura Cabral from Lisbon to Rio de Janeiro.

Palácio Nacional da Ajuda

Cresting the hill behind the monastery complex is the neoclassical Palácio Nacional da Ajuda. Although the palace contains sumptuous decorative features, the heavy 19th-century style is not comparable with the national palaces of Queluz (see pp. 168–169) or Sintra (see pp. 159–160).

The painted ceilings, statues, tapestries, decorative objects, and furniture were all enjoyed by King Luis and his Italian wife, Maria Pia, after their marriage in 1862, and by their son, King Carlos I.

Palácio Nacional da Ajuda

🗺 48 B2
✉ Largo da Ajuda
☎ 213 637 095
🕐 Closed Wed.
💲 €€

palacioajuda.pt

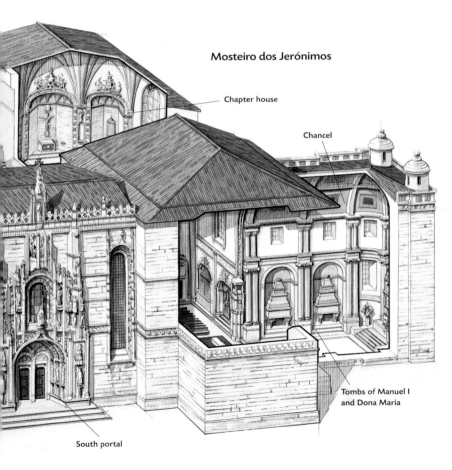

Mosteiro dos Jerónimos

Chapter house

Chancel

Tombs of Manuel I and Dona Maria

South portal

Museu Colecção Berardo

🅰 48 B1

✉ Praça do Império

☎ 213 612 878

museuberardo.com

Museu de Arte Popular

🅰 48 B1

✉ Avenida de Brasília

☎ 213 011 282

🕐 Closed Mon.– Tues.

💲 €

patrimoniocultural .gov.pt

An unexpected element is Carlos's neo-Gothic painting studio and its simple wooden furniture, which decidedly differs from the formal reception rooms of the upper floors, dripping with chandeliers. Carlos was the royal painter par excellence, and much of his prodigious output hangs in the palace at Vila Viçosa (see pp. 186–187) in the Alentejo.

Centro Cultural de Belém

Closer to today in spirit is the massive geometric form of the Centro Cultural de Belém; it opened in 1999. Design shops and cafés flank the monumental main steps leading to the cultural center's inner sanctum where the auditoriums are located. The **Museu Colecção Berardo** houses over 800 works covering all major modern artistic movements from 1900 to the present. In addition to José Berardo's private collection of modern and contemporary

art, temporary exhibitions also focus on contemporary art and design. The cultural center's lively bar and restaurant with terrace are great places for a drink or snack.

Belém Docks Area

From the cultural center, take the nearby pedestrian underpass beneath the riverfront avenues to reach the Belém docks and the **Padrão dos Descobrimentos** *(tel 213 031 950, padraodos descobrimentos.pt, closed Mon. Oct.–Feb., €).* This massive 1960 monument dedicated to Portugal's age of discoveries is shaped like a ship's prow and peopled by a cast of historical figures led by Prince Henry, the driving force behind Portugal's overseas discoveries (see pp. 23–26). A sidewalk mosaic depicts a huge compass and map of the world.

Next to the monument is the often-overlooked **Museu de Arte Popular,** housed in the last surviving pavilion from Lisbon's 1940 Exposition. Inside is a delightful display of rural folk art and clothing; ceramics, basketwork, wooden carts, and rugs are also prominent.

From here, it's only a short walk along the river to Lisbon's much photographed architectural gem, the **Torre de Belém.** Built in 1519 to protect Lisbon against English and Dutch pirates, this work of the brothers Francisco and Diogo de Arruda originally stood on a midstream island; when the 1755 earthquake affected the course of the river, the fort became attached to the riverbank. A masterpiece of

A Craving for Pastry

Your last stop in Belém should be Lisbon's most illustrious pastry shop, **Pastéis de Belém** *(Rua de Belém 84–92, pasteisdebelem. pt),* on the monastery side of Belém. This labyrinthine tearoom dates back to the 19th century, when it first supplied patrons with it famous custard tarts, allegedly made from a still secret recipe created by the neighboring monks. Azulejo-faced walls create a colorful backdrop for boisterous Lisbonite families devouring a daily total of about 7,000 of these delicious treats. Remember this one gastronomic tip: Sprinkle your tart with cinnamon.

The shield-shaped battlements of the iconic Torre de Belém guard the Tejo River's north bank.

Gothic and Manueline styles, the tower also incorporates Moorish-style watchtowers and Venetian loggias with openwork tracery. The combination manages to look entirely harmonious. If the lines are long to reach the tower's top-floor terrace, enjoy looking up at its rope carving, armillary spheres, and the unique shield-shaped battlements decorated with the cross of the Order of Christ.

One of Belém's more unique museums, the **Museu Nacional dos Coches** *(Av. da India 136, tel 210 732 319, museudoscoches. pt, closed Mon., €€)* displays one of the world's best collections of 18th- and 19th-century carriages in a new building. It is still possible to visit the **Picadeiro Real** *(Royal Riding School, tel 213 610 850, closed Mon., €)* once the royal stables and now part of the exhibition, where the museum used to be located.

MAAT

Opened in 2016 and heralded as Lisbon's new cultural hub, the **Museu de Arte, Arquitetura e Tecnologia** *(Av. de Brasília, tel 210 028 130, maat.pt, closed Tues., €€)*, known as MAAT, is made up of two distinctive parts: The colossal red-brick Tejo Power Station, a fine example of 20th-century Portuguese industrial architecture (formerly the Museu da Electricidade), and a brand-new, ultramodern building dedicated to national and international art and architectural exhibitions. Sensitive landscaping and its riverfront location make this a popular spot. ■

Torre de Belém
🅰 48 A1
✉ Avenida da Índia
☎ 213 620 034
🕐 Closed Mon. & holidays
💲 €€

torrebelem.pt

MUSEU CALOUSTE GULBENKIAN & AROUND

Another of Lisbon's cultural focal points lies around the Praça de Espanha, to the north of Baixa, and centers on the world-famous Museu Calouste Gulbenkian. A couple of other sites, notably the Casa-Museu Dr. Anastácio Gonçalves and the bucolic bliss of the tropical greenhouses of the Parque Eduardo VII, equally merit visits.

■ The wide-ranging Gulbenkian collection includes 18th- and 19th-century European paintings.

Museu Calouste Gulbenkian

🅰 49 E4
✉ Avenida de Berna 45A
☎ 217 823 000
🕐 Closed Tues.
💲 €€€ (includes entry to Centro de Arte Moderna)
🚇 Metro: São Sebastião, Praça de Espanha. Bus: 746

gulbenkian.pt

The Gulbenkian

The museum stands in a large, grassy park dotted with sculptures and ponds. It displays the vast, eclectic collection—some 6,000 works of art ranging from Mesopotamian sculptures to French Impressionism paintings—of Armenian Calouste Sarkis Gulbenkian (1869–1955; see sidebar opposite).

The superbly designed, low-lying building was brilliantly conceived to offer constant interaction between the art displayed inside and nature; the art is presented in

a series of rooms and halls whose large windows overlook two courtyards or the surrounding grounds. The layout groups the art according to chronology, geographic origin, and medium.

The Eastern World: The first three rooms exhibit artwork from the **Egyptian, Greek, Roman,** and **Mesopotamian** civilizations. Keep your eyes peeled for the Egyptian head of an old man, a beautiful green schist sculpture dating from about 2000 B.C., and the large ninth-century Assyrian bas-relief from the palace of Nimrud, superbly sculpted in alabaster.

The next two rooms display an extremely rich and large collection of **Eastern Islamic art.** Gulbenkian was especially drawn to this art because he grew up in Istanbul under the Ottoman Empire. This section overflows with priceless ceramics in glowing turquoises and greens, carpets, manuscripts, tiles, and mosque lamps from Syria. The unusual 13th- to 14th-century Persian ceramic mihrab (prayer niche) is stunningly executed, combining Koranic quotations and vegetal motif decoration.

Move into the **Oriental room** to see exquisite Japanese lacquerware, Ming porcelain, 17th- and 18th-century biscuit ware, Chinese jade stones, and much more.

The Western World: From the Oriental room, you leave the Eastern world for the Western. The richly stocked **galleries of European art of the 14th to 17th centuries** showcase some medieval carved ivories and illuminated manuscripts of the 10th century before moving on to a chronological display of exceptional paintings—among them Rembrandt's "Portrait of an Old Man." The next two rooms are devoted to **18th-century French decorative arts:** myriad tapestries, silverware, and typically ornate furniture.

A side room contains **sculpture from the 18th century.** Look for Jean-Antoine Houdon's (1741–1828) graceful marble statue of Diana as well as the

work of Renaissance sculptor Andrea della Robbia. From here you head into a succession of four rooms that masterfully display **European paintings of the 18th and 19th centuries.** Gaze upon the turbulent "Wreck of a Transport Ship" by J. M. W. Turner (1775–1851), the moody pastel of a winter scene by Jean-François Millet (1814–1875), and the much reproduced "Boy Blowing Bubbles" by French Impressionist Édouard Manet (1832–1883).

The last gallery of the museum devotes space to an exceptional collection of art nouveau glass

Calouste Sarkis Gulbenkian

Born and raised in Turkey, Gulbenkian began collecting while in his teens and was systematically purchasing high-quality art by the turn of the 20th century. As his oil-magnate fortunes flourished, Gulbenkian astutely bought, exchanged, and donated works of art, while placing some on loan in museums in London, Paris, and Washington. In 1942, as World War II raged, he immigrated to Lisbon, where he remained until his death. In accordance with his wishes, a foundation was set up for his art collection to be held "under one roof." The museum finally opened in 1969.

and whimsical **jewelry by René Lalique** (1860–1945). The most sophisticated piece is arguably the "cat's choker," a technical exploit incorporating diamonds, rock crystal, and gold, yet entirely sober in its total impact.

Downstairs, two generously scaled halls are used for temporary exhibitions, and a very pleasant

Centro de Arte Moderna

🅰 49 E4

✉ Rua Dr. Nicolau de Bettencourt

☎ 217 823 474

🕐 Closed Tues.

💲 €€€ (includes entry to Museu Calouste Gulbenkian). Free on Sun.

🚇 Metro: São Sebastião, Praça de Espanha

gulbenkian.pt

Casa-Museu Dr. Anastácio Gonçalves

🅰 49 E4

✉ Avenida 5 de Outubro 6–8

☎ 213 540 923

🕐 Closed Mon.

💲 €

🚇 Metro: Picoas, Saldanha

blogdacmag. blogspot.com

Estufa Fria de Lisboa

🅰 49 E4

✉ Parque Eduardo VII

☎ 213 882 278

💲 €

🚇 Metro: Picoas, Saldanha

estufafria.cm -lisboa.pt

cafeteria spills out onto a terrace overlooking the grounds.

Centro de Arte Moderna

Next door to the Gulbenkian is the less frequented **Centro de Arte Moderna,** opened in 1983, which offers a full panorama of 20th- and 21st-century Portuguese art as well as some British art. It boasts both temporary and permanent exhibits culled from the museum's permanent collection.

Casa-Museu Dr. Anastácio Gonçalves

In the heart of this upscale residential and commercial district is the Casa-Museu Dr. Anastácio Gonçalves. This museum's decorative arts collection numbers some 2,000 pieces and once belonged to physician António Anastácio Gonçalves (1889–1965), a friend of Gulbenkian who frequented the same artistic and literary circles.

The elegant, muted calm of the 19th-century mansion Casa Malhoa, named after the 19th-century painter to which it once belonged, makes a suitable backdrop for the wide-ranging collection. The tapestries, silverware, and European furniture of the 17th, 18th, and 19th centuries are noteworthy, but the Chinese porcelain takes pride of place. Highlights include ceramics from the Song dynasty; a vast collection of Ming "blue-and-white" porcelain, much of which was destined for export; and a good selection of "green" and "pink" porcelain from the Qing dynasty.

Parque Eduardo VII

This enjoyable park to wander around in lies immediately west of the Casa-Museu Dr. Anastácio Gonçalves, behind Lisbon's largest and most popular department store, El Corte Inglés. The Parque Eduardo VII (Av. da Liberdade, tel 213 882 278) was named after the British King Edward VII, who paid a visit to Lisbon in 1903 soon after his coronation.

After taking in the long views of the Baixa and castle from the top of the hill, head down to the main greenhouse, the luxuri-

---

INSIDER TIP:

Pack a lunch and take a break from the bustle of city life in the shady, sculpture-filled gardens of Lisbon's Centro de Arte Moderna.

—EMMA ROWLEY
National Geographic contributor

---

ant **Estufa Fria de Lisboa.** This unheated greenhouse was first planted in 1910 and shaded by a slatted roof to let rain into water channels, which course through what amounts to a mini-tropical forest. Tree ferns, banana palms, aspidistras, rubber plants—they are all there. Close by is the smaller **Estufa Quente** (hothouse), where the vegetation is even more tropically exuberant, and the **Estufa Doce** (sweet greenhouse), home to cacti and succulents. ∎

PARQUE DAS NAÇÕES

Bordering Lisbon's working docks, Parque das Nações (Park of the Nations) is the capital's architectural showcase built for Expo 98. Its buildings have been converted into attractions and modern residential units, making it a cultural, riverfront playground for Lisbonite families.

■ The dramatic Oceanário de Lisboa is a popular tourist destination.

The park's centerpiece is the **Oceanário de Lisboa** (tel 218 917 000, oceanario.pt, €€€). This striking glass-and-steel oceanarium is mirrored in a large expanse of water and reached via a two-tier bridge. Inside you'll discover 25,000 specimens of marine animals and plants from all the world's oceans. The diversity of life in the enormous central tank will keep you spellbound.

Álvaro Siza Vieira's visually stunning Portuguese Pavilion, with its swooping suspended roof, is now occupied by government offices, but the nearby **Pavilhão do Conhecimento** (Knowledge Pavilion; tel 218 917 100, pavconheci mento.pt, €€) houses a science and technology museum with fun interactive exhibits.

The most visible of the other Expo structures is the 460-foot-tall (140 m) **Torre Vasco da Gama,** now part of the Myriad hotel. The great views over the city and river from this tower rival the novelty of those from the **Telecabine** (cable car; tel 218 956 143, telecabinelisboa .pt, €) that transports people from one end of the park to the other.

From any point along the park's riverfront promenade, you cannot help but see the breathtaking 10.7-mile-long (17.2 km) **Ponte Vasco da Gama.** The bridge—Europe's longest—starts beside the park and sails to the horizon in low-level minimalist style. ■

Parque das Nações

🅰 49 G4

🚇 Metro: Estação do Oriente

portaldasnacoes.pt

AZULEJOS

If there is one decorative element you cannot escape in Portugal, it is tiles. Tiles are everywhere, from church interiors to mansion staircases, restaurants, palace bedrooms, building facades, terraces, and even the Lisbon metro. The Moors first introduced the technique of tilemaking into Portugal, and contact with other cultures over the centuries enriched the craft. The result is the famous Portuguese azulejo, a painted ceramic tile.

■ Azulejos adorn the staircase at Lisbon's Palácio dos Marqueses de Fronteira.

The word azulejo derives from the Arabic *al-zulaycha,* meaning "little polished stone," which probably referred to the individual tesserae used in mosaics. The Moors specialized in geometric designs; this stylistic tradition remained long after the *reconquista* rid Portugal of the Moors. The first use of wall tiles on non-Moorish structures in Portugal was at the abbey of Alcobaça and at Leiria in the 13th century. But it wasn't until the early 16th century, with the introduction of the Hispano–Moorish style, that the use of tiles truly flourished. Manuel I greatly admired this decorative style imported from Seville,

Spain; his endorsement of its use on Sintra's Palácio Nacional (see pp. 159–160) began a wall-tiling craze that would last for centuries.

An Abundance of Azulejos

Renaissance motifs gradually crept in, and soon entire wall panels were not merely decorative, but illustrative as well. These early illustrative panels typically showed religious scenes painted in blues and yellows, but the expansion of the Portuguese empire soon introduced exotic inspiration and colors. Toward the end of the 17th century blue-and-white tiles became the dominant choice, no doubt inspired by imports of Ming porcelain from China. The two main centers of Lisbon and Coimbra produced lyrical panels depicting hunting scenes, nursery stories, and more.

After the 1755 earthquake, multicolored tiles came back into fashion and people discovered that the tiles kept out the damp. Thus many of Lisbon's new houses were entirely faced in tiles, visible today in the Bairro Alto and Alfama districts. The 19th century was the golden era of tiling, as Brazilian emigrants reinforced the practice and the introduction of mechanical printing methods made tiles more affordable.

Porto also has some prime azulejos, notably the São Bento railway station, which is the work of Jorge Colaço from the turn of the 20th century. His superb blue-and-white azulejos are typical of that period, which loved aping the 18th-century style. However, art nouveau soon brought its own decorative adaptations to architectural structures.

After a few decades of neglect, the 1950s saw a ceramic art revival and, in Porto particularly, architecture and azulejos worked in tandem. Since then, the Lisbon metro has become the standard-bearer by systematically commissioning azulejos for each new station, starting with abstract designs by Maria Keil in 1959. To learn more about azulejos, visit the National Tile Museum in Lisbon (see p. 72).

■ Azulejos adorn the facades of many houses in Porto's old quarter of the Ribeira.

EXPERIENCE: Paint Your Own Azulejo

Take inspiration from the tiles in Portugal and paint one yourself. In Estoril, 16 miles (25 km) from Lisbon, **Art Paradise in Portugal** (Av. Portugal 616A, tel 963 589 797 or 214 681 571, artparadiseinportugal .com) is a creative arts studio run by the exuberant Margarida Alberty. The studio offers both one-off tile-painting experiences (€15/hr.) and three-day workshops (€60/day, 6 hr. a day) and extended stays that include sightseeing and accommodation if needed.

Several methods of painting tiles can be covered, such as tracing, transferring, stenciling, and traditional Portuguese style (where designs are punched with a needle and then passed over with charcoal to transfer the design to the tile); these tiles are usually painted with shades of blue. Alberty's website gives details of the workshops and costs, but it is best to call her directly, as she is more than happy to tailor your experience to your individual needs and time restrictions.

More Places to Visit in Lisbon

Fundação Oriente Museu

Occupying a former 1930s warehouse used to store salt cod, this museum pays homage to Portugal's historical links to the East. Divided into two main exhibition areas, the first traces Portuguese presence in Asia, with exhibits from colonial outposts and trading areas dating from 1500 to the 1900s. The second, known as the Kwok On collection, is a superb collection of Cantonese marionettes, musical instruments, and books. *museudooriente.pt* 🅰 48 D2 ✉ Avenida de Brasília, Doca de Alcântara ☎ 213 585 244 🕐 Closed Mon. 💲 €€

Jardim Botânico da Universidade de Lisboa

Part of the Museu Nacional de História Natural e da Ciência, this well-hidden gem was designed as a scientific garden with species from all over the world; the first were planted in 1873. The tropical palms and cycads (very rare, living fossils) are outstanding. At the main entrance just behind the Natural History Museum, look for the gigantic Moreton Bay fig *(Ficus macrophylla),* its aerial roots now as thick as tree trunks. And don't miss the pipal tree *(Ficus religiosa),* the species under which Buddha is said to have gained enlightenment. *museus.ulisboa.pt* 🅰 49 E3 ✉ Rua da Escola Politécnica 58 ☎ 213 921 808 💲 €

Jardim Zoológico

Not the cheapest day out, but adults and children alike will enjoy the well-kept Lisbon Zoo, which boasts some 300 species. Highlights include the enormous primate enclosure, the dolphin and sea lion show, and the crocodile pool. *zoo.pt* 🅰 48 D4 ✉ Estrada de Benfica, 158–160, Sete Rios ☎ 217 232 900 💲 €€€

Museu Nacional de Arte Antiga

This cultural highlight, in the residential district overlooking the Alcântara docks, is well worth the effort to visit. This national art collection was set up in 1884 to house much of the fantastic artwork that the state inherited from the monasteries on their closure. Since then the museum has overflowed from a 17th-century mansion into a beautiful baroque chapel and a 1940s annex. A vast collection of European art and decorative arts takes up the majority of the ground floor. It primarily spans the Middle Ages to the early 19th century, with masterful works on display. The next floor up holds rooms dedicated to artwork from Portugal's former colonies and trading partners as well as Portuguese and Chinese ceramics and silver and gold jewelry. The top floor is devoted to Portuguese painting and sculpture. There's also a pleasant garden café and terrace. *museudearteantiga.pt* 🅰 49 D2 ✉ Rua das Janelas Verdes ☎ 213 912 800 🕐 Closed Mon. 💲 €€

Museu Nacional do Azulejo

Even if ceramic tiles do not specifically interest you, the exhibits of the National Tile Museum, in the former convent of Madre de Deus, will stimulate your imagination. The museum traces the evolution of the Portuguese style from its early Moorish geometric designs through the Mudejar style of the late 15th and 16th centuries and the classic illustrative blue-and-white azulejos of the 16th and 17th centuries, up to modern abstract designs. Also displayed are imported tiles from Andalucia (Spain), Italy, and even Goa (India). You will also see the convent's fabulous church of Madre de Deus and chapter house, another feast of gold leaf and huge azulejo panels; spot the crocodiles depicted on the left. The Manueline cloister has some lovely 18th-century geometric-patterned panels. *museudoazulejo.gov.pt* 🅰 49 G3 ✉ Rua da Madre de Deus 4 ☎ 218 100 340 🕐 Closed Mon. 💲 €€

The perfect setting for vineyards, baroque masterpieces, remote, traditional villages, and the always magnetic Porto

PORTO E NORTE

■ A common souvenir: the ubiquitous ceramic cockerel from Barcelos

PORTO E NORTE

Wild and highly cultivated, starkly barren and lushly green, deeply traditional yet spiced with modern accents: Portugal's Norte embodies numerous contradictions in its modestly scaled yet mountainous expanse. Dividing it from the Centro region is its star attraction, the majestic Douro River, whose valley is not only the source of the profitable port and wine industry but also a spectacular must-see.

The Douro and other rivers that crisscross the region—from the Minho, which acts as a natural border with Spain in the far north, to the Lima and Cávado Rivers—make the Porto e Norte region of Portugal, divided into the Minho, Douro, and Trás-os-Montes areas, more fertile than the rest of the country. They also bring a string of spa establishments to the touring agenda. And, not least, they help nurture acres of vines, which produce refreshing *vinho verde* (green wine), red and white table wines, and the heavier port

wine that has brought fame and fortune to one of Europe's oldest cities—Porto.

However much these rural areas are becoming depopulated, you cannot fail to be seduced by timeless and unhurried scenes. Bescarved old ladies in black sit knitting in the shadows of doorways, while marginally younger ones stride past with basins of vegetables balanced on their heads. Men well past their prime steer tractors through fields and orchards. Then you notice a child sitting, playing on his mobile phone.

Gems of the Porto e Norte Region

To explore this region, the obvious launchpad is Porto, an enchanting city with plenty of cultural and gastronomic offerings, a breezy beach, and sweeping views over the mouth of the Douro. The lush and verdant Douro Valley, which shelters acres and acres of vineyards growing on rhythmically terraced hillsides, lies within easy reach. As does the pious, though industrialized, city of Braga, home to a 12th-century cathedral and the striking sanctuary of Bom Jesus on its outskirts. Lighter in spirit, the UNESCO-listed World Heritage town of Guimarães is considered the birthplace of the Portuguese nation. Head north to discover Viana do Castelo, a delightful, easygoing town on the Lima estuary. On the northeastern side, toward the Spanish border, is the starker, poorer, though very beautiful, area of Trás-os-Montes. Its capital, Bragança, although historically significant, is quite isolated. In between stand daunting ranges of granite hills rising to bare summits of rocky scree (including those of the national park, Peneda-Gerês), memorable for giant boulders, long-horned bulls, wild ponies, goats, wild boar, and deer. These dramatic landscapes and a succession of charming villages make up the soul of northern Portugal. ■

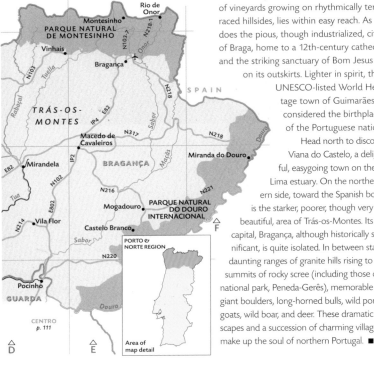

RIo de Onor

Montesinho

PARQUE NATURAL DE MONTESINHO

Vinhais

Bragança

SPAIN

TRÁS-OS-MONTES

Macedo de Cavaleiros

Miranda do Douro

Mirandela

BRAGANÇA

N216

Mogadouro

PARQUE NATURAL DO DOURO INTERNACIONAL

Vila Flor

Castelo Branco

PORTO & NORTE REGION

N220

Pocinho

GUARDA

CENTRO p. 111

Area of map detail

PORTO

Portugal's second largest city, with more than one million inhabitants, Porto boasts several highlights on its unrivaled riverside location. You can admire the city's steep slopes from the deck of a *rabelo* (a traditional sailboat used for transporting barrels of port, now motorized as a tour boat) on its circular "six bridges" tour. Alternatively, relax at one of the modern cafés lining the quays of Vila Nova de Gaia (Porto's left-bank nucleus of wine lodges and warehouses), or stop on the iconic 1886 Dom Luís I bridge that mimicked Gustave Eiffel's designs.

 Porto's graphic bridges; in the foreground is Gustave Eiffel's Ponte de Dona Maria Pia.

Porto

 74 A1

Visitor Information

✉ Rua Clube dos Fenianos 25 & Rua Sampaio Bruno w. Praça da Liberdade (kiosk) & Sé, Calçada Dom Pedro Pitões 15

☎ 223 326 751

visitporto.travel

From any one of these spots you will see the dense urban fabric that has been woven since Phoenician and Roman times when Porto was known as Cale (Greek for "beautiful"), later adding Portus (port) to become Portus-Cale—thus the origin of the national name. Narrow alleyways, rough cobblestones, and tortuous steps riddle the northern riverbank while church spires vie with draped laundry to set the most atmospheric stage. You

will need energy and muscles to negotiate the steep streets.

Maritime at heart, with strong trading and shipbuilding traditions, Porto played an important role in the Portuguese expeditions of the 15th century. However, its boom came in the 18th century, thanks to the profitable port trade and the acumen of English entrepreneurs. This, too, was the heyday of baroque, a style that left its mark on many a church in Porto and smaller inland towns. Landmarks such as the Cathedral and the church of São Francisco, although both much older in origin, were blanketed in baroque carvings, paintings, and other features. More visible still is the Torre dos Clérigos, a towering baroque original that has become another Porto icon. Equally common are the azulejos (glazed tiles) that decorate walls from the Cathedral cloister to the railway station.

History aside, Porto is a lively, notoriously hardworking town. Relaxation is at hand in the beach bars of nearby Foz and downtown at a string of bars and restaurants, which can be delightfully old-fashioned or stylishly chic. Contemporary culture is catered to at the starkly modern Fundação de Serralves and in a dedicated street of art galleries (see p. 84), and the shopping urge can be quenched in a central pedestrianized area. Above all, however, you should make a beeline for the bustling **Ribeira** area down by the river: Boats come and go, giant signs of port brands monopolize the horizon, and café tables spill out into the sun. Here the character of Porto really comes alive.

In & Around Praça da Liberdade

Stand in the middle of Praça da Liberdade, beside the equestrian statue of Dom Pedro IV, and feel the pulse of 19th-century Porto—its institutions, industries, and commerce. This sloping north–south rectangle creates an unofficial border between the more down-at-heel eastern side of town, the upscale

> ## Unusual Tours
>
> Food and wine enthusiasts can sign up for a four-hour tour exploring some of Porto's most historic neighborhoods and their old-world eateries and cafés whilst learning about traditional Portuguese food and drink, such as *bolinhas de bacalhau* (cod fritters), *bifanas* (pork sandwiches), and the national Super Bock beer. Be sure to pace yourself. Additional offerings by **Blue Dragon Tours** (*Av. Gustavo Eiffel 280, tel 222 022 375, bluedragon.pt*) include eco-friendly walking, bicycle, and Segway tours around Porto. For those still unaware, Segways are two-wheeled electric vehicles that seem to defy any laws of balance. Be assured, driving one is much easier than it looks. Tours are led by knowledgeable guides who aim to take their visitors slightly off the beaten track while still covering all the main points of interest.

avenues to the west, and the World Heritage–listed Baixa/Ribeira area to the south.

The avenues connecting Praça da Liberdade and the adjoining square to the north, Praça General Humberto Delgado, are lined with the headquarters of major banks and businesses, all watched over by the **Paços do Concelho** (City Hall) at the far northern end. Next door is the city's main tourist office. This area is a major social crossroad of the city, where businesspeople cross paths with beggars, housewives, and schoolchildren. As always, Porto is able to let its hair down: Head down to the Ribeira Square on any weekend night and the streets will be buzzing. And on any warm day of the week, sidewalk cafés add a leisurely tone. The lower square

Praça da Liberdade

 Map p. 83

is also a hub for Porto's excellent bus network, allowing easy connections with São Bento, the central railway station, just a little way east. The older area of Porto, classified as a World Heritage site, starts at the southern edge of Praça da Liberdade.

Porto's central food market, the **Mercado Municipal do Bolhão** (corner of Rua de Sá da Bandeira & Rua Formosa, closed Sat. p.m. & Sun.), stands one block east of City Hall. Its vast, galleried interior brims with stalls selling produce from the entire region. This striking ironwork structure has been open since 1851. One block farther east is the pedestrianized **Rua de Santa Catarina,** once a popular bourgeois

promenade and now Porto's shopping mecca, boasting international fashion chain stores and a large mall, Via Catarina.

Toward the southern end of the street is the renowned **Café Majestic** (Rua de Santa Catarina 112, tel 222 003 887, cafemajestic .com, closed Sun.), a belle epoque wonder of sinuous lines, gilded woodwork, mirrors, and beaming cherubim. Designed by architect João Queirós, it opened in 1921 under the name Elite, but the city's intelligentsia only started flocking to its marble tables the following year, after it changed its name to Majestic. After a decades-long heyday, the café began to decline, and by the 1960s it was in a ruinous state. Closure and

EXPERIENCE: Discover the Art of Making Port

Tightly controlled and regulated by the Portuguese government, port, a fortified, sweet dessert wine of which there are several varieties, is unique to the upper Douro Valley. Learn the port production process on a tour around one of the port wine lodges of Vila Nova de Gaia. Although these tours are aimed at the tourist market, they are usually informative and it's always fun to see a lodge interior; take a sweater, as the lodges can be chilly. Try **Sandeman** (Largo Miguel Bombarda 47, tel 223 740 533, sandeman.com, €€) or **Porto Cálem** (Av. Diogo Leite 344, tel 916 113 451, calem.pt, €€).

As you tour the lodge, you'll discover that the common feature of all ports is the addition of brandy during the fermentation process. Once about half the sugar from the pressed grapes has turned into alcohol, the vintner mixes the wine with a healthy dose of high-proof grape brandy.

This stops the fermentation process in its tracks, leaving a sweet and robust raw product. What happens next depends greatly on the vintner. If the grapes are from a superior crop year, the port is designated as vintage. It is usually then mixed with other fine pedigree grapes, set in wooden casks for two years, and bottled to age. After a few decades, this finest of ports is ready for sipping.

Common ports are aged longer in wooden casks and are potable immediately on bottling. Ruby port is a fruity wine, lighter than vintage ports. Tawny port is produced from younger, often quite concentrated and aggressive wines. It is thus aged much longer than a ruby—up to 40 years in many cases—mellowing the flavor. The name "tawny" comes from the faded color the wine takes on after so many years in wooden casks. Lightly chilled dry white port makes an ideal aperitif.

refurbishment led to the café's reopening in 1994 with the crystal gleaming once again. Today, though touristy, it is a mandatory stop on the Porto circuit.

On the opposite, western side of Praça da Liberdade rises the **Igreja** and much photographed **Torre dos Clérigos.** The baroque church and tower together form a compact, oval-shaped city block.

INSIDER TIP:

For great photos of traditional tiles, check out the São Bento railway station, Capela das Almas on Rua de Santa Catarina, and Pérola do Bolhão, opposite the market.

—EMMA ROWLEY
National Geographic contributor

The work of the prolific Italian architect Nicolau Nasoni, they date from 1735 through 1748. Although there are more striking church interiors in the city, the Igreja's facade is notable for the oval eyeglass. Make the effort to climb the 225 steps to the top of the 248-foot-tall (76 m) tower for the fantastic views.

A few steps north of here stands another towering baroque edifice, the **Igreja do Carmo** *(Rua do Carmo, tel 222 078 400).* Apart from the impressive main facade, the church's side facade is equally worth noting: Its large tiled panel by Silvestre Silvestri depicts Carmelite nuns taking the veil. Immediately next to it stands the **Igreja dos Carmelitas** *(Rua do Carmo, tel 222 050 279),* which presents a less harmonious 17th-century mix of neoclassical and baroque styles.

For a complete contrast in both style and function, head around the corner to see Porto's most illustrious bookstore, **Livraria Lello e Irmão** *(Rua dos Carmelitas 144, tel 222 002 037, livrarialello.pt, closed Sun.),* a 1906 neo-Gothic extravaganza complete with stained-glass ceiling. It has since been classified as a national heritage site. Although the bookstore is a place of business, it is surprisingly tolerant of sightseers who stop in to view the lavish interior designed by the French engineer Xavier Esteves.

The Ribeira

Although inland and near the Atlantic coast, Old Porto exudes atmosphere, history, and the color of daily life that one typically finds in a Mediterranean port. The steep, winding streets of the riverfront Ribeira quarter offer fleeting vistas over the Douro below, where the quays are a major focal point for visitors and locals alike. Two churches—the Sé and dazzling São Francisco—join the Palácio da Bolsa, the old stock exchange, as the monumental highlights.

Sé: The massive edifice of the Sé (Cathedral) rises above the rocky hillside, its twin bell towers built in the solid gray granite with which northern Portugal is so well endowed.

Torre dos Clérigos

🗺 Map p. 83

✉ Rua de São Filipe de Nery

☎ 222 145 489

💲 €

torredosclerigos.pt

Sé

🗺 Map p. 83

✉ Terreiro da Sé

☎ 222 059 028

🕐 Cloister closed Sun. a.m.

💲 €

A symphony of dazzling gilded and carved woodwork greets visitors to Porto's São Francisco.

Igreja de São Francisco

🅰 Map p. 83
✉ Rua do Infante D. Henrique
☎ 222 062 125
💲 €

Despite 12th-century origins, the Sé underwent such a radical face-lift in the late 17th and early 18th centuries that most of the original Romanesque purity has been lost. Yet again, Italian Nicolau Nasoni was responsible for much of the baroque overlay as well as for the adjacent bishop's palace.

The pleasingly bare triple-aisled nave leaves the main focus on the extensively modified transept and chancel. On the left is the **Chapel of the Holy Sacrament** and its magnificent altar—made in phases between 1632 and the 19th century—a superlative example of the prowess of Portuguese silversmiths. Look, too, for the graceful 14th-century statue of Our Lady of Vandoma—an incarnation of the Virgin Mary, the patron saint of the Sé—that stands in a heavily gilded niche. More lashings of Brazilian gold dazzle in the baroque main altarpiece, framed by Nasoni's wall paintings. A doorway to the right of the

nave leads to the **cloister** where the rhythm of Gothic arches contrasts with seven azulejo panels dating from 1731. These illustrate Solomon's "Song of Songs" and the Life of the Virgin. A feast of treasures lies in wait in the 18th-century chapter house, from rich brocade vestments, statuary, and silver crowns to a coffered, painted ceiling, azulejos illustrating moral allegories, and a massive carved-wood candelabra. In the corner of the cloister, the **Chapel of St. John** houses the impressive stone sarcophagus of João Gordo and a graceful 14th-century statue of Our Lady of Batalha. Don't miss Nasoni's grand staircase that leads to the upper gallery. Faced in tiled panels depicting rural and mythological scenes, it offers extensive views across Porto.

Igreja de São Francisco:
As if the Sé were not enough, the Ribeira's other monumental draw is the Igreja de São Francisco. Again victim of a

late 17th- to early 18th-century baroque makeover, São Francisco is quite staggering in its ornamentation: Virtually the entire surface is blanketed in gilded, carved wood in a riot of vines, cherubim, and birds and other animals. Begun in 1245, the church and former monastery were not completed until 1425, when they hosted Dom João I after his marriage to Philippa of Lancaster. Centuries later, after the baroque additions were complete, the decorative excess so shocked the clergy that no services have been held there since.

Today the most spectacular element remains a high-relief **altarpiece,** positioned to the left of the nave. Illustrating the Tree of Jesse in polychrome and gilded wood, it depicts 12 kings of Judah in the branches of a tree that rises out of the body of Christ to end with the Virgin and Child. This sculptural tour de force was made in the 1720s by Filipe da Silva and António Gomes, two little-known local artisans. More naif in style is the 13th-century granite statue of St. Francis in a niche to the right of the entrance. Opposite the church, the rebuilt monastery holds a small **museum** of interesting ecclesiastical iconography as well as some unusual catacombs.

Behind São Francisco stands the **Palácio da Bolsa,** Porto's stock exchange. This late 19th-century neoclassical building claims a succession of highly decorated and richly furnished halls that can be visited with a guided tour. The star attraction is the **Pátio das**

Nações, only rivaled by the glitter and inscriptions of the **Arabian Room,** a pastiche of the Alhambra in Granada, Spain.

Beyond the Center

Porto's urban sprawl now extends west from the Baixa to the beaches of Foz do Douro. In between lie several sites and spots to relax in after a day navigating downtown's backstreets. Nor should the port lodges of Vila Nova de Gaia be forgotten.

Casa da Música

Opened in 2001, the imposing **Casa da Música** (Av. da Boavista 604–610, tel 220 120 220, casadamusica.com), designed by Dutch architect Rem Koolhas, has firmly established itself as Porto's principal cultural venue. Home to Porto's Symphony Orchestra and the Casa da Música Choir, it offers a full program of musical events and performances for all tastes and ages.

Museu Nacional de Soares dos Reis: Close to the Baixa area, this elegant museum is devoted to fine and decorative arts. It was founded by Pedro IV in 1833 as Portugal's very first museum to safeguard the art heritage from convents that were closing their doors; it soon became a showcase for academic artists. What was then known as the Museu Portuense was moved to its present site, the 18th-century Palácio dos Carrancas, in the 1940s, acquiring additional collections of decorative and 20th-century art.

(continued on p. 84)

Palácio da Bolsa
- Map p. 83
- Rua Ferreira Borges
- 223 399 000
- Closed Nov.– Mar.
- €€

palaciodabolsa.pt

Museu Nacional de Soares dos Reis
- Palácio dos Carrancas, Rua D. Manuel II
- 223 393 770
- Closed Mon.
- €€

museusoaresdos reis.pt

A WALK THROUGH THE RIBEIRA

Porto's topography is best dealt with by following a generally downhill direction. This walk winds past major sites and through back alleys to end at the Douro River's edge.

Views from the Cathedral take in a jumble of houses and the landmark Torre dos Clérigos.

From the equestrian statue in Praça da Liberdade, head south and cross two side streets at the left-hand corner of the square to reach the Praça de Almeida Garrett. In front of you is the **Estação de São Bento ❶**. Enter the train station to admire the large 1930s azulejo panels by Jorge Colaço illustrating daily life and historic battles. Return toward the statue, turn left, and walk up the steep Rua dos Clérigos toward the highly visible church and **Torre dos Clérigos** (see p. 79) ❷, passing a fascinating mix of shops. As you round the corner at the top, look for the highly decorative fruit, vegetable, and *bacalhau* shop **Casa Oriental** (*Campo dos Mártires da Pátria 111, casaoriental.pt*) and an 18th-century **pharmacy** (*Campo dos Mártires da Pátria 122*).

In front of you rise the forbidding walls of Porto's former prison and Court of Appeal. Closed down in 1974, it reopened in 1997 as

NOT TO BE MISSED:

Estação de São Bento • Torre dos Clérigos • Centro Português de Fotografia • Sé

the **Centro Português de Fotografia ❸** (Portuguese Center for Photography; *Largo Amor de Perdição, tel 220 046 300, closed Mon. & a.m. Sat.–Sun., cpf.pt*). It stages some groundbreaking photography exhibitions.

Heading Downhill

Now turn to the left of this building down Rua dos Caldeireiros, a typical working-class street complete with dripping laundry, flags, and people on balconies and in workshops below. Walk past the intersection of Rua das

Flores to reach the busy Rua de Mouzinho da Silveira. Cross again to a wall fountain and turn right up Rua do Souto. This lively street leads you to the remaining sections of Porto's 12th-century walls, the **Muralha Fernandina** ❹, originally 3,000 feet (900 m) long and averaging 30 feet (9 m) in height. The **Sé** ❺ (see pp. 79–80) is now in sight: Turn right at a fork, walking through an arch to the vast esplanade fronting the Cathedral. This gives you one of Porto's best views down to the river.

Walk back through the arch toward the next church steeple. Steps lead down to a small square and lookout terrace with, on the left, the **Museu de Arte Sacra e Arqueologia** (*Largo Dr. Pedro Vitorino 2, tel 223 395 020, closed Sun. & Mon. a.m., €*) ❻ installed beside a church. This small museum displays religious artwork and

some archaeological artifacts. Continue down Rua de Santana, turn left into Rua da Bainharia and left again down atmospheric Rua dos Mercadores, full of the sounds of music and hammering from workshops. At the bottom turn right into Rua do Infante Dom Henrique. At No. 8 you pass the arcades of the former factory, **Feitoria Inglesa,** built in the late 1780s for Porto's English business community. Cross the road, turn left, and stroll down to the riverfront cafés and restaurants of Praça da Ribeira.

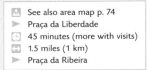

⊠ See also area map p. 74
▶ Praça da Liberdade
🕒 45 minutes (more with visits)
↔ 1.5 miles (1 km)
▶ Praça da Ribeira

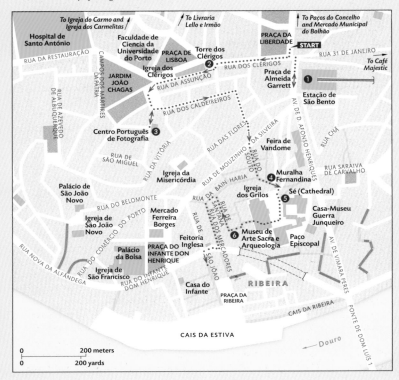

**Fundação
de Serralves
Museu de Arte
Contemporânea**

✉ Rua D. João de
Castro 210

☎ 226 156 500

$ Museum &
park €€. Park
only €

🚌 Bus: 201
from Praça da
Liberdade

serralves.pt

The decorative arts section offers the most interest, whether in the Portuguese ceramics, Asian pieces (look for the hand-painted Japanese screen dating from the 1600s), or Iron Age jewelry from Povoa de Varzim. Do not miss the unusual raised patio garden, its azulejo-faced wall fronting a pleasant outdoor café.

Far more cutting-edge artwork can be seen two blocks north of here in the **Rua de Miguel Bombarda.** This is where the majority of Porto's contemporary art galleries are conveniently located (*most closed Sun.–Mon. & a.m.*).

Parque da Cidade

For some downtime, head to Portugal's largest urban park, at the bottom of Avenida da Boavista, which stretches over 83 hectares toward the Atlantic Ocean. Its gentle contours and architectural stone features are the work of landscape architect Sidónio Pardal. The park makes for a relaxing afternoon or a great spot for a picnic.

Fundação de Serralves Museu de Arte Contemporânea: The jewel in Porto's cultural agenda, the Fundação de Serralves Museu de Arte Contemporânea lies far to the west. This lively and ambitious arts center stands on a verdant hillside in a residential area. The extensive 44-acre (18 ha) park is as important as the museum interior; sculptures (including interesting works by Ângela de Sousa, Claes Oldenburg, Richard Serra, Alberto Carneiro, and Dan Graham) dot the lawns. Some 2 million euros have also

been invested in revamping the modernist gardens.

Originally designed to showcase the pristine, pink art deco mansion, Casa de Serralves, in which the museum first opened in 1989, the lake, woods, fountains, arboretum, and rose garden are now a popular destination for weekend strollers. One place not to miss is the delightful teahouse. **Casa de Serralves** often houses exhibitions, presenting an opportunity to admire the superb interiors courtesy of Lalique, Ruhlmann, and other leading French designers of the period.

Major exhibitions of contemporary art and performances are now staged within the massive white minimalist structure designed by Porto's celebrity architect, Álvaro Siza Vieira, which opened in 2000. The infrequently shown permanent collection—and then only a few pieces at a time—covers international art movements from the 1960s to the present. Bonuses come in the form of an excellent bookstore and a rooftop café-restaurant.

Foz do Douro: From the arts center, it is less than a mile to Foz do Douro, a town that grew up at the very mouth of the Douro River around the fort of **São João da Foz.** Today Foz extends about 2 miles (3 km) north up the coast to merge with the more industrial **Matosinhos,** where old fish-preserving factories have been converted into hip waterfront nightclubs. Foz itself is really one long avenue and a balustraded promenade bordering beaches of coarse sand and rocks. The restaurants that line the beachfront serve excellent seafood. Few beachgoers venture into the chilly water other than bodysurfers, but the breezy cafés make an invigorating escape from downtown Porto, only a half-hour bus ride on weekends.

Vila Nova de Gaia

Back in central Porto, the other main draw for visitors is across the river: the port lodges of Vila Nova de Gaia. Try to go there on foot via the upper level of the Ponte Dom Luís I: Vertigo and staggering views from the bridge are assured. At ground level, dozens of port companies vie to lure in passersby for tastings and, they hope, acquisitions. These enterprises are very much geared to busloads of tourists, yet they are worth a look if the history of port interests you. Some port lodges offer tours of their facilities so you can learn about portmaking (see sidebar p. 78). Otherwise, the riverfront bars facing the colorful facades of the Ribeira are a great place to sip a drink as sunset nears. ■

■ The signature neomodernist planes of the spectacular Fundação de Serralves

DOURO VALLEY

However much the beauty of the Douro Valley is extolled, it is easily beaten by the reality. Little can prepare you for the grandeur of its terraced slopes carved out of the schist or for the changing panoramas of the river itself. Whether seeing the valley by boat, train, or car, it will leave an indelible mark.

■ Vineyards cover every inch of hillside in the Douro Valley, no matter how steep the slope.

The Douro meanders 528 miles (850 km) from its source in Spain to its mouth at Porto, carving vertiginous ravines from the schist and granite rock en route. Once a turbulent river of rapids and narrow ravines, it has been tamed considerably by the construction of eight dams. The river's most spectacular stretch in Portugal runs between Mesão Frio and Pinhão. The hill terracing along here is so dense and rhythmical that it is apocryphally said to be the only man-made feature visible from space other than China's Great Wall. And it has been like this for some 2,000 years.

This is quintessential port country and the world's first official wine region, established in 1756 and still going strong today, as witnessed by omnipresent brand-name placards among the vines—whether Sandeman, Taylor, or Ferreira. Sadly, the pretty *rabelos* (sailboats) that transported barrels of the nectar downriver to Porto were retired decades ago and are used today only occasionally as tour boats and, every June, in a race. Tanker trucks have supplanted them. On the other hand, elegant *quintas* (rural estate houses) still monopolize the steep riverbanks, and villages are mainly concentrated in interior valleys.

INSIDER TIP:

For a wonderful view
of the Douro Valley
head to the viewpoint
at São Leonardo de
Galafura between Vila
Real and Peso da Régua.
There you'll also find
poems carved in the
rocks.

—MARGARET ROBERTS
National Geographic contributor

Tucked in among the vineyards
are pockets of fruit orchards and
olive and almond trees; come in
February for a visual feast of pink
and white almond blossoms.

The official capital of the
Douro and seat of the Port-Wine
Institute is **Peso da Régua,** usually
shortened to Régua. It can easily
be bypassed; it has little character
and even fewer sites, but it does
act as an important transportation
hub for the area. You can take a
train or boat trip from here or
head for the quayside storehouses
where various port companies
offer tastings.

Lamego

The charming town of Lamego
sits some 7 miles (11 km)
south of Régua. Its most striking site is **Nossa Senhora dos
Remédios** *(tel 254 614 392),* a
Douro version of Braga's more
famous Bom Jesus do Monte
(see pp. 98–99), as this 18th-
century church similarly crowns
a baroque staircase bristling with
ornamentation. Climb or drive

up for the views. To see a stunning interior, head to Lamego's
Sé, or Cathedral *(Largo da Sé,
tel 254 612 766),* located at the
lower end of the tree-shaded
and café-lined esplanade. Dating
from the second half of the 12th
century and partly rebuilt in the
16th century, it was extensively
reworked in the 18th century
by the Italian architect Nicolau
Nasoni. Crane your neck to
view the ceiling illustrated with
biblical stories, and don't miss
the lovely 16th-century cloister,
accessed from outside, filled
with a perfumed rose garden
and two ornate chapels.

A significant though modestly
scaled historical site lies just
2 miles (3 km) northeast
of Lamego: the chapel of **São
Pedro de Balsemão** *(tel 254
600 230, closed Mon.)* in the village of Balsemão. Said to date
from the seventh century, it is
thus the second oldest sanctuary

Peso da Régua
🗺 74 C1
Visitor Information
✉ Rua da
Ferreirinha
☎ 254 312 846

Lamego
🗺 74 C1
Visitor Information
✉ Avenida
Visconde
Guedes Teixeira
☎ 254 612 005

portoenorte.pt

EXPERIENCE:
The Grape Harvest
The Douro Valley comes alive during the
annual *vindima* (grape harvest), which
usually occurs in mid-September. You can
witness hundreds of local villagers picking
and trampling the grapes in large granite
lagares (tanks) at several of the *quintas* in
the region that open their doors to tourists then. For full information on which
quintas are open to visitors at harvesttime,
call or visit the **Rota do Vinho do Porto**
*(Peso da Régua, Rua dos Camilos 90, tel 254
320 130, ivdp.pt)* office. Some quintas offer
a full visitor package year-round, with
multilingual audio tours and tastings.

Tarouca

🗺 74 C1

Visitor Information

✉ Avenida
Prof. Leite
Vasconcelos

☎ 254 781 461

on the Iberian Peninsula. The small, colonnaded chapel displays Byzantine and Visigothic features and contains the heavily carved sarcophagus of a Porto bishop, who died in 1362, as well as later baroque additions.

Rail Trips Along the Douro

Traveling by train is an effortless and spectacular way to see the Douro Valley. Tracks run parallel to the river for 62 miles (100 km) of the 110 miles (175 km) between Porto and Pocinho. The most stunning ride is from Pinhão to Tua and then north beside the Tua River to Mirandela: Feats of engineering, mind-blowing landscapes, and endless vineyards are assured.

Tarouca

Another impressive monument can be seen at Tarouca, 9 miles (15 km) to the southeast of Lamego. Here, lost at the bottom of a pretty valley, stands the semi-ruined **São João de Tarouca,** a massive 12th-century Cistercian monastery (Portugal's first), currently undergoing excavation. The adjacent **church** (tel 254 678 766, closed Mon.) is in a far better state. The sacristy contains no fewer than 4,700 azulejos, each one with a different illustration. Walk through the tiny village following the gushing water channels downhill, to reach the river, a tributary

of the Douro, and its Roman-esque bridge.

Pinhão

Farther east on the north bank, modest Pinhão is the Douro's great highlight, mostly for its setting. It sees most traffic during harvesttime, when truckloads of grapes thunder in from the vineyards to be pressed; otherwise, the village is quiet and offers a handful of restaurants and hotels. Pinhão's landmark is the unusual **railway station** where walls are decorated with azulejo panels depicting local life. If heading north from here by car, consider two equally spectacular routes that wind through terraced hills; one goes to Alijó and the other to Sabrosa, birthplace of the great navigator Ferdinand Magellan.

Alternatively, cross the Douro again and drive 12 miles (19 km) east to the village of **São João da Pesqueira,** home to some magnificent manor houses as well as a lookout point that affords what is considered the most breathtaking view of the Douro. This spot also claims a sanctuary, **São Salvador do Mundo,** once visited by young girls in search of husbands. History tells the story of Baron Forrester, an Englishman who was active in the development of the region. He lost his life when his boat capsized in the Valeira rapids below this lookout point; supposedly he was loaded down with gold coins. A fellow passenger survived, allegedly buoyed up by her ballooning Victorian crinoline. Is there a moral to this Douro tale? ∎

AMARANTE

On the northern edge of the Douro region, straddling the Tâmega tributary, lies the attractive and historically significant town of Amarante—a mecca for poets and painters. Amarante is picture-postcard stuff: Its 16th-century monastery stands beside the arches of an 18th-century granite bridge, both framed against distant hills and reflected in the willow-edged river.

Wander through the steep cobbled streets of the old town to see a wealth of handsome 16th- to 18th-century houses. At the top of this web of streets, do not miss the evocative ruins of the **Solar dos Magalhães,** a manor house sacked by Napoleon's troops under Marshal Soult in 1809. The bridge at Amarante was where the calamitous French invasion was definitively halted by Portuguese troops after a two week standoff, after which the French burned down most of the old town.

■ **The monastery of São Gonçalo sits above the Tâmega River.**

The 1540 monastery of **São Gonçalo** looms above, its church fronting a large square with an outdoor café. Gonçalo was a 13th-century preacher who, after falling for the beauty of this spot, built a hermitage and bridge here, thus founding the town. His tomb, in a chapel to the left of the main altar, still attracts immense veneration; you are quite likely to see worshippers kissing the toes of his effigy. As the patron saint of marriage, his statue is often touched by those despairing of finding their mates. The rest of the church interior displays impressive baroque wood carving.

Museu Amadeo de Souza Cardoso *(tel 255 420 272, amadeo souza-cardoso.pt, closed Mon., €)* occupies the upper monastery floor; access is to the side of the church. It is dedicated to cubist painter Souza Cardoso (1887–1918), an Amarante native who studied in Paris in the company of Modigliani and others. His art hangs beside an assortment of works by Portuguese modernists. ■

Amarante
🗺 74 B2
Visitor Information
✉ Largo Conselheiro António Cândido
☎ 255 420 246
baixotamega.pt

VILA REAL & ENVIRONS

Nestling in the foothills of the Serra do Marão, Vila Real is resolutely modern while harboring a relaxing historic center. Its greatest claim to fame is the renowned Casa de Mateus, which sits in verdant splendor just outside town.

Casa de Mateus graces the label of Portugal's bestselling 20th-century export: Mateus Rosé.

Vila Real

74 C2

Visitor Information

✉ Avenida
Carvalho
Araújo 94

☎ 259 308 170

The presence of a university in Vila Real (meaning Royal Town) creates a youthful and lively atmosphere in what is otherwise a semi-industrialized town of 25,000 inhabitants that has turned its back on its aristocratic past. It is sandwiched between the beautiful hill ranges of the Alvão (to the north) and the Marão (to the southwest) on the Corgo, a tributary of the Douro; the wilder Trás-os-Montes region unfolds to the east. This strategic location makes Vila Real an obvious stop before or after touring Casa de Mateus, 2 miles (3 km) to the east. In the center, restaurants

and shops line a grid of pedestrian streets east of the main avenue, Avenida Carvalho de Araújo. Souvenir hunters will find black pottery from Bisalhães and wool products from the Alvão and Marão hills.

The Gothic cathedral stands on the main avenue, but its rather dull interior is for die-hards only. More interesting is the facade of the 15th-century **Casa de Diogo Cão** (*Av. Carvalho Araújo 19, closed to the public*), right next to the Town Hall. Diogo Cão, who discovered the mouth of the Congo River in Africa, was born here. A few doors away, the **Palácio dos Marqueses de Vila**

Real presents another singular facade, this one notable for its battlements and ornate Manueline windows.

Beyond Vila Real

Vila Real's greatest attraction is the **Casa de Mateus,** 2 miles (3 km) from town. Hidden from the road by a screen of vegetation, the beautiful 1740s manor house boasts baroque ornamentation at its best, thanks to the great Italian architect Nicolau Nasoni. Surround this with a lovely park landscaped with manicured boxwood hedges, lofty centennial cedars, tiered pools, and formal alleys of flower beds, and you have a very worthwhile destination. Guided tours take you through the main reception rooms (see sidebar below); some rooms are off-limits because the seventh Count of Vila Real still lives here. The Casa de Mateus Foundation, set up in 1970 to promote the arts, has transformed a barn into a concert hall.

In complete contrast to such baroque excess, it is worth going 4 miles (7 km) farther southeast,

just beyond the village of Constantim, to the sanctuary of **Panoias** *(tel 259 336 322, closed Mon.–Tues. a.m., €).* This ancient site, fenced in on the edge of a village, consists of a series of huge granite boulders, including several that are inscribed in Latin and carved with troughs. Thought to have been used for both animal and human sacrifices, the stone monuments bring a very different perspective of these lands and its former people.

The **Serra do Marão** is part of the **Parque Natural do Alvão,** a 17,840-acre (7,220 ha) protected area between Vila Real and Mondim de Basto. In this rural area, thatched-roof granite houses and *espigueiros* (raised stone granaries, common throughout the north) dot the higher elevations. Pigs, goats, and long-horned Maronesa cattle graze in the fields, while eagles, falcons, wolves, and otters populate the wilder areas. The most popular beauty spot in the area is the thundering 985-foot-tall (300 m) waterfall of **Fisgas de Ermelo.** And no visit to these hills would be complete without sampling the delicious smoked sausages, a local specialty. ∎

Casa de Mateus

🅰 74 C2

Visitor Information

✉ N322, Mateus

☎ 259 323 121

💲 €€

casademateus.com

Wonders of Casa de Mateus

This elegant baroque masterpiece displays furniture and ornaments that typify the tastes of a prosperous family of the period. Treasures include the superb hand-carved chestnut-wood ceilings and doors; Cantonese porcelain of the 17th and 18th centuries; family portraits; and Japanese, French, English, and Spanish furniture. The Ladies' Room contains a beautiful Indo-Portuguese table in tortoiseshell and mother-of-pearl. A small museum displays rich vestments, reliquaries, religious sculptures, and documents. The library contains books from the 16th century to the present. Copperplate engravings by Fragonard for *The Lusiads* by Luís Vaz de Camões (1524–1580), the Portuguese Shakespeare, prove the Mateus family's long support of the arts, as this valuable first illustrated edition dates from 1817.

PORTUGUESE WINE

Few countries can claim such a globally known and appreciated wine as port. However, this tends to overshadow Portugal's other wonderful wines, such as the light *vinho verde* (green wine) of the Minho, the smooth and robust reds of the Alentejo, the velvety reds from Colares, and the sweet Muscatel from Setúbal.

■ Despite modernization, many tasks—such as decanting—are still done by hand.

One reason for their low profile is that, until very recently, most vineyards were small; as a result, exports were mainly white vinho verde, red Dão, Madeira dessert wine, and that 1960s classic, Mateus Rosé. Recent decades, however, have seen vast improvements in vineyard quality and scale. Modernization means that Portugal's untapped potential is at last being realized.

In a world where standardization is increasingly the rule, Portuguese wines stand out as individuals, refusing to bow to

superstar grape varieties that dominate production elsewhere. Here, producers rely on indigenous grapes such as Touriga Nacional (used in port and Dão wines), Tinta Roriz (the same as the Tempranillo grape used in Spain's *rioja* wines), Malvasia Fina (a local variety of the famous Greek grape used in the Douro's sparkling wines), Alvarinho (the basis of many vinhos verdes), and Periquita (widely used in reds of the Setúbal Peninsula and Alentejo). Nor have tried-and-tested methods been entirely abandoned either;

you still find some producers in the south aging wine in clay vessels.

Then & Now

Wine production dates back to the Phoenicians, who introduced it to southern Portugal in 600 B.C. and traded it around the Mediterranean. Since then, Greeks, Celts, Romans, Visigoths, and even Moors have enjoyed the local tipple. Yet it was the English who kick-started the port trade. In 1678, a Liverpudlian merchant discovered port when he added brandy to a sweet, heavy Douro wine to prevent the wine from souring en route to England. Soon barrel loads of the fortified wine were being shipped to England and a 1703 trade treaty sealed the deal; port and English merchants were inextricably bound and profits soon boomed. A few decades later, Portugal's prime minister, the Marquês de Pombal, introduced the world's first production standards and controlled areas in the Douro Valley.

All was not smooth sailing though: The late 19th century saw vineyards devastated by the phylloxera plague, and a few decades later by shifts in agricultural focus. Since Portugal joined the European Union in 1986, however, modern procedures have transformed its wine industry and its previously incomprehensible classifications.

■ Portugal's grapes produce the curiously named *tinto verde* and port wine.

With nearly 988,000 acres (400,000 ha) of vines flourishing in granitic, shale, sandy, or clay soils, domestic consumption is around 53 liters (11.5 gallons) per capita a year, placing Portugal among the world's top five consumers. In years gone by, wines tended to remain within their production regions. This is no longer the case and all but the most simple establishments will offer a choice of wines from different regions. If in doubt, order the *vinho da casa* (house wine); you are unlikely to hit a bad note.

Where to Savor Portugal's Wines

Wine flows freely in Portugal and forms a central part of any social gathering. For this reason alone, dedicate some time to exploring the subtleties of Portuguese wine, whether rustic brew or elegant vintage. Here are some great atmospheric venues that offer the traveler a special experience:
Free tastings: Sala Ogival, Praça do Comércio, Lisbon, tel 213 420 690, or **Palácio da Bolsa,** Rua das Flores 8–12,

Porto, tel 223 323 072, viniportugal.pt, closed Sun. (Nov.-Mar.)
Port: Port Wine Institute, Rua de São Pedro de Alcântara 45, Lisbon, tel 213 475 707, closed Sun., or **Portologia,** Rua de São João 28–30, Porto, tel 222 011 050
Vinho verde: Solar do Alvarinho, Rua Direita, Melgaço, tel 251 410 195
Table wines: Wine Bar do Castelo, Rua Bartolomeu de Gusmão 11, Lisbon, tel 218 879 093, viniportugal.pt

GUIMARÃES

Historical status, gastronomy, the church, and a dash of contemporary panache all combine in this seductive medieval town that is classified as a World Heritage site. With rare architectural harmony and intelligently pedestrianized, Guimarães is a must-see highlight of Portugal's north.

 Visitors may walk the ramparts of Guimarães's faithfully restored 10th-century castle walls.

Guimarães
🗺 74 B2
Visitor Information
✉ Praça de S. Tiago
☎ 253 421 221
**guimaraes
turismo.com**

With Porto only 30 miles (50 km) away, Guimarães is hardly out of touch, and this shows in the style of many shops and restaurants in the town. Yet the nation of Portugal was founded here back in the 12th century, when Afonso Henriques, heir to the county of Portucale, chased out the Moors and declared himself king (see pp. 22–23). His regal seat was the castle that dominates Guimarães, built in the 10th century to protect the monastery of Nossa Senhora da Oliveira.

The old town lies between the gardens of the Alameda and bustling commercial Largo do Toural to the south, and the hilltop park, castle, and palace to the north. An obvious starting point is the main square, the **Largo da Oliveira,** which is separated from the adjacent Praça da Santiago by an attractive arcaded walkway. Above this veranda were the old Council Chambers, now the **Museu de Arte Primitiva Moderna** *(tel 253 414 186, closed Sat.–Sun.)* of marginal interest. Beside this stands the atmospheric old Hotel da Oliveira (see p. 243). In the warmer months, much of the square is invaded by sidewalk cafés, great places from which to admire the Gothic shrine fronting the church of the monastery of **Nossa Senhora da Oliveira.**

This medieval church (*closed lunchtime*) has undergone numerous alterations; today only the cloisters and the chapter house remain Romanesque; little is left of the monastery. The lovely buildings now house the remarkable **Museu Alberto Sampaio** (*Rua Alfredo Guimarães, tel 253 423 910, culturanorte.gov.pt, closed Mon., €*), stuffed with church treasures, including medieval tomb sculptures and one of Portugal's finest collections of silverware. Look for the magnificent gilded silver triptych, allegedly taken from the Castilians at the Battle of Aljubarrota in 1395. Dom João I's tunic from that same battle is also displayed. But do not let the exhibits monopolize your attention: The **chapter house, cloisters,** and **ancient priory buildings** are equally magnificent.

Outside, on the corner of this street, a small open shrine houses carved figures of the Passion: It is one of five left from an original seven, erected in 1727 to represent the **Stations of the Cross.**

To the west, the ultramodern **Centro Internacional das Artes José Guimarães,** built on the site of the former municipal market, is known locally as the Plataforma das Artes e Criatividade (Arts and Creativity Platform), or PAC. Dedicated to contemporary art, the award-winning building holds a museum, art exhibitions, and artists' studios.

Guimarães's other major attraction is the **Paço dos Duques de Bragança,** a striking fortified palace bristling with brick chimney pots that stands in a small park. Near ruins since the court moved out in the 16th century, the palace was fully restored in the 1930s to its original 15th-century appearance, complete with massive proportions, huge fireplaces, Aubusson tapestries, Persian rugs, coffered ceilings, and granite walls. Outside stands a statue of Afonso Henriques, founding king of the Portuguese nation.

Penha

Aficionados of heights and views shouldn't miss the verdant summit of Penha, the highest point in the Serra de Santa Catarina, right on the outskirts of Guimarães. It's reached via cable car; the Teleférico da Penha (*Parque das Hortas, tel 253 515 085, turipenha .pt, closed Mon.–Thurs. Nov.– Mar., €*) **rises 1,300 feet (400 m) in 10 minutes.**

On the hill just above the Paço dos Duques de Bragança is the chapel of **São Miguel do Castelo** (*tel 253 412 273*). This simple, unadorned chapel dating from the 12th century is where Afonso Henriques is said to have been baptized. Notice the etched stone tombs of Portugal's first warriors set into the floor. At the very top of the hill looms the **Castelo de Guimarães** (*tel 253 412 273*), built in the 10th century to guard the monastery against attacks by the Normans and Moors. It, too, has been fully restored, and a steep climb up the keep will reward you with fine views. ∎

Centro Internacional das Artes José Guimarães (PAC)
- ✉ Avenida Conde Margaride 175
- ☎ 253 424 715
- 🕐 Closed Mon.
- $ €

ciajg.pt

Paço dos Duques de Bragança
- ✉ Rua Conde D. Henrique
- ☎ 253 412 273
- $ €€. Free Sun.

pacodosduques.gov.pt

BRAGA & ENVIRONS

An old saying goes: "Porto works, Lisbon plays, and Braga prays." Braga is indeed renowned for its numerous churches and, above all, its Sé. Yet this industrious town is also home to enthusiastic diners, giving the center a lively atmosphere. Just beyond the high-rise suburbs are four major religious sites and the ancient settlement of Citânia de Briteiros.

Braga

🗺 74 A2–B2

Visitor Information

✉ Avenida da Liberdade 1

☎ 253 262 550

cm-braga.pt

While most of the main sites are religious in nature, Braga offers much more for visitors. The city's origins lie in Roman times when, as Bracara Augusta, it was an important commercial crossroads, but successive occupations by the Suevi, Visigoths, and finally the Moors left it in virtual ruins. Status and prosperity returned in the 11th century when the resident archbishop of the newly liberated town assumed ecclesiastical authority over the entire Iberian Peninsula. Later, when a 16th-century successor embarked on a frenzied building campaign, the city gained Renaissance fountains, squares, mansions, and churches. These were further embellished in the 18th century, although Braga's formal ecclesiastical status ended in 1716, when Lisbon took over the patriarchate.

The best time to experience the city's intensity of faith is during Easter Week: Braga's spectacular

■ The mountainside setting of S.C. Braga's stadium makes it a unique destination for soccer lovers.

processions peak on Maundy Thursday. June 23 and 24 bring more parades, dancing, bonfires, and fireworks to celebrate the solstice and the feast of St. John the Baptist.

Braga's City Center

Start your visit in the **Rossio da Sé** in the center of a pedestrianized area. This plaza is named for its **Sé** (Cathedral). Much of the original Romanesque structure lies hidden under a wealth of late Gothic and baroque additions. Notice the beautiful altarpiece carved out of white stone and the statue of the nursing Virgin Mary, thought to be the work of French Renaissance artist Nicolas de Chanterenne.

The treasury—the **Tesouro Museu da Sé Catedral de Braga** (tel 253 263 317, closed Mon., €)—is the highlight. A guided tour shows off a breathtaking hoard of precious objects acquired by the prelates over the centuries, from gold and silver chalices to ivory or crystal crucifixes, gold thread altar cloths and vestments to platters of jewels. It perfectly illustrates the wealth and lavish way of life the bishops enjoyed.

The tour also takes in the magnificent carved baroque choir and massive organs before ending downstairs at two chapels. The Gothic **Capela dos Reis** (Chapel of the Kings) contains the rather ghoulish, mummified body of a 14th-century archbishop as well as the tombs of Henry of Burgundy and his wife, Teresa, the parents of Portugal's first king, Afonso

Henriques. Opposite, the Capela de São Geraldo is dedicated to Braga's first archbishop, who died in 1108; his tomb, set into a heavily gilded altarpiece, stands surrounded by 18th-century azulejos that portray his life.

Opposite the Sé, on Rua do Souto, is the **Antigo Paço Episcopal** (former bishop's palace), its rather forbidding facade enclosing three sides of a square. Much of this 14th- to 18th-century edifice is occupied by municipal offices, but enter

---

INSIDER TIP:

Be sure to stop by Rua da Violinha, one of the most typical streets of Braga's medieval town, and admire the interior of the medieval wall.

—ISABEL LEITÃO
Founder, À Descoberta de Braga tours

---

the doorway to the left to have a look at the beautifully carved and painted library ceiling (closed Sat.–Sun.). Behind the former palace is the **Jardim de Santa Bárbara,** a vividly colorful and immaculately tended garden.

By far Braga's most evocative site is the much underrated **Museu dos Biscainhos** (tel 253 204 650, closed Mon., €). This manor house museum stands west of the pedestrian area, just outside **Porta Nova,** the 18th-century arch that once marked

Citânia de Briteiros

Farther afield, roughly halfway between Braga and Guimarães, you step back 2,000 odd years to the largest Celtiberian settlement in Portugal, Citânia de Briteiros *(tel 253 415 969, €)*. Tiered, defensive walls surround the foundations of more than 150 buildings, two of which have been reconstructed, although the site's better finds are now in Guimarães's archaeological museum, the **Museu Martins Sarmento** *(Rua Paio Galvão, Guimarães, tel 253 415 969, closed Mon.)*, named for the first archaeologist to excavate here in 1875. Briteiros nonetheless makes an evocative, rural setting and the site is being upgraded to provide better visitor facilities, including a restaurant. Be wary about visiting during the heat of the day.

the entrance to town. The rambling house provides a remarkable window on the social history of Portugal's nobility, greatly helped by multilingual information sheets in each room. The tiled walls and painted, stuccoed ceilings are mainly 18th century, although some elements date from a century earlier, when the core of the house was built. A revealing feature is the raised platform on which the women of the house used to sit, sewing and embroidering, in a kind of social purdah. Close by is the room for social gatherings *(partidas)*, a development that came in the mid-18th century and inspired card and game tables, musical instruments, and even tea and coffee sets. More important, it brought women out into society.

Striking decorative items include Ming porcelain, glassware, silverware, and jewelry, while furniture ranges from Indo-Portuguese pieces to Japanese lacquer. The stables and fabulous kitchen can be visited on the way to a lovely baroque garden where towering chestnut and magnolia trees give plenty of shade and peeling sculptures add atmosphere, making it an evocative retreat for a summer's day.

Four Venerated Religious Centers

The much photographed **Bom Jesus do Monte** sits about 4 miles (6 km) east of Braga high on a hill. This church, a major pilgrimage spot, crowns a magnificent double baroque stairway. By the time the staircase was complete, after several decades, architectural styles had changed and, as a result, the church itself is neoclassical and less fancy.

The climb is not as bad as it looks, and it must be undertaken if you wish to have a close look at the chapels, terra-cotta figures, and allegorical fountains that decorate each level. You will gravitate from the Stations of the Cross at the bottom to the intermediary Five Senses (which all worthy believers should overcome) and finally attain the symbols of the three virtues: Faith, Hope, and Charity.

Serious pilgrims accomplish the climb on their knees; most people simply walk. Alternatively, Portugal's oldest **funicular** *(€)*, dating from 1882, creaks up to the top every half hour during daylight, and there is also a road that winds up to the church and nearby hotels. Try to time your visit for sunset and settle on a garden bench, in the terrace café, or in the panoramic restaurant: The sky explodes into dramatic color in front of you, while the lights of Braga slowly come on below. The entire hilltop is a popular weekend escape for locals since there are walks and pony rides in the woods behind.

Three miles (5 km) west of Braga is the important sanctuary and pilgrimage spot **Santúario Nossa Senhora do Sameiro** that venerates the Virgin Mary. It commands extensive views over the Minho area, but has little architectural interest.

On the northwestern side of Braga, the Visigothic chapel of **São Frutuoso de Montélios** *(usually open Tues.–Sun. 2 p.m.– 4:30 p.m.)* now stands engulfed by sprawling suburbs. Located on one of Portugal's medieval pilgrimage routes to Santiago de Compostela, in Spain, this is one of Portugal's oldest chapels, dating from the seventh century. In the 18th century it was incorporated into a church, but its simple, cruciform structure and capitals are clearly visible.

Also on the northwestern side of Braga and a complete contrast both in scale and style to São Frutuoso is the stunning **Mosteiro de São Martinho de Tibães** *(tel 253 622 670, cm-braga.pt, closed Mon., €).* This sprawling monastery was founded in the 11th century, soon acquired immense power and wealth, and eventually became the father of all Benedictine monasteries in

Portugal. The late 17th century saw a period of massive expansion and embellishment, leaving an astonishingly rich interior that is now considered one of Portugal's greatest baroque landmarks. Abandoned for more than a century, the monastery was rescued by the Portuguese state in 1986. Its restoration work is ongoing. A state-of-the-art exhibition space has been created in one wing to house a historical center.

■ Countless stone heads, statues, and urns adorn the zigzagging staircase at Bom Jesus do Monte.

One of the monastery's highlights, apart from the dazzling rococo church, is a vast, somewhat overgrown baroque garden fashioned out of the hillside, a wondrous place of fountains, water channels, arbors, an oval lake, and box-hedged paths, with steps leading up to the reconstructed Chapel of St. Benedict. The latter was an enlightened attempt by the monks to symbolize the ascent into heaven. ■

VIANA DO CASTELO &
THE NORTHERN MINHO

The northwestern corner of Portugal is full of inspiring contrasts, from a charming main town (Viana) to windswept beaches and a succession of fortified outposts along the Minho River. Inland lie the lush Lima Valley and the rugged Peneda-Gerês National Park (see pp. 104–105).

Every year the Minho's string of festivals brings out glorious costumes and masks.

Viana do Castelo

74 A3

Visitor Information

Praça do Eixo Atlântico

258 098 415

Closed Mon. Sept.–June

vivexperiencia.pt

Viana do Castelo

Viana is a pleasant surprise with pedestrianized streets, a wealth of Renaissance and baroque architecture, good restaurants, and an easygoing atmosphere.

In this prosperous little port of 15,000 inhabitants you can still find fishermen's wives selling the daily catch west of the town center near the port, while raucous seagulls screech overhead. Embroidery is another Viana specialty; look for the local household linen. If you are in the region August 20 to 23, enjoy the revelries of the spectacular festival of Nossa Senhora d'Agonia (see sidebar opposite).

The heart of the town is the lively, café-lined **Praça da República** and its focal point, the **chafariz,** a tiered Renaissance fountain. Overlooking this from the northern end is the **Antigos Paços do Concelho** (Old Town Hall) and immediately opposite, the Venetian-style **Hospital da Misericórdia,** a former alms-house. The impressive caryatids and loggias (dating from 1589) shelter stone seats at ground level, invariably used by locals waiting to enter the municipal offices inside. Next door is the church of the **Misericórdia** itself *(tel 258 822 350, open Sun. a.m. only)*, rebuilt in 1714 and replete with exceptional azulejos by António de Oliveira Bernardes.

The main concentration of historic buildings in the web of narrow streets south of here includes the 15th-century **Hospital Velho,** a beautiful vaulted structure. Close by is the **Sé** (Cathedral); Gothic and Romanesque elements grace a lovely facade, but the interior is somewhat dreary.

Head to **Rua São Pedro** for a string of Manueline mansions, then make for the other side of this main north-south avenue and the **Museu de Artes Decorativas** *(Largo de São Domingos, tel 258 809 305, closed Mon., €)*. Housed in a slightly dilapidated 1720s mansion, it has a wonderful sense of history heightened by remarkable azulejos by Policarpo de Oliveira Bernardes, lofty coffered ceilings, and the personal character of the collection. You will see an illuminating display of 17th- and 18th-century Portuguese faïence, some from Viana itself—much of it in blue and white and designed to replace Ming imports from China—as well as Indo-Portuguese furniture, drawings, inlaid cabinets, and a lavish bedroom. Also worth a quick visit is the costume museum, **Museu do Traje** *(Praça da República, tel 258 809 306, closed Mon., €)* on the main square.

In addition to a bridge by the prolific Gustave Eiffel, Viana's riverfront also boasts the striking 16th-century castle of **Santiago da Barra** *(closed to public)* guarding the river mouth. Above, on the Monte de Santa Luzia, you can climb the dome of neo-Byzantine **Templo de Santa Luzia** *(tel 258 823 173, templosantaluzia.org, €)* for panoramic views of seemingly idyllic beaches below; better still, indulge in a sunset cocktail on the terrace of the *pousada (tel 258 800 370)*.

Finally, step back in time aboard **O Navio** *Gil Eannes (tel 258 809 710, fundacaogileannes.pt, €)*. Built in the city shipyard during the 1950s, it originally supported cod fishermen in the North Atlantic as a hospital ship. Now fully restored, almost the entire ship can be visited.

The Minho Coast

Although only thick-skinned swimmers brave the waves on

EXPERIENCE: Nossa Senhora d'Agonia Festival

If you are in the Minho around August 20, you will undoubtedly be caught up in the revelries of the spectacular festival of Nossa Senhora d'Agonia, when groups from across the Minho converge on Viana. There are marching bands, street performances, *gigantões e cabeçudos* (people dressed as giants with enormous heads), and lots of *bombos* (drums). The highlight is definitely the street parades, when participants display their elaborate regional costumes and the women don their fine gold filigree jewelry; the more gold the higher the status. Contact the tourist office *(tel 258 098 415)* or visit the festival's website *(vianafestas.com)* for exact dates and the program of events.

Caminha

74 A3

Visitor Information

Praça Conselheiro Silva Torres

258 921 952

Closed Sun.

cm-caminha.pt

Valença do Minho

74 A4

Visitor Information

Loja de Turismo, Porta do Sol

251 823 329

Closed Sun.

visitvalenca.com

Monção

74 A4

Visitor Information

Praça Deu-la-Deu

251 649 013

---

these beautiful Atlantic beaches, the shores are popular for sunbathing and for surfing. The main beach just south of Viana, **Praia do Cabedelo,** can be reached by ferryboat *(Margem Rio Lima, open July–Aug. only).* Head 7 miles (11 km) north of Viana for the surfing beach of **Afife,** separated from the main road by fields of corn, for now with only a couple of beach bars for "development." A few miles farther, the small family beach resort of **Vila Praia de Âncora** is immediately followed by **Moledo.** The latter's beach is much calmer and the water shallower, making it safer and slightly warmer for swimming. From here, you get a good view of a tiny island fort guarding the estuary of the Minho River. Between Moledo and Caminha, an extensive pine forest crossed by boardwalks borders a broad white sandy beach.

In **Caminha,** have a look at the medieval and Renaissance buildings that surround **Praça Conselheiro Silva Torres,** the central square, as well as the **Igreja Matriz** *(tel 258 921 413, open p.m. Sat.–Sun. only).* The church claims one of the most finely carved and coffered ceilings in Portugal. You can also take a 10-minute car ferry *(tel 912 253 809)* across to the town of A Guarda in Galicia to visit the well-maintained Celtiberian settlement of **Santa Tecla.**

Continuing along the Minho River, the next stop is the fortified town of **Valença do Minho,** once a very important stronghold. Below the massive 17th-century

ramparts sprawls a modern border town of little interest, but walk or drive up to the two polygonal fortresses and you enter a curious hybrid world of Spanish and Portuguese cultures. Resolutely aimed at droves of Spanish day-trippers,

---

INSIDER TIP:

The Monção area produces excellent white Alvarinho wine, perfect paired with a dish of local lampreys (baby eels).

—EMMA ROWLEY
National Geographic contributor

Valença's cobbled streets are lined with tapas bars and shops selling cheap items. During weekdays when it is quieter, it offers a pleasant wander to admire the bastions, cannon, watchtowers, fountains, churches, and harmonious 17th- and 18th-century houses. **Porta do Sol** is the best entry; a footbridge connects the two fortresses.

Less adulterated by commercial concerns, but displaying an equally defensive character, the medieval stronghold of **Monção,** 10 miles (16 km) east, offers a relaxed, attractive setting around the verdant main square, **Praça Deu-la-Deu.** Two churches are of some interest, the partly Romanesque **Igreja Matriz** *(Rua da Glória)* and the early baroque **Misericórdia** *(Praça Deu-la-Deu),* where cherubs dance across a wood-paneled ceiling in front of an elaborate Renaissance altarpiece. ∎

PONTE DE LIMA

Plumb in the middle of *vinho verde* territory, beside the Lima River, is this immaculately preserved "oldest town in Portugal." There are no major monuments, but it is a natural point between Viana and the interior mountains, and between the northern border with Spain and Braga. The twice-monthly market is a major event locally and the oldest market in the country.

Ponte de Lima's historical claim to fame was its medieval role as a stop on the pilgrimage road to Santiago de Compostela from the religious hotbed of Braga. The graceful, arched granite bridge remains from those days, with five arches of an even older Roman section, built for military purposes, on the western bank. Here, too, are very pleasant gardens laid out according to themes and surrounding a small **Museu Rural** *(closed a.m. & Mon.).*

Town Attractions

Ponte de Lima's central focal point is the attractive main square, **Largo de Camões,** which hosts an 18th-century fountain and relaxing pavement cafés. On alternate Mondays, the entire riverside springs to life with a sprawling market which has been held, virtually uninterrupted, since 1125. The old town's architectural styles range from Romanesque to neoclassical. Wander around and enjoy the facades, many enhanced by window boxes or doorway pots, and note the Romanesque doorway of the parish church. Shops sell local specialties: linen, elaborate Minho costumes, and life-size models of woolly sheep.

The modest **Museu dos Terceiros** *(Av. 5 de Outubro, tel 258 240 220, closed Mon., €)* is housed in two churches—one of which, the **Igreja dos Terceiros,** with its baroque front, was built in 1745. The museum displays religious iconography, 16th-century Mudejar tiles from Spain, and some fine wood carving. ∎

Ponte de Lima
- 🗺 74 A3

Visitor Information
- ✉ Torre da Cadeia Velha, Passeio 25 Abril
- ☏ 258 240 208

▪ **Tree-lined, cobblestoned paths offer relaxing strolls beside the Lima River in Ponte de Lima.**

PARQUE NACIONAL DA PENEDA-GERÊS

Vaguely resembling a horseshoe, the park curls around the Spanish border in the far north of the country. Portugal's first national park, it was set up in 1971 to protect some remote, very traditional villages as well as flora and fauna, and it is one of the last refuges of the Iberian wolf and golden eagle. A partnership with the bordering Spanish national park ensures a larger protected habitat.

At Junceda, near Campo do Gerês, boulder-strewn landscapes rise to more than 2,700 feet (863 m).

Parque Nacional da Peneda-Gerês

🗺 74 B3

✉ Largo da Misericórdia 10, Ponte da Barca

☎ 258 452 250

natural.pt

Peneda-Gerês covers 190,000 acres (77,000 ha), roughly between the towns of Castro Laboreiro in the north and Caldas do Gerês in the south, and is crossed by the Lima, Homem, and Peneda Rivers. Four mountain ranges (serras), rich in granite and some schist, dominate the terrain—the highest peak, in the Serra do Gerês, rises to 5,044 feet (1,538 m)—creating a series of peaks and valleys edged with undulating foothills. Yet the ancient megaliths (particularly around Castro Laboreiro and Mezio) and

strange granite formations, the remnants of ancient glacier activity, are far more impressive.

The park straddles the Mediterranean and northern Europe biosystems, making for a wide range of flora and fauna, the former being particularly impressive in April and May, the perfect time for hiking in the area. But beauty has a price—rain. The hills of the Serra da Peneda receive Portugal's highest rainfall, nourishing luminous green meadows much in favor with the local long-horned barrosão cattle. Several species of oak trees dominate the lower elevations while

EXPERIENCE: Walking Through Wolf Territory

Get up close with the wild and untamed Peneda-Gerês region by tracking one of its rarest residents, the endangered Iberian wolf. Depending on how much time you have available, it is possible to hike for anything from one to eight days with **Ecotura** (*Lugar do Queimadelo, Castro Laboreiro, Melgaço, tel 967 442 217, ecotura.com*). Knowledgeable guides lead small groups along centuries-old shepherd paths and known wolf trails, searching for wolf tracks and pointing out the ancient traps once used to catch these much

feared creatures. They explain the importance of wolves to this northern region and their miraculous ability to survive extinction despite man's efforts (until recent years) to be rid of them. Guide and owner Pedro Alarcão suggests that the best time to visit is in September and October, when the probability of spotting a wolf is greatest. A one-day hike (8.5 hr.) costs about €40 per person, including lunch. If wolves do not interest you, Ecotura offers a range of other trips in addition to year-round horseback riding.

the higher reaches see typical moorland vegetation, including seas of brilliant yellow gorse, broom, heather, pine, and fir trees. If you are lucky, you will see the wild Gerês lily; endemic to the park, it grows in wooded areas, but only in select locations. Park denizens include roe deer, wild boars, otters, foxes, wild ponies, and raptors.

Most of the park's infrastructure is concentrated in a buffer zone that encircles the spectacular, higher-elevation core region, which should not be missed. Try to avoid the area around Caldas do Gerês on weekends and holidays, when it gets extremely crowded.

Nossa Senhora da Peneda

An unexpected sight in such a raw, craggy setting and dwarfed by a sheer granite cliff is the sanctuary of **Nossa Senhora da Peneda,** a graceful baroque building with a zigzagging stairway inspired by Braga's Bom Jesus. The long flight of steps is

flanked by 14 chapels, each one depicting a major event in the life of Christ. The sanctuary was inspired by the reported vision of the Virgin by a local shepherdess in the 13th century. If you visit around September 7, you will see one of Portugal's most important pilgrimages. The sanctuary is in the most rewarding northern part of the park, where you will discover some of the traditional rural lifestyles the park protects— despite the population's ongoing drift to the cities.

Traditional Life

To gain a sense of the customs of the region, visit the town of **Terras de Bouro,** just outside the southwest corner of the park. Its ethnographic museum, **Museu Etnográfico de Vilarinho da Furna,** reveals the traditional life once enjoyed in Vilarinho das Furnas, a village submerged by the reservoir next to Campo do Gerês in 1972. Building stones were saved to build the museum. ∎

Museu Etnográfico de Vilarinho da Furna

- ✉ São João do Campo, Terras de Bouro
- ☎ 253 351 888
- 🕒 Closed Mon.
- 💲 €

NOTE: If you wish to stay overnight in the park's core region, relatively comfortable rooms in private village houses are available as are a selection of established bed-and-breakfasts. There are also campsites at Travanca, Vidoeiro, and Entre Ambos-os-Rios. For details, visit *adere-pg.pt* or *turismo ruraleparquesdecampismo geres.com.*

DRIVE INTO PARQUE NACIONAL DA PENEDA-GERÊS

Less about specific sites and more about rural scenery, this drive takes you from Ponte de Lima up into the rugged mountains of Peneda-Gerês National Park, before circling back along verdant riverbanks to Ponte da Barca.

■ *Espigueiros* (raised stone granaries), often built in clusters, are unique to northern Portugal.

Leave **Ponte de Lima ❶** by following signs for the A3 to Valença/Espanha. Enter the toll road and then turn off immediately toward Ponte da Barca. This road (N202) takes you past typical Minho vine-draped pergolas, wooded slopes, and villages. You soon reach **Arcos de Valdevez ❷** *(visitor information, Rua Prof. Mário Júlio Almeida Costa, tel 258 520 530)*, a pretty town on the Vez River. Turn left at the first traffic circle to cross the river, then right after the bridge. After a stroll along the scenic river, return to the town entrance and follow signs to Soajo (N202). After passing the tiled church of **São Paio**, turn right, and take the first left.

The road climbs through pine and eucalyptus groves to wild, rockier terrain of heather, terraced hillsides, and distant mountains. At

NOT TO BE MISSED:

Ponte de Lima • Soajo *espigueiros* • Castelo do Lindoso • Ponte da Barca riverside

Portela do Mezio ❸ you leave the buffer zone and enter the national park. There is a small **visitor center** *(park headquarters in Braga, tel 253 203 480)*, and ancient megaliths lie off the road to the right. The road now descends to **Soajo ❹**, famous for its 24 *espigueiros* (raised stone granaries). Drive straight on to a stone monument and turn left; after 200 yards (180 m) the espigueiros come into view beside the road. Return to the main road; turn right and right again to see Soajo's main square and pillory. Leave by the way you came and then, after a sharp right-hand bend, turn right up a steep cobbled road signposted **Gavieira.**

This road leads through a landscape of gorse, pine trees, black sheep, horses, goats, and long-horned *barrosão* cattle. Switchbacks offer stunning views to the southeast before the road reaches a rocky pass at 4,644 feet (1,416 m). From here it twists up to the village of **Adrão ⑤**, a mile or two past which is one of the best lookout points in the area. Pull over to admire the sheer granite slopes and deep verdant valleys sprinkled with hamlets below, with the religious sanctuary of **Peneda** nestling beneath the rock face to the far north. From here backtrack for about a mile (1.6 km) to a road beside a vertical rock face, which is only marked by a sign that warns against cattle. Turn left up this very narrow, vertiginous road, which offers more spectacular views over the hills and valley. The **Barragem do Alto Lindoso** (dam) in the Peneda River is soon visible below.

Paralleling the Lima

After passing a roadside chapel at **Paradela,** cross the Lima River dam and continue uphill toward **Lindoso ⑥.** Make for the medieval tower and lichen-clad stones of the **Castelo do Lindoso** *(Lugar do Castelo, tel 258 578 141, natural.pt)* which provides information on the national park and houses a small photo exhibit and arms section. Far more impressive, however, are the 60-odd **espigueiros** grouped just outside the walls.

Leaving Lindoso, turn left onto the main road (N304-1). This snakes 18 miles (29 km) beside the river to **Ponte da Barca ⑦** *(Rua Conselheiro Rocha Peixoto, tel 258 455 246, closed Sun.–Mon.).* The old town's draw is its idyllic river frontage—an attractive 15th-century bridge, pillory, and open market hall.

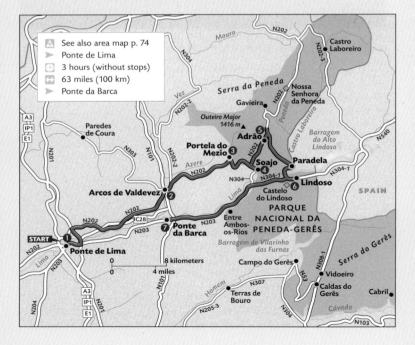

See also area map p. 74
Ponte de Lima
3 hours (without stops)
63 miles (100 km)
Ponte da Barca

BRAGANÇA & ENVIRONS

The walled town of Bragança, in the far northeast, dominates the Trás-os-Montes. This is Portugal's least prosperous area—a marked contrast to areas farther west. Broad plateaus, wide valleys, and traditional villages are protected to the north in the Parque Natural de Montesinho.

Bragança's dramatic medieval citadel rises above the surrounding modern town.

Bragança
- 75 E3

Visitor Information
- ✉ Avenida Cidade de Zamora
- ☎ 273 381 273
- 🕑 Closed Sat.–Sun.

Museu Militar
- ✉ Cidadela (castle keep)
- ☎ 273 322 378
- 🕑 Closed Mon.
- 💲 €

exercito.pt

Bragança is a town with an unusually rich aristocratic past. Visible from miles away, its historic center extends from its defensive hilltop citadel, started by Dom Sancho I in the 12th century and enlarged over the following centuries. Crenellated stone walls, arched gateways, staircases, ramparts, a towering keep, a pillory, and cobbled, flowery streets all create a strikingly harmonious setting. The keep (1409–1449), one of Portugal's most beautiful, houses the somewhat dull **Museu Militar,** but it offers memorable panoramic views from its roof. Across the esplanade stands the town's oldest church, **Santa**

Maria, a charming late 16th- to early 17th-century building.

Just behind this stands Bragança's most unusual site, the **Domus Municipalis** *(closed Mon.),* the oldest town hall in Iberia. The pentagonal structure, perforated by arched openings, is a rare civil building in Romanesque style, thought to date from the early 15th century. The upper floor appears to have been designed for meetings, while below lies a cistern *(ask for a key in the Museu Militar).*

From the citadel, streets snake downhill into a more baroque, 18th-century quarter and beyond that to a recklessly conceived 20th-century extension. The **Sé,** or Cathedral *(Praça da Sé),* occupies the central position in the old quarter, fronted by a 1689 stone crucifix and surrounded by emblazoned seigneurial mansions. Bragança has a wealth of these impressive, mainly 17th- and 18th-century houses—testimony to its grandiose past as the fiefdom of the dukes of Bragança. The Cathedral's 17th-century **sacristy** is well worth visiting. Its paneled ceiling relates the life of St. Ignatius de Loyola, founder of the Jesuits who controlled this church for two centuries.

Downhill from here, toward the citadel, is the beautiful church of **São Vicente** (*Largo do Principal*), Romanesque in origin but much altered in the 17th and 18th centuries. The result is a profusion of dazzling baroque gilt.

For a glimpse of a mansion interior, head for the nearby **Museu do Abade de Baçal,** where a varied collection of ethnographic and decorative arts is displayed in the former bishop's palace. It is presented in a very modern, imaginative fashion. The ground floor shows gold Iron Age *fibulae* alongside local ironwork and Roman *stelae*. Upstairs, look for a 16th-century triptych that illustrates the martyrdom of St. Ignatius; it is one of the museum's most valuable works. Finally, don't miss the ancient granite sow at the entrance: You will see many more throughout the region.

Parque Natural de Montesinho

Nudging the Spanish border, the Parque Natural de Montesinho covers an area of 185,250 acres (75,000 ha) in which approximately 90 traditional villages harbor a dwindling population of 9,000. Like Peneda-Gerês (see pp. 104–105), the park was created more to preserve a rural lifestyle than to protect flora and fauna. The granite and schist hills and valleys of this northern part of Trás-os-Montes are known as *terra fria* (cold land), in contrast to the *terra quente* (hot land) of olives, almonds, and figs farther south. Montesinho has archaic roots, visible in the simple slate-roofed stone houses, surnames of Visigothic origin, dialects, and sometimes pagan rituals. The easiest villages to reach from Bragança are **Rio de Onor** and **Montesinho** itself, both about 14 miles (22 km) to the north. ■

Museu do Abade de Baçal

- ✉ Rua Conselheiro Abílio Beça 27
- ☎ 273 331 595
- 🕐 Closed Mon.
- 💲 €

Parque Natural de Montesinho

- 🗺 75 D3–D4, E3–E4

Visitor Information

- ✉ Parque Florestal de Bragança, 5300–000 Bragança
- ☎ 273 300 400
- 🕐 Closed Sat.–Sun.

natural.pt

montesinho.com

EXPERIENCE: Traditional Montesinho Life

For a hands-on taste of traditional Transmontano life, head north out of Vinhais to the tiny hamlet of Travanca. Set in the heart of Parque Natural de Montesinho, **Casa da Fonte** (*Travanca, tel 933 289 612, casadafonte.com, double room €50*) offers comfortable accommodation in refurbished village houses and will arrange for guests to take part in various traditional activities, most of them free of charge or for a nominal fee. Choose from a day with a local shepherd herding his flock or, depending on the season, trout fishing or hunting for small game and wild boar. It is also possible to try your hand at archery, crossbow, and pistol shooting.

More Places to Visit in the Norte Region

Barcelos

Barcelos, 14 miles (21 km) west of Braga, is known for its vast Thursday market and a curious, brightly painted clay cockerel. The latter is ubiquitous throughout Portugal in countless forms as a symbol of justice. Legend holds that a cockerel rose from its lifeless state on a judge's platter to protest the innocence of an unjustly sentenced pilgrim. Other than market day, Barcelos is a sleepy place with two main sites: The **Paço dos Duques** (*tel 253 412 273*), an open-air archaeological museum, is laid out in the ruins of the palace of the counts of Barcelos, overlooking the Cávado River. The **Museu de Olaria** (*Rua Cónego Joaquim Gaiolas, tel 253 824 741, museuolaria.pt, closed Mon., €*) displays pottery from all over Portugal.

🅰 74 A2 **Visitor Information** ✉ Largo Dr. José Novais 27 ☎ 253 811 882 🕐 Closed Sun. in winter

Chaves

This small spa town on the Tâmega River was developed by the Romans as much for its strategic position as for its thermal waters. The main monument is the massive keep, the **Torre de Menagem** (*tel 276 340 500*) that overlooks the Roman bridge and the river. Inside is a modest military museum with maps detailing the attacks at Chaves by Luso and Wellesley (later Lord Wellington) on French troops in 1809. You can climb to the battlements for sweeping views.

The tower fronts the main cluster of monuments at the heart of Chaves's medieval quarter: the town hall, a rather limited ethnographic museum, the parish church, and an elaborate pillory. Crowning the hilltop behind is the impressive **Forte de São Francisco,** most of which has now become an upscale hotel. Chaves's other attraction is its delicious local cured ham and sausages.

🅰 74 C3 **Visitor Information** ✉ Terreiro de Cavalaria ☎ 276 348 180

Vidago Palace

Commissioned in 1908 by Dom Carlos, Vidago Palace (*tel 276 990 920, vidago palace.com*) **was intended as a luxurious holiday home for the royal family, where they could come to take the region's famous therapeutic waters. Dom Carlos was assassinated before its completion, but Vidago Palace went on to become one of Iberia's most luxurious hotels, attracting royalty from across Europe. More than one hundred years later, a total refurbishment saw its belle epoque features meticulously restored and modern luxuries added, including a state-of-the-art spa at which to enjoy the benefits of the famous waters.**

Mirandela

Built on a hillside sloping down to the Tua River, the lively market town of Mirandela lies at the head of the stunning narrow-gauge railway from Tua in the Douro Valley. The evocative old quarter rises beside a 16th-century bridge of 20 unequal arches. Mirandela's most interesting site is the town hall, housed in a lovely 18th-century mansion, the **Palácio dos Távoras.** The **Museu Municipal Armindo Teixeira Lopes** (*Rua João Maria Sarmento Pimentel, tel 278 201 590, closed Sat. a.m. & Sun.*) offers an overview of mainly 20th-century Portuguese art. The main draw, however, lies in its market building where, even outside Thursday, the main market day, shops sell delicious regional products—goat and sheep cheeses, cured ham, extra virgin olive oil, honey, jams, and of course wines.

🅰 75 D2 **Visitor Information** ✉ Rua D. Afonso III, next to the train station ☎ 278 203 143 or 800 300 278 🕐 Closed Sat. p.m. & Sun.

A land of fortified hill villages, giant boulders, creamy sheep cheese, and Portugal's most august university

CENTRO

Azulejos adorn a town wall in Viseu, one of the Beiras area's many well-kept secrets.

CENTRO

Now officially known as the Centro region, this area is still often referred to by its former name of the Beiras and its subdivisions *alta, baixa,* and *litoral* (high, low, and coastal), to which you could easily add a fourth, the mountainous spine of the Serra da Estrela. To the west of this massif lie outgoing, dynamic towns, while on its eastern side a string of defensive castles and walled towns face the old enemy, Spain.

■ Musicians in traditional costume entertain passersby in the heart of Coimbra's shopping district.

These medieval outposts evolved over centuries of conflict, but long before that the Romans had left their mark at Conímbriga, to the west. Today this area remains the sociocultural heart of the Beiras in the form of Coimbra. This lively, attractive university town entrances the visitor with its cultural sites, fado music, gastronomy, outdoor activities, and a number of nearby bucolic escapes.

Although the coastline boasts sandy beaches and pine forests, the sea is cool and the waves big, making the shore less of a priority than the interior. The exception is Aveiro, an engaging little town built on canals, with two relaxed beach resorts a short distance away. Every other place of interest in the Beiras is small scale, possesses several churches, and, often, a castle. Closer to the Serra da Estrela, you enter a dramatic region peppered with gigantic granite boulders,

dolmens, and cromlechs; north of here, spanning the border between the Beiras and the Trás-os-Montes area, the Vale do Côa

(Côa Valley) displays exceptional paleolithic rock art. There is ample evidence of early Celtic, Swabian, and Arab presence, while the historically strong Jewish community has in recent years made something of a comeback.

Craftwork is omnipresent, whether the black pottery of the mountains, the intricately decorated ceramics of Coimbra, or the fine porcelain produced at Vista Alegre, near Aveiro. In the field of textiles, the leader is Castelo Branco, thanks to a tradition of embroidered bedspreads, while beautiful woolen blankets are woven in the villages of the Serra da Estrela. From here, too, come sheepskin products and the region's famous sheep cheese, *Queijo da Serra*. In gastronomic terms, the Beiras offer a tantalizing menu of dishes ranging from hearty mountain cuisine (meat or game based) to the fresh seafood of the coast, and several excellent wines. ■

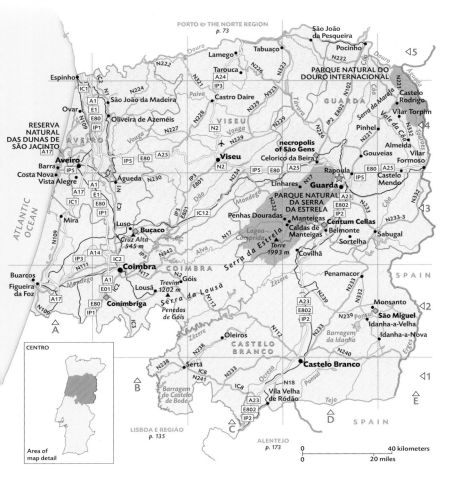

AVEIRO & ENVIRONS

Aveiro has a split personality. Past its sprawling metropolis you'll discover a picturesque town built on a network of canals, earning it the epithet "Venice of Portugal." Aveiro is also distinguished as the country's city-museum of art nouveau, a member of the Réseau Art Nouveau Network along with Barcelona, Budapest, and Havana, among others.

■ Cheerfully painted beach huts line the seafront of Costa Nova.

Aveiro

🗺 113 A4

Visitor Information

✉ Rua João
Mendonça 8

☎ 234 420 760

**centerofportugal
.com**

Museu de Aveiro

✉ Avenida de
Santa Joana

☎ 234 423 297

🕐 Closed Mon.

💲 €

**patrimonio
cultural.pt**

It is hard to believe that Aveiro was once a port. Today, a wide highway connects the town with the coast, crossing a tidal lagoon area that once was the harbor before silting up some 400 years ago in the wake of a disastrous storm. The next two centuries saw an economic decline; prosperity eventually returned on the shoulders of salt workers and seaweed gatherers, as well as a burgeoning ceramics industry in neighboring Vista Alegre. Aveiro itself nurtured a renowned school of baroque sculpture. It is now Portugal's third industrial center, after Lisbon and Porto.

Aveiro's compact town center can easily be covered on foot. Then, cruise along the canals (*Douro Acima, tel 911 745 461, douroacima.pt or contact tourist office*), perhaps in a motorized version of the attractive local *moliceiros* (flat-bottomed sailboats).

Aveiro's signature site is the fabulous **Museu de Aveiro,** housed in splendor in the former **Convent of Jesus,** home to an order of cloistered nuns from 1461 to 1834. The refectory, with its 17th-century tiled walls and Manueline lectern, is lovely, while the church is a dazzling extravaganza of gilded baroque, including a massive stepped altarpiece. The beautiful ceiling illustrates the life of São Domingo, and oil paintings from 1729 depict the life of Santa Joana, the convent's most celebrated resident. Mementos of Princess Joana, later beatified, abound. She spent 18 years here before her death, in 1490. A silver reliquary containing her relics is in the small embroidery room, where she spent her last days; an elaborate baroque marble tomb, commissioned after her sainthood in 1693, stands in the lower choir.

Upstairs, the museum collection offers a wide-ranging feast of paintings, sculpture, woodwork, furniture, and silver, dating from the 15th to 18th centuries. Don't miss the 18th-century convent pharmacy: It contains interesting traditional herbal medicines.

Just across the square, fronted by the Gothic **crucifix of São Domingos,** stands the early 15th-century **Sé** *(tel 234 422 182),* formerly part of a Dominican monastery. Much altered over the centuries, the Cathedral's dominant style is baroque.

The heart of the town lies across the bridge where, in a small web of quaint backstreets, you will discover **Largo da Praça do Peixe,** a large square surrounding the fish market. Seafood restaurants are plentiful, with excellent low-cost eateries on the upper floor of the market.

As Portugal's art nouveau capital, Aveiro also boasts a dozen or so not-to-be-missed buildings including Casa de Major Pessoa, now home to the **Museu de Arte Nova** *(Rua Dr. Barbosa*

Magalhães 9, tel 234 406 485, closed Mon., €). Its detailed stone façade is laden with flowers, arabesques, and wrought-iron embellishments; inside await tile panels depicting motifs of birds, animals, and flowers as well as interesting exhibits and the Casa de Chá (see p. 245).

Beyond Aveiro

Immediately north of the surfing beaches and family resorts of **Barra** and **Costa Nova** is a long spit of land edged by sand dunes, the **Reserva Natural das Dunas de São Jacinto** *(access via ferry from Aveiro or Barra, or road from Ovar; entrance is restricted, reservations advised).* The nature reserve no longer teems with the incredible diversity of birdlife for which it was once known, yet is still interesting. ∎

Reserva Natural das Dunas de São Jacinto

▲ 113 A4
☎ 234 331 282 or 960 335 438
🕐 Closed Sun.
💲 Guided visits 9:30 a.m. & 2 p.m. €

natural.pt

> **EXPERIENCE: Making Doces Conventuais**
>
> To satisfy your sweet tooth and learn how Aveiro's local and much acclaimed *ovos moles* and other *doces conventuais* (sweet egg-based delicacies) are made, visit the **Oficina do Doce** *(Rua João Mendonça 23, Letra JKL–Galeria Rossio, tel 234 098 840, oficinadodoce.com),* located on the town's central canal. Visitors are invited to watch demonstrations and try their hand at making their own ovos moles in the traditional manner, by filling the delicate wafer shells with sticky yolky filling before cutting out the shapes with scissors. Naturally, at the end, everyone gets to taste their handiwork. Reserve your spot at the Oficina do Doce or at the **Aveiro Welcome Center** *(Rua Clube dos Galitos 2, tel 234 420 760, rotadabairrada.pt).*

COIMBRA & AROUND

Coimbra, Portugal's third largest city, was the country's first capital and remained a royal residence for centuries before power shifted to Lisbon. The city's vibrant character draws energy and life from the students and traditions of the Universidade de Coimbra, the country's oldest and most prestigious university. Groups of students stroll about in their swirling black capes, and the Renaissance university itself crowns the hill that is the geographic center of this city.

Stepping up a hillside across the Mondego River, the engaging town of Coimbra never fails to appeal.

Coimbra

🗺 113 B2

Visitor Information

✉ Largo da Portagem & Praça da República

☎ 239 488 120; 239 857 186

turismodocentro.pt

Below, bordering the Mondego River, a typical provincial town of northern Portugal unfolds—the old, narrow streets now pedestrianized and the outskirts peppered with invasive apartment blocks. Across the river sit two major convents and the road south to Conímbriga, a once flourishing and major Roman settlement (see p. 122). In this direction, too, lie the hills of the Serra da Lousã that edge the western end of the massive Serra da Estrela (see pp. 128–129). Although gaining in popularity as a nature retreat, it is still overshadowed by the more famous forest of Buçaco and the neighboring spa at Luso, both to the north of Coimbra.

Coimbra's university was established in 1537 after Lisbon's university, founded in 1290, was forcibly exiled here (see p. 27). As such, Coimbra's academic institutions remain concentrated and traditions deeply entrenched. The *repúblicas* (student lodgings), established by royal decree in medieval days, continue to thrive, furthering the values of community life and democracy. Come here in early May and you will experience the **Queima das Fitas**—the symbolic burning of faculty ribbons to kick off a month of intensive study leading to exams, and an excuse for wholehearted carousing and heavy drinking. Another offshoot of Coimbra's intellectual bent is the local fado (see sidebar p. 118)—a more complex and mournful song than its emotional Lisbon cousin, and strictly the preserve of men.

Universidade de Coimbra

Fortresslike in appearance, the hilltop university demands energy and good calf muscles to reach it from the lower town. The classic approach is up the back-breaking flight of stairs, Quebra-Costas, reached through the Arco de Almedina, an old Moorish gateway; however, you might want to keep this for your descent and climb up via the gentler slope of the Couraça de Lisboa.

At the university's heart is a U-shaped structure that started life as a Moorish fortress in the 10th century. The colossal scale and sturdiness were designed to symbolize the power of the caliphate of Córdoba, the first center of Moorish rule in the Iberian Peninsula. In 1130, Portugal's first king, Afonso Henriques, chose to move here from Guimarães and it thus became a royal palace, the Paço Real. Portugal's oldest royal residence, it was regularly inhabited until the 15th century, when it

was abandoned. It only assumed its present identity as part of a university in 1537. Numerous alterations have been made over the years, giving it Manueline and baroque features. It is nonetheless surprising on a winter's day to see students huddled on wooden benches in lecture halls; the only changes in the last century or so appear to be the addition of electric heaters.

Courtyard Buildings: On entering the main courtyard from the monumental square Praça da Porta Férrea, you face the Gerais (Law School), the Capela de São Miguel, and, on the far left, the university's most

Universidade de Coimbra

✉ Paço das Escolas, Praça da Porta Férrea

☎ 239 859 884 or 239 424 744

uc.pt

River Ride on the Mondego

For some of the best views of the city of Coimbra, hop aboard the **Basófias** (*Cais do Parque Dr. Manuel Braga, tel 969 830 664, basofias.pt*) riverboat for a 50-minute cruise (€€) along the banks. Excursions set off from the quay, south of the Santa Clara Bridge. In addition to cruises, this company also offers *tuk-tuk* tours of the city, which can be paired with the boat trip (€€).

---

outstanding site, the library, or Biblioteca Joanina. The colonnaded gallery on your right, the **Via Latina,** was built in the late 18th century to improve access to the Manueline **Sala dos Capelos** and the **Sala do Exame Privado.** These rooms close to the public when university ceremonies take place. The Sala dos Capelos is a vast, imposing hall with a ceiling

EXPERIENCE: Coimbra Fado

Lisbon fado, sung by both men and women, originated in the taverns of the oldest and poorest districts of the city; Coimbra fado is the domain of black-cloaked, male students who typically sing in the streets after dark, like roaming troubadours (see pp. 58–59).

For a closer insight into this intrinsic part of Coimbra culture, be sure to visit the cultural center **Fado ao Centro** (Rua do Quebra Costas 7, tel 239 837 060 or 913 236 725, fadoaocentro.com, €€), down the steps opposite the Cathedral. The center puts on daily fado concerts of a high standard, hiring only the finest of the city's musicians. Concerts start at 6 p.m. and last 50 minutes. Alternatively, pop in to the afternoon rehearsal at 4 p.m. Reservations are advised for the evening concert.

painted by Jacinto da Costa and a gallery of rather stiff royal portraits. Don't miss the balcony with far-reaching views over the city and beyond.

Reached via the Gerais, the **Capela de São Miguel** mixes Renaissance and baroque styles with panache. The chapel's vaulted ceiling is covered in delicate paintings, the walls partly faced in azulejos, and the altar home to a gilded retable by Bernardo Coelho. Pride of place, however, goes to the magnificent organ (1733) in its carved and painted chinoiserie casing. Next door the small *tesouro* (treasury) displays church plate, vestments, and paintings. Wander upstairs in this building to get a feel for 21st-century student life.

The adjoining **Biblioteca Joanina**—its baroque beauty much extolled and much photo-graphed—easily surpasses all the other buildings for sheer visual delight. *(Purchase timed passes at the office beside the baroque clock tower.)* Three lofty, interconnecting halls arguably offer the world's most lavish library setting thanks to the

INSIDER TIP:

Join in one of the most traditional activities of Coimbra's residents: Walk at sunset along riverside Avenida de Conímbriga, to watch as the setting sun illuminates the old town.

—TINO SORIANO
National Geographic photographer

perspective paintings of the ceil-ings and the intricately carved and painted bookcases, again charged with subtle chinoiserie motifs. Tapering, carved columns sup-port shelves bearing some 30,000 volumes and 5,000 manuscripts, the upper levels accessed by lad-ders. The allegorical paintings of the last and most sumptuous hall honor Dom João V, founder of the library. A statue of the corpu-lent man stands outside, his back turned to the view over town, which you can enjoy from the esplanade terrace.

Churches of Note: Two churches, the **Sé Nova** (New Cathedral) and **São Salvador,** are squeezed between the academic buildings; however, a short walk downhill takes you to the far more interesting **Sé Velha,** or Old Cathedral. This beautifully sober structure, originally Romanesque, dates from 1140, making it Portugal's oldest cathedral. It owes its austere design to two Frenchmen. Sixteenth-century Sevillian tiles and elegant Mudejar-style arches above the transept give visual weight to the otherwise bare stone interior. The focal point is the Gothic altarpiece, all high-relief and vivid colors, designed by Flemish masters Olivier de Gand and Jean d'Ypres. The chapel to the right, the **Capela do Sacramento,** contains a Renaissance work by João de Ruão: sculpted figures of Christ and his disciples, the four evangelists, and Mary with baby Jesus. A delightful 13th-century cloister on the nave's right side, built at a higher level than the rest of the church, has an unusual view of the hilltop university buildings.

From here, souvenir shops selling Coimbra's distinctive blue-and-white ceramics signal the way down to the bottom of the hill via the Quebra-Costas. As this is the main pedestrian access to the university, it caters equally to the needs of students in the form of bookstores, record shops, and cyber cafés. Coimbra's best stores for fashion and sundries line the wide pedestrian street at the bottom, the **Rua Ferreira Borges.**

Coimbra's Lower Town

A lovely square, the Praça 8 de Maio, fronts the important **Igreja de Santa Cruz.** Founded in 1131 by the canons of St. Augustine (the azulejos along the right wall of the nave depict the saint's life), this church houses the tombs of Portugal's first two kings, Afonso Henriques and Sancho I, their recumbent statues the work of sculptor Nicolas de Chanterenne. He was also responsible for the superb Renaissance

Sé Velha
- ✉ Largo da Sé Velha
- ☎ 239 825 273
- 💲 €

sevelha-coimbra.org

Igreja de Santa Cruz
- ✉ Rua Martins de Carvalho 3
- ☎ 239 822 941
- 🕐 Closed Sun. a.m.

igrejascruz. webnode.pt

■ **A wealth of chinoiserie, Coimbra's Biblioteca Joanina—now a museum—is arguably the world's most lavish library.**

■ The Gothic monastery of Santa-Clara-a-Velha

museum, the **Casa Museu Bissaya Barreto** (*Rua da Infantaria 23, tel 239 853 800, cmbb.pt, closed Sun.–Mon. Oct.–Apr., €*). The late 19th-century mansion holds the eclectic collection of local surgeon and scholar Bissaya Barreto (1886–1974): 16th- to 19th-century azulejos and books, sculptures, Portuguese paintings, Chinese porcelain, baroque furniture, and more.

Across the wide Alameda is the lovely **Jardim Botânico** (*Calçada Martins de Freitas, tel 239 855 215, uc.pt/en/jardimbotanico*), 32 acres (13 ha) of formal gardens designed in 1774 by English architect William Elsden, under the reforming aegis of the Marquês de Pombal. Internationally known for its studies of flora and seed bank, the garden's exotic trees take you on a tropical world tour, as do the two greenhouses. The oldest trees grow in the Quadrado Grande, the Great Square, reached by a long stairway.

Santa Clara-a-Nova

The imposing convent of Santa Clara-a-Nova (*Rua da Rainha Santa Isabel, tel 239 441 674, closed Mon., cloister €*), sits across the Mondego River. Started in 1649, it became home to the Clarist nuns who were forced to abandon their previous convent, the Gothic **Santa Clara-a-Velha** (*Rua das Parreiras, tel 239 801 160, closed Mon., guided visits by appt., €€*) due to repeated flooding. Its ruins still stand by the river. The strongest site in the existing church is the 17th-century silver-and-crystal tomb

pulpit and, with João de Ruão, contributed sculptures to the portal. Do not miss the tiled and vaulted chapter house and the elegant Manueline cloister (€), the work of Manuel Pires. In the far corner is the entrance to a sleekly redesigned space, **Memórias de Santa Cruz,** exhibiting a dazzling array of statues, reliquaries, silver, and paintings belonging to the former monastery.

In contrast to these ecclesiastical and academic diversions, the southeastern side of Coimbra offers a small but personal

of Queen Isabel, the sainted wife of Dom Dinis I; the original 1330s tomb, a carved block of limestone sitting on six lions, is behind a wrought-iron grille at the end of the lower chancel. The patron saint of Coimbra, she is feted in July every even-numbered year; some years the procession was so long that it took four hours to cross the bridge.

Coimbra's Outskirts

Out in the rolling hills of **Lousã,** a wild, protected area about 18 miles (29 km) southeast of Coimbra, are remote mountain

Góis, tel 235 778 938, trans serrano.com), arranges guided walks or jeep tours.

The forest of **Buçaco,** equally bucolic but endowed with a strong spiritual bent and human imprint, lies 15 miles (24 km) to the north of Coimbra. This magical place was first used by Benedictine monks in the sixth century as a retreat; in the 17th century it was walled and planted by the Order of Barefoot Carmelites. The result is a rare display of some 300 exotic trees together with local varieties, all of which surround quaint little shrines, grottoes, ponds, and fountains. The **Vale dos Fetos** (Valley

Lousã
🗺 113 B2
Visitor Information
✉ Rua Dr. João Luso
☎ 239 990 040

Luso
🗺 113 B3
Visitor Information
✉ Rua Emídio Navarro 136
☎ 231 939 133

Medieval Love

Coimbra was the setting for Portugal's version of Romeo and Juliet, a real-life, tragic love story centered around the convent of Santa Clara-a-Velha. The beautiful Inês de Castro, a lady-in-waiting, lived here; Pedro, the crown prince, although married to the Infanta Constanza, fell hopelessly in love with

her. Fearful of her Spanish family's influence, Dom Afonso IV had Inês executed in 1345, unaware that Pedro had secretly married her after Constanza's death the year before. The afterlife united the ill-fated lovers: Their tombs now stand together in the magnificent abbey of Alcobaça (see pp. 145–147).

villages made of local schist and oak and chestnut, and pine forests home to wild boar and deer. The highest point, **Trevim,** at 3,950 feet (1,202 m) gives fantastic views over all central Portugal, while just below stand the striking quartzite cliffs of **Penedos de Góis.** The excellent English handbook "Lousã Mountain," published by the Coimbra Tourist Board, contains detailed maps and wildlife information, and a local organization, Trans Serrano (Barrio de S. Paulo 2,

of Ferns) is particularly attractive while the highest point, the **Cruz Alta,** has views to the sea.

On weekends the forest fills up with day-trippers, who also head for the spa town of **Luso,** 2 miles (3 km) downhill. You can drink the water at the town's thermal springs, **Termas de Luso** (Rua Álvaro Castelões 63, tel 231 937 910, termasdoluso.pt), have treatments or massages, or indulge yourself at the extravagant, turreted palace hotel that overshadows the ruins of the former convent. ■

CONÍMBRIGA

First inhabited by Neolithic peoples, then by the Celts, and finally the Romans, Conímbriga is Portugal's largest and most significant Roman site. It lies 9 miles (15 km) south of Coimbra in a rural setting of olive trees and woods—altogether a rewarding excursion.

The Casa dos Repuxos is one of the impressive Roman remains at Conímbriga.

**Museu e Ruínas
de Conímbriga**

☎ 239 941 177

💲 €

conimbriga.pt

The Celtic suffix "briga" points to the importance of the existing settlement when the Romans arrived in 138 B.C., but it was during the first-century A.D. reign of Emperor Augustus that Conímbriga really flourished, acquiring public baths, a forum, and an aqueduct, as well as villas. It became a prosperous stop on the road between Lisbon and Braga. In 468, the Swabians managed to breach a third-century defensive wall and the Romans gradually began to abandon the area; by the eighth century, Conímbriga was deserted, allowing Coimbra to rise in power and scale.

Today, the **Museu de Conímbriga** *(tel 239 941 177, patrimonio cultural.gov.pt, €)* offers a good introduction to the archaeological site. Look closely at the scale model of the forum in order to project this onto the ruins you will visit. Sculptures, mosaics, and fragments of stucco and wall paintings present a clear picture of what life was like in this far westerly Roman outpost.

The site is large enough to demand water and a hat if you are visiting on a hot summer's day. A route past the most significant sections and superb mosaic floors is well marked, and you can clearly see a stretch of the Roman road to Braga. At the front, a large canopy shelters an area of fountains and water channels, while just outside the wall stand the crumbling remains of the House of Cantaber, the largest in Conímbriga. ■

VISEU

Viseu is a small town that leaves an indelible aesthetic and atmospheric mark. It lies at the center of the Dão wine-producing area—part of that swathe of northern Portugal dominated by granite, visible in numerous dolmens, churches, and fortresses of the outlying countryside.

Viseu's compact and well-preserved old quarter is a delight to wander: Every street holds some architectural interest, and enticing craft and food shops sell products from the Serra da Estrela (see pp. 128–129). Viseu's main sites cluster around the cathedral square, Adro da Sé.

INSIDER TIP:

The painter Vasco Fernandes has been honored with a wine named for his pseudonym, Grão Vasco. One of his masterpieces, "S. Pedro," is part of the brand image.

—JOANA PAIS
Representative, Sogrape Vinhos

Adro da Sé

The 16th-century Paço dos Tres Escalões stands, recently restored, on one side of the square. A former bishop's palace, it now houses an impressive art museum, **Museu Grão Vasco.** Viseu's main historical claim to fame was a school of painting developed in the 16th century by Vasco Fernandes

(circa 1475–1543) and Gaspar Vaz (died circa 1568) that had strong Flemish influences. Fernandes was better known as Grão Vasco and it is this name that has become attached to the art museum, which displays a large collection of his work beside other European paintings of the same period, sculpture, ceramics, fabrics, and furniture. Look for Fernandes's superb painting "Adoration of the Magi," a seminal work due to the fact that the black king, Balthazar, was replaced by a native Brazilian complete with feathered headdress; this reflected Portugal's "discovery" of Brazil in 1500. Altogether, there are 14 paintings by the Viseu school that once made up the altarpiece in the Sé.

The masterful **Sé** (Cathedral), with its forbidding granite bell towers, faces the museum. Built between 1289 and 1313, its main structure bridges Romanesque and Gothic styles, although later radical remodeling endowed it with a baroque facade and Manueline vaulting inside. The magnificent triple nave is flooded with light thanks to multiple windows and lateral light sources, drawing the eye to the grand altarpiece, a classic of baroque gilded artistry. In front are elaborately carved baroque choir stalls and, typical of

Viseu

🗺 113 C4

Visitor Information

✉ Viseu Welcome Center, Casa do Adro, Adro da Sé

☎ 232 420 950

🕐 Closed Sat.–Sun.

Museo Grão Vasco

✉ Largo da Sé

☎ 232 422 049

🕐 Closed Mon.

💲 €

patimoniocultural.pt

Museu de Arte Sacra

- ⊠ Catedral, Adro da Sé
- ☎ 232 436 065
- 🕐 Closed Mon.
- 💲 €

the dynamism of this small town, ultracontemporary altar furniture designed by Luís Cunha in 1992. Look for the niche containing a silver reliquary arm displaying the bones of São Teotónio (1082–1162), who was a prior of this cathedral before founding Santa Cruz in Coimbra.

To the side of the main entrance is the **Manueline cloister,** a superb example of Portuguese Renaissance architecture. Don't miss the lateral doorway, a feat of Romano-Gothic stone carving incorporating a bas-relief Virgin and Child. This stood undetected for centuries until restoration work in 1918 uncovered it. At the back of the cloister you can see a beautiful **vaulted chapel** and, above, the small **Museu de Arte Sacra** that displays the church treasury: Rich vestments, chalices, and Limoges enamel caskets contrast with an 11th-century silver reliquary of

St. Ursula from Germany that looks surprisingly modern.

The church of **Misericórdia,** a modest but harmonious rococo building, stands alone on one side of the square, while an unusual dungeon tower and canons' veranda (a raised open walkway) flanks the square's fourth side.

Other Sites

Below the Sé stands a statue of the Portuguese king Dom Duarte (1391–1438), watching over an area of bustling shopping streets. Head downhill to **Rua Direita,** a long winding pedestrian street that in medieval days was the shortest route to the citadel (ironically, *direita* means "straight"). Stop at No. 90 to admire the **Casa da Viscondessa de Treixedo,** now a bank, with its ornate window frames and elegant portals—typical of this modest yet engaging town.

Renovation of the old market, **Mercado 2 de Maio** on Rua Formosa, has produced a large paved area dotted with trees and pools and surrounded by chic boutiques, the entire face-lift designed by Porto's renowned architect Álvaro Siza Vieira. A new stylized roof is due to be added in the next few years. The weekly market is on Tuesday, while June 24 sees the procession of Cavalhadas, and later in summer Viseu stages the São Mateus fair; all are excuses to sample local kid (goat), sausages, smoked meats, and chestnuts washed down with Dão or Jeropiga, the local tipple made from partially fermented must. ∎

■ **The 18th-century rococo church of the Misericórdia is one of a trio of monuments on the rim of Viseu's Adro da Sé.**

GUARDA

A somewhat bleak yet fascinating sensation unfolds at Guarda, stemming from its remote, mountainous location just 23 miles (37 km) from the Spanish border. Guarda is in fact Portugal's highest town at 3,463 feet (1,056 m).

Wedged between the mountains of the Serra da Marofa to the northeast and the more imposing Serra da Estrela to the southwest, Guarda was founded in 1199 by the second king of Portugal, Sancho I. A frontier town that guarded the border with Spain—hence the name—Guarda needed a strong defensive system, including citadel walls with five gates. Only two gates remain.

The heart of this small town is dwarfed by a massive fortified **Sé** *(tel 271 212 993, closed Mon.)*, complete with flying buttresses, pinnacles, and gargoyles. Construction began in 1390 and lasted nearly 150 years. The most imposing of the Cathedral's three entrances, in flamboyant Gothic style, opens onto the triangular Praça Luís de Camões. Inside, the triple-aisled Gothic nave leads to a high altar displaying a superb Renaissance limestone carving: The work of João de Ruão and Nicolas de Chanterenne, it depicts the life of Christ through a hundred biblical figures.

The main road north from this square, **Rua Francisco de Passos,** takes you past 16th- and 17th-century houses, antique shops, and the church of São Vicente to a medieval warren that was once the **Judiaria**

Guarda's forbidding and fortress-like Sé

(Jewish quarter). Here cobbled streets, vaulted doorways, and one-storied houses, some now derelict, were built against granite rocks. At the far end, at Largo do Torreão, a small garden offers views north.

Guarda also boasts the modest **Museu da Guarda,** housed in a 17th-century seminary. Four rooms cover local history from ancient times to the Renaissance, and there are temporary arts and crafts displays. Also worth seeing on this same street are the colorful, baroque church of the **Misericórdia** and the **Torre dos Ferreiros,** a tower that was part of the town's original fortifications. ∎

Guarda
🗺 113 D3
Visitor Information
✉ Praça Luís de Camões
☎ 271 205 530

Museu da Guarda
✉ Rua Alves Roçadas 30
☎ 271 213 460
🕐 Closed Mon.
💲 €

patrimonio
cultural.pt

DRIVE: TOURING THE FORTIFIED VILLAGES OF THE SERRA DA MAROFA

This circular tour takes you north from Guarda to four medieval villages that, despite their relative proximity, all developed different styles of fortifications.

A statue of Jesus—at 3,200 feet (975 m)—embraces the Serra da Marofa near Castelo Rodrigo.

Set off from Guarda following the N221 signs to Pinhel, through the suburbs and the village of Rapoula, past dry-stone walls, vines, orchards, and a sprinkling of light industry. The landscape soon changes to barren, granite-strewn slopes where you should watch out for a roadside dolmen, **Anta de Pêra do Moço.** Beeches, oaks, and chestnuts flank the road, and at **Gouveias** views open up to the west past conical haystacks and vineyards. Superficially modern, the villages you pass are still traditional; you may meet a donkey cart, so don't drive fast.

Huge boulders in a bleak landscape herald **Pinhel ①** *(visitor information, Rua de Santa Maria, tel 271 410 000)*, a venerable town with remains of a 14th-century castle and a military history going back to Roman times. Steep, cobbled streets lead to the old quarter. The Rua do Castelo winds past pretty lichen-clad houses

NOT TO BE MISSED:

Pinhel • Castelo Rodrigo • Almeida

to a flattened hilltop dominated by two sturdy towers with far-reaching views. Leave Pinhel along the main road past the cemetery, turning left at the bottom of the hill. The road skirts the valley before crossing the Côa River, passing terraced olive trees, then twisting through more dramatic boulder-strewn landscapes.

Castelo Rodrigo ② comes into view at an intersection. At the top of the hill, visit the citadel. Although almost overrestored, the semi-ruined **palace of Cristóvão de Moura** *(Rua do Relógio, tel 271 311 277)* is an evocative site; villagers burned it down in 1640—they suspected their ruler conspired with the Spaniards. There are many striking buildings in the citadel, but few people live there; those that do run restaurants or shops.

Rejoin the main road and turn left on the N332 toward Almeida. As you drive through the village of **Vilar Torpim,** note the stately *quinta* (manor house) on your right. Eventually **Almeida** ❸ appears on the horizon. Its massive medieval, moated fortress, built in the Vauban form of a 12-pointed star *(visitor information, Portas de São Francisco, tel 271 574 204)*, was later used as an ammunition depot, which Napoleon's troops blew up in 1810. Walk along the ramparts and explore the attractive, well-preserved streets inside the walls.

Return to the N332 south, toward Vilar Formoso. Just outside of Almeida, at the IP5/

Guarda sign, turn right onto the N340, soon crossing the Côa again. About 5 miles (8 km) farther turn left at the road marked Castelo Mendo (N324). This passes under the IP5 highway. Turn left at an intersection and drive to the stone archway guarded by two granite boars that fronts the medieval village of **Castelo Mendo** ❹. Look at the church of Misericórdia with its beautiful Mudejar (Hispano-Moorish) ceiling, the 23-foot-high (7 m) pillory, and typical granite houses. From here return to Guarda on the N16.

- 🗺 See also area map p. 113
- ▶ Guarda
- 🕐 2 hours (more with stops)
- ↔ 69 miles (110 km)
- ▶ Guarda

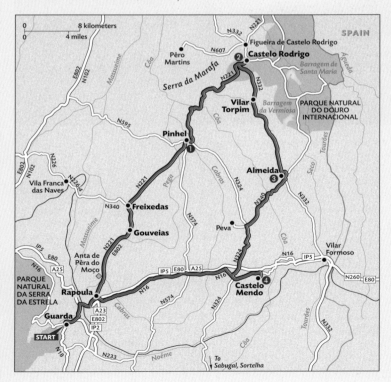

SERRA DA ESTRELA

Something of a moving feast, as its wild beauty is claimed by every town that borders it, the Serra da Estrela is Portugal's highest mountain range. This 250,000-acre (101,000 ha) expanse, protected as a natural park, creates a formidable barrier between the more urban west and the rural emptiness of the eastern Beiras.

Winter in the Serra da Estrela brings enough snow for skiing.

Serra da Estrela
🗺 113 C3, D3–D4
Visitor Information
✉ Rua Sacadural Cabral, Celorico da Beira
☎ 271 742 109

✉ Rua Dr. Esteves de Carvalho 2, Manteigas
☎ 275 981 129
🕐 Closed Sun. in winter

natural.pt

Sandwiched between the Mondego and Zêzere Rivers, the rugged peaks of the Serra da Estrela rise to their highest point, 6,537 feet (1,993 m), at **Torre.** The spot is marked by a 23-foot-high (7 m) tower erected in 1817, which brings the elevation to exactly 2,000 meters. This, too, is where the ski slopes are. Just below lies a natural lake, **Lagoa Comprida,** and several artificial lakes that are now generating electricity. This entire massif is the ideal place for slow drives, hiking, sampling creamy

mountain cheese, wrapping up in local wool blankets, listening to the tinkling of sheep bells, and exploring the many seductive mountain villages.

Viseu, Guarda, and Belmonte are the classic starting points for visiting this area, yet villages such as Manteigas and Linhares bring you much closer to the Estrela soul, especially in gastronomy. Indulge in hearty mountain food such as smoked sausages and ham, curd cheese (served with pumpkin jelly), roast kid or boar, young lamb, black pudding with cabbage, or grilled mountain trout. Desserts are equally varied, often egg based, and may incorporate honey, cheese, chestnuts, or rice. Wash it all down with a robust Dão wine.

The shepherd dog is another unique feature of the Serra da Estrela; it is thought to be one of the purest and most ancient species of dog in the Iberian Peninsula. Large, muscular, with thick golden fur and a docile temperament—though quite capable of confronting the wolves of the Serra—they are the prized companions of the shepherds.

Hill Towns

At the far northern end of the range, **Celorico da Beira,** with its castle, narrow streets, Gothic doorways, and Manueline windows, makes a striking place to enter the mountains. A local cheese fair is held at the market building every other Friday between December and May.

Just across the Mondego River lies the **necropolis of São Gens.** It dates from Visigothic days (eighth and ninth centuries) and contains 46 stone tombs hollowed out of the rocks and overlooked by the sculptural **Penedo do Sino** (Rock of the Bell).

Your next stop should be **Linhares**—arguably the most attractive village in the Serra da Estrela—which started life around 580 B.C. as a *castro* (fortified hill village). There is plenty of medieval ambience between the castle and its ramparts built on the rocks, local houses, and delicious traditional cuisine.

Smack in the center of the massif, in the pastoral Zêzere Valley, lies **Manteigas,** sheltered by surrounding hills at 2,296 feet (700 m). Handwoven blankets, carpets, sheepskin items, and tinware are made here. Up above Manteigas, along a dizzily twisting road, is the popular mountain resort of **Penhas Douradas,** known for its typical hill town architecture.

NOTE: For information on rural bed-and-breakfast accommodations, contact the offices of **Adruse** (Largo Dr. Alípio de Melo, Gouveia, tel 238 490 180, adruse.pt).

EXPERIENCE: Trekking the Glacial Valley

The wildness of the Serra da Estrela is best experienced by leaving the car and getting out on foot, especially during crisp and snowy winter months. In addition to hikes all over the north of Portugal, adventure company **Borealis** (Rua do Mormeiral s/n, Rebordões Santa Maria, Ponte de Lima, tel 910 910 930, borealis.pt), based in Ponte de Lima, offers a day-long hike (€€€€€) through the central massif of the Serra da Estrela, known as the Penhas Douradas. Qualified guides introduce visitors to the Zêzere Valley, one of Europe's largest glacial valleys, passing giant granite blocks, frozen mountain lakes, and thick pine forests. Hiking boots and adequate clothing are a must and trekking poles are recommended.

A short distance south is the spa **Caldas de Manteigas;** its sulfuric waters are said to be good for rheumatism, skin problems, and respiratory troubles. The modern spa only operates between March and November. In this area, beside the river, you will see stone houses with roofs thatched in rye straw and broom, and numerous waterfalls cascading down the slopes. ∎

CASTELO BRANCO & AROUND

It may not be the most scenic town in the Beiras, but industrious Castelo Branco has a couple of unusual sites and is a useful stopover on the way to border villages with colorful pasts. It also acts as a bridge between the Beiras interior and the Tejo Valley to the west and the Alentejo region to the south.

Natural and man-made formations aesthetically collide in the village of Monsanto.

Castelo Branco
113 D1
Visitor Information
Avenida Nuno
Álvares 30
272 330 339

Thought to have pre-Roman origins, Castelo Branco achieved prominence under Dom Afonso Henriques when it was part of the land donated to the Knights Templar, the military and religious order that reached its apogee during the Middle Ages. The oldest and highest part of Castelo Branco has a few sections dating to this period. Here the narrow cobbled streets strung with laundry and birdcages make an atmospheric place to wander, but the main interest lies downhill at the **Antigo Paço Episcopal.** This former bishop's palace boasts beautiful gardens studded with baroque statuary and clipped box hedges. The vegetal work of art dating from 1725 also incorporates fountains and ponds, altogether creating a rare baroque time capsule. Inside the palace is the **Museu de Francisco Tavares Proença Junior** (*Largo Dr. José Lopes Dias, tel 272 344 277, closed Mon., €*), a museum big on portraits of bishops and clerical vestments. The most striking exhibits are the 16th-century Flemish tapestries illustrating the story of Lot and a beautiful display of *colchas.* Castelo Branco's most desirable product, a colcha is a delicately embroidered linen bedspread that can take more than a year to complete—and is priced accordingly. A guided tour takes in an embroidery workshop where these spreads are made.

Fortified Villages

A string of remote villages well worth investigating lie northeast of Castelo Branco. The fortified village of **Penamacor,** 31 miles (50 km) away, was inhabited successively by Romans, Goths, and Moors. There are fine panoramic views from the hilltop ruins of the 13th-century castle and keep. The older streets of Penamacor display lovely portals

---

INSIDER TIP:

Be sure to pick up as a souvenir some of Castelo Branco's hand-embroidered linen, for which the region is renowned.

—CARRIE BRATLEY
Journalist, Portugal News

---

and windows. In particular take a look at the **church of the Misericórdia** (closed Sun.), with its Manueline porch and gilded altarpiece, and the 16th-century **convent of Santo António** (closed Sun.), with its chapel, ornate pulpit, and richly gilded wood carvings.

Slightly closer to Castelo Branco is **Monsanto,** often claimed to be Portugal's most traditional village and certainly a magnificent sight clinging to the base of a granite escarpment beside the Ponsul River. This whole region is one of alternating plains and rocky outcrops, rendering castles practically invisible as they fade into their rocky bases. Monsanto came to prominence under the Templars who built the citadel in the 12th century. The entire village is astonishing, with steep alleyways cutting through rows of granite houses, some of which bear coats of arms and/or elaborate Manueline windows. The highly fortified **castle** has a long history of sieges. Monsanto's victories are celebrated on the first weekend of May by the Festa das Cruzes (Festival of Crosses), during which a flowerpot is thrown from the ramparts in lieu of a calf that once symbolized to besiegers that the inhabitants still had plenty to eat. The church ruins of the Romanesque **São Miguel** that stand next to the castle preserve some exceptional capitals. Fabulous views take in the **Barragem da Idanha,** an artificial lake.

The tiny village of **Idanha-a-Velha** sits only 8 miles (12 km) southwest of Monsanto, yet feels completely different. Thanks to an illustrious past peopled by Romans, Swabians, Visigoths, Moors, and Templars, the village boasts some fine archeological ruins. The **Cathedral** undoubtedly started as a mosque: Islamic influence is visible in its vaulted chapel and unusual, asymmetrical proportions. The village's Roman walls have been preserved, and a small gallery beside the Cathedral displays Roman stelae (inscribed stone slabs). ∎

Monsanto
△ 113 D2
Visitor Information
✉ Rua Marquês da Graciosa
☎ 277 314 642

Idanha-a-Velha
△ 113 D2
Visitor Information
✉ Rua da Sé
☎ 277 914 280

LIVING LIKE NOBILITY

European countries all have a rich architectural heritage, but there are few where visitors can actually stay in grandiose private houses. Portugal stands out for its guest accommodations in *quintas* (rural estate houses, usually quite elegant) or *solares* (aristocratic manor houses) that often cost far less than hotels with equivalent comforts, and which are generally outfitted with period furniture and family heirlooms.

■ *Quintas* and *solares* may be grand or stately, but the hospitality is always warm and friendly.

While some quintas date back to the 15th century, most of Portugal's solares were built between the mid-1600s and mid-1700s. After decades of austerity under Spanish domination, the year 1640 marked the return of the Portuguese monarchy and the consequent craze for baroque. In the north, the booming port trade with England led to frenzied building of beautiful quintas in vineyards of the Douro Valley, while elsewhere in the country, the landed gentry were reaping

the rewards from the riches of Brazil. This period of prosperity peaked in the first half of the 18th century under João V. Some 200 years later, in tandem with Portugal's general decline, many of these properties were in semi-ruinous states, their hereditary owners unable to finance necessary repairs or restoration.

A solution was dreamed up in the early 1980s by a cash-strapped count living in Ponte de Lima: He converted his family manor house into paying-guest accommodations and threw open his doors to visitors in search of authentic, albeit faded, grandeur as a place to stay. Although the idea was not new in countries such as Ireland or England, it was for Portugal, which had been living on the margins of Europe, both literally and metaphorically, for so long.

The idea caught on, government and European Union subsidies followed, and *turismo de habitação* (literally "home tourism") gradually changed the face of rural Portugal. Villages that were once cut off from the outside world gained a new lease on life, employment opportunities multiplied, and a network of stunning properties throughout the country has been made available to visitors. Not least, there is a dialogue between villagers and guests staying at the local "big house," and between owners (who generally speak English and French) and their visitors.

Manor houses may offer just two en suite guest rooms, complete with four-poster beds, creaking floorboards, hand-carved wardrobes, and exquisite bed linens, or they may have converted outbuildings into a dozen rooms. In all cases, however, the hospitality is remarkable and, the more out of the way a place is, the more spectacular the breakfast may be. In working quintas guests may witness winemaking or other agricultural practices, and in all of them the exterior surroundings will be as delightful as the interior. The only possible drawback is a surfeit of opulence, as Portuguese decorative style tends toward the heavily ornate. If you can handle that and an occasional lack of heating in winter, then you are destined for noble style.

Guests in *quintas* and *solares* often have full run of a house.

A Home Fit for a King

Though rustic in style, **Quinta da Comenda** *(quintadacomenda.net)* is one of the Centro region's most historically important manor houses. Older than the nation itself, the *quinta* belonged to Dona Tareja, mother of Portugal's first king, Afonso Henriques. In 1143, she gave it to her brother, who in turn handed it over to the recently established Order of the Knights of Malta. Afonso Henriques and his son, who incidentally was the Order's first grand master in Portugal, were frequent visitors. The house remained in the hands of the Knights of Malta until 1834, when religious orders were abolished in Portugal and their lands handed to the monarchy. The quinta was then left to ruin until it was bought by the present owners in 1984. They have lovingly restored it and turned its lands over to organic farming. For information on staying here or at any of Portugal's other manor houses, visit *solaresdeportugal.pt* or *manor-houses-portugal.com*.

More Places to Visit in Centro

■ Shimmering salt flats edge the Mondego River at Gala, just south of Figueira da Foz.

Belmonte

The birthplace of Pedro Álvares Cabral, the European who claimed Brazil for Portugal in 1500, Belmonte is dominated by the semirestored ruins of a **castle** *(tel 275 911 488)*. Don't miss the view of the mountains through an elegant Manueline window. In front, to one side, is a reproduction of the simple wooden cross used by Cabral in the first Mass held on Brazilian soil. The neighboring **São Tiago** church has 400- to 500-year-old frescoes and the tombs of the Cabrals. More significant today is the 1997 **synagogue** that lies downhill in the old Jewish quarter. Belmonte's Jewish community has seen a strong resurgence in recent times and is now Portugal's largest. The impressive Roman tower **Centum Cellas,** 2.5 miles (4 km) to the west, is thought to have formed part of a Roman villa and played a role on the tin trade route between Mérida (in Spain) and Braga.

🅰 113 D3   **Visitor Information** ✉ Castelo de Belmonte ☎ 275 911 488

Figueira da Foz

Figueira is the closest beach resort to Coimbra: It lies just 28 miles (45 km) west at the mouth of the Mondego River. High-rises dominate the shoreline, but the resort offers a broad sandy beach, rolling waves loved by surfers, a casino, and a lively festival in late June. The estuary is overlooked by the 16th-century **Forte de Santa Catarina,** where Wellington landed the first British troops in 1808. For a quieter, more scenic setting, head a few miles north to the smaller resort of **Buarcos,** backed by the Serra da Boa Viagem, a hillside of eucalyptuses, pines, and acacias.

🅰 113 A2   **Visitor Information** *cm-figfoz.pt* ✉ Avenida 25 de Abril 19 ☎ 233 422 610

Sortelha

This dramatic, often windswept border village commands far-reaching views from its fortified summit. The granite walls, keep, and majestic Gothic gateways seem to grow out of the landscape. Inside, the medieval core has been extensively restored; it springs to life Easter through summer. Craft shops and a handful of bars and restaurants follow the same rhythms. The village still makes an evocative destination out of season.

🅰 113 D3   **Visitor Information** ✉ Largo do Corro ☎ 271 750 080 or 800 262 788 🕐 Closed Mon.

Portugal's heart—a time capsule of castles, palaces, monasteries, and small towns radiating from Lisbon, and an exhilarating coast

LISBOA E REGIÃO

◾ Batalha monastery's intricate Manueline stone tracery

LISBOA E REGIÃO

The prosperous Lisboa e Região region, comprising the Estremadura and Ribatejo areas, bridges the mountainous north of Portugal and the hotter, flatter south, while encircling Lisbon and the Tejo estuary. Portugal's cultural epicenter, this region features four magnificent World Heritage sites, lavish and grandiose royal palaces, a major pilgrimage destination, relics of the Peninsular War, Moorish castles, and the favorite resort for exiled kings and aristocrats in the 1930s.

The infrastructure of the Estremadura and Ribatejo areas, more densely populated than others, threatens to overwhelm the charm of the Lisboa e Região region, but pockets of natural beauty remain: from lovely coastal spots, including continental Europe's western extremity at Cabo da Roca, to the romantic and verdant Serra de Sintra. Many places—Sintra, Cascais, Estoril, Mafra, Óbidos, Peniche, Santarém, and Setúbal—can be seen on day trips from Lisbon, but such visits only hint at their character.

Only extended stays reveal what gives these towns their special atmosphere, be it surfers riding the waves at Guincho, bells tolling at Batalha's monastery or Mafra's palace, the roulette wheel of Estoril's casino, bottlenose dolphins in the Sado Estuary, or morning mists rising above the palaces and forest of Sintra. Add clusters of windmills, immaculate, whitewashed villages, and a few dinosaur footprints, and you have an unrivaled feast of diversity—paralleled in the succulent, affordable seafood and range of regional wines.

Evidence of Great Wealth

This land of kings and queens reached its high point during Portugal's age of discoveries—the 15th and 16th centuries—when newfound riches financed major renovations. Manueline details on Gothic structures became commonplace. Sintra's Palácio Nacional is the quintessential example and displays Europe's most varied and extensive decorative wall tiling. Meanwhile, brooding high above Tomar, the Convent of Christ is a masterpiece of Renaissance, Manueline, and Gothic styles. Older still, the rebuilt Moorish castle of Óbidos, a traditional wedding gift from every Portuguese king to his queen since 1282, embraces a web of cobbled, flower-clad streets. Fast forward to the height of baroque and you have the vast palace and monastery of Mafra, closely followed by the rococo Queluz palace, now engulfed by the outer suburbs of Lisbon. Finally, there is cosmopolitan seaside Cascais, a magnet for the idle rich between the two World Wars and Portugal's version of the French Riviera. ∎

NOT TO BE MISSED:

Eating freshly grilled fish at Nazaré   140

The monasteries of Batalha and Alcobaça   143–147

Drinking *ginjinha* (cherry liqueur) from a chocolate cup in Óbidos   148–149

A boat ride to the fairy-tale Castelo de Almourol   153

Sintra's amazing palaces   158–163

Watching the world go by with a cold drink at a Cascais beach café   166–167

The Tróia Peninsula's pristine beaches   172

LISBOA E REGIÃO

Lisbon ✪

Area of
map detail

N109
Figueira
da Foz   A14   IP3   ◁6

A17   CENTRO
                               p. 111

                    IC2
Liz
PINHAL DE LEIRIA   N109   Pombal   IC8   Pedrógão
                          A1   IC8   Grande   ◁5
                          E1
Carride   E80   Alvaiázere
                                           N110
A17   Zêzere
Marinha   Leiria   Ferreira
Grande   do Zêzere
N242   A8   Batalha   N113   Ourém
Sítio   IC1   Fátima   Aqueduto   Barragem do
Nazaré   Alcobaça   Pedreira   dos Pegões   Castelo de Bode
Praia Gralha   da Galinha Tomar
São Martinho   Alvados   Serra   Santo   Zêzere   Sardoal   Mação
do Porto   Grutas de   de Aire   Antonio   River   N2
RESERVA NATURAL   Foz do Arelho   Alvados   Torres   Constância   IP6
DA BERLENGA   Caldas   Santo António   Novas   Castelo de   Tejo
Ilhas Berlengas   da Rainha   Entroncamento   Almourol   Abrantes
Remédios   Óbidos   PARQUE NATURAL   Golegã   N243
Cabo Carvoeiro   Peniche   DAS SERRAS DE AIRE   Chamusca   N2   Bemposta
Praia de São   IP6   E CANDEEIROS   SANTARÉM   Alpiarça
Bernardino   Rio Maior
Lourinhã   Bombarral   A15   IP6   Asseca   RIBATEJO   Valley   N118
Praia de   Cadaval
Santa Cruz   Serra de   Santarém
ATLANTIC   Montejunto   A1   IC10   Almeirim   Muge   ALENTEJO
OCEAN   Torres   E1   N114   Sorraia   p. 173   ◁3
               Vedras   A8   E80   A13
N247   N1   Coruche   N251   Couço
Praia de   Alenquer   N118
Ribeira de Ilhas   N9   Arruda dos   A10   Vila Franca   Santo Estêvão   N119   N114
Ericeira   Vinhos   A8   de Xira   IC11
Mafra   LISBOA   A9   Alverca   Vale do Calção   Lavre
PARQUE NATURAL   IC1   do Ribatejo
DE SINTRA-CASCAIS   A21
Praia das   Azenhas   RESERVA NATURAL
Maçãs   do Mar   DO ESTUÁRIO
Colares   Sintra   DO TEJO
Praia Grande   Parque e   A9
Praia da   Palácio N. da   N118   A13
Adraga   Pena   Amadora   IC11
Cabo da Roca   Serra de   LISBON (LISBOA)
Praia do   Sintra   Palácio   SETÚBAL
Guincho   A16   Nacional   Almada   Montijo   ◁2
Cascais   Estoril   de Queluz   Barreiro   A12
Costa do Estoril   Caparica   Amora   IP1   ALENTEJO
               Costa da   Amora   E1   Palmela   N10   p. 173
               Caparica   A2   E90   IP1
Vila Nogueira de Azeitão   Setúbal   A2
PARQUE NATURAL   Setúbal Peninsula   Forte São Filipe   E1   D
DA ARRÁBIDA   Serra da Arrábida   Praia de Figueirinha   IP1   N253
Sesimbra   Portinho da Arrábida   N253-1
Cabo   Lapa de Santa   Tróia   Alcácer do Sal   ◁1
Espichel   Margarida   Peninsula   N261
               Baía de   Comporta   RESERVA NATURAL
               Setúbal   DO ESTUÁRIO
                                    DO SADO   Sado

0   20 kilometers
0   10 miles

LEIRIA & AROUND

Sprawling over a wide valley, Leiria appears deceptively large. In reality the compact center is sandwiched between the Liz River and a hill rising to the castle above. There are few sites, but Leiria makes an enjoyable lunch stop on the monastery trail of Batalha, Alcobaça, and Tomar or en route to the beaches.

■ Leiria's unusually designed castle entices visitors to walk uphill.

Leiria

🗺 137 B5

Visitor Information

✉ Jardim Luís de Camões

☎ 244 848 771

Castelo de Leiria

✉ Largo de São Pedro

☎ 244 839 670

cm-leiria.pt

Dom Dinis I and his queen, Santa Isabel, chose Leiria as their base in the 14th century. Walk or drive up to the principal residence, the unusual-looking **Castelo de Leiria.** Afonso Henriques, who recaptured the fabulous site from the Moors in 1135, built the original castle. In the years that followed, historical vicissitudes led to Leiria being overshadowed by Santarém and Lisbon, and the castle fell into semi-ruin. Dom Dinis restored it, and several decades later João I built a palace extension on the south side, incorporating

loggias, Gothic bays, and a vast hall, while maintaining the flanking towers.

Inside the walls, you enter a large garden courtyard, beyond which lie the keep, dungeons, royal palace, and the attractive ruins of **Nossa Senhora da Pena,** a church adorned with Gothic and Manueline features. The keep houses a museum of medieval armor, the **Núcleo Museológico** (closed Mon.).

Head for Leiria's pedestrianized main square, the **Praça Rodrigues Lobo,** at the heart of the attractive historical center; its 17th-century arches are still

Pilgrimage to Fátima

Fátima, 10 miles (16 km) southeast of Leiria and Portugal's most important shrine, acts as a beacon to four million pilgrims annually. Although Fátima is hard to recommend to anyone other than fervent believers—the town is little more than a pilgrims' dormitory that has grown haphazardly since 1930—it is symbolically fascinating. Some pilgrims still arrive on their knees, while others hold candlelit vigils at religious festivals. In 1917, three young children allegedly witnessed a series of appearances by the Virgin Mary. The dates of her first and last visitations, May 13 and October 13, draw an estimated 100,000 pilgrims from all over the world. Pope John Paul II visited the site three times and canonized two of the children in 2000, and Pope Francis visited in May 2017. The neoclassical basilica seats 900; the new basilica—notable for its vast, unsupported ceiling design—seats 9,000 (fatima.pt).

INSIDER TIP:

Make the effort to stop in Fátima to look inside the controversial new basilica. This architectural masterpiece seats 9,000 and has no internal pillars.

—EMMA ROWLEY
National Geographic contributor

intact. An antiques and handicrafts market takes place here on the second Saturday of the month. While exploring the backstreets around the square, you will encounter the **Sé,** a Renaissance cathedral fronted by a striking row of tiled houses converted into a nightclub.

Beyond Leiria

The countryside surrounding Leiria is of much interest. Europe's largest continuous pine forest, the **Pinhal de Leiria,** stretches north and west of town: About 10 million trees blanket 28,400 acres (11,500 ha) crisscrossed by long straight roads. First planted by Dom Dinis I, the forest was later enlarged to halt encroaching sands and to supply shipbuilders with materials during Portugal's age of discoveries. Today, it is the source for Leiria's wood and paper industries, the latter dating back to 1411.

South of Leiria is the **Parque Natural das Serras de Aire e Candeeiros,** a pocket of wild beauty stretching over a rugged limestone massif that holds several interesting sites. Evoking memories of a time gone by, traditional windmills (*moinhos da Pena*) dot the hills; some now serve as accommodations. A series of dinosaur footprints at **Pedreira da Galinha** are thought to date back to the mid-Jurassic period, about 175 million years ago. Here, too, are four separate caves (*grutas*) with exceptional stalactite and stalagmite formations. The **Grutas de Alvados** and neighboring **Grutas de Santo António** offer the most variety and scale. ∎

Parque Natural das Serras de Aire e Candeeiros

🗺 137 B4–C4

Grutas de Alvados & Grutas de Santo António

🗺 137 C4
☎ 249 841 876
🕐 Closed Mon. Sep.–June
💲 €€

sogrutas.com

COASTAL ESTREMADURA

The long straight coastline of the Estremadura area links the Beira Litoral (dominated by Figueira da Foz) to the north with Lisbon's playground resorts to the south. Magnificent sweeps of white sand, impressive dunes, dramatic surf, and spectacular cliffs are a haven for sunbathing, sailing, and surfing, as well as scuba diving and sportfishing in some areas.

■ Pleasure boats bob gently in Nazaré's harbor. The town is the largest resort on the Estremadura coast.

Nazaré
🗺 137 B4
Visitor Information
✉ Avenida Vieira Guimarães, Mercado Municipal
☎ 262 561 194

São Martinho do Porto
🗺 137 B4
Visitor Information
✉ Rua Vasco da Gama
☎ 262 989 110

Nazaré

You'll find the largest, loudest resort at Nazaré, where a long, sandy beach ends abruptly at a 361-foot-high (110 m) cliff crowned by the district of **Sítio.** Steep steps, a road, or a **funicular** *(tel 262 569 070, €)* will take you to the top, where a lookout point surveys the main resort area below, the fishing harbor at its southern end, and the original hilltop town, **Pederneira.**

The name Nazaré derives from a statue of the Virgin said to have been brought back from Nazareth by a monk in the fourth century and rediscovered in the 18th century; this naturally gave rise to a church, **Nossa Senhora da Nazaré,** on Sítio's

main square. Every September 8 a major pilgrimage kicks off the town's festival. Next to the lookout point stands Nazaré's most significant site, the tiny **Ermida da Memória,** which a very thankful nobleman built to commemorate the perceived miracle that saved his life in 1182. Azulejos—added centuries later—illustrate the incident in great detail. From here, a short walk to the headland brings you to a lighthouse and another spectacular view. In July and August the town is packed, but out of season Nazaré makes an enjoyable, scenic stop.

São Martinho do Porto & Around

The low-key family resort of São Martinho do Porto sits 8 miles (13 km) south of Nazaré. Its popularity stems from its almost circular bay with calm, shallow waters that are ideal for swimming and wading. Every morning the quay sees small boats unloading mountains of sardines from trawlers anchored in the bay, later replaced by pleasure boats. Stroll north along the quay, past a string of restaurants, then through a short tunnel to see waves crashing against the rocks. On the headland above, you can see a number of

(continued on p. 142)

EXPERIENCE: Surfing in Portugal

Portugal may be a relatively small country, but it boasts some big waves along its 765 miles (1,230 km) of coast, many of which provide ideal surfing conditions as the large Atlantic rollers pound its shore. Cool water temperatures do little to deter year-round surfing enthusiasts.

These waves attract much international attention. In 2011 some of the world's most experienced big wave riders descended on the small fishing town of Nazaré, where a giant swell had been predicted at Praia do Norte (praiadonorte.com.pt). Using a Jet-Ski to tow in, Garrett McNamara, who spent many years chasing the world's biggest waves, successfully caught a 90-foot (27.4 m) wave, smashing the previous world record of 77 feet (23.5 m) set by Mike Parson in 2001. In 2018, the Portuguese surfer Hugo Vau rode an even bigger one. In addition, global surf hot spots such as Peniche and Ericeira frequently feature on the world surfing circuit, attracting the world's top, professional surfers to Portugal's most challenging breaks. Most years, it's possible to catch a glimpse of the sport's biggest names, like surfing megastar Kelly Slater or John John Florence and Gabriel Medina, as they come through on the world tour.

Portugal boasts top surfers of its own, with the national team winning the European Championships in 2011. Watch for national pro-surf names such as Frederico Morais, Vasco Ribeiro, and up and coming junior champions such as Teresa Bonvalot.

Where to Surf

Thanks to the high profile of these international surf events and the growing accessibility of surf equipment, surfing has exploded in Portugal over the last 20 years. Head to the beach near any good-size town at the weekend and the waves

---

INSIDER TIP:

Portugal boasts hundreds of kilometers of superb surf, but my favorite spot is Coxos in Ericeira. But be warned, it's not for the fainthearted.

—FILIPA LEANDRO
Former national surf champion

---

will be dotted with boards. Favorite beaches in the Lisbon area include **Carcavelos**, popular with beginners, and **Guincho**, also a windsurf mecca; a short drive north, **Ericeira, Peniche,** and **Nazaré** attract a more experienced crowd. In the north, the windy beaches to the north of **Viana do Castelo** have great waves; in the south, the **Sagres** area offers marginally warmer waters. The Alentejo coast provides

countless options; the most popular being **Arrifana** and **Praia do Amado.**

Surf Schools

Portugal's surf can be dangerous for the novice or the ill-informed. Even experienced surfers should consult with locals, as many breaks have hidden rocks and reefs; currents are strong and often unpredictable. There are calm spots, however, and a growing number of good surfing schools are making the sport safe for people of all ages and abilities to enjoy the thrill of the waves. To master them yourself, consider the following locations and surf schools:

Carcavelos: Carcavelos Surf School, Windsurfcafé, Praia de Carcavelos, tel 962 850 497 or 966 131 203, carcavelossurfschool.com

Foz do Arelho: Call Martim at Foz Camp, Rua Francisco Almeida Grandela 109, tel 912 534 748, surfcamp-portugal.eu

Sagres: International Surf School, tel 914 482 407, surfsagres.com

Viana do Castelo: Surf Clube de Viana, Rua Manuel Fiúza Júnior 133, tel 962 672 222, surfingviana.com

Peniche

🏔 137 A4

Visitor Information

✉ Rua Alexandre Herculano

☎ 262 789 571

cm-peniche.pt

NOTE: Accessing the Ilhas Berlengas Motorboats to the islands run daily year-round from the Peniche jetty, depending on sea conditions and passenger numbers. Companies include **Viamar** *(tel 262 785 646, viamar -berlenga.com).*

recently built ocean-view condominiums, and 1 mile (1.6 km) farther, at **Monte do Facho,** a viewpoint looks south to Foz do Arelho (see p. 149) and to the bay of São Martinho do Porto. A few art nouveau buildings surround Largo Vitorino Frois, but modern blocks have marred the southern end.

Peniche & Cabo Carvoeiro

A former island, Peniche joined the mainland in the 16th century, when silt formed an isthmus. Modern high-rises conceal an attractive harbor, complete with old bulwarks, walls, and a star-shaped 16th-century fortress. Formerly a prison for political dissidents and testimony to the horrors of Salazarism, the fortress will soon become the seat of the National Museum of Resistance and Freedom. The coastal town of Peniche is famed for bobbin lacework; it comes center stage on the **Dia da Rendilheira** (Lace Day), the third Sunday of July.

The fortress faces the large harbor that has given Peniche its status in Portugal's fishing and canning industry; fish conserving goes back to Roman times. Fish restaurants clustered around the harbor and fort area specialize in delicious *caldeirada de peixe* (fish stew), as well as barbecued sardines and steamed lobster. Sun and surf worshippers will find beautiful sandy beaches and world-class surfing spots nearby, especially along the Baleal isthmus. Like Cabo Carvoeiro, a 2.5-mile-long (4 km) peninsula edged by stratified rock formations, eroded rock stacks also rise out of the sea. A lighthouse at the peninsula's end offers fantastic views in all directions. A few hundred yards before this, at the hamlet of **Remédios,** a charming little tiled chapel, **Nossa Senhora dos Remédios,** is the focal point of a cult that developed following the discovery of the Virgin Mary's image in a cave in the 12th century. A simple cross on the rocks outside indicates the supposed spot. An equally dramatic stretch of cliffs and rock stacks lies to the south of Peniche, between the beaches of **São Bernardino** and **Santa Cruz.** ∎

Ilhas Berlengas

Ilhas Berlengas, a 40-minute boat ride from Peniche, are surrounded by a wonderful marine reserve. The red-ocher granite formation of the isles is estimated to be some 280 million years old. Crystalline water and several inlets, islets, creeks, and grottoes create a beautiful day-trip destination, perfect for swimming, snorkeling, and diving.

The main island, **Berlenga Grande,** *(berlengas.eu)* boasts little more than a crumbling 17th-century fort at the end of a causeway. There are basic accommodations, a campsite, a small restaurant, and a lighthouse. A coastal path circles the island, providing marine views and opportunities to see abundant birdlife. The Berlengas constitute some of the most important breeding grounds for seabirds on the Iberian Peninsula. You can also rent a rowboat to explore the grottoes.

BATALHA

This late Gothic fantasy was inspired by Dom João I's victory in 1385 over the Castilians at the Battle of Aljubarrota, just 1 mile (1.6 km) away. In gratitude, the king founded the monastery, dedicated it to the Virgin Mary, and named it Santa Maria da Vitória.

■ The Batalha monastery is a masterpiece of Portuguese Gothic and Manueline art.

Today the complex is more commonly called Batalha for the nearby small town. The fact that this magnificent abbey is a World Heritage site has not, however, slowed the traffic thundering along a major highway just a couple of hundred yards away. Bristling with pinnacles, buttresses, gargoyles, and delicate stone tracery, this ornate structure took 145 years to build, from 1388 to 1533.

While Alcobaça's importance (see pp. 145–147) lies in religious practice and its social spin-offs, Batalha is more symbolic of political confidence. Its rise coincides with the beginning of Portuguese maritime expansion. Announcing this on the vast esplanade outside is an equestrian statue of Nuno Álvares Pereira, who led the Portuguese forces at Aljubarrota. The beautiful limestone facade behind the statue was the work of the master craftsman Huguet, who took over from Afonso Domingues on his death in 1402. Mateus Fernandes, the third main architect, was responsible for the stunning Manueline entrance to the Unfinished Chapels and much of the decorative detail in the Royal Cloister. His tomb is in the main nave.

Batalha

🗺 137 B5

Visitor Information

✉ Praça Mouzinho de Albuquerque

☎ 244 765 180

Mosteiro de Santa Maria da Vitória–Batalha

☎ 244 765 497

€ €€

mosteirobatalha .gov.pt

The church interior has both a vast, imposing scale and an uncomplicated appearance, the only decorative elements being the stained-glass windows depicting the life of Christ. To the right is the **Founder's Chapel,** another tour de force by Huguet, although the original ceiling collapsed in the 1755 earthquake. Here, enclosed by a vaulted, octagonal structure, are the elevated tombs of Dom João I and his English wife, Philippa of Lancaster; tombs of their descendants, including Henry the Navigator, are set into wall niches.

Off the left of the nave lies the striking **Royal Cloister,** a rhythmic

the unknown soldier (in fact, two soldiers), under permanent guard of honor, is located in the chapter house. Opposite, the former **refectory** houses the original 15th-century sculptures from the west porch; copies stand in their former location. Beyond lies the **Dom Afonso V Cloister,** more human in scale and less ostentatious than the Royal Cloister, which houses a stone-carving workshop at the back.

Batalha's last site is arguably its most outstanding: the **Unfinished Chapels.** This octagonal structure is entered from outside the chapter house. Commissioned by Dom Duarte I (1391–1438), designed

EXPERIENCE: Making Artisan Breads

Portugal is famous not only for its windmills, but also for the excellent bread made by its bakers. **CataVino** *(tel 914 367 836, catavino.net),* whose main headquarters in Portugal are in Porto, gives you the chance to organize an unforgettable experience—a workshop where you'll observe and participate in the making of true traditional bread: You'll get to mill the grain, knead the dough, and finally bake the bread in a clay wood-burning oven. The activity can be organized in a characteristic, picturesque village, and will be a great way to see

and experience this ancient craft firsthand and make a fun day out for all the family, in a typical local atmosphere.

You can begin your experience with a walk to the mill to grind the grain; a traditional, hearty lunch is provided in a village house before guests spend the afternoon preparing and baking their bread; at the end of the day, everyone sits down to enjoy their freshly baked bread with local cheeses, olive oil, and a glass of wine. You'll need to reserve in advance. The personnel will certainly be able to satisfy your needs.

feast of intricate Manueline carving that was added to the original Gothic structure. To one side is the **chapter house,** where unsupported star-vaulting meets at a center point formed by João I's coat of arms. If you notice an unexpected military presence in the complex, you will soon understand why: The tomb of

by Huguet, and completed by Mateus Fernandes, it was intended as Duarte's family pantheon—yet only he and his queen were buried there. The breathtaking riot of embellishment—especially the lacelike carving of the doorway and the deeply incised pillars— is all dramatically open to the elements. ∎

ALCOBAÇA

The small town of Alcobaça is dominated by just one attraction, its magnificent Cistercian abbey dating from 1153. A World Heritage site since 1985, the abbey is noted for its evocative interior, which propels you back to the Middle Ages.

A view from behind the altar reveals the purity, scale, and grandeur of Alcobaça's Cistercian design.

Occupying a prime spot at the confluence of the Alcoa and Baça Rivers, massive in scale, austere yet serene in atmosphere, and stunningly beautiful in its detail, the **Mosteiro de Santa Maria de Alcobaça** was modeled on France's Clairvaux, and it soon became one of the most powerful Cistercian abbeys.

Alcobaça was completed in the mid-1200s. It flourished for six centuries, during which the abbot acquired immense regional power and owed no allegiance to the king. From the late 16th century on, the monks turned to art and literature, producing superb sculptures and building up one of the

richest libraries in Portugal. The monastery peaked in the late 18th century. Agriculture blossomed and the kitchens turned out feasts of gastronomic largesse: The frugal Cistercian life—the eschewal of wealth, privileges, and ostentation—had been put aside. In 1810, French troops pillaged the abbey. And after the government banned all religious orders in 1834, Alcobaça was abandoned.

Not all the abbey can be visited, but what you do see is breathtaking. The main entrance leads through a Gothic portal into the **church,** where soaring vaults span a triple nave extending 348 feet (109 m)—the largest church

Alcobaça

🅰 137 B4

Visitor Information

✉ Rua 16 de Outubro 7

☎ 262 582 377

Mosteiro de Santa Maria de Alcobaça

☎ 262 505 120

💲 €€

mosteiroalcobaca .gov.pt

in Portugal. Simplicity and purity reign; the main altar consists of just one crucifix and a statue of Christ. In the south transept, look for a terra-cotta relief depicting the life of St. Bernard made by the monks in the 17th century. The most famous highlight is the pair of 14th-century tombs of the star-crossed royal lovers, Inês de Castro and Pedro I. Positioned at opposite sides of the transept, these tombs display virtuoso sculptures and friezes in keeping with their tragic love story (see sidebar p. 121).

At the back of the chancel is a baroque sacristy; only the exqui-sitely carved Manueline doorway and vaulted lobby survive from

the 16th-century Renaissance sacristy destroyed by the 1755 earthquake. Here, too, is the Royal Pantheon: Look for the stylized tomb of Lady Beatriz.

At the front of the church, a side entrance leads through the ticket office to the Cloister of Dom Dinis, or **Cloister of Silence.** Built in the early 14th century, with an upper story added two centuries later, the elegant cloister encloses orange trees, box hedges, and an unusual octagonal lavabo on the north side. The cloister

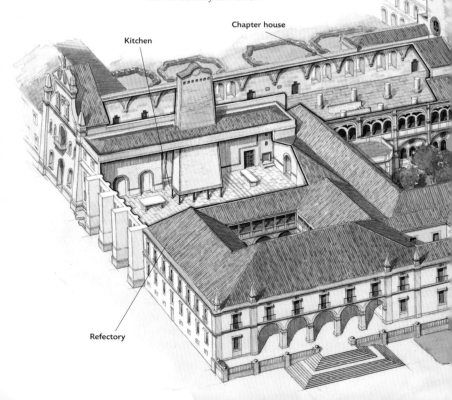

Chapter house

Kitchen

Refectory

leads to the **chapter house,** containing larger-than-life-size statues; a vast dormitory above; and, on the northern flank, the Monks' Hall, kitchen, and refectory. Note how the Monks' Hall steps down to accommodate the natural slope of the land, although its unity was destroyed when a staircase was added during a 1940s renovation.

The huge 18th-century **kitchen** was seemingly built for giants.

Completely tiled, its two vast fireplaces (up to seven oxen could be roasted at once) and massive stone tables are backed by a row of water tanks fed by the Alcoa River. Next door, the **refectory** holds a delicately carved, niche pulpit from where a monk would read as the others ate in silence. Today this vaulted hall houses an 18th-century statue of the Virgin and Child, transferred from the altar in the 1940s. ■

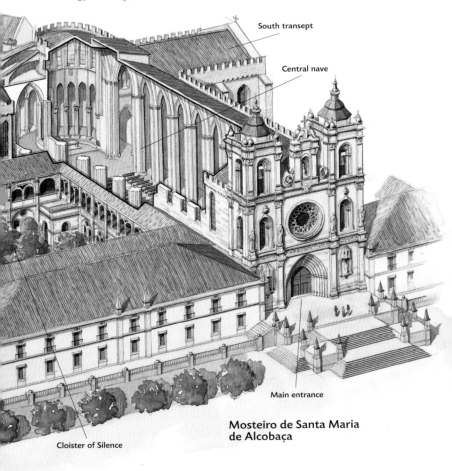

South transept

Central nave

Main entrance

Mosteiro de Santa Maria de Alcobaça

Cloister of Silence

CALDAS DA RAINHA & ÓBIDOS

Just 3 miles (5 km) separate these two Estremaduran towns, yet they are worlds apart. Caldas is a venerable old spa town with an unbeatable ceramics tradition, while Óbidos is an attractively spruced up, historical village geared almost exclusively to visitors. Their contrasts make Caldas and Óbidos an intriguing combination.

Caldas da Rainha

🗺 137 B4

Visitor Information

✉ Rua Provedor de São Paulo 1

☎ 262 240 005

Museu de Cerâmica

✉ Palacete do Visconde de Sacavém, Rua Dr. Ilídio Amado

☎ 262 840 280

🕐 Closed Mon.

💲 €

patrimoniocultural .gov.pt

Caldas da Rainha

Caldas da Rainha (Queen's Baths) started life in 1484 when Queen Leonor, the wife of João II, was struck by the curative properties of the local sulfuric springs and founded a hospital. After peaking in popularity, the spa town took a new lease on life with the impetus of ceramicist Rafael Bordalo Pinheiro (1846–1905). By introducing modern techniques, this artist inspired a school of whimsical designs (the cabbage-leaf plates are the most famous) that transformed the 400-year-old local craft tradition.

The **Museu de Cerâmica** displays pieces from all over the world. Upper rooms are devoted to the extraordinary animal and plant forms developed in Caldas. Lobsters, mussels, basketweave, sweet corn, and berries—all are rendered realistically, bringing some pieces to the brink of kitsch. The top floor exhibits contemporary ceramic work.

Of the four other art museums in town, the **Museu Malhoa** holds the most interest. Standing in a leafy park fronting the spa complex, this art deco museum highlights local painter José Malhoa (1855–1933) as well as other Portuguese artists and ceramicists. On the eastern side of the park, stop at the **Faianças Artísticas Bordalo Pinheiro factory** (*Rua Rafael Bordalo Pinheiro 53, tel 262 839 380, eu.bordallopinheiro.com*), to buy faïence earthenware at factory prices. A 20-minute tour (€) of the museum is available, if arranged in advance.

Óbidos

South of Caldas da Rainha, the fortified village of Óbidos will not disappoint—although in high summer the crowds can be overwhelming. Dom Dinis I was the man responsible for its popularity: In 1282, he gave the former Moorish castle to his wife-to-be, Isabel of Aragon, as a wedding gift. This tradition was

■ Caldas da Rainha comes alive at its morning fruit and vegetable market, a classic social crossroads.

EXPERIENCE: Festival Fun in Óbidos

Twice a year, Óbidos celebrates two of Portugal's most entertaining festivals. In late April, it hosts the **International Chocolate Festival** *(festivalchocolate.cm-obidos.pt)*, a time when the narrow streets and castle area are filled with stands displaying every conceivable form of chocolate, including huge chocolate sculptures; and top chefs hold demonstrations and workshops. Children are well catered to, with a dedicated child's area hosting activities and street shows.

In July and August, Óbidos is transformed with the arrival of the **Mercado Medieval** *(mercadomedievalobidos.pt,*

closed Mon.–Wed.). Before entering the market area, visitors are encouraged to enter into the spirit of the fair and trade in their clothes for medieval costumes; the price of the costume then gives you free entry. Inside, the castle grounds teem with street performers, musicians, and stalls. Vendors sell spit-roasted meat with hunks of bread in brown paper and clay goblets of wine, which are eaten at long wooden trestle tables.

Both festivals are great fun, but aim to arrive early, as they get incredibly busy. Check the websites for exact dates, times, and prices.

INSIDER TIP:

If you are a fan of chocolate, don't miss the International Chocolate Festival, held every year in Óbidos, usually in April.

—TINO SORIANO
National Geographic photographer

---

repeated by all future kings until 1833. In 1951, the transformation of the castle into a state inn (see p. 248) prompted extensive restoration of the village. Today the crenellated battlements enclose cobbled streets flanked by whitewashed houses with ultramarine or saffron yellow borders, walled gardens, 14 churches and chapels, and many craft shops. You can make a mile-long (1.6 km) circuit of the ramparts, starting at the castle or the main gate.

The village heroine was the baroque painter Josefa de Óbidos (1630–1684), who left her native Seville to settle here. A couple of her paintings are in **Santa Maria,** a charming Renaissance church built over Visigothic and Moorish structures. The future Afonso V married his eight-year-old cousin Isabel here in 1441; he was 10. The walls are blanketed in azulejos and paintings by Josefa de Óbidos hang to the right of the altar. Across the square from here, the attractive portico beside the pillory once held the market.

To the south, the 1380 **Porta da Vila** (Town Gate) has some impressive 18th-century azulejos within its angled form. This gateway plays a major role during the two-week-long, torchlit Easter processions. Another highlight is the concert series held June through September in an amphitheater just outside the walls. For hopping nightlife, head to the coast to **Foz do Arelho,** 3.5 miles (6 km) due west of Caldas. ■

Museu Malhoa
- ✉ Parque Dom Carlos I, Caldas da Rainha
- ☎ 262 831 984
- 🕐 Closed Mon.
- 💲 €

patrimoniocultural.gov.pt

Óbidos
- 🗺 137 B4

Visitor Information
- ✉ Rua Porta da Vila
- ☎ 262 959 231

obidos.pt

TOMAR

Tomar is a lot more than a one-monastery town. Its medieval origins, nonetheless, blossomed with its magnificent *castelo* (castle) and Convento de Cristo (Convent of Christ), the former headquarters of the powerful Knights Templar in Portugal.

■ A statue of a bruised Christ presides over a shadowy section of the evocative Convento de Cristo.

Tomar
🗺 137 C4

Visitor Information
✉ Avenida Dr. Cândido Madureira (corner of Pé da Costa de Baixo)
☎ 249 329 823

Convento de Cristo
☎ 249 324 090
💲 €€
conventocristo.pt

Tomar's old town is a delight: Whitewashed houses line cobbled streets, flowers reach over garden walls and perfume the air, willows drape the banks of the Nabão River, and walking paths twist through a wooded hillside. The web of old lanes harbors Portugal's oldest surviving **synagogue** (*Rua Dr. Joaquim Jacinto 73, closed Sun.*). Built in 1430, the synagogue lost its function in 1496 when Jews were forced to convert or be expelled. The vaulted room, now the **Museu Luso-Hebraico Abraão Zacuto,** displays tombstones with Hebrew inscriptions and Jewish memorabilia. One

block north, Tomar's late 15th-century church **São João Baptista** (*Praça da República*) boasts one of the finest views in town. Stand in its flamboyant Gothic doorway to take in the magnificent 12th-century convent walls high above and the 18th-century town hall on the opposite side of the square. The modern town on the river's right bank has less interest, but Tomar makes an enjoyable place to stay while on the monastery trail.

Convento de Cristo

The massive hilltop Convento de Cristo is a remarkably

INSIDER TIP:

The Convento de Cristo in Tomar is a fascinating place to visit and learn about the Knights Templar.

—LACEY GRAY
National Geographic *magazine editorial coordinator*

harmonious blend of Romanesque, Gothic, Renaissance, and Manueline styles; its labyrinthine cloisters, galleries, staircases, corridors, terraces, and halls resound with atmosphere.

The Knights Templar—a military order founded by crusaders in Jerusalem in 1119—began building the monastery in 1160, and construction continued on and off for four centuries despite a change in ownership in the 1300s (see sidebar this page). The complex changed hands again in 1834, when the government banned all religious orders and the castle became the residence of the count of Tomar.

Beyond a vast esplanade and broad staircase, you will find the main entrance tucked into the side of the massive rotunda— the back of the original fortified church. Before entering, have a good look at the fabulously decorated **south porch** of the church. Inside, arrows direct you along one of two self-guided routes laid out over the three-story edifice: The full tour of this World Heritage site lasts 60 to 90 minutes; a shorter one takes 30 to 45 minutes. Strategically

placed information panels (in Portuguese and English) elucidate the sites you see.

Exploring the Convent:
Begin your tour in the old sacristy, from which you enter two adjoining Gothic cloisters, the **Claustro do Cemitério** (Cemetery Cloister) and the **Claustro da Lavagem** (Laundry Cloister). The circuit brings you past some remarkable early 17th-century azulejos on the walls of the first cloister, the burial ground for knights and friars. The Laundry Cloister has two large reservoirs at its center. More chapels and the new sacristy follow before you reach the superb church.

The 16th-century **church** incorporates the original 12th-century structure, the Romanesque *charola,* or rotunda, that resembles in layout Jerusalem's Holy Sepulchre. The 16-sided

Order of Christ

Fearful of the Knights Templar's growing power, Dom Dinis I banned the Templars in 1314, replacing them with the Order of Christ, which moved to Tomar from Castro Marim (in the Algarve) in 1356. This order's prestige peaked the following century when, under its grand master, Prince Henry the Navigator (1418–1460), it financed Portugal's pioneering expeditions to Africa and India. Wealth from these forays funded much of Tomar's outstanding Manueline detail and also that of Lisbon's Jerónimos monastery (see pp. 60–64). The order's status subsequently waned and, in 1834, disappeared completely with the suppression of all religious orders.

charola has an exuberantly decorated octagonal oratory at its center. The riot of paintings, statues, and murals adorning the octagon mix illustrations of the life of Christ with symbols of royal power. The decorative works in the charola and the nave behind, with its raised choir area, are by the prolific Manueline architect Diogo de Arruda, though the Spaniard Juan de Castilla finished them.

EXPERIENCE:
Festa dos Tabuleiros

There's nothing quite like Tomar's other claim, the legendary four-day-long **Festa dos Tabuleiros** (Festival of Trays; *tabuleiros .org*), held every four years in early July (The latest celebration occurred in 2019.) Although officially honoring Isabel, the saintly wife of Dom Dinis I, the event is thought to have pagan roots. The most spectacular procession features 400 young girls (traditionally virgins) dressed in white, each balancing on her head a tray piled high with bread and paper flowers. The next day bread and wine are distributed to Tomar's poorest families. Plan ahead if you'd like to attend, as hotels fill well in advance.

From here, arrows point you downstairs to the convent buildings; the route enters through the **Claustro Principal** (Great Cloister). This outstanding example of Renaissance structure and Manueline decoration dates from 1529. Look for typical Manueline rope motifs on the back wall to the right as you enter the cloister.

As you exit to a terrace overlooking the intimately scaled **Claustro de Santa Bárbara** (St. Barbara's Cloister), you get your first glimpse of Tomar's much photographed **Manueline window.** This masterpiece of carved stone, designed by Diogo de Arruda, combines maritime motifs with royal emblems and is surmounted by the cross of the Order of Christ. A spiral staircase in the northeastern corner of this terrace leads up to more terraces, which offer good views of the convent, especially the terrace at the far end of the Claustro Principal, which has lovely views over the friars' garden and the picturesque chapter house ruins.

Further striking sites include the lofty corridor leading to the **monks' cells** and, finally, on the lowest floor, the kitchen and refectory. The tour ends at the neighboring **Claustro da Micha** and **Claustro das Hospedarias,** the latter, the Hospitality Cloister, designed for receiving visitors. You exit through the north face of the convent.

Nearby Curiosities

West of the monastery, on the road to Leiria (see pp. 138–139), looms the **Aqueduto dos Pegões.** This starkly designed aqueduct was built in the early 17th century to supply the convent with water; its 180 arches span 4 miles (6 km). Another curious monument stands on the convent's other side, halfway down the hill: the unused mausoleum of Dom João III, the 16th-century **Ermida de Nossa Senhora da Conceição** (*inquire at monastery*). ∎

TEJO VALLEY

The longest river in Iberia, the Tejo (Tagus) flows 687 miles (1,100 km) from its source in Spain through Portugal to empty into the Atlantic at Lisbon. The area of the Ribatejo (meaning "banks of the Tagus") derives its name from the river, as does the Alentejo (meaning "beyond the Tagus"), to the south.

The island-bound Almourol castle, built by a Templar knight, epitomizes the medieval citadel.

The Tejo snakes through the Ribatejo, its banks alternating between dense pine forests and patchy industrial installations, which conceal some unusual sites. Portugal's most overtly romantic castle, the **Castelo de Almourol,** sits majestically on a rocky island in the river, 14 miles (22 km) south of Tomar. Built by a grand master of the Knights Templar in 1171 on the site of a Roman fort, it inspired countless legends and literary references, but the castle was abandoned when its defensive function became obsolete. A small boat (€) ferries visitors to and fro.

Farther east is **Abrantes,** a surprisingly attractive town once you penetrate its industrialized outskirts. An extensively renovated 12th-century **castle** *(tel 241 371 724, closed Mon.)* crowns the narrow streets of the old quarter. A Visigothic necropolis, the governor's palace, and the beautifully restored 15th-century church of **Santa Maria** (now a museum) all stand within the castle walls. The church holds exceptional tombs, statuary, tiles, Roman pieces, and a rare wooden Gothic-Manueline retable. Between Almourol and Abrantes, scenic **Constância,** overlooking the confluence of the Tejo and the Zêzere Rivers, is just the place to while away a lazy afternoon, wandering along the cobbled streets and alleys. ∎

Castelo de Almourol

🗺 137 C4

✉ Vila Nova da Barquinha tourist office, Largo 1° de Dezembro

☎ 249 711 550 or 927 228 354

🕐 Closed Mon. Oct.–Apr.

cm-vnbarquinha.pt

Abrantes

🗺 137 D4

Visitor Information

✉ Esplanada 1° de Maio

☎ 241 330 100

SANTARÉM

Famous for bullfights and festivals, Santarém is Ribatejo's district capital. It was described by José Saramago as "a Sleeping Beauty castle, without the sleeping beauty," referring to its sense of remoteness on the vast plains of the region.

In Santarém and in neighboring Ribatejo towns such as Golegã, the Lusitano horse is highly revered.

Santarém

137 C3

Visitor Information

Rua Capelo e Ivens 63

243 304 437

Despite a lack of major sites, Santarém has plenty of character. The high point of the year is the 10-day agricultural fair held in early June, featuring bullfights (sometimes), bull-running, and horse racing; an ongoing taurine theme is reflected in Santarém's witty sidewalk mosaics.

A Jesuit seminary church, **Nossa Senhora da Conceição** (*Praça Sá da Bandeira, closed Mon.*), is notable for its lengthy azulejo frieze. For elegant Gothic architecture, head to the **Igreja da Graça** (*Largo Pedro Álvares Cabral, closed Mon.–Tues.*); the church's rose window was carved from a single stone. The tomb of Pedro Álvares Cabral, who laid claim to Brazil for Portugal in 1500, is inside. The older **São João de Alporão** church, a few minutes north of here by foot, houses the **Museu Arqueológico** (*Largo Zeferino Sarmento, tel 243 377 290, patrimoniocultural.pt, closed Mon.–Tues.*). The undisputed highlight is the elaborate tomb of Duarte de Meneses, a military commander who died at the hands of the Moors in Morocco in 1464. The 15th-century **Torre das Cabaças,** opposite the museum, displays an imaginative exhibit on the theme of time with old sundials and clock mechanisms. You can climb to the top for views, although those from the **Portas do Sol,** the remains of a Moorish citadel overlooking the Tejo on the southeast side of town, are better. ■

TORRES VEDRAS

Vineyards and towers characterize the landscape around Torres Vedras, which lies at the heart of the Estremadura area. The bleak Serra de Montejunto range looms to the east, while the surf-pounded beaches of the Atlantic lie west.

Both red and white wines are produced in the undulating vineyards of **Arruda dos Vinhos** to the south and **Bombarral,** 17 miles (27 km) to the north, where the train station is plastered with azulejos illustrating the wine-growing culture. For military historians, however, the region is known for one thing only: the Duke of Wellington's famous defensive Lines of Torres Vedras built during the Peninsular War to protect Lisbon against attack.

Wellington's Anglo-Portuguese troops constructed two roughly parallel lines of trenches and redoubts over a 12-month period (1809–1810), severely altering the landscape in the process. The 152 towers armed with 600 cannon stretched from the coast to the Tejo River. When General Masséna led 65,000 French soldiers in the third invasion of Portugal (the first two having failed), he entered through Almeida in the east. After advancing toward Lisbon, he soon realized the impregnability of Wellington's system (which included roads, ditches, and embrasures), so he retreated to Santarém. Finally, without supplies, he made the final retreat that ended the French invasions.

The remains of one of the towers, the **São Vicente fortress,** stands in Torres Vedras. The **Museu Municipal Leonel Trindade** details the Napoleonic invasion and has a scale model of the Lines of Torres Vedras. Be sure to admire the azulejos that blanket the cloister walls of this former convent and the exhibit on ceramics. Also of interest are a ruined 13th-century **castle** on the edge of town and, on the main square, the church of **São Pedro** with a rich baroque interior and an unusual Manueline portal depicting winged dragons. Behind stands a distinctive Gothic fountain with vaulted arches, the **Chafariz dos Canos.** ■

Torres Vedras
⚐ 137 A3
Visitor Information
✉ Rua 9 de Abril
☎ 261 310 483
🕐 Closed Sun.

■ Typical 18th-century blue-and-white azulejos mix pastoral and spiritual scenes in the church of São Pedro.

Museu Municipal Leonel Trindade
✉ Convento da Graça, Praça 25 de Abril
☎ 261 310 485
🕐 Closed Mon.
💲 €

MAFRA

You cannot miss the massive bulk of the palace, monastery, and basilica of Mafra as it looms over the plain north of Sintra. This is yet another of Portugal's heavyweight sites, this time an ode to concentrated baroque detail, scale, and pomposity.

■ The palace and basilica at Mafra reveal strong German baroque and Italian neoclassical influences.

Mafra
🗺 137 A3
Visitor Information
✉ Avenida das
    Forças Armadas
    28
☎ 261 817 170

cm-mafra.pt

Mafra is a place of mind-boggling statistics: some 50,000 workers, 13 years of construction, 880 rooms, 154 stairways, and 4,500 doors and windows carved out of Portuguese and Italian marble and exotic woods from Brazil. Dom João V commissioned the complex in 1717 to fulfill a vow he made when his wife bore him an heir. The German architect Johann Friedrich Ludwig of Ratisbon (1670–1752) headed the project, backed by an army of Italian artists, craftsmen, and masons.

Initially funded by Brazilian gold, the building costs eventually bankrupted the Portuguese economy. In 1807, little more than 70 years after its completion, the royals fled to Brazil in the face of the French invasion (see sidebar opposite). With them went most of the palace furniture and objets d'art. After the return of the monarchy, in 1821, Mafra was used only sporadically, but it was from here that the last king, Dom Manuel II, left for exile in 1910.

The Basílica

The long, umber-colored facade of the palace flanks the white marble Basílica, crowned by two bell towers containing

92 Flemish-made bells. The sober, neoclassical interior of the church was inspired by St. Peter's in Vatican City but, like the facade, has a strong German baroque flavor. Look for the 14 marble statues of saints and numerous bas-reliefs crafted by the Mafra school, a body of Italian and Portuguese sculptors based in the palace from 1753 to 1770.

If in town on the first Sunday of the month, do not miss the monthly organ recital in which the Basilica's six organs—designed to be played together—are put through their paces.

Palácio Nacional de Mafra

The one-hour guided tour (tel 261 817 550, palaciomafra. pt, closed Tues., €€) to the **palace** and **monastery** begins at the Queen's Entrance, midway along the left-hand facade. Long corridors and vast salons with painted ceilings—all furnished with 19th-century pieces that replaced the originals—characterize the palace. The main site is the stunning rococo **library** with its checkered marble floor and barrel-vaulted ceiling. The ornately carved wooden bookcases hold some 40,000 volumes, including numerous incunabula and codices dating from the 15th century on. At the back of the palace, the monastery displays monks' cells, a pharmacy, and an infirmary with a section once reserved for insane Franciscans.

Outdoor Havens

The royals and the monks passed many an hour in the **Jardim do Cerco,** the formal French-style garden that lies north of the palace. The vast **Tapada Nacional de Mafra** (Portão do Codeçal, tel 261 814 240, tapadademafra.pt, guided walks €€–€€€)–a 2,023-acre (819 ha) walled preserve home to wild boars, deer, civet cats, and even wolves—encircles the entire complex of Mafra. You can tour this delightful enclave by electric train, mountain bike, or guided walk. ■

Royal Exodus

The flight of the Braganças to Brazil in 1807 marks one of the lowest points in Portuguese history. Portugal was in serious decline: The costly extravagance of Mafra had depleted the country's coffers, Britain and France had eclipsed Portugal on the political world stage, and Napoleon's army was sweeping across Europe. As the French drew closer, the Prince Regent, Dom João, under pressure from the British envoy, made a fateful decision both for the Portuguese crown and for its colony Brazil.

On November 29, 1807, a day before the French entered Lisbon, Dom João and his queen, Dona Carlota, took to the seas. A convoy of three dozen frigates, brigantines, sloops, and corvettes, with 10,000 members of the royal court on board, set sail for Brazil under British escort. The ships also carried the paraphernalia of an empire: the royal carriage, a piano, several tons of documents, and favorite objets d'art. The exodus signaled the end of Portugal's heyday.

SINTRA

Verdant, romantic, and intensely evocative, Sintra never fails to seduce. Blessed with a microclimate that nurtures a varied, exuberant flora, from mosses to massive sequoias, its centuries-long popularity has produced unforgettable palaces and mansions.

■ The towering white chimneys of Sintra's national palace rise unmistakably above the town center.

Sintra

🗺 137 A2

Visitor Information

✉ Praça da República 23

☎ 219 236 114

cm-sintra.pt

High in the hills above the Estoril coast just west of Lisbon, Sintra is a radical contrast to the capital both in style and in climate, the latter being distinctly moist. Together with the surrounding Parque Natural de Sintra-Cascais (see p. 169), which encompasses forested hills dotted with palatial follies, the town is justly classified as a World Heritage site. You can see Sintra in a day, but try to stay a night or two in this delightful retreat, once the preserve of monarchs and European aristocrats, artists, and poets—including Lord Byron.

The town straggles along a road that winds uphill from the train station to the square in front of the national palace. Alternatively, coming by car from Estoril or Lisbon takes you through **São Pedro,** a satellite village about 1 mile (1.6 km) from Sintra that brims with antique shops. West of the main square, a turnoff curls up to the Moorish castle ruins and the Palácio da Pena, both high above the town, while the main N247 continues out of Sintra to snake through the *serra* (hills) to Quinta da Regateira, the Palácio de Seteais, the park of Monserrate, a few villages, and, eventually, the coast. There are some lovely walks in the area and, even if you take a bus or taxi up to the Pena Palace, you should try to walk down to see Sintra's many art nouveau mansions and to enjoy fabulous views.

If you are in Sintra on the second or fourth Sunday of the month, don't miss the tempting market that takes over the center of São Pedro. Music lovers should aim to visit in June or July, when an international music festival is held. At any time you can indulge in Sintra's famed *queijadas* (see sidebar this page) and typical mountain fare of Negrais suckling pig, Mercês pork, roast kid, or veal, washed down with Colares red wine.

Queijadas

Sintra's most famous culinary export are its *queijadas.* **Best translated as "cheesecakes," though in no way resembling the cheesecake that most people are familiar with, these small sweet cakes are made with cheese, eggs, milk, sugar, and cinnamon and surrounded in fine crispy pastry. They are best experienced with a** *galão* **(milky coffee served in a glass), in Sintra's café** **Piriquita** *(Rua das Padarias 1, tel 219 230 626, piriquita. pt);* **wrapped in paper rolls, packs of six are also available to carry out.**

INSIDER TIP:

Linger in the moss-bottomed forest that engulfs the winding path to the palace—it's as fairy-tale as the hill-topping edifice itself.

—JOHNNA RIZZO
National Geographic
magazine editor

Palácio Nacional de Sintra

Dominating the *vila velha* (old town), the magnificent yet confusing Palácio Nacional de Sintra, Portugal's oldest palace, spans more than eight centuries of history from its Moorish origins until the end of the monarchy in 1910. Over the course of time it underwent numerous extensions—notably in the 14th, 15th, and 16th centuries under kings Dinis I, João I, and Manuel I, respectively. The palace was a convenient retreat from the heat of Lisbon and served as a luxury hunting lodge.

It displays superb decorative arts of the Manueline period, when the western tower and east wing were added, as well as extensive Mudejar (Hispano-Moorish) tiling, the oldest still in place in Europe.

The entrance, through the Gothic main porch and up a spiral staircase, leads into the largest room in the palace, the **Sala dos Cisnes** (Swan's Room), used for banquets and dances and, even today, for official receptions. Although most of the palace miraculously survived the 1755 earthquake, this vast hall did not; however, it was harmoniously rebuilt and the 27 swans faithfully repainted on the ceiling.

Outside in the **central patio,** the heart of João I's palace, do not miss the tiled grotto. An antique version of a refrigerator, the grotto's walls are now entirely faced in 18th-century azulejos that conceal tiny waterspouts, but a series of Manueline frescoes lie underneath the tiles. From here the route takes in the unusual **Sala das Pegas** (Magpies' Room),

Palácio Nacional de Sintra
✉ Largo Rainha D. Amélia
☎ 219 237 300
💲 €€

parquesdesintra.pt

so-named for its ceiling paintings depicting 136 magpies spouting the king's motto, *Por Bem* (For the Best). Another stunner is **King Sebastian's bedroom,** with its Italian marquetry four-poster bed and original vine-leaf tiles. Most of the inlaid furniture elsewhere

---

EXPERIENCE: Sintra Hills Adventures

For some great views of the Sintra hills, its palaces, and surrounding countryside, get off the main roads on a thrilling 4x4 trip. **Muitaventura** *(Rua Marquês de Viana 31, Largo da Feira, Sintra, tel 211 931 636 or 967 021 248, muitaventura.com)* offers half- and full-day jeep safaris *(€€€€€)* through the natural park with frequent stops to admire the scenery. For those who would prefer a more eco-friendly option, **Silencetour** *(tel 912 942 942, silencetour.pt)* has 1- to 2.5-hour excursions on specially adapted off-road Segways *(€€€€€)* on tracks around the Sintra reservoir and Peninha area. Call for full details and reservations.

---

is 17th- and 18th-century Indo-Portuguese, with exceptions such as the spectacular Murano glass chandelier in the north wing.

From the **Sala das Sereias** (Room of the Sirens) you enter the **Arab Room,** formerly João I's bedroom, which displays a rare, dazzling juxtaposition of tile techniques and patterns. Continuing on, you find yourself in the vast, square **Sala dos Brasões** (Blazons Hall), which juts out over the gardens and tenders views to the Atlantic. Paintings of stags holding 74 coats of arms of the Portuguese nobility dance, and portraits of Manuel I's children cover the

room's coffered dome ceiling. Altogether this tour de force combines heraldic decoration, gilded cornices, and azulejo panels illustrating hunting scenes that stand more than 13 feet (4 m) tall. Note the typical Manueline details of ropes and plants framing the doorway.

Although the northern wing rooms that follow are less impressive, pay special attention to Dom Dinis's 14th-century **chapel,** which Manuel I redecorated with cut-tile flooring, frescoes of doves (repainted in the 1940s), and a Mudejar ceiling. Afonso VI, who was imprisoned in the palace for six years by his brother Pedro II, died of apoplexy while attending Mass here in 1683. Last but not least come the astonishingly scaled 15th-century **kitchens** with their 108-foot-high (33 m) conical chimneys, unique in Europe, and tapped spring water. They are still used today during official receptions. To recover from the decorative excess, take a walk around the gardens to be soothed by trickling fountains.

News Museum

One of the latest Sintra attractions, located in the center of town, is the **News Museum** *(Rua Visconde de Monserrate 26, tel 210 126 600, newsmuseum. pt, closed Mon.–Tues., €€; reserved for private events and group visits in Oct.–Mar.).* As the name implies, it is dedicated to the history of news, with intriguing multimedia displays offering relief from monument overload. Portuguese history, war, propaganda, and freedom are among the topics covered, and visitors are encouraged to participate by recording their own news item for radio, TV, or Internet.

MU.SA—Museu de Artes de Sintra

Before plunging further into Sintra's magical past, anyone desiring a visual feast of another kind should visit **MU.SA, the Museu de Artes de Sintra** *(Av. Heliodoro Salgado, closed Mon., €)*, in the new part of town. Housed in a converted 1924 casino, this museum is chock-full of stunning modern art and is run by the municipality.

Parque e Palácio Nacional da Pena

The fairy-tale **Palácio Nacional da Pena,** colorful and turreted, was the creation of Prince Ferdinand of Saxe-Coburg. Begun in the 1840s, the palace sits on the foundations of a 15th-century monastery and commands a prime hilltop setting. The highly cultured Ferdinand (1816–1885), the Portuguese prince regent for two years, was a grand master of the Rosicrucian Order, and numerous Masonic symbols can be spotted throughout his palace.

Your 10-minute walk up from the parking lot brings into focus otherworldly archways, minarets, crenellated towers, and a drawbridge before you finally arrive at the palace courtyard, where tiles and vibrant color take over. The passageway through the densely carved **Triton Arch**—its shell, coral, and vine symbolizing the link between sea and earth—leads to a Manueline cloister (all that remains of the original monastery), and a chapel containing an alabaster altarpiece by Nicolas de Chanterenne. Next, a series of small rooms decorated in tiles, shellwork, porcelain fragments,

Parque e Palácio Nacional da Pena

🅰 137 A2

✉ Parque da Pena, Sintra

☎ 219 237 300

💲 Palace & park €€ mid-Oct.–Mar., €€€ Apr.–mid-Oct.
Park only €€

parquesdesintra.pt

▪ Quinta da Regaleira is a World Heritage site within the "cultural landscape of Sintra."

■ An initiation well (or inverted tower) was used for ceremonial purposes that included tarot initiation rites.

stucco, and trompe l'oeil plasterwork overflow with opulence: Chandeliers, lamps, and objets d'art culminate in the hand-carved furniture of the **Indian Room.** Above all, relish the fabulous views to the southwest from the terrace at the back.

In the foreground, the Parque da Pena–500 acres (200 ha) of semiwild terrain with ferns, lakes, a few fountains, massive boulders, and rare species of trees–hugs the granite slopes of the serra around the palace. The entry ticket comes with a map outlining a 1.5-hour walk. The highest point, the **Cruz Alta,** is on the southern flank and has views reaching as far as Lisbon.

Two possible routes lead downhill from the palace: The first, the Calçada da Pena, winds through the forest and past art nouveau mansions to São Pedro, from where it is a mile (1.6 km) walk to Sintra's center; the second

leads down to the eighth-century **Castelo dos Mouros** (tel 219 237 300, €€), where ruined battlements offer more stunning views north over the valley as well as a whiff of Moorish past. From here you can zigzag down steps and paths to the Romanesque church of **Santa Maria** to reach Rua Marechal Saldanha, which leads back to Sintra's main square.

More Sintra Sites

Be sure to see the **Chalet & Garden of the Countess of Edla** (Estrada da Pena, tel 219 237 300, parquesdesintra.pt, €€). Painstakingly restored and opened to the public in 2011, this former recreational chalet was built between 1864 and 1869 by Fernando II for his second wife, Elisa Henster, Countess of Elda. The outside is painted stucco made to resemble a log cabin; its interior is full of decorative details, including inlaid cork ceilings, murals, and tile floors.

Another of Sintra's whimsical sites is the **Quinta da Regaleira,** *(tel 219 106 650, regaleira.pt, €, guided tours €€–€€€€),* an early 1900s palace that has a striking garden. Even more than the Pena Palace, this *quinta* abounds in esoteric references, and mixes neo-Gothic and neo-Manueline architectural styles with classic Romantic abandon.

The eccentric, highly cultured millionaire António Carvalho Monteiro (1848–1920), after making his fortune in Brazil, commissioned Luigi Manini, the Italian architect responsible for the palace of Buçaco, to build this dream palace. Like Pena, it teeters on the brink of kitsch, but the gardens have an inimitable atmosphere with their fountains, lakes, grottoes, statues, and the famous **Poço Iniciático** (Well of Initiation). The well is the high point: Steps take you down to what feels like the bowels of the Earth, where you stand on an eight-pointed star before following underground stepping-stones through a passage out into a decorative courtyard.

Nearby, the **Palácio de Seteais** is now a luxury hotel (see p. 250) with fine views over extensive gardens to the distant sea. Built in the late 18th century by the Dutch consul, Daniel Gildemeester, it later witnessed the signing of the 1808 Convention of Sintra—an agreement that led to Napoleon's army withdrawing from Portugal (they reinvaded the following year). The interior boasts delicate murals, grand staircases, and antique furnishings.

From the Palácio de Seteais, 2.5 miles (4 km) of road twist through beautiful forest to the magnificent **Palácio e Parque de Monserrate** *(Estrada da Monserrate, tel 219 237 300, parquesdesintra.pt, €€).* The palace and estate name derives from a religious order that owned the land when it was leased to Gerard DeVisme, the first of several English owners (see pp. 164–165), including Francis Cook, who commissioned the surviving Orientalist extravaganza. Decades of neglect ended in the 1990s with much needed restoration; the domed palace, a classic Romantic structure, is now open to visitors. Be sure to admire the very English lawn in front of the palace, the first such lawn in Portugal, watered by underground ceramic pipes.

While the English lawn is novel, the 81-acre (33 ha) gardens are truly outstanding. These were the pride and joy of the Cook family, who exploited the humid climate to nurture tree ferns from Australia and New Zealand, Montezuma cypresses from Mexico, rhododendrons from the Himalaya, and countless other species. A walk through the park (allow an hour or so) is a delight. Take in the chapel ruins sheltered by massive ficus trees. The ornately carved Arch of India, brought back by Cook following the Indian Mutiny in 1857, stands just east of the palace. A little farther on, the old stables have been converted into a restaurant and café with inviting outdoor tables under the trees. ■

SINTRA'S ENGLISH ECCENTRICS

The role of the English in Portugal has been prominent ever since their traders developed the profitable port wine industry. Not all were businessmen, however. Their influence began in the 14th century, when John of Lancaster and his band of crusaders helped the Portuguese fight the Moors; thanks to the local tipple, the English army was seldom sober.

■ The architecture of the Monserrate Palace evokes Sintra's early Moorish conquerors.

Soon after, in the 1380s, Philippa of Lancaster, daughter of John and the wife of João I, gave royal patronage to her countrymen's commercial interests. For the next 500 years wine, cork, salt, and oil were exchanged for cod and cloth from England, an enduring relationship that also brought a new breed of Englishmen to Portuguese shores: English merchants and minor aristocrats in search of mild climes and copious sources of inebriation. English communities flourished in Porto and Lisbon, their members meeting at specific hotels, restaurants, clubs, and churches. Among them were the men who brought both fame and scandal to Sintra: William Beckford, the poet Lord Byron, and Sir Francis Cook.

Monserrate's English Tenants

Lesser known but equally instrumental in raising Sintra's profile, the merchant Gerard DeVisme made his fortune importing wood from Brazil. In 1790, this Englishman of French Huguenot stock leased Monserrate, a prime property overlooking a valley outside Sintra (see p. 163). DeVisme first replaced a semi-ruined chapel with a neo-Gothic mansion, and then he set about creating a new "ruined" chapel in the woods below. Still visible today, draped in vegetation, this picturesque folly was Sintra's first contrived Romantic structure—the blueprint for moody ruins lost in time.

DeVisme's time at Monserrate ended just a few years later, when ill health forced his return to England. In his place soon came William Beckford, Orientalist scholar, author of *Vathek,* notorious snob, and reputedly the wealthiest man in England. Beckford had been forced into exile in 1785 for alleged homosexual relationships. After acquiring the tenancy of Monserrate, he wasted little time in criticizing DeVisme's "barbarous gothic" structure, yet he partied hard there in the late 1790s, raising a few local eyebrows in the process. But his tenure barely outlasted DeVisme's.

Years of abandonment followed Beckford's departure, witnessed in 1809 when the 21-year-old English poet Lord Byron made his famous three-day visit to Sintra with his friend John Hobhouse. Lured by the estate's reputation for elegance—and decadence—the two English visitors, according to Hobhouse's diary, found the mansion "deserted and bare of all furnishings." Yet Sintra's fascination struck again and Byron wrote: "The village is perhaps, in every respect, the most delightful in Europe ... Palaces and gardens rising in the midst of rocks, cataracts and precipices, convents on stupendous heights—a distant view of the sea and the Tagus." Byron's epic poem *Childe Harold I* also famously extols Sintra, referencing "Cintra's glorious Eden."

In 1855, Sir Francis Cook, a textile millionaire, bought the property. He proved to be the most industrious of all its owners and was named viscount of Monserrate by the king in 1870. After hiring the American architect James

Lawrence's Hotel

Opened by the British Lawrence Oram family in 1764, Lawrence's Hotel claims to be the oldest in Iberia—and although this may be hard to verify, what is certain is that this Sintra landmark offered hospitality to many visiting English eccentrics. In 1809, Lord Byron visited Sintra as part of his Grand Tour and stayed at Lawrence's, as did William Beckford before acquiring Monserrate. In Byron's wake followed the cream of Portuguese 19th-century Romantics and intellectuals, putting Lawrence's firmly on the Sintra map. Today it is fully restored and still open to guests (see p. 250).

Knowles, Jr., to build an Orientalist fantasy palace, Cook orchestrated the park's now famous landscaping. The vast undertaking required more than 2,000 people to build the palace and another 50 to plant the park. It remained in the Cook family until after World War II, when they could no longer afford its upkeep. Their departure brought to an end a line of particularly colorful English inhabitants.

■ **Monserrate's rampant vegetation and decorative features never fail to appeal.**

COSTA DO ESTORIL

Lisbon's favorite coastal playground, the Estoril coast hugs continental Europe's western-most point, Cabo da Roca. The shoreline stretches west from Estoril in a virtual continuum of hotels, restaurants, and condominiums, and curls around the Cabo Raso to the wild and unspoiled Parque Natural de Sintra-Cascais and the Guincho beach. North of here is Cabo da Roca and a string of lovely beaches.

Cabo da Roca's 1846 lighthouse emits a beam visible 26 miles (42 km) out to sea.

Cascais
137 A2
Visitor Information
✉ Praça 5 de Outubro, Antigo Ed. dos Bombeiros
☎ 912 034 214

There is a marked difference between the diverging coast-lines at Cabo Raso. To the east, south-facing beaches are calm and sheltered, with plentiful distractions. The western coast, north of Cabo Raso, up to Cabo da Roca and beyond, is wild and often very windy, with dramatic cliffs and pounding surf, and amazing beaches both north and south of Cabo da Roca.

Cascais

A genteel air still clings to the older part of Cascais behind the fishing harbor, where cobbled pedestrian streets offer an enticing lineup of restaurants and fashion boutiques. An 800-year-old tradition of fishing endures, although the dethroned kings who brought fame to Cascais between the two World Wars are long gone. Entirely rebuilt after the 1755 earth-quake, Cascais rose to promi-nence in 1870 when King Luís I moved the summer court here from Sintra and set up residence inside the Cidadela fort. In his wake came a flood of wannabes, further encouraged by the new fashion for sea bathing. The western end of Cascais, where the old mansions are located, once harbored Umberto II, Italy's last king; Juan Carlos of Spain, who was a resident during his long exile prior to 1975; and even Salazar, Portugal's infamous dictator.

Cascais centers on the **Praia da Ribeira,** the beach where fishermen bring in their catch every morning. To one side stands the fish market, behind are the pedestrian shopping streets, and around the bay to the west is the 16th-century **Cidadela.** The fort sits on a promontory overlooking the bay and harbor; it was one of several defensive keeps built to protect Lisbon against attack. The fort is now home to a *pousada* and various fashionable restaurants.

Walk some 100 yards (90 m) along the waterfront to the **Museu dos Condes Castro Guimarães** (tel 214 815 304, closed Mon., € guided tour), a typical, turreted, 19th-century Cascais mansion, which stands beside a sea inlet. The sumptuous interior displays a rich private collection of decorative arts, including some lovely Indo-Portuguese furniture, early 20th-century Portuguese paintings, and a vast library. Opposite here is the Cascais Marina, good for a stroll and a bite to eat.

Farther along this coastal avenue is the **Boca do Inferno** (Mouth of Hell)—the most visited site in Cascais—where waves thunder through a gorge. Walk down over the rocks to the little platform for a good view.

The **Casa das Histórias–Paula Rego** (tel 214 826 970, casadas historiaspaularego.com, €), one block back on Avenida da República,

houses a fabulous collection by the world-renowned, Cascais-born Paula Rego. Her paintings are considered by some to be sinister and oppressive, depicting controversial social realities. Anyone desiring a quick dip or a chance to sunbathe should head for **Praia da Rainha** and **Praia da Conceição,** two beaches just east of the old quarter.

Estoril

Though cheek to cheek with Cascais, **Estoril** lacks the former's air of faded grandeur and range of restaurants. The small **Museu dos Exílios do Estoril** upstairs in the Correios, a sober art deco building designed by Adelino Nunes in 1942, illustrates the town's history. Around the corner is Estoril's highlight: Europe's largest **casino** (tel 214 667 700, casino-estoril.pt, closes at 3 p.m., game room €€), which fronts a large formal garden leading to the sea. Follow in the footsteps of exiled royals, Ian Fleming, Orson Welles, and other notable personalities and

---

An Iconic Gelateria

Santini (Av. Valbon 28F, tel 214 833 709, santini.pt), recently renovated, has been part of Cascais life since the late 1940s. A favorite with the then exiled Italian royal family, the gelateria quickly became fashionable and has remained so ever since. The recipes for their ice creams are closely guarded, with dozens of delicious flavors produced from natural ingredients. Which flavor is best is subject to debate, but rest assured, they are all amazing. Additional branches are in Lisbon, Estoril, Carcavelos, and Porto.

Museu dos Exílios do Estoril

✉ Avenida Marginal 7152A, Estoril

☎ 214 815 930

🕑 Closed Sat.–Sun.

indulge in anything from roulette to slot machines, or watch the nightly cabaret. To maintain lower adrenaline levels, head for the small beaches for a swim.

Palácio Nacional de Queluz

In the hinterland between Cascais and Lisbon, one major site stands out: the 18th-century **Palácio Nacional de Queluz** *(Largo do Palácio, Queluz, tel 219 237 300, parquesdesintra.pt, €€).* Standing in the shadows of high-rises and highways, this once gracious royal palace fell into a sorry state of disrepair, but many millions of euros of restoration work has returned the interiors and formal gardens to their former glory. Now your attention will be drawn to the exterior and to the famous pink façade that has recently been repainted in its original cobalt blue color. One wing, the Queen Maria Pavilion, is still used by visiting heads of state; another section is a *pousada* (inn).

The palace was the brainchild of Prince Pedro (1717–1786), the brother of King José. French architect Jean-Baptiste Robillon

masterminded the transformation of a country house into this small-scale Portuguese imitation of Versailles, in which rococo gilding, elaborate paneling, and stuccowork dominate. Despite exceptional details and craftsmanship in the 22 rooms, the overall impression is one of decorative excess. Nonetheless, the palace does showcase a valuable collection of Portuguese furniture, Arraiolos carpets, royal portraits, jewelry, and Chinese and European porcelain. Of outstanding interest is the **Sala do Trono** (Throne Room), an echo of the Hall of Mirrors at Versailles, where glossy parquet floors and mirrored walls reflect glittering chandeliers beneath a gilded, stuccoed ceiling. More unusual is the **Sala de Don Quixote,** where Dom Pedro IV died; eight pillars support a circular ceiling and wall paintings depict scenes from the Cervantes novel.

Also designed by Robillon, with more than a nod to the French landscape designer Le Nôtre, the extensive **gardens** hold many surprises. Great whimsicality produced the completely tiled walls of the **canal**—the 18th-century azulejos depict river and seaport

Vagaries of Palace Life

The palace of Queluz has had a checkered record of residency. Despite its extravagant transformation from country house to summer palace in the mid-18th century, engineered by Prince Pedro (1717–1786), the brother of King José, the palace initially saw little use. An exception was Pedro's wife (and niece), Queen Maria I, who lived here for many years while her

melancholic eccentricity accelerated into insanity. In 1794, a fire at Lisbon's Ajuda palace brought the royal family to Queluz on a permanent basis, but this residency, too, proved to be short lived; in 1807 the royals fled to Brazil. Over the next century, until the end of the Portuguese monarchy, Queluz was inhabited only sporadically.

scenes. The royal family would view these while sailing up and down the waterway, listening to chamber music played in a nearby pavilion. This reflects the original plan for Queluz as a pleasure palace for summer entertainment. Today the summertime tradition continues—from equestrian exhibitions Wednesdays at 11 a.m. to evening concerts. You can take a pleasant stroll through the formal gardens dotted with statues and descend to a lower, more Italianate level of pools and fountains, but you will not escape the muted roar of traffic.

Cabo da Roca & Environs

Back on the coastline that is part of the **Parque Natural de Sintra-Cascais,** the geographic highlight is **Cabo da Roca,** continental Europe's most westerly point. High on a windswept cliff, 460 feet (140 m) above the waves, the lighthouse has become something of a pilgrimage spot, where a tiny tourist office writes out certificates. The 360-degree views are fantastic, and a cliffside cross marks the actual most westerly point *(there are buses from Colares & Cascais).*

Beyond the cliffs to the south, backed by sand dunes and pine trees, is the beautiful **Praia do Guincho,** a popular surfing beach where the European Windsurfing and World Surfing Championships are held. Notwithstanding a couple of hotels and a few seafood restaurants that dot the rocky coast to the south, the coast preserves its unspoiled nature. The beaches north of Cabo da

Roca are reached from Colares, except for the lovely but often overcrowded **Praia da Adraga,** accessed from Almoçageme. The neighboring **Praia Grande** (also accessible from Almoçageme, and notable for its clifftop dinosaur footprints and bodyboarders slaloming the waves below) and

---

INSIDER TIP:

Do not approach the cliff edge at Cabo da Roca; tourists have disappeared while trying to take that perfect picture.

—EMMA ROWLEY
National Geographic contributor

Praia das Maçãs, farther north, are lovely beaches, but **Azenhas do Mar** is the most striking. Here, colorful houses cling to a cliff from where a road winds down to the shore. If the tide is low, you can enjoy a tranquil swim in a saltwater pool carved out of the rocks.

The last stop on this section of Estremaduran coastline, due west of Mafra, is **Ericeira.** This popular little resort has a lively atmosphere, a fishing harbor, and a quaint old center around its clifftop church and main square. Three beaches lie within walking distance and a few more within a short drive, including **Praia de Ribeira de Ilhas,** another surfing championship beach. Restaurants are plentiful and the nightlife hops, mostly due to the weekend influx of Lisbonites. ∎

Parque Natural Sintra-Cascais

🅐 137 A2–A3

Visitor Information

✉ Avenida Barão Almeida Santos 10–12, Sintra

☎ 219 247 200

parquesdesintra.pt

Cabo da Roca

🅐 137 A2

Visitor Information

✉ Cabo da Roca, Azóia

☎ 219 280 081

Ericeira

🅐 137 A3

Visitor Information

✉ Rua Dr. Eduardo Burnay 46

☎ 261 863 122

ericeira.net

cm-mafra.pt

SETÚBAL PENINSULA

Jutting impudently into the Atlantic Ocean south of Lisbon, the Setúbal Peninsula presents an eclectic mix of beaches, light industry, hills, vineyards, and nature reserves. On summer weekends, beachgoing Lisbonites pour across the two bridges spanning the Tejo River.

Portugal's fourth largest port, Setúbal is home to more than 2,000 small boats.

Setúbal Peninsula

137 B1–B2

Visitor Information

✉ Travessa Frei Gaspar 10, Setúbal

☎ 265 539 130

Sesimbra

137 B1

Visitor Information

✉ Largo da Marinha 26–27

☎ 212 288 540

Whatever the tourist literature says of **Costa da Caparica** and the sandy beach to the south, you cannot ignore the blight of development at its northern tip. Yet surfers from the capital head here in droves and, apart from the breakers, enjoy fabulous views north to the Serra de Sintra. In summer an electric train services the beach strip, which includes fossilized limestone cliffs backed by an immense pine forest. Between here and Sesimbra are industrial pockets as well as eucalyptus and pine forests.

Sesimbra & Around

The fishing port of **Sesimbra** occupies a strategic position in the southwestern corner of the peninsula, its medieval **castelo** (castle) standing above increasing modern development. Inside the castle walls stand the ruins of a Romanesque church, **Santa Maria,** and a pleasant café. Down below, quaint narrow backstreets end at a deep sandy beach, its placid waters protected by a headland and guarded by the fort of Santiago. Brightly painted fishing boats fill the harbor west of the center; they supply the excellent seafood restaurants in town.

Seven miles (11 km) west lies the windswept **Cabo Espichel,** boasting a cliff-edge lighthouse, magnificent views, and a 13th-century sanctuary.

EXPERIENCE: Dolphin-Watching in the Sado Estuary

Dolphins have inhabited the waters of the Sado Estuary for many years; the earliest recorded sighting was in 1863 and it is believed that a pod has been in residence ever since. Today it is believed the group of bottlenose dolphins (*roaz* in Portuguese) numbers 28.

You can witness these highly active cetaceans riding the bow waves of boats, reaching speeds of up to 27 miles (40 km) an hour, on a three-hour catamaran excursion with **Vertigem Azul** (*Edifício Marina Deck, Rua Praia da Saúde 11D, Setúbal, or Marina Tróia, tel 265 238 000 or 916 982 907, vertigemazul.com, €€€€€*). Trips set off from either Setúbal or the marina on the Tróia Peninsula and cruise in both the estuary and the coastal waters of Tróia and Arrábida. A biologist narrates the tour, giving you insights into dolphin life—for example, each dolphin eats up to 44 pounds (20 kg) of food a day.

The **Serra da Arrábida—** the hill range that runs parallel to the coast between Sesimbra and Setúbal—creates an unexpected enclave of Mediterranean-style landscape; it is a protected nature reserve. Rising to 1,640 feet (500 m), the *serra* is clad in Portuguese oaks, vineyards (famed for their muscatel grapes), and aromatic herbal scrub. Various mammals include genets, weasels, badgers, and wildcats, while in the air you might spot Bonelli's eagles, kestrels, buzzards, swifts, and bee-eaters. The hillside cradles a picture-postcard Franciscan **monastery,** founded in 1542. Its whitewashed buildings with tiled roofs, terraces, pergolas, and shrines spill down the hillside in complete harmony with their surroundings.

Immediately below the monastery is an absolute gem: the crescent-shaped beach and village of **Portinho da Arrábida.** Protected from the north winds by the hills and edged by transparent waters, the village makes an idyllic spot for a seafood lunch. Close by is the **Lapa de Santa Margarida,** a sea cave where the area's oldest traces of human presence (200,000–400,000 years old) were found. The **Forte de Santa Maria,** built in 1670 to protect the monks against Moorish pirate attacks and now a marine biology center, guards the western end of the beach. Farther east lies **Galapos** beach, much favored by scuba divers, followed by **Praia de Figueirinha,** a white-sand beach popular with windsurfers. Terrible forest fires in 2004 rendered part of this coastal road inaccessible, but thankfully all signs of the fire have disappeared—smaller roads currently serve the beach towns.

Setúbal & Around

The road to Setúbal along the crest of the massif offers views both north to Lisbon and south across the Sado Estuary. The hamlets along this route produce excellent Azeitão sheep cheese and velvety honey, as well as the sweet wine, Moscatel de Setúbal. In **Vila Nogueira da Azeitão** you can try the Moscatel at the **José Maria da Fonseca** winery (*Rua José*

Setúbal (town)
🗺 137 B2
Visitor Information
✉ Avenida Luísa Todi 486
☎ 265 534 402

*Augusto Coelho 11, tel 212 198
940, jmf.pt, reserve for tastings).*

Setúbal itself is a large, chaotic seaport that looks straight across at the Tróia Peninsula. Portugal's fourth port after Sines, Porto, and Lisbon, it counts sardines and oysters, not tourists, as its major priorities. This fact makes it a relaxing, offbeat place to stay, with an abundance of excellent seafood restaurants. To the west is the massive 16th-century **Forte de São Filipe,** built to fend off Moorish and English attacks. It overlooks the estuary and town. Down below, the town center

---

INSIDER TIP:

The Sado Estuary is amazing for birding any time of year, but try to visit between November and February, when the migratory flamingos are here.

—PEDRO NARRA
*Wildlife photographer & owner,
Vertigem Azul*

---

straddles the tree-lined Avenida Luisa Todi, with harbor facilities to the south and a maze of pedestrian streets to the north off Praça de Bocage.

One site not to be missed is the excavated Roman remains of a fish condiment factory visible through the transparent floor of the tourist office. Elsewhere, the 15th-century **Igreja de Jesus** *(Praça Miguel Bombarda, closed Sun.–Mon., hours vary)* is a landmark

of early Manueline design. Although this Franciscan church underwent misguided cement restoration in the 1940s, the lovely pink Arrábida stone portal remains intact, as do the striking twisted columns, polychrome tiles, and vaulted chancel. The remarkable 14-panel altarpiece has migrated to the adjoining gallery, **Galeria de Pintura Quinhentista** *(Rua do Balneário de Dr. Paula Borba, tel 265 537 890, closed Sun.–Mon.)* to join a rich collection of Renaissance art. Note: Sections of this museum may be closed for renovation.

You can visit the **Sado Estuary** by boat, preferably a typical sailing galleon *(Troiacruze, tel 265 228 482, troiacruze.com),* or by car via the 10-mile-long (17 km) **Tróia Peninsula.** Hikers should pick up a handbook outlining walks from the Sado reserve office *(Praça da República, tel 265 541 157)* in the harbor.

Follow signs to Tróia Cais to take a 15-minute **ferry ride** *(Atlantic Ferries, tel 265 235 101, atlanticferries.pt, €€€)* to the tip of this finger of land. The road runs south to pine-edged dunes (a botanical reserve) and blissful beaches on the Atlantic side, and fishing villages on the estuary side. With luck you will spot otters or dolphins, and storks, herons, and egrets are common. One of the most traditional villages is **Carrasqueira,** where boats moor at rickety raised walkways jutting out into a lagoon. This is accessed from the N253, running eastward from Comporta, at the base of the peninsula, to Alcácer do Sal (see p. 196) in the Alentejo. ■

Sweeping plains and hills clad in cork oaks, olive trees, and vineyards, where hilltop villages date from Moorish and medieval days

ALENTEJO

■ Hand-painted ceramics of the Alentejo

ALENTEJO

Rural, unspoiled, blissfully empty, and full of breathtakingly big horizons, the Alentejo covers almost a third of Portugal, yet has barely one-tenth of its population. Here the pace slows palpably. Old ladies gossip in doorways, and old men gather on sunny benches or keep the bars in business. The sun bounces off whitewashed walls, and gnarled olive trees or cork oaks greet you around every corner.

Bordered to the north by the Tejo River (the name of the region derives from words meaning "beyond the Tejo"), to the south by the Algarve, and to the east by Spain, the Alentejo boasts a stunning Atlantic coastline, until recently barely exploited. Apart from the oil-refinery and port town of Sines, the Alentejo offers a succession of captivating small hill towns and villages, each one home to specific craft traditions and, more often than not, a medieval castle. Nor does history end there: On deserted hillsides animated only by sheep, you will find silent menhirs, dolmens, and cromlechs going back millennia.

Three District Capitals

The main interest radiates from three district capitals: Évora, Portalegre, and Beja. Évora lies at the center of high culture, both inside its walls and in nearby towns such as Estremoz, Vila Viçosa, and Elvas. Industrial Portalegre opens the way to some beautiful villages, to the Lusitanian horse stables of Alter do Chão, and to the Serra de São Mamede natural park, a wild, hilly region that is perfect for hiking. Dominating the plains to the south, Beja links up easily with seductive small towns such as Serpa and Mértola, as well as the protected natural park of the Guadiana Valley. And to the west are the beaches: endless stretches of sand alternating with dramatically high cliffs from where fearless anglers pitch their lines.

An asset of the region is the abundance of signposts and surprisingly good roads, making it possible to drive from north to south in under four hours, despite the lack

of major highways. Although the Spanish and Algarve borders are delineated by craggy hills, most of the Alentejo is composed of easily negotiated low-lying, rolling hills. Its villages are built for the intense summer heat: narrow streets lined with orange trees and low, white and saffron yellow or cobalt blue houses with tiny windows.

The cuisine features hearty lamb, pork, kid, chicken, and game conjured into delicious dishes with chickpeas, coriander, clams, and lashings of virgin olive oil. The smooth red wines made from Aragonês, Periquita, and Trincadeira grapes or the delicate, slightly tart whites of Roupeiro and Antão Vaz grapes are delicious. Today's winemaking methods are highly modernized, but a few small-scale producers still age wine in clay vessels, an ancient Alentejo tradition. ■

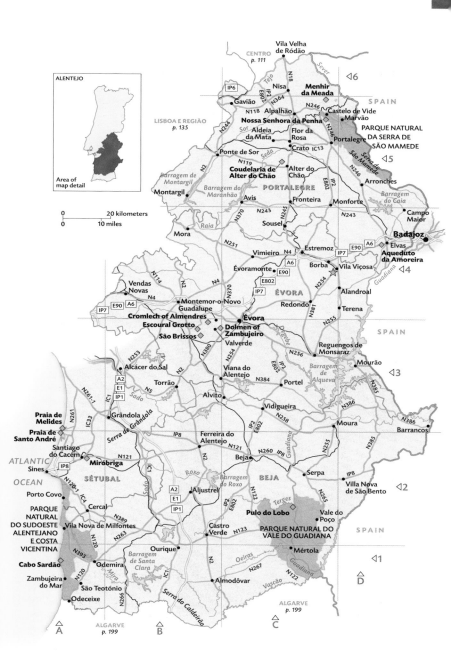

ÉVORA & AROUND

There is a distinctly aristocratic feel to Évora, the largest town in the Alentejo, whose population of 50,000-plus includes a large percentage of university students. Ringed by sturdy walls and topped by a cathedral towering above terraced houses, it is both unmistakable and beguiling.

Évora
🅰 175 C3
Visitor Information
✉ Praça do Giraldo
☎ 266 777 071
cm-evora.pt

The maze of cobbled streets seems to have no rhyme or reason: Square after square is doggedly asymmetrical, flowers spill over archways, and farms, convents, and modern apartment blocks nudge the outskirts. Around each corner there seems to be a mansion, a flamboyant church, or an exceptional structure. Many buildings date from Évora's Renaissance heyday.

■ Évora's impressive aqueduct, built in the 1530s, plays a curious multifunctional role.

Portugal's annexation by Spain in 1580 announced the end of Évora's glory and the beginning of a gentle decline. Yet restoration has done wonders and the entire town is now a World Heritage site. As a bonus, the nearby hills contain impressive megalithic sites, while Montemor-o-Novo and Évoramonte offer medieval castles drenched in atmosphere (see pp. 180–181). There are even a few bullfights in summer.

Évora's unusual urban pattern can be explained by the multiple layers of civilization, starting with the Romans. Then came the Moors, whose imprint is evident in the northern quarter, and finally the Portuguese rulers, who left an array of Gothic, Renaissance, Manueline, neoclassical, mannerist, and baroque architectural styles. The old Jewish quarter (bet. Rua dos Mercadores e Rua da Moeda) has its own distinctive layout. If you have a car, leave it outside the walls; parking spaces within are rare and the one-way streets a challenge.

The main hub is the triangular and arcaded **Praça do Giraldo,** a spot for relaxing and sipping a coffee by the 16th-century fountain and church of Santo Antão. This fountain and numerous others throughout the town draw water from the **Água da Prata** (silver water) aqueduct, which spans Rua do Cano, an unspoiled neighborhood well worth exploring in the northwest of town. The 1530s aqueduct was the work of Francisco de Arruda, of Torre de Belém fame (see p. 64).

Lower Évora

It is an easy walk downhill from Praça do Giraldo to lower Évora and the **Igreja de São Francisco** (*Praça 1° de Maio*). The church's Gothic-Manueline style dates from the years of Manuel I and João II; their royal emblems, an armillary sphere and pelican, respectively, decorate the large Manueline doorway. But the most famous site is inarguably the adjoining **Capela dos Ossos** (Bones Chapel; €). The Franciscans built this ossuary to induce meditative qualities among their brethren. Embedded in the walls and columns are the bones and skulls of some 5,000 people, collected from overflowing cemeteries, and—even more cheerful —two mummified corpses; in contrast, the ceiling is beautifully and delicately painted.

Recover from the ossuary on a shaded bench in the **Jardim Público** immediately south of the church. The restructured palace of Manuel I dominates this park.

Then stroll northwest past the shops and restaurants of the former Jewish quarter, cutting through to Rua Serpa Pinto to the **Convento de Santa Clara** (*tel 266 088 771, closed Sun.–Mon.*). This 1450s church and Franciscan convent was once home to the saintly princess Dona Joana. It boasts a superbly painted ceiling, carved wood, and decorative azulejos of the 16th and 17th centuries.

Upper Évora

Uphill from Praça do Giraldo you'll come to upper Évora and the main concentration of Évora's monuments and atmospheric backstreets. The twin towers of the fortress-like **Sé** (Cathedral; *tel 266 759 330*) reign over Évora. The transitional Romanesque-Gothic style of the Cathedral dates from the late 12th century, with subsequent additions including the impressive 14th-century stone Apostles adorning the main portal. The Cathedral proudly claims that the pennants of Vasco da

---

INSIDER TIP:

When you are in Évora, be sure to see the Bones Chapel. It's entirely covered with human skeletons from medieval times.

—MIGUEL CONDEÇO
Product manager, Cooltour Lx

Gama were blessed here in 1497, before his fleet set sail on its historic voyage to the East. The Cathedral's **cloister** and **treasury** (€), accessed via the south tower, are the main interest inside. The dazzling church plate, statuary, paintings, and heavily embroidered ecclesiastical robes show evidence of Évora's influential role in Portuguese history. The lovely 14th-century

■ Évora's 1,900-year-old Templo Romano was only unearthed a century ago.

Museu de Évora

⛰ Map p. 179

✉ Largo do Conde
de Vila Flor

☎ 266 730 480

🕐 Closed Mon.

💲 €

museudevora.pt

cloister boasts the tombs of four archbishops, and stairs in each corner spiral up to great views from the walls.

INSIDER TIP:

For the best food in Évora, book a table at O Fialho; it has been serving traditional food made from quality regional ingredients for three generations (see p. 252).

—EMMA ROWLEY
National Geographic *contributor*

Around the corner from the Sé you are confronted by the visual anomaly of the second-century **Templo Romano** (*Largo do Conde de Vila Flor*). It is also called the Templo de Diana, although there

is no proof that it was ever dedicated to this goddess; Jupiter is currently considered a contender. This ruin certainly tops any in Portugal. Encircled by structures that are some 1,400 years younger, it makes a moving site. The temple's granite Corinthian columns and their Estremoz marble capitals stand in surprisingly good condition, perhaps because the temple was converted into a medieval fortress and only exposed in the 19th century.

Évora's Roman past is also on show at the **Termas Romanas** (*tel 266 777 000, closed Sat.–Sun.*) inside the Câmara Municipal on Praça de Sertório. At the back of the lobby, a glazed wall overlooks the remains of Roman baths from the first century A.D.

Facing the Roman temple, the 16th-century **bishop's palace** houses the newly renovated **Museu de Évora.** Look in particular for Jean Pénicaud's beautiful "Passion Triptych" (1510–1540), an unusual work of enamel on copper; Francisco Henriques's large and expressive painting of "Prophet Daniel Releasing Chaste Suzanne" (1508–1512); and two lovely paintings by Josefa de Óbidos, which reveal her great feel for light. The exquisite marble tomb sculptures exemplify the quality craftsmanship of Évora in the 15th century.

Just next door, the former **Convento dos Lóios** dates from 1485 and is now the very elegant Pousada Convento de Évora (see p. 252). The **Igreja dos Lóios,** a private family church, stands a few doors away and serves as the pantheon for its owners, the Dukes of Cadaval. The breathtaking azulejos are the 1711 work of António de Oliveira Bernardes. Both the church and adjacent **Palace of the Dukes of Cadaval** are open to visitors *(tel 967 979 763, palaciocadaval.com, closed Mon., €)*. Wedged between the convent and church, the

Igreja dos Lóios & Palace of the Dukes of Cadaval

🗺 See below

✉ Largo do Conde de Vila Flor

☎ 967 979 763

🕐 Closed Mon.

💲 €

palaciocadaval.com

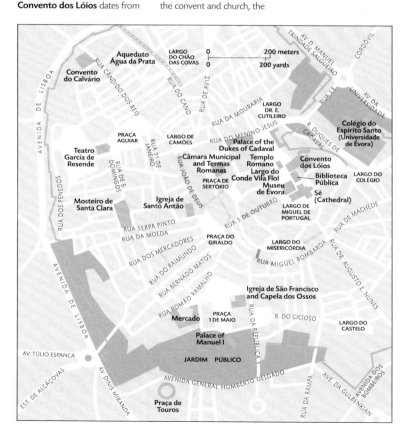

Évora's Environs
📍 175 B3–B4, C3

Escoural Grotto
📍 175 B3
✉ Herdade da Sala, Lugar da Fonte Nova, Montemor-o-Novo
☎ 266 857 000
💲 € (Tours Tues.–Sat.; reserve at least 24 hours ahead)

Biblioteca Pública, founded in 1805, protects a valuable collection of documents related to Portugal's age of discoveries.

Évora's Environs

Évora's surroundings offer a fascinating range of sites, from incredible megaliths studding the hills to the delightful towns of Montemor-o-Novo and Évoramonte.

Megaliths Tour: The entire north of the Alentejo region is peppered with Neolithic structures dating from between

EXPERIENCE: Évora's Megaliths by Bike

To experience firsthand the mysteries of prehistoric Alentejo, you need to get up close to its Neolithic megaliths and soak up the surrounding atmosphere. One of the best ways to visit the stones is by bike, quietly pedaling and enjoying the ancient ambience. **Bikeiberia** *(Largo Corpo Santo 5, Lisbon, tel 969 630 369 or 213 470 347, bikeiberia.com)* offers a one week guided tour *(€1900, 6 nights & 7 days)* that departs from Évora. The itinerary is moderately difficult with daily legs of 14 to 41 miles (23 to 66 km). There are stops along the route to admire archeological sites, olive groves, vineyards, forgotten villages, and breathtaking views.

Montemor-o-Novo
📍 175 B4
Visitor Information
✉ Largo Calouste Gulbenkian
☎ 266 898 103

cm-montemornovo.pt

4000 and 2000 B.C. The megaliths are open-air and access is not restricted. If you are short of time, limit yourself to the **Cromlech of Almendres.** Ten miles (16 km) west of Évora, the cromlech stands on a hillside of cork oaks just beyond the

village of Guadalupe. Ninety-five menhirs (vertical stones) form an oval that aligns with the equinoxes. If you are there alone, it is an extremely powerful site, made more so with the view of Évora on the plain below. A lone 8-foot-tall (2.5 m) menhir is signposted on the way up to the cromlech, hidden behind grain bins.

The **Dolmen of Zambujeiro,** near the village of Valverde, measures almost 20 feet (6 m) long, making the prehistoric monument the largest in Iberia. A last site on this trail is the unusual dolmen-chapel at **São Brissos.** If you're interested in even older history, visit the caves at **Escoural Grotto** *(advance reservations required),* a few miles west of the Zambujeiro dolmen. The cave paintings of animals are thought to date from 18,000 to 13,000 B.C.

Montemor-o-Novo: The town of Montemor-o-Novo lies a short distance northwest of the megaliths, yet tourists often mistakenly bypass it. The presence of Moorish kings, Christian knights, and Portuguese royalty is undeniable. The decisions to go on the voyages of discovery to India and to build the University of Coimbra were made in the palace here, the ruins of which are visible on the southern edge of the citadel that crowns the hill.

From the 13th through the 15th centuries, Montemor wielded enormous economic and religious sway, but from the 16th century on, the population moved downhill to create the "new" town. Visit the landscaped **citadel;** the 16th-century Dominican **Convento da Saudação** at the entrance serves as a residential workshop for performing artists.

A few worthwhile sites in the town below include the **Igreja Matriz** (*Largo São João de Deus, closed Mon.*). It and the adjoining 17th-century convent were built on the birthplace of St. John of God (1495–1550), a Franciscan who founded the Order of Brothers Hospitallers; his statue stands outside. An annex of the convent, the **Galeria Municipal** (*Terreiro de São João de Deus, closed Sat. a.m. & Sun.*) stages interesting exhibitions by young artists, as does a gallery in the **Convento de São Domingos** (*Largo Prof. Dr. Banha de Andrade, tel 266 890 235*).

Évoramonte: Some 19 miles (30 km) northeast of Évora, Évoramonte is really a castle with a village attached as an afterthought. Towering above the plains, the **Castelo de Évoramonte** (*tel 268 950 025, closed Mon.–Tues. a.m.*) has three floors and four corner towers seemingly held together with stone knots on each facade—odd, but typical of the House of Bragança, whose motto *Despois vós, nós* (After you, us) played with the second meaning of *nós:* "knots."

Built in 1531 after an earthquake devastated the original fortifications of Dom Dinis I, and based on a design by Diogo de Arruda, the new castle imitated the French château of Chambord.

Ninety-five menhirs form the magical Cromlech of Almendres, a site probably once used for ritual prayers and meetings.

Its Renaissance style contains a superb, empty interior of rib vaulting and sturdy columns topped by carved capitals. A tight spiral staircase linking the floors eventually brings you to a roof terrace once used for shooting practice. Today it is yet another of Portugal's perfect lookout points.

The main street beside the castle runs along the walled ridge to end at the 16th-century church of **Santa Maria,** whose impressive interior is only open during services. Have a look, too, at the local handicrafts displayed and sold at the tourist office. ∎

Évoramonte
🅰 175 C4
Visitor Information
✉ Rua de Santa Maria
☎ 268 959 227
🕐 Closed Mon.–Tues.

PORTUGAL'S SEPHARDIC JEWS

Portugal's Sephardic Jews played a significant role in the country's burgeoning economy and made major scientific and economic contributions that enabled the glorious discoveries of the 15th and 16th centuries. The word "Sefarad" is actually Hebrew for "Spain" and refers to the Jewish communities that flourished in the Iberian Peninsula for centuries, before their dissolution at the end of the 15th century.

The first records of Jewish presence in Portugal date from the late fifth century, when the Visigoths replaced Roman rule. From then on, this minority took root and by the 12th century Santarém had become home to the first national synagogue. Later, synagogues appeared in Porto, Viseu, Guarda, Torre de Moncorvo, Covilhã, Évora, and Faro. Wherever there were more than 10 Jews, a commune *(aljama)* was founded, centering

■ The 1460 synagogue of Tomar saw only a few years of use before the 1497 expulsion of Jews.

on a synagogue that served not only as a place for prayer but also as a mouthpiece for edicts by the king and by the head rabbi.

Portugal's Jewish community was encouraged to help the newfound nation in its struggle with its Moorish occupiers and populate the reconquered lands; however, the early 13th century saw the first friction between Jews and Catholics. Afonso II soon passed repressive legislation that forbade Jews to have Christian servants or to be appointed to official positions. Sancho II later scaled back this attempt to reduce the Jews' status, but complaints were made to the pope about such a "lax" approach. Under the enlightened Dom Dinis I

(1279–1325), the Sephardic communities were answerable to their head rabbi through representatives in each of their main centers.

Each community had a school and a Beth Hamidrash, where the scriptures were read and analyzed, as well as a Genesim for the study of the Torah. The community's livelihood came from medicine, handicrafts, and agriculture, but the Jewish community truly excelled in commerce, contributing greatly to the national economy but at the same time stirring up envy.

The Spanish Inquisition's Effect

Proof of their prosperity was the growing number of Jewish communities, which multiplied from about 30 in 1400 to more than 100 by the 1490s, with an estimated population of 30,000 (3 percent of the total population). The largest communities were in Lisbon, Évora, Santarém, and Covilhã. The rapid rise resulted from the influx of immigrants fleeing anti-Semitism in Spain. The last wave came in 1492, when the Spanish rulers Ferdinand and Isabel had completed their *reconquista*. The large Sephardic community in Spain was told to convert or go into exile, and 50,000 to 70,000 Jews fled across the border to Portugal.

Unfortunately, their sanctuary was short-lived. In 1497, in order to marry Isabel, daughter of the Spanish monarchs, Manuel I was forced to impose the same maxim as in Spain. Some Jews emigrated to the colonies and the rest were forcibly converted to Christianity (adopting surnames such as Cruz, Trindade, and Santos). In 1536 the situation worsened when João III allowed the Inquisition to be set up by papal edict; the first auto-da-fé took place four years later. Nearly five centuries on, a Crypto-Jewish community was discovered in Belmonte, still worshipping in secret after all those years. The last part of this sorry chapter of Portuguese history came in 1989, when President Mário Soares made a public apology to the Jewish people.

ESTREMOZ

Estremoz is arguably the Alentejo's most impressive fortified town, thanks to its massive Vauban-style walls and gateways. There are two sections: the older, walled quarter, and the more functional 17th- and 18th-century town below that nonetheless holds plenty of interest.

■ Panoramic views of the Alentejo are assured from Estremoz's 13th-century Torre das Três Coroas.

Estremoz

⛰ 175 C4

Visitor Information

✉ Rossio Marquês de Pombal

☎ 268 333 541

Try to reach the hilltop quarter by sunset to watch the colors paint the hills to the west, or alternatively, target Saturday morning, when the town's main square below welcomes a huge and colorful market. Estremoz is strikingly agricultural, increasingly involved in wine production with no fewer than 15 wineries now on its outskirts. It is also the largest of the Alentejo's three main marble-producing towns.

The Walled Town

The medieval quarter is dominated by the palace and castle, most of which is now a sumptuous inn, the Pousada Castelo Estremoz–Rainha Santa Isabel (see p. 251). Only the iconic machicolated keep, the **Torre das Três Coroas,** remains from the original medieval castle, which was blown up in 1698. Rebuilt, the castle was later sacked by the French army in 1808, but it remained standing. Legend says that the castle owes its survival to the protective ghost of the widow of Dom Dinis I, St. Isabel, who died here in 1336 and whose statue stands outside. Today you can admire the reception areas of the palatial pousada, which offers free access to the keep and its fabulous views. Do not miss the **Capela da Rainha Santa** (Queen Isabel's Chapel; *closed Mon.; get key from the Galeria de Desenho in the Museu Municipal*) tucked behind, where magnificent azulejos illustrate the life of the saintly queen.

Across the square, the **Museu Municipal** (*Largo Dom Dinis, tel 268 339 219, closed Mon., €*) is housed in a charming 16th-century building. Wide-ranging exhibits include rural artifacts, reconstructed period rooms, cork sculptures, and traditional clay figurines, some of which are miniature masterpieces. The terraces display architectural fragments, and a potter's workshop gives demonstrations. The prominent **Galeria Municipal Dom Dinis** (*Largo Dom Dinis, closed Mon.*), originally Dom Dinis's Audience Hall, sits on a corner of the square. Admire the carved Manueline capitals on the colonnaded porch and the striking clock tower before stepping inside to view the marble interior. Downhill from this cluster, a residential quarter houses a large Romany population. And halfway down the main street, look for a courtyard lined with raised, numbered doorways, once military barracks and evidence of the town's role in the intermittent wars with Spain.

Outside the Walls

It is a short walk or drive from the city walls down to the main square, the vast **Rossio Marquês de Pombal.** Flanked by trees, churches, and harmonious 17th- and 18th-century architecture, this social and commercial hub always harbors a few market stalls along its southern side. Vendors sell everything from local cheese to sheep- or goat-skin products, ceramics, sausages, and vegetables; they multiply greatly on Saturdays. The 17th-century **Igreja dos Congregados** towers over the market stalls. The church's blinding white

---

EXPERIENCE:
Visit a Local Winery

The Alentejo area is dotted with small-scale *adegas* (wineries) that you can visit, all on the Rota dos Vinhos (Alentejo Wine Route). A wonderful one in the Estremoz area is **J. Portugal Ramos** (*Vila Santa, Estremoz, tel 268 339 910, jportugalramos.com, closed Sun., €€–€€€€*), which offers a variety of tours and tastings, plus lunch and tapas (be sure to book in advance). You see the whole winemaking process, from grape pressing and fermentation to aging and bottling, then you are invited to try a selection of the estate wines. Tasting number 4 offers the broadest selection and includes some of the estate's finer wines. For information on other participating adegas on the wine route, visit *vinhosdoalentejo.pt*.

---

marble interior is accessible through the modest, upper-floor **Museu de Arte Sacra** (*tel 967 528 298, closed Mon., €*). You'll also be given access to the rooftop terrace; the 360-degree view takes in the baroque **Igreja de São Francisco** on the opposite side of the square. This church shows off more local marble and, above all, a Tree of Jesse of carved gilded wood to the left of the altar. ∎

VILA VIÇOSA & BORBA

Vila Viçosa and Borba are joined by the tradition and the spirit of marble, but beyond that they differ greatly. Vila Viçosa is a one-palace, one-castle town, while Borba, just a few miles distant, is a much more cheerful place—maybe it has something to do with the robust red wine it produces.

■ The Sala dos Duques and the rest of the royal palace at Vila Viçosa reflect a regal splendor.

Vila Viçosa
🏛 175 C4
Visitor Information
✉ Praça da República
☎ 268 881 101
cm-vilavicosa.pt

What Vila Viçosa shares with Borba is an abundance of marble; the 2.5 miles (4 km) between the two towns is one uninterrupted stretch of quarries. In Borba, door frames, wainscoting, and front steps of even humble dwellings are of the subtly veined white marble, while Vila Viçosa boasts more than 20 marble-clad churches.

Vila Viçosa

Vila Viçosa's famed **Paço Ducal** *(Terreiro do Paço, tel 268 980 659, closed Mon.–Tues. a.m., €€),* or Duke's Palace, could rival Versailles, albeit on a mini scale. The fourth Duke of Bragança commissioned the palace in 1501; the construction took more than a century, with further additions made once the Braganças acceded to the Portuguese throne in 1640. The result is a megafacade 360 feet (110 m) long, although it is surprisingly shallow. The 78 rooms once saw a stream of noble visitors, some coming to enjoy the *tapada* (hunting ground) across the road, others to watch bullfights on the huge square (Terreiro do Paço).

The penultimate king to live here, Carlos, left an indelible mark in dozens of accomplished paintings in postimpressionist style. Tragically, Carlos set off from the palace one February morning in 1908 never to return; he and his son, the crown prince, were assassinated later that day in Lisbon. His rooms remain relatively unchanged from when he lived here.

The obligatory one-hour guided tour of the palace is, for the moment, only in Portuguese (though some guides speak some English and are happy to explain a little); so to best grasp the sophistication of the Braganças consult the English catalog, which details the main features covered during the tour. The palace still contains a wealth of decorative arts, from Brussels and Gobelins tapestries to Venetian chandeliers, 17th-century frescoed ceilings, Chinese porcelain, Italian majolica, and Arraiolos and Persian carpets. The **Sala dos Duques** (Room of the Dukes) honors the dukes of Bragança: the Italian artist Giovanni Domenico Dupra painted 18 of their portraits on the ceiling.

One of the more revealing sections is the last addition made to the palace, the 1762 **new wing** of apartments. More intimately scaled, these rooms give a good idea of the monarchs' personal interests, whether Dom Carlos's wardrobe of uniforms or his wife Amélia's own drawings of botany and architecture. The **kitchens** are the final site on the tour. They gleam with copper pans once swung by no fewer than 26 chefs and sous-chefs, while still more attendants slaved in the pantry. Other tours take in the carriage museum, the impressive armory, and the porcelain collection.

You exit the palace grounds via the **Porta do Nó,** an interestingly carved marble and schist gateway that incorporates several knots, the symbol of the Braganças, into its design. Follow the main avenue south from the palace to reach the castle walls. Inside, a small community huddles up beside the 14th-century Gothic **Nossa Senhora da Conceição,** built on the ruins of the original church. Recently fully restored, the church is home to some rich azulejo panels. The **Museu de Caça e Arqueologia** (tel 268 980 128, closed Mon.–Tues. a.m., €), inside the castle complex, has an hour-long guided tour dedicated to hunting and archaeology.

To fully grasp the importance of marble to this region's history and economy, make a quick stop at the **Museu do Mármore Raquel de Castro** (Av. Duque D. Jaime, Olival da Gradinha, tel 268 889 310, closed Mon., €), located in a former train station on the northern edge of town. Photographs and three-dimensional models take you through the extraction and transformation process.

Borba

Borba's interest is far more prosaic. Once you have seen the main square, **Praça da República,** dominated by a huge marble fountain and overlooked by a modest town hall, head toward the castle turrets. Opposite them, a cobbled street leads uphill to the 16th-century church of **São Bartolomeu,** around which a handful of antiques and secondhand goods shops spill their wares. Borba's wine is now one of Portugal's best, celebrated during the wine festival held every November. The **Festa do Vinho e da Vinha** (Wine and Vineyard Festival) enlivens the little town for about 10 days with wine-related events, as well as with concerts and street artist performances ■

Borba
🗺 175 C4
Visitor Information
✉ Avenida 25 de Abril
☎ 268 891 630

PORTALEGRE & SERRA DE SÃO MAMEDE

Somewhat out on a limb, nudging both the Spanish border and that of the Beiras area, Portalegre is not on the main tourist circuit. It is, however, the gateway to the hills of São Mamede and to a number of offbeat villages in the Alentejo plains.

A lone watchtower projecting over the rock face of Marvão surveys the Serra de São Mamede.

Portalegre

175 C5

Visitor Information

Rua Guilherme Gomes Fernandes 22

245 307 445

Surrounded by vineyards that give way to oak and chestnut forests, Portalegre's most visible site from afar is not, for once, a castle or a cathedral, but the belching twin chimneys of a cork-processing factory founded in the 19th century. Historically, however, Portalegre's prosperity stemmed from textile manufacturing, and its international fame derived from its tapestries that vied with those of Aubusson.

The Robinson cork factory has been relocated to an industrial park on the outskirts of town, and the old factory and adjoining

Igreja de São Francisco have been restored. The factory, now **Museu Robinson** (*Rua D. Iria Gonçalves Pereira 2A, tel 245 307 532, fundacaorobinson.pt, closed Sat.– Sun.*), tells the story of cork and its importance to the region.

A strong drive for renewal is apparent throughout the town with work on the old town walls, renovating the castle, creating a regional crafts market, building underground parking lots, and more. At its heart, Portalegre has a rich history whose imprint is apparent in the baroque mansions within its walls, as well as a 16th-century **Sé** *(Praça do Município, closed Sun. p.m.–Mon.)* containing mannerist paintings. The Cathedral's facade, redone in the 18th century, is a fine example of baroque workmanship.

Across the road, the former seminary now houses the **Museu Municipal** *(Rua José Maria de Rosa, 245 307 525, closed Mon., €)* and its rich collection of religious and decorative arts: Look for the 15th-century Spanish pietà in carved wood, a rare 17th-century ebony tabernacle, and some striking Arraiolos rugs. From here, the pedestrianized Rua 19 de Junho, lined with baroque houses, runs southeast through the Porta de Alegrete to the **Praça da República,** an architecturally harmonious square filled with outdoor cafés. The castle is just north of here, but little remains.

Portalegre's unique cultural site lies downhill from the Sé at the **Museu da Tapeçaria,** honoring

Guy Fino, the cofounder of the town's tapestry revival in 1946. A personal docent guides you past looms, a wall of 1,150 different colors of wool (more than 5,000 are in fact used), and a chronological display of tapestries from 1947 (the earliest depicts the huntress Diana) to simpler, more graphic 1990s pieces by Lourdes Castro.

Around Portalegre

The bewitching village of **Crato** lies 21 miles (34 km) due west of Portalegre. Its historical significance dates from 1350, when it headquartered the powerful Order of the Knights Hospitaller (later the Order of Malta; see sidebar below), and its castle hosted two royal weddings (Manuel I and João III). Today the town is a sleepy but beautiful little place, all saffron yellow and white, with some stunning medieval, Manueline, and baroque architecture. All streets

Museu da Tapeçaria

✉ Rua da Figueira 9
☎ 245 307 530
🕐 Closed Mon.
💲 €

mtportalegre.pt

Crato
🗺 175 C5

Knights Hospitaller in Crato

Formed in 11th-century Jerusalem to protect pilgrims to the Holy Land, the Order of the Knights Hospitaller of St. John of Jerusalem became one of the most powerful political forces in Europe. Dislodged from Jerusalem and then Cyprus by Muslim forces, they eventually settled on the island of Malta in 1530. Their troubles did not end there; in 1565 the Ottoman Empire waged a bloody war against them in an aim to remove them from the Mediterranean. After huge loss of life, the Muslim forces retreated, allowing the knights to use their enormous wealth to rebuild their stronghold and regional influence.

Crato became home to the Portuguese branch of the Knights Hospitaller in 1340, when it was moved from the Porto area onto lands donated by Sancho II. Crato castle housed the order until 1356, when Prior Álvaro Gonçalves Pereira ordered the building of the Flor da Rosa palace-monastery, a mile (1.6 km) down the road. Its architecture is defensive, giving the appearance of a castle rather than a religious building; its cloister bears the cross of Malta, as the order later became known.

It is possible to spend the night in the imposing 14th-century monastery tower, as it is now home to the very comfortable Pousada Mosteiro do Crato (see p. 252).

Flor da Rosa

🅰 175 C5

Visitor Information

✉ Mosteiro de Santa Maria de Flor da Rosa

☎ 245 997 341

lead to the elegant **Praça do Município.** Here you'll find the **Museu Municipal do Crato** *(tel 245 990 115, cm-crato.pt, closed Mon., €),* housed in a handsome baroque mansion and focusing on megalithic artifacts (there are 72 sites nearby), Roman pieces,

near the village of Aldeia da Mata, and of **Penedos de São Miguel.** The last stop on this circuit, **Alter do Chão** is another noble village dominated by a castle, replete with ornate fountains and baroque mansions. Yet the main attraction is the world-famous stud farm of **Coudelaria de Alter** *(Tapada do Arneiro, tel 245 610 060, alterreal.pt, closed Mon., €€)* where Alter Real Lusitanian horses are bred and trained. An exhibit details the 250-plus-year history of the former royal stables. You can tour the stables, riding school, and falconry section.

EXPERIENCE:
Ballooning Over the Alentejo Plains

To fully appreciate the open plains of the Alentejo, take to the air. Whether skimming above the cork oaks and cattle or sailing silently above castles and whitewashed villages, there is no better way to get the Alentejo into true perspective. **Wind Passenger Ballooning** *(tel 243 660 006 or 927 585 536, windpassenger.pt)* offers year-round ballooning adventures from a variety of locations across the region, starting at €160 per person. **Emotion** *(tel 925 508 116, emotionportugal.com)* also offers balloon rides and other outdoor activities. Call or check websites for full details.

Alter do Chão

🅰 175 C5

Visitor Information

✉ Palácio do Álamo

☎ 245 610 004

Serra de São Mamede

🅰 175 D5

and the Order of Malta. Don't miss the picturesque ruins of a 13th- to 17th-century **castle** on Crato's eastern edge.

One mile (1.6 km) north of Crato, the satellite village of **Flor da Rosa** grew around its 14th-century fortified monastery. This massive construction stands in scenic isolation, with a couple of village streets curling round it, the interior now converted into the strikingly modern Pousada Mosteiro do Crato (see p. 252). From here, head 5 miles (8 km) due west to see the largest dolmens in the area, that of **Tapadão,**

Serra de São Mamede

Look north from Portalegre and you see the abrupt hills of the Serra de São Mamede, which rise to 3,000 feet (1,027 m). Much of the range lies protected as a 78,000-acre (31,750 ha) **natural park.** Hiking opportunities abound in this area; local tourist offices and the park headquarters in Portalegre *(Rua Augusto César de Oliveira Tavares, tel 245 309 189, natural.pt, closed Sat.–Sun.)* provide trail maps, and a number of overnight shelters *(casas abrigo)* dot the hills.

North, the population is scattered between farms, quintas (rural estate houses), enclosed tapadas (hunting grounds), and hamlets of two-story houses. In the more inhabited south, low, whitewashed dwellings alternate with the typical monte (estate) of the Alentejo. Visitors generally target the small town of Castelo de Vide, straddling a ridge, and the village of Marvão, just 6 miles (10 km) away.

Castelo de Vide, with its castle ruins, web of idyllic flowery, cobbled streets, and majestic main square, is the more charming of the two since it has a life outside tourism. There is little specific interest in the main church, **Santa Maria da Devesa** (1749), but follow Rua Santa Maria uphill to enter the castle walls and a delightful maze of medieval streets. On exiting the walls, follow steps and picturesque alleys into the **Judiaria,** the old Jewish quarter, centered on the Rua da Fonte. On the corner is a tiny two-room synagogue thought to date from the 15th century. At the bottom of the hill, look for the elaborate Manueline fountain with its raised roof and endless supply of pure mineral water.

Megalith aficionados should head north to see the largest known menhir in the Iberian Peninsula, the 23-foot-tall (7 m) **Menir da Meada.** Another short excursion south leads to **Nossa Senhora da Penha,** a hilltop sanctuary with fabulous views north over Castelo de Vide.

To the east lies **Marvão,** named after a ninth-century Moorish horseman, Ibn Maruan. This extraordinary village seems to grow out of the granite outcrop. True walkers should take the ancient paved path to the summit, while lesser mortals can drive up to the gateway (it is possible to drive in, but best to utilize the carpark outside the walls). The medieval citadel, a stronghold that guarded the region against Spanish attacks, is so complete that it is classed as a World Heritage site; however, the population has dwindled to a mere 180 souls, leaving Marvão with a distinctly artificial "museum" atmosphere.

Wander the town's narrow streets and alleyways to enjoy Renaissance doorways, wrought-iron grilles, and Manueline windows. Don't miss the undeniably beautiful pillory before heading uphill to the **castle,** which has magnificent views in every direction. A Gothic church on the Largo de Santa Maria houses the **Museu Municipal** *(tel 245 909 132, €),* which exhibits a motley collection of statues, a 14th-century fresco, historical costumes, and a Roman skeleton from excavations at nearby Pombais. ∎

Castelo de Vide
⌖ 175 C5
Visitor Information
✉ Praça Dom Pedro V
☎ 245 908 227
castelodevide.pt

Marvão
⌖ 175 D5
Visitor Information
✉ Largo da Silveirinha
☎ 245 909 131

Hillside Offerings

The Serra de São Mamede offers an incredibly diverse range of plants and wildlife because it bridges two ecological zones: Atlantic and Mediterranean. The terrain of quartzite, limestone, schist, and granite supports some 800 plants, including oaks, chestnuts, cork oaks, olive trees, and rare mosses and lichens. There are no great rarities among the serra's wildlife, but more than half of Portugal's nesting birds, including the eagle owl, Bonelli's eagle, several vulture species, and the great bustard, are found here. Also seen are Europe's largest bat colony and endemic Iberian species such as Bosca's newt, the Iberian midwife toad, and Schreiber's green lizard. You may also spot the odd fox, red deer, storks (white and black), genets, otters, wild boars, and Egyptian mongooses.

DRIVE TO THE GUADIANA VALLEY

From the marble quarries of Vila Viçosa, this drive takes you through the historical villages, olive groves, and grainfields of the central Alentejo to reach Europe's largest artificial lake, Lago Alqueva, in the Guadiana Valley.

Cork oaks and olive trees stud the banks of Lago Alqueva, Europe's largest artificial lake.

From **Vila Viçosa** ❶ (see pp. 186–187) follow directions south to Alandroal, leaving town on the N255. After some marble quarries, the road slices through undulating olive groves for 16 miles (25 km) until an unannounced turnoff on the left to **Alandroal** ❷ (*visitor information, tel 268 440 045*); be prepared for it. As you drive into town you will see the 13th-century **castle** on your right. Park at a square in front of the raised entrance where an 18th-century marble fountain cools the air. Walk in to enjoy the atmosphere of this towering but empty structure, built for the Order of Avis. Nearby shops specialize in tin, wood, and schist handicrafts.

Leave via the corner diametrically opposite the arch, following a sign to **Terena** ❸ (sometimes referred to as Terena de São Pedro). Stay on the N255 for 17 miles (28 km), winding

NOT TO BE MISSED:

Terena • Menir do Outeiro • Monsaraz • Lago Alqueva

through open landscapes where only sheep and shepherds dwell. Soon the silhouette of Terena's castle appears on the horizon. Turn left at the sign and drive up to the immaculate village of whitewashed houses, where two main streets run parallel to end at the **castle square.** Wander around the grassy quadrangle inside the castle walls; climb to the ramparts for views and the faint echoes of sheep bells.

Return to the N255, passing the fortified, stone sanctuary of **Nossa Senhora da Boa Nova,** thought to date from the early 14th century. After about 6 miles (10 km) on the

N255, follow a sign for Monsaraz left through the hamlet of **Aldeia da Venda,** after which the road follows the contours of the hillside with distant vistas east and north through olive and eucalyptus groves. The road eventually runs through the typical whitewashed village of Motrinos. From here follow signs left to Monsaraz. After a couple of miles you will see a sign for *"anta"* (dolmen). This short circuit takes you to three impressive megaliths, including Europe's most notable phallic menhir, the **Menir do Outeiro ❹**, that of **Belhoa,** and the dolmen of **Olival da Pega.** The circuit takes little more than 20 minutes and ends at Telheiro, at the base of **Monsaraz ❺.**

Drive up to this hilltop village, following signs until you can park. In peak season this may be some distance from the main gateway; Monsaraz is a very popular Alentejo destination. This stunning walled enclave, closed to cars, features cobbled alleyways, elegant facades, a ruined castle, numerous craft shops, and the church of Santa Maria da Lagoa. The tiny **Museu de Arte Sacra** *(tel 266 508 040)* beside the church displays a 14th-century fresco.

Leave Monsaraz by following signs to Mourão, which take you down to the N256. This road crosses the Guadiana River where it merges with the 96-square-mile (250 sq km) **Lago Alqueva ❻**. Continue to follow signs to **Mourão ❼.** This small fortified town boasts a 17th-century church set into the walls of its castle where, again, the interior has been left to the elements.

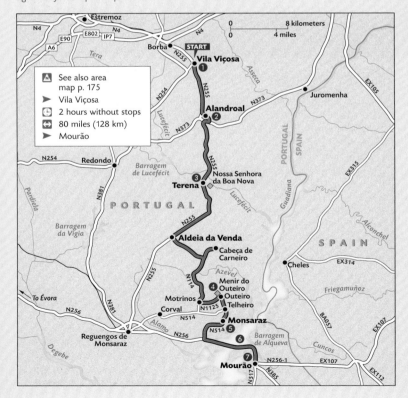

BEJA, SERPA, & MOURA

The three fortified towns of Beja, Serpa, and Moura in the plains of southern Alentejo make an obvious triangular tour. All have great historical impact, medieval fortifications courtesy of Dom Dinis, and varying degrees of character.

■ The crenellated walls and towers of Beja's splendid castle

Beja
🏰 175 C2
Visitor Information
✉ Castelo de Beja, Largo Dr. Lima Faleiro
☎ 284 311 913

Serpa
🏰 175 C2
Visitor Information
✉ Rua dos Cavalos 19
☎ 284 544 727

Beja

The principal town of southern Alentejo, with 20,000 inhabitants, Beja towers above the agricultural plains, visible from some 20 miles (32 km) away. The town boasts a well-maintained old quarter and a massive, restored **castelo,** featuring a 138-foot-high (42 m) keep, the tallest in the Iberian Peninsula, which you can climb for sweeping views. Just opposite, Beja's oldest church, Santo Amaro, houses the **Núcleo Visigótico** (*Largo de Santo Amaro, tel 284 321 465, closed Sun., €*), an informative display of rare fragments from the seventh and eighth centuries. The same square sees Beja's lively fair on the first Saturday of every month—a good

place to pick up a live rabbit or chicken.

Your ticket to the Visigothic exhibit also gives access to the **Museu Regional** (*Largo de Nossa Senhora da Conceição, tel 284 323 351, closed Mon., €*), located in a magnificent 1459 Gothic-Manueline convent. It stands dramatically alone on a large square south of the elegant **Praça da República,** Beja's historic heart. A dazzling array of wall tiles, including 16th-century Mudejar designs, line the cloister galleries and the chapter house; the latter's ceiling is painted in delicate tempera designs. The full-length "São Vicente," by Mestre do Sardoal, hangs next to an anonymous painting of St. Vincent's martyrdom in a room devoted to 16th- and 17th-century paintings.

Serpa

Small Serpa, 19 miles (30 km) east of Beja, has a greater atmosphere than Beja and feels engagingly forward looking. The crenellated walls enclose narrow cobbled streets, churches, mansions, and some good restaurants. Park your car outside the town walls and take a look at the gnarled, thousand-year-old olive trees before heading to the main square, **Praça da República,** and its outdoor cafés. Its **Torre do**

Relógio (Clock Tower) looms over a wide staircase leading up to the church of Santa Maria and the **castelo**. A small **Museu Arqueológico** (tel 284 544 663, closed Mon.) displays artifacts from the Stone Age to Roman and Moorish times. This upper part of town harbors a web of picturesque narrow lanes as well as the town's most grandiose mansion, the 17th-century **Palácio do Conde do Ficalho** (closed to the public).

South of the square at the clock museum, **Museu do Relógio** (Rua do Assento, tel 284 543 194, museodorelogio.com, closed Mon., €), guided tours take you through rooms crammed with 1,100 watches and clocks. The waterwheel and aqueduct on the Rua dos Arcos, on the western side of the town walls, are worth a look as well. Before you leave, be sure to sample Serpa's famous sheep cheese, *queijadas* (cheesecakes), and robust Pias wine.

Moura

Far less sophisticated, Moura, 19 miles (30 km) north of Serpa, has strong Moorish connections and highly rated olive oil and mineral water. Its name stems from the legend of a Moorish bride-to-be who let Christian hordes through the town gates under the mistaken impression that her fiancé was among them. The result? Her suicide from a turret. The most you will see of this past is the **Poço Árabe,** a 14th-century well (Largo da Mouraria, tel 285 253 978, closed Mon.) in the **Mouraria** (Moorish quarter), a web of streets south of the castle. The dilapidated **castle** was erected on the site of a Moorish fort, of which one lathe-and-plaster tower remains. ■

Moura

🗺 175 C3

Visitor Information

✉ Moura Castle, Largo de Santa Clara, Pátio dos Rolins

☎ 285 251 375 or 285 250 400

EXPERIENCE: Alentejo Pottery Workshops

While in the Alentejo, try your hand at one of the region's distinctive crafts: pottery. Most regions in Portugal produce their own distinctive designs using locally found materials and methods passed down through the generations. The *oleiros* (potters) of the Alentejo have for centuries made rough, utilitarian pieces from local clay; these earthenware pieces would rarely be decorated or even glazed. As demand for the rustic cooking pot declined, many *olarias* (potteries) simply went out of business, while others adapted and began producing more elaborate pieces using colored glazes to depict the bright floral or fruit designs that are now found across the region.

You can experience an olaria firsthand by signing up for a half-day pottery workshop with **Rotas do Fresco** (Rua 5 de Outubro 20, Vila Nova de Baronia, Alvito, tel 284 475 413 or 911 158 698, rotas compadres.pt, minimum of 4 people, €€€€€), north of Beja. After a brief demonstration, you'll spend the first hour and a half making your own pot using local clay and a traditional, foot-powered wheel. Your pot is then fired and can either be collected the next day or (time permitting) posted to your hotel. During the second half of the workshop you get the chance to demonstrate your decorative skills painting a ready-made piece, which you can take away with you.

ALENTEJO'S COAST

A blissful stretch of semiwild beaches and cliffs edged by a capricious ocean, the Alentejo coast—known locally as the Costa Vicentina—extends some 62 miles (100 km) from the Sado Estuary south to Odeceixe, on the Algarve border. A handful of villages provide services.

Striated rocks and cliffs create vertiginous lookout points, such as at Cabo Sardão.

Alentejo coast
📖 175 A1–A3

Santiago do Cacém
📖 175 A2
Visitor Information
✉ Parque da
   Quinta do
   Chafariz
☎ 269 826 696
🕐 Closed Sun.

**turismo.cm
-santiagocacem.pt**

The lone blemish on the coast is the halfway point of Sines with its petrochemical installations and large shipping port. Otherwise, only low-key villages punctuate the sandy beaches north of Sines and the dramatically chiseled cliffs and coves to the south, protected as far as Sagres as part of the **Parque Natural do Sudoeste Alentejano e Costa Vicentina** (*tel 283 322 735, natural.pt*). To some, the year-round cold water, a constant wind blowing off the Atlantic, and limited facilities are a downside, but a growing number of chic guesthouses cater to

those who relish these aspects. Rice fields and salt marshes characterize the landscapes around **Alcácer do Sal,** a pretty riverside town famous for its storks and their vertiginous nests. Southwest of here lie the lagoons and beaches of **Melides** and **Santo André,** both rich in birdlife and offering good windsurfing and fishing. A strip of fine white sand between the lagoon and the sea invites breezy, scenic strolls, and a cluster of modest fish restaurants offers the local specialty, eel stew.

South of here and inland, scenic **Santiago do Cacém** is

one of the Alentejo's fortified hilltop towns; it was named for the Order of Santiago, which controlled it from 1336 to 1594. The town makes a good base for access to the coast.

Sites in town start at the lively **food market** (*Mercado Municipal, Largo do Mercado, closed Sun.*), where you can stock up on delicious local products. From here it is a steep walk up attractive cobbled streets to the castle. At the gates is the **Igreja Matriz** (*closed Mon.–Tues.*), a lovely church with a theatrical baroque interior. Walk around the castle walls. Below, on the main square, the **Museu Municipal** is housed in the old city jail and displays local ethnographic and archaeological pieces beside some fine antiques.

INSIDER TIP:

In autumn the Sagres Peninsula and southern Alentejo coast become a mecca for birdwatchers. You may see up to 2,000 Eurasian griffon vultures at once!

—SIMON WATES
Owner, Algarve Birdwatching

The Roman site of **Miróbriga** lies in the hills about a mile (1.6 km) to the east. Boasting a small, modern museum, it is a lovely rural spot for sitting in the shade of cypress trees, watching sheep and musing on the Roman past. The first- and second-century ruins include the foundations of

Badoca Safari Park

If you're looking for a fun family outing, check out Badoca Safari Park *(Herdade da Badoca, Vila Nova de Santo André, tel 269 708 850, badoca.com, €€€€),* 10 minutes from Santiago do Cacém. The park offers activities and attractions for all ages, including a one-hour safari ride in tractor-pulled trailers to observe giraffes, zebras, and gnus; a Tropical Forest area, filled with exotic birds; an interactive lemur sanctuary; and an adventure area complete with a wild rafting ride and 23-foot (7 m) trampolines.

baths, a forum with a temple to Venus, and villas. Portugal's only Roman hippodrome, where Lusitanian horses once raced, is half a mile (0.8 km) away.

South of Sines

The coast south of Sines, part of the natural park, joins the Algarve's Costa Vicentina (see p. 218). Although cliffs dominate the landscape, there are idyllic coves and beaches in between, served by three low-key resorts. One, **Vila Nova de Milfontes,** in season has an upbeat feel plus a long causeway and a small ivy-clad castle, now an upscale guesthouse.

Farther south is the dramatic headland of **Cabo Sardão** and its lighthouse. Follow the dirt road to the top of the cliff and look down the sheer drop to the pounding surf below. Another 8 miles (13 km) south brings you to **Zambujeira do Mar,** a little resort overlooking a lovely beach backed by cliffs. A breath-stopping clifftop path leads south to more wild beaches inaccessible by car. ∎

Museu Municipal
- ✉ Praça do Município, Santiago do Cacém
- ☎ 269 827 375
- 🕐 Closed Sun.–Mon.

Ruínas Romanas de Miróbriga
- ✉ Cumeadas, Santiago do Cacém
- ☎ 269 818 460
- 🕐 Closed Mon.
- 💲 €

Vila Nova de Milfontes
- 🅰 175 A2
- **Visitor Information**
- ✉ Rua António Mantas
- ☎ 283 996 599

More Places to Visit in the Alentejo

Elvas

This handsome town lies just 8 miles (12 km) from the Spanish town of Badajoz. You cannot miss the impressive 17th-century fortifications, which include two hilltop forts north and south of the massive curtain walls, nor the **Aqueduto da Amoreira,** built between 1529 and 1622. At the heart of Elvas is the harmonious **Praça da República,** a square overlooked by a cathedral whose exterior was altered from its original 18th-century Manueline design. Uphill from here is the old Arab quarter; be sure to see the **Largo de Santa Clara** with its elaborate marble pillory. Beyond is the medieval **castelo** *(tel 268 626 403, closed Sun.–Mon., €),* a castle built by

■ The ambitious aqueduct of Elvas was financed by Portugal's first royal water tax.

Dom Sancho and remodeled in the 15th century, now housing a small military museum. The architecture of the town's attractive maze of cobbled streets, archways, emblazoned facades, and stairways gives a strong sense of the progression from Moorish citadel to medieval bastion and 17th-century stronghold. This last period of development is more visible in the southern part of town. 🅰 175 D4 **Visitor Information** ✉ Praça da República 2 ☎ 268 622 236

Mértola

Mértola is the last outpost of southeastern Alentejo before the hills of the Algarve. It is a fascinating little town, with handicraft workshops (notably weaving, ceramics, and jewelry) and Roman and Moorish remains. Idyllically sited on the Guadiana River, Mértola's historic nucleus lies around a restored **castelo,** where a towering keep exhibits Visigothic artifacts *(closed Mon.).* Just below, archaeological excavations are revealing significant Roman finds. The adjacent church of **Igreja de Nossa Senhora da Anunciação** *(closed Mon., guided tours through tourist office)* was a former mosque; horseshoe arches and the former mihrab are still intact. Down by the river stands Mértola's oldest site, the **Torre do Rio,** a tower built during the Roman era to defend the river port. On the street above, the **Museu de Mértola–Arte Islâmica** *(closed Mon.)* presents an impressive display of Moorish ceramics and gravestones; note the brick cupola made by Moroccan artisans in 2002. Mértola is a good base for canoeing, cycling, and horseback riding; wild boar features on many restaurant menus. *visitmertola.pt* 🅰 175 C1 **Visitor Information** ✉ Rua da Igreja 1 ☎ 286 610 100

Pulo do Lobo

This extraordinary gorge and waterfall in the **Parque Natural do Vale do Guadiana** is well signposted and reached via an easy 10-mile (16 km) dirt road, west from the village of Vale do Poço on the N265, or from the N122 connecting Beja and Mértola. The deserted landscape fosters black storks, Bonelli's eagles, and royal owls, and the fragrant shrubs are rich in myrtle and rosemary. The 44-foot (13.5 m) fall in the riverbed, known as the *corredoira* (runner), probably was created by erosion and drops in sea level during the Quaternary period. *natural.pt* 🅰 175 C2

Portugal's favorite playground, with lovely beaches, great golf courses, and buzzing nightclubs along the southern coast

ALGARVE

Sardines, an Algarve staple, usually grilled

ALGARVE

The name Algarve derives from the Arabic *Al-Gharb,* meaning "the west," pointing to the roots of Portugal's southernmost region, once the Moors' western outpost. A thousand years on, a wall of tourist development extending from Faro west to the beaches of Lagos obscures that past. Yet inland, you will discover delightful swathes of unspoiled landscapes.

Geographically important due to its position near the Mediterranean and the Atlantic, the Algarve was successively fought over by Phoenicians, Romans, Moors, and Christians, today replaced by armies of sunseekers. Portuguese boats set sail on 15th-century voyages of discovery from the port of Lagos, while Sagres remains symbolic as the purported site of Prince Henry's school of navigation. Few buildings remain from before the 1755 earthquake; the epicenter lay 125 miles (200 km) southwest of Cabo de São Vicente.

Every summer, the Algarve's population swells from some 350,000 to more than 1,000,000; nearly half of all visitors to Portugal

head straight to this coast. The unfailing lure boils down to three essentials: a sunny year-round climate, beautiful sandy beaches, and scenic golf courses. In addition, some of Portugal's top restaurants cater to a sophisticated cosmopolitan clientele. Faro, where the recently upgraded airport is located, constitutes the mid-way point between the more low-key eastern Algarve and the brasher, package-holiday heaven around Albufeira. Faro, too, is where you will get your first glimpse of the lagoons and islets of the Parque Natural da Ria Formosa. Toward the eastern end of this park lies the charming town of Tavira, one of the region's best kept secrets with plentiful offerings from history and

gastronomy to peaceful island beaches. In the far west, the Costa Vicentina is home to some of Europe's most spectacular beaches and is frequented mainly by surfers and campers.

The low, undulating *serra* (hills) to the north and east remains scenic. Between the serra and coast lies the intermediary band known as the Barrocal—the true agricultural heart of the Algarve. Local market stalls brim with cherries, strawberries, and melons in summer and grapes, figs, and almonds in fall.

You cannot really go wrong here in your choice of food, as the Moors' legacy reveals itself in local cuisine. Try the delicious *bolinhos de amêndoa* (small marzipan cakes). Sardines and tuna have long been favorites from the deep; clams and other shellfish are steamed in the ubiquitous *cataplanas* (copper pans with domed lids) or stewed with rice. In the hills, pork and poultry enter the menu, joined in autumn by hare soup and stewed partridge. Choose a wine from one of the vineyards near Lagoa, Lagos, Tavira, or Portimão. They produce fruity, full-bodied wines, continuing a

tradition developed by the Phoenicians, and expanded upon by the Romans.

Algarve's cornucopia of attractions for the mind, body, and spirit will certainly please even the most discerning visitor. ■

NOT TO BE MISSED:

The wealth of birdlife in the lagoons of the Ria Formosa   202

Eating grilled sardines riverside in Portimão   205

Picking up a memento from Loulé market   207–208

A day at the spa in Monchique   211

Playing a round of golf at a top course   212–213

Watching the sunset from Cabo de São Vicente   217

FARO & COASTAL ALGARVE

Centered on the southern coast of the Algarve, Faro is the point of arrival for most visitors. To the east lie the low-key towns of Olhão and Tavira, while west as far as Lagos is a succession of idyllic beaches backed by burgeoning development.

Coastal Algarve

🅰 200–201 B1–F2

Visitor Information

✉ Avenida 5 de Outubro 18–20, Faro

☎ 289 800 400

visitalgarve.pt

The Faro airport lies a short distance from town, right beside the lagoons, salt pans, and sandbank islands that characterize the eastern half of the Algarve. Protected as **Parque Natural da Ria Formosa** *(natural.pt),* they extend some 30 miles (48 km) northeast to beyond Tavira.

This important habitat for birds claims the least tern and purple gallinule among its rarities, as well as more common waterbirds. Some of the Algarve's quietest beaches are found on the *ilhas* (islands) off Faro and Tavira. To the west the shoreline heaves with high-rises and holiday developments; and yet the beauty of the ocher cliffs and white sandy beaches remains undiminished. Albufeira is the hub of this stretch.

Faro

Faro has an attractive historic center that, apart from a diabolical one-way road system common to many Portuguese towns, is user-friendly. Known as Ossonoba in pre-Roman days, Faro was once one of southern Portugal's most important settlements. It was much developed in the eighth century by the Moors, integrated into Portugal in 1249, and declared capital of the Algarve in the mid-1800s.

Enter the walled **Vila-Adentro** (Inner Town) from the north through the **Arco da Vila,** a monumental gateway added in 1812. This brings you past 19th-century government buildings to the impressive **Largo da Sé,** dominated by the **Sé** *(tel 289 806 632 or 289 823 018, closed Sat. p.m.–Sun., €).* Only the bell tower

■ Idyllic beaches line the Algarve coast.

and main entrance remain from the original 1251 church, thanks to pillaging by English troops in 1596 and the earthquake in 1755. Look at the azulejos and baroque retable, and then climb the bell tower for fabulous views. The curious shrine across the courtyard dates from before the earthquake; this

INSIDER TIP:

From Faro, hop a boat to Ilha Deserta for flamingos. Before you head off, be sure to look for the nest of Faro's pet pelican just inside the old walled city's main entrance.

—JOHNNA RIZZO
National Geographic contributor

area was a children's cemetery and the entire structure was constructed from skulls and bones. The peaceful walled quarter ends to the south at defensive ramparts built by ninth-century Arab ruler Ben Bekr, with towers added three centuries later. To the northeast lies the old *mouraria* (Arab quarter) and a network of pedestrianized shopping streets centered on Rua de Santo António.

East of Faro

From Faro to Olhão, lagoons and islands edge the coastline. The popular beaches of **Ilha da Culatra** and **Ilha da Armona** can be reached by boat from Olhão.

Olhão: This town is a bit of an anomaly—far from being a beach resort, it's the region's largest fishing port, complete with trawlers, canning factories, and a lively fish market. It has an attractive, bustling air about it, and the pedestrian streets behind the harbor are a joy to wander. Lined with picturesque, peeling facades of both humble and aristocratic buildings, these cobbled streets start at the modest 17th-century parish church on Avenida da República and end at the **Mercado Municipal** (City Market) on the waterfront, where vendors at the morning fish market hawk a fantastic array of creatures. Beside the market, the verdant grounds of the **Jardim Patrão Joaquim Lopes** host Olhão's main festival of seafood and folk music during the second week of August.

Tavira: The last stop east is Tavira, arguably the Algarve's most unspoiled town. The Romans developed their fish-salting industry here, and later Tavira flourished under Moorish rule; in the 15th century, it was the chief port for supporting Portuguese overseas garrisons. This led to city status, in 1520. Decline followed in the 17th and 18th centuries, due in part to the silting of the sea channel, plague outbreaks, and the 1755 earthquake. Tuna fishing and canning again revived Tavira's fortunes, and recently it began dabbling in tourism. *Flor de sal* (salt flakes) is another local industry; the flakes are obtained

Faro
201 D1
Visitor Information
Rua da Misericórdia 8–11
289 803 604

Olhão
201 E1
Visitor Information
Largo Sebastião Martins Mestre 6A
289 713 936

Tavira
201 F2
Visitor Information
Praça da República 5
281 322 511

■ Dusk falls over the tiled roofs of Albufeira's whitewashed cubic houses.

by skimming off young crystals from the salt pans between May and October. The rest of the year ordinary salt is farmed.

Despite the town's attractive Mediterranean-style architecture along the Gilão River, Tavira has successfully escaped major development. It strives to achieve status as the Algarve's cultural hub through exhibitions, concerts, and innovative structures. The palm-lined river frontage—with two central bridges, one of which is originally Roman, fishing boats, and low whitewashed houses—is a classic picture-postcard scene. And there are plenty of outdoor cafés from which to enjoy the view.

Towering above is the hilltop **castelo,** originally Moorish and rebuilt by Dom Dinis. The castle interior blooms with ficus, hibiscus, and bougainvillea, and the top affords panoramic views. On the way up from Rua da Liberdade, you pass the church of the

Misericórdia *(Travessa da Fonte, Rua da Galeria, closed Sun.)* with its beautiful Renaissance facade by André Pilarte, the master mason who also worked on Lisbon's Jerónimos monastery (see pp. 60–64). Inside, look at the statues and gilded retable of the main altar. Just past the church, the **Museu Islámico** *(tel 281 320 540, closed Sun.–Mon., €)* gives insight into Tavira's Islamic past. At the top of Rua da Galeria, stop to see the **Palácio da Galeria** *(tel 281 320 540, closed Sun.–Mon., €)* and its exhibitions of contemporary art.

Beside the castle stands the Gothic church of **Santa Maria** *(closed Sat. p.m.–Sun.),* dating from the 13th century but much altered since, and with huge external clocks defying all sense of proportion. Another of Tavira's numerous churches is **Igreja de Santiago,** immediately downhill from Santa Maria. It was built on a former mosque and is home to some valuable baroque statues. Just behind the church a rare camera obscura is installed inside an old water tower: the **Torre de Tavira.** *(Calçada da Galeria 12, tel 281 322 527, torredetavira.com, closed Sat.–Sun., €).* It offers a 15-minute journey through Tavira in real time, giving a fascinating overview.

West of Faro

Some 25 miles (40 km) west of Faro, **Albufeira** is Portugal's most popular package resort town; it is submerged in a sea of development as well as a bewildering network of roads. Despite souvenir shops, bar signs in English and German, and roaming packs of sunburned revelers, the old part of Albufeira to the west maintains some character, with narrow streets of whitewashed houses perched above the beach. The surrounding hills are alive with chaotic vacation apartments, while the modern eastern extension, **Montechoro,** is dedicated to eating, drinking, and entertainment.

The entire seafront is pedestrianized, so you can stroll from one beach to the next. **Praia dos Pescadores,** fronting the old town, provides a whiff of Albufeira's past in colorful, painted fishing boats. Immediately west, **Praia do Peneco** is often jam-packed with sunbathers, but venture beyond to **Praia da Galé,** or east to **Praia da Oura** and **Olhos de Água,** and you come to vast stretches of sand and pretty coves that are far less crowded. Most of the Algarve's golf courses concentrate between

Praia da Oura and Faro, notably at **Vilamoura.**

The most photographed beach, **Praia da Rocha,** lies farther west, due south of **Portimão,** whose only claim to fame is sardines (see sidebar below). This beach kicked off tourism in the Algarve in the 1950s and 1960s, drawing crowds to its very scenic red-ocher cliffs, craggy outcrops, and clear water. Today the central thoroughfare, Avenida Tomas Cabreira, is lined with tourist

facilities, and a ruined **fort** at the mouth of the Arade River now overlooks a marina. **Carvoeiro,** 3 miles (5 km) south of Lagoa, is yet another picturesque fishing village on a cliff-backed cove that has seen a recent radical transformation. Immediately east is **Algar Seco,** a popular beauty spot of eroded cliffs and extraordinary rock formations. ∎

Albufeira

◭ 200 C1

Visitor Information

✉ Rua 5 de Outubro

☎ 289 585 279

Praia da Rocha

◭ 200 B1

Visitor Information

✉ Avenida Tomas Cabreira

☎ 282 419 132

Sardines

Grilled sardines, one of Portugal's most typical dishes, can be found in any coastal town between May and October; however, many would argue that the best place to eat sardines is riverside in Portimão. So famous is Portimão for its grilled sardines that in 1994 it staged a Sardine Festival, now a firm fixture on its annual calendar. For a week in August, the Zona Ribeirinha (riverbank area) serves over 80,000 visitors grilled sardines with a hunk of bread, roasted green-pepper salad, and a jug of wine. Stalls sell local delicacies and crafts and the evenings feature live music and dancing. For more information, contact the Portimão Tourist Office *(tel 282 430 165).*

EXPERIENCE: Follow the Cork Route

As you travel around central and southern Portugal, you'll see acres upon acres of the cork oak—*Quercus suber*. The cultivation of this evergreen tree has been of vital importance to the national economy for centuries. Immerse yourself in the heritage and tradition of cork by spending a day with **Algarve Rotas** (*Eco-Cork Factory, Sítio da Mesquita Baixa, São Brás de Alportel, tel 965 561 166, algarverotas.com, €*), following the cork route.

Cork oaks have been a valuable Portuguese resource for centuries.

Based out of São Brás de Alportel, north of Faro, **Algarve Rotas** takes visitors through the whole cork process, from the tree to the factory, explaining its heritage and traditions. You'll walk through cork groves along ancient trails, explore rural life as it has been for hundreds of years, and watch cork masters at work using traditional methods.

The cork harvest is still done by hand, June through August, using age-old and totally natural methods. Harvesters use a small axe to cut sections of bark, which they then pry off in strips, using the handle of the axe. As you follow the cork route, you'll learn Portugal produces some 50 percent of the world's cork and is home to one-third of the world's cork oak forests. Today, the cork oak accounts for about 16 percent of Portugal's foreign trade income.

Cork oaks need abundant and evenly distributed rainfall as well as short dry summer periods, mild winters, clear skies, lots of sun, and deep siliceous soil. All these conditions come together especially well in central and southern Portugal, with the very best quality cork coming from the Algarve and parts of the Alentejo.

The trees take 25 to 30 years to reach maturity, by which time their bark—the cork—is ready to be harvested. The tree will then take 9 to 10 years to grow new bark and be ready for harvest again.

Portugal presently has some 650 companies working in the cork sector, equipped to produce all types of cork items for domestic and industrial use: cigarette tips, flooring, table mats, floats, and insulation for such diverse areas as shipping, homes, and even the space program. This in addition to the 40 million stoppers it produces daily.

Feira da Serra

Another way you can become more acquainted with the cork oak is to attend the Feira da Serra (Mountain Market), an annual event that takes place the last weekend in July in São Brás de Alportel. In addition to finding all types of regional craftwork for sale here, you will have the opportunity to see cork artisans at work, making a range of items from hats and belts to table mats and purses.

For more information contact the tourist office in São Brás de Alportel (*Largo de São Sebastião 23, São Brás de Alportel, tel 289 843 165*).

INLAND ALGARVE

Many people forget there is more to the Algarve than beaches. It also possesses captivating inland destinations and a gently rolling *serra* (hills). This is where you should head for authenticity, handicrafts, whitewashed villages, a Roman spa, and great walking territory.

It is little more than 20 miles (32 km) from the coast north to the Alentejo border, so a drive into the hills is an easy day trip. You'll also find welcome relief from the hordes. The A22 highway, which extends from the Spanish border west to Lagos, forms a quasi-frontier between the coastal infrastructure and a quieter, more rural hinterland. This region, known as the Barrocal, is where fertile limestone soil nurtures the Algarve's fruit orchards.

As you head toward the hills and negotiate the web of roads encircling **Almancil**, try not to miss the church of **São Lourenço** *(tel 289 395 451, closed Sun. & Mon. a.m., €)*, visible beside the N125. Although remodeled during the heyday of baroque, it was originally Romanesque and is regarded as one of the Algarve's greatest cultural gems. The cupola, walls, and ceiling are faced in a masterful display of azulejos illustrating the life of St. Lawrence. This is the 1730 work of Policarpo de Oliveira Bernardes who, together with his father António, created many tiled masterpieces found throughout Portugal.

Loulé

North of Almancil, crowds descend upon Loulé every Saturday morning for the huge food and handicrafts **market** staged in a field on the west side of town. This tradition goes back to 1291, when the founding of a fair made Loulé a major trading crossroads. Dried figs, almonds, and honey (all favored by the Moors) are among the local staples on offer, as is rock salt.

Loulé
🗺 201 D2
Visitor Information
✉ Avenida 25 de Abril 9
☎ 289 463 900

■ The stunning azulejos in Almancil's São Lourenço church depict the life and martyrdom of St. Lawrence.

Carnaval in Portugal

Carnaval, known in some parts of the world as Mardi Gras, traditionally marks the final days of feasting and celebration before the restraint and fasting of the Christian season of Lent. Running now for more than a hundred years, the Loulé Carnaval parade claims to be the oldest in Portugal. Locals do all they can to capture the atmosphere of a Brazilian Carnaval, with samba bands, scantily clad dancers, and elaborate floats; only the tropical Rio weather evades them, as the February Carnaval falls in the middle of Portugal's winter.

Fonte Benémola
△ 201 D2

Rocha da Pena
△ 201 D2

Few people know that Loulé sits above miles of underground galleries where exceptionally pure salt is mined. Nonperishable items for sale at the market include copperware, leather goods, and wickerwork handmade in area villages.

Because the market is very tourist oriented, you may want to explore Loulé on another day when the sleepy atmosphere returns. The Moorish-style market hall on the corner of Praça da República has a daily **food market** (closed Sun.) as well as some handicrafts, and just behind lies the small but attractive old quarter. The **castelo** and **Museu Municipal** (Rua D. Paio Peres Correia 17, tel 289 400 885, museudeloule.pt, closed Sun., €) houses a reconstructed traditional kitchen, in keeping with Loulé's gastronomic concerns. The museum exhibits a predictable collection of Neolithic, Roman, and Moorish artifacts, and from there steps take you up to the castle walls and turret. Far more interesting are the craft shops

concentrated in the street behind the castle, Rua da Barbaçã. Loulé and Almancil both have strong gastronomic reputations, so if you want a true dining experience away from the coast, indulge yourself here.

North of Loulé

The typical Algarve villages of Querença and Salir nestle on either side of the **Fonte Benémola.** Entered from **Querença,** Fonte Benémola is a protected, idyllic little valley crossed by walking trails. Near the Algibre River, you will pass willows, ashes, oleanders, and tamarisks, while the higher slopes foster carob trees, wild olives, oaks, and aromatic herbs. Fauna is limited to otters, bats, and a wide variety of birds. A little farther north is the very pretty whitewashed village of **Salir**—visually dominated by a rather nondescript church and water tower—that safeguards the significant remains of a castle. Follow the "ruínas" signs to see extant ramparts now incorporated into several picturesque houses and gardens. Although modestly signposted, they are among Portugal's few surviving examples of Moorish fortifications constructed of taipa, a Moorish building material made of sand, pebbles, clay, and lime. The outpost was subsequently captured by the Knights of Santiago, who prepared their 1249 assault on Faro from here.

A couple of miles west of Salir, the steep walls of the limestone outcrop **Rocha da Pena**—another protected area with nature trails for visitors—rises to 1,600 feet (474 m). It offers sublime views from the summit looking north to the rugged serra and south to the sea. You may spot Bonelli's or royal eagles, as well as genets, mongooses, and foxes among the juniper, arbutus, and pepper trees.

You can drive north of this outcrop and circle round to **Alte,** another picturesque village of whitewashed houses edged in *platibandas* (decorative plaster borders, often painted yellow or blue), clinging to a hillside. The church dates from the 13th century, when it was founded by the wife of Alte's ruler in thanks for his safe return from the Crusades; it has been altered since. The tiled walls and painted ceiling of the main chapel date from the 18th century, but the Sevillian tiles of the chapel of São Sebastião are 16th century. While the church is attractive, the most popular draws in Alte are its fountains, the **Fonte Pequena** and **Fonte Grande** (respectively small and large), signposted at the bottom of the village, which once produced water to turn the wheels of nine mills. One of them, the Moinho da Abóboda, still stands.

Silves

Another enclave of interest, the hill town of **Silves,** sits beside the Arade River. Once the Moorish capital of the Algarve, borne out by its towering red sandstone castle, Silves is today a prosperous, well-organized town. Your first port of call should be the massive **castelo** *(tel 282 440 837, €),* which was landscaped in the style of an Arab garden in 2005. An outsize

Alte
⚐ 201 D2

Silves
⚐ 200 C2
Visitor Information
✉ EN 124—Parque das Merendas, Silves
☎ 282 098 927

EXPERIENCE: Bird-Watching in the Algarve

Bird-watching may not be what first comes to mind when you think of the sun-soaked Algarve, but the coast and interior hills actually shelter some significant bird-life. Coastal areas are home to diverse coastal and seabird species, including the rare red-billed chough; while inland, cork forests and scrubland provide the ideal habitat for bee-eaters, hoopoes, azure-winged magpies, and raptors such as kestrels and short-toed eagles.

Birding is possible at any time of year, although there are fewer species to be found between June and August. Spring marks the arrival of summer breeders and the start of the migration period, especially among waterbirds; autumn is the best time to observe large numbers of migratory seabirds and raptors.

Ornithologist Simon Wates, a longtime resident of the area and owner of **Algarve Birdwatching** *(tel 912 824 053, algarve birdman.com, €€€€€),* leads tours that are tailored to your interests and time constraints—call well in advance to arrange a trip. Or try **Becool Travel** *(tel 308 810 671, algarve-birdwatching.com).*

If you would rather head off on your own, try to find a copy of A Birdwatchers' Guide to Portugal and Madeira (Prion Birdwatchers' Guide Series, 1988) by H. Costa, C. C. Moore, and G. Elias. Although old, it is still one of the best birding guides to Portugal on the market. Alternatively, check out the **Portuguese Society for the Study of Birds** *(spea.pt/en),* which offers some great information on birds and bird-watching in the area.

bronze statue of Sancho I, who first conquered Silves from the Moors in 1189, greets you outside the castle's double gateway. Inside, excavations have revealed 12th- and 13th-century Almohad structures, and it is thought the Moors occupied the site for some 500 years. One of their 11th-century rulers was Al-Muthamid, a poet-king whose works are still widely read in Arab countries. Apart from archaeological excavations and the garden, the area inside houses an *aljibe* (cistern), once the town's water supply; you can climb the castle's ramparts for fabulous views.

Steps lead from the castle entrance to the **Sé** (Cathedral), which dates from 1189 and preserves a simple Gothic nave with numerous tombs of Crusaders. Next door is the simple little **Igreja da Misericórdia,** a church built in the late 16th century. Down the cobbled streets at the base of the hill, the modern **Museu Arqueológico** *(Rua da Porta de Loulé 14, tel 289 400 885, €),* illustrates the rich archaeological history of Silves from Neolithic times onward.

The **Municipal Market** in Silves, just past the Ponte Romana, is worth a visit to pick up local produce and delicacies; Saturday morning is the best, when stalls spill out onto the square.

Serra de Monchique

From Silves, the drive up into the cool Serra de Monchique, due north of Portimão, takes you into densely wooded hills of eucalyptuses, chestnuts, cork oaks, and pines, with occasional splashes of wild rhododendrons.

Medronho & the Arbutus Tree

Distilled from the fruit of the arbutus tree, commonly known as the strawberry tree, *medronho* is the (exceedingly) alcoholic drink of choice in the Algarve.

For generations, there were dozens of village distilleries producing medronho; with the advent of European Union health and safety legislation, most of these ancestral home breweries were forced to close. Thankfully several converted their facilities and continue to produce this excellent *aguardente.* Be sure to try a high-quality brand and do not drive afterward.

To taste and buy the best, go to **Loja do Mel e do Medronho** *(Largo 5 de Outubro, Monchique, tel 967 735 783).* For the full medronho story, head east to **Casa do Medronho** *(Rua de Aljezur 14, Marmelete, tel 282 955 121, casadomedronho.com),* a working museum where visitors learn about the whole distilling process.

Caldas de Monchique owes its wealth to the hot springs that pour from its mountainside.

The volcanic soil, combined with the humid climate, makes the hill range particularly fertile. Be sure to stop at the viewpoint that overlooks the tight terracing (originally Roman) around the spa town of **Caldas de Monchique** to take in its incredibly panoramic scene. Hedonistic Romans favored the spa for treating their digestive troubles, 19th-century Spanish bourgeois flocked to take its waters, and today resort fugitives seek out its serenity. You can indulge in a treatment at the sulfurous **Termas de Monchique** (*tel 282 910 910, monchiquetermalresort.com*), wander the streets lined with pastel-hued buildings, or simply enjoy the gardens overlooking the ravine.

A few miles farther north lies the small town of **Monchique** itself, where you can explore the ruins of a 17th-century Franciscan monastery and admire the Manueline portal of the parish church. The town is a hub for hikers and horseback riders, and its good selection of basketware, leatherware, woolen garments, and honey will please any shopper. The town's monthly **market** is held on the second Friday of the month; it's a great place to pick up local crafts such as wooden and cork items and a good selection of basketware. They also sell hand-painted wooden children's chairs and the local folding scissor-style stools, thought by some to be of Roman origin. Vendors also peddle the local firewater, *medronho*, made from fermented arbutus berries (see sidebar opposite).

Five miles (8 km) from Monchique is the Serra's highest point at Fóia, more than 3,000 feet (900 m) up. ■

Monchique
🄰 200 B2
Visitor Information
✉ Largo de São Sebastião
☎ 282 911 189

A GOLFING TRADITION

Portugal's love affair with golf dates from the end of the 19th century. Porto Niblicks ("niblick" is the old name for a lofted golf club, the equivalent of today's nine iron) was the first golf club, its creation linked to British involvement in the wine city of Porto. Lovers of the game, the British established courses wherever they lived—notably in the countries of their empire or, in the case of Portugal, where they had trading interests.

A breathtaking view of the Atlantic Ocean is the backdrop for Algarve's numerous golf courses.

The Porto Golf Club (it has dropped "Niblicks") still exists 10 miles (16 km) south of Porto beside the beaches of Espinho. It's the second oldest course in continental Europe.

The number of golf clubs grew in the 1920s and '30s to accommodate wealthy Portuguese patrons and the increasing number of tourists from Britain and France flocking to fashionable Cascais and Estoril. Porto's second course, Miramar, appeared in 1932, but the main growth centered around Lisbon, notably the Estoril course, which was played on by exiled European royals such as the Duke of Windsor, the former King Edward VIII.

Golf & the Algarve

Today the Lisbon region boasts 23 courses, notably Penha Longa at Sintra, host to many European tour events; Oitavos Dunes in Cascais; Quinta do Peru, south of the Tagus; and Tróia Resort, south of Setúbal. The largest expansion, however, has been in the Algarve, where there are now 37 golf courses—and with good reason: It is perfect golf country. The climate is mild in winter, and summer sea breezes cool even the most hot-tempered golfer.

The very first course on the Algarve goes back to 1921; it was a small, rudimentary course between Portimão and Praia da Rocha that was abandoned during World War II. The turning point came with the arrival of Sir Henry Cotton, a former British Open champion who began semiretirement in the Algarve in the late 1950s. He designed three courses and remained most proud of his first, Penina, which was built on a former rice field in 1964. The Portuguese Open was played there in 2004.

Today Vilamoura, with six courses, is the center of Algarve golf. The first one, the Old Course, was designed in 1969 by Frank Pennink; it was arguably the most popular course until the grand unveiling of the challenging Arnold Palmer–designed Victoria course in 2004, which hosted the 2005 World Cup championship.

Several Algarve courses are perfect for beginners, such as Pine Cliffs, just east of Albufeira. The golf club's first president was

■ European royals once played on the Estoril course.

former Formula One world champion Nigel Mansell. The nine-hole course overlooking the sea might be short, but there are some hazardous holes, notably the sixth where you have to drive over a huge ravine to land on the putting green. Known as The Devil's Parlour, it is a devilish little hole that can ruin an otherwise delightful stroll over the clifftop course. With such illustrious precedents and such views, golf in the Algarve is unlikely to decline. (See p. 261 for a listing of several Algarve courses.)

EXPERIENCE: Improve Your Swing

With its delightful climate and wealth of courses, the Algarve is the perfect place to improve your swing if your golf game is a little over par. Spend a few days at one of the Algarve's many golf schools or take an organized golf vacation; a wide selection of programs are available, catering to all levels. Here are three good choices.

At Dutch-owned **East Algarve Golf Academy** (tel 925 459 558, east-algarve golf.com), their slogan is "keep it simple" and their lessons do just that. Beginners are taught basic swings while the more experienced can improve specific aspects of their game. Their three- and four-day clinics, aimed at lowering your handicap, cover both technique and tactics training,

including mental game coaching. Prices start at about €425.

At **Lester's Golf Academy** (tel 967 979 576, lesters-golf.com), PGA professional Peter Lester hosts four- to seven-night golf vacations. Starting at €450 per person, these include accommodation in a Vilamoura hotel, transfers to the golf course, and daily lessons.

During winter months, British golf specialist **David Short** (tel 0044 1637 879 991, davidshortgolf.co.uk) brings his golf clinics to the Algarve, with guests spending the morning in class and the afternoon playing the most prestigious courses in the region. Costs run starting from €1,500 for a weeklong clinic.

LAGOS

Lagos's name reflects its role in the Portuguese age of discoveries, when the town was the operational center for Prince Henry the Navigator (1394–1460) to plan his African forays. Its status grew further in 1573, when it became the capital of the Algarve until 1756.

■ The fantastically eroded coastline at Ponta da Piedade

Lagos

🗺 200 B1

Visitor Information

✉ Praça Gil Eanes

☎ 282 763 031

Today Lagos is an attractive, relaxed town, its walled harbor guarded by the modest 17th-century **Forte da Ponta da Bandeira** *(tel 282 761 410, closed Mon., €)*. Here you can learn about Lagos's role during Prince Henry's time. A statue of the prince presides over the nearby **Praça do Infante,** a verdant square with an unmarked but significant arcaded building in its northwest corner—the site of Europe's first slave market, in 1444.

A short walk takes you to the fabulous **Igreja de Santo António,** entered through the **Museu Municipal** *(Rua Gen. Alberto da Silveira, tel 282 762 301,*

closed Mon., €). This displays interesting archaeological pieces as well as cork, azulejos, and vestments, but the church is the showstopper. Within its gilded baroque interior, azulejo-faced walls and a painted ceiling counterbalance the remarkable retable.

To recover from this visual excess, explore the pedestrian streets that run north to **Praça Gil Eanes.** Don't miss **Rua da Barroca;** its sidewalks are cobbled with marine designs.

Lovely nearby beaches include the broad sweep of **Meia Praia** to the east and a string of coves with calm waters and some impressive grottoes and sea stacks, particularly at **Praia de Dona Ana,** south of Lagos. A walking path from **Praia do Pinhão** leads around the headland as far as **Porto de Mós.**

If in need of a break from the idyllic beaches of the Algarve, head to the well-maintained **Parque Zoologico de Lagos** *(Medronhal–Quinta Figueiras, Barão de São João, tel 282 680 100, zoola-gos.com, €€€)* a few minutes outside Lagos. Birds are the stars of the show here, but there are also small mammals, reptiles, and an adventure playground to keep the kids happy. Great effort has been made to keep animals in their natural habitat and enclosures are often secured by moats rather than bars. ■

SAGRES

The reality of Sagres reinforces a distinct sensation of teetering on the edge of Europe, a final blip on the map. Little happens in this small town other than the ebb and flow of surfers, and the main attraction is a fort symbolizing its past glory.

Sagres is indelibly linked to Prince Henry the Navigator: This is where he supposedly founded his school of navigation. Although he lived and died (in 1460) nearby

INSIDER TIP:

The countryside surrounding Sagres is delightful year-round, but in spring it is filled with the color and smell of wildflowers.

—ANA CARLA CABRITA
Owner, Walkin'Sagres

and his expeditions set off from Lagos, no proof exists of this school. Yet Sagres is an extraordinarily evocative place, occupying a flat, three-pronged promontory that was for centuries one end of the known world. Surprisingly, it still has this quality about it, particularly in the off-season. Surfers and windsurfers flock here year-round, giving the town an alternative feel and spawning low-key bars and cheap restaurants. A trail of their parked campers snakes north up the Costa Vicentina.

The main site at the tip of the windswept promontory is the **Fortaleza de Sagres** *(tel 282 620 140, €)*. Renovated in 1993, it encloses, among other things, a small 16th-century church and

the famous "wind rose." This giant mariner's compass built in stone was uncovered in 1921, but little else is known about it—yet another Sagres mystery. Walk along the promontory's mile-long (1.6 km) path to enjoy fabulous views of pounding surf and soaring eagles.

A couple of miles west lies the barren **Cabo de São Vicente** (Cape of St. Vincent) with its lighthouse and, just before it, the old fort of **Beliche,** where visitors flock to watch the sun set behind the cape. Down below Sagres itself is the beach of **Mareta,** while around the headland to the east, fishing boats moor at the **Porto da Baleeira.** At the next beach along the coast, the lovely **Praia do Martinhal,** windsurfing is king. ■

Sagres

◭ 200 A1

Visitor Information

✉ Rua Comandante Matoso

☎ 282 624 873

■ The 16th-century Sagres fortress stands watch over a desolate but spectacular headland.

DRIVE TO CABO DE SÃO VICENTE

This leisurely drive takes you along the undeveloped western Algarve coast between Lagos and Europe's most southwesterly point—Cabo de São Vicente.

Cabo de São Vicente's cliffs rise nearly vertically some 246 feet (75 m).

From the fort on the seafront of **Lagos** (see p. 214), drive west out of town, following signs to Sagres on the N125. Turn left at the signpost to **Luz ❶,** a small seaside town just a couple of miles off the main road. Follow signs down to the *praia* (beach). Park near the yellow-and-white church of São Vicente and take a stroll along the palm-lined promenade, overlooking rock pools and the crescent-shaped beach backed by cliffs.

Follow the one-way system out of town and signs to Burgau past a stretch of vacation apartments before regaining the countryside. At **Burgau,** cross an intersection and then follow signs to Forte de Almadena. A rough road leads you into empty hills dotted with small farms. At a sign for **Praia das Cabanas Velhas ❷,** turn left down a dirt road to an idyllic little cove, and the discreetly designed modern **Cabanas Beach Restaurant** *(tel 968 871 974).*

> **NOT TO BE MISSED:**
>
> **Praia das Cabanas Velhas • Salema • Nossa Senhora da Conceição**

Back up on the road, continue west for a half mile (0.8 km) before turning left along another dirt road to **Forte de Almadena.** This ruined 16th-century fort was built for King João III and commands beautiful views west from its headland position. The coastal road winds downhill before crossing the old riverbed of the Almadena, now full of pampas grass and oleanders. This rutted road ends at a junction where you turn left onto a steep paved road to **Salema ❸,** a charming little fishing port.

Leave by returning uphill and following signs to Vila do Bispo. At the main road (N125) turn right, then left opposite a huge tourist development. Keep driving until you see a sign for **Guadalupe** to the right, where you take a parallel road past grazing donkeys. After about a mile (1.6 km) you come to a tiny 13th-century chapel venerating **Nossa Senhora de Guadalupe ❹**; this is where Prince Henry the Navigator is said to have prayed while living in Raposeira, a short distance farther west. Keep driving on this side road to rejoin the N125, and then follow a sign, just after Raposeira, left to the **"monumentos megalíticos."** Here, numerous ancient menhirs lie scattered in the shrub of a high headland, and sweeping views take in the lighthouse at Cabo de São Vicente. The **Bateria do Zavial,** a ruined 17th-century

fortification, lies at the end of this road, from where you circle back to Raposeira. At the N125, follow signs to nearby Vila do Bispo.

Vila do Bispo to the Cape

Drive into **Vila do Bispo ❺** and park near the beautiful yellow-and-white baroque church, **Nossa Senhora da Conceição,** on the main square. If it is open, you will see a dazzling early 1700s interior of azulejos, gilded woodwork, painted ceilings, and ornate retables. Wander the side streets before rejoining the main road to continue to Sagres (see p. 215). After driving through town, turn right at a traffic circle to Cabo de São Vicente, and then cross a barren heath to the 1632 fortress of **Beliche.** Beyond is the lighthouse of **Cabo de São Vicente.**

See also area map p. 200
► Lagos
⏱ 1.5 hours without stops
↔ 38 miles (60 km)
► Cabo de São Vicente

COSTA VICENTINA

Europe's most spectacular beaches edge this wild coastline that descends the Alentejo coast and wraps around into the Algarve. This is an area for surfing and hiking; the daunting Atlantic waves are rarely safe for swimming.

Blissfully unspoiled low hills border the Costa Vicentina.

Parque Natural do Sudoeste Alentejano e Costa Vicentina

⛰ 200 A1–A3

Visitor Information

✉ Rua João Mendes Dias 46A, Aljezur

☎ 282 998 673

natural.pt

Museu Municipal de Aljezur

✉ Largo 5 de Outubro, Aljezur

☎ 282 991 011

🕐 Closed Sun.–Mon.

💲 €

This inviting coast—protected as part of the **Parque Natural do Sudoeste Alentejano e Costa Vicentina**—is noted as much for its geologic formations as for its plants, birdlife, and estuaries.

Rough roads end at breath-taking viewpoints over deserted beaches backed by craggy cliffs and edged by breakers. Infrastructure is still almost nonexistent—only an occasional restaurant or beach bar, and accommodations are limited to private rooms or small guesthouses. There is an easy though rough road from **Carrapateira,** on the main N268, to the beach of **Pontal,** a blissfully broad sweep of sand and dunes. **Arrifana,** 9 miles (14 km) farther north, is a long stretch

of white sand with a pretty little fishing harbor and the ruins of a 17th-century fort built to protect the tuna fishermen. Farther north again, the neighboring beaches of **Amoreira** and the 5-mile-long (8 km) **Monte Clérigo** have striking rock formations and some visitor facilities.

Aljezur, the crossroads for this stunning string of beaches, makes a pleasant place for lunch. Two rivers, the Aljezur and the Cerca, meet at the center of town. The ramparts of a 10th-century Moorish fort, badly damaged in the 1755 earthquake, stand atop the hill, while downhill, the **Museu Municipal** displays local items that highlight the history of this evocative region. ■

An island hothouse for subtropical plants, where botanical beauties clad breathtakingly steep cliff edges

MADEIRA

■ *Strelitzia*, or bird-of-paradise—one of Madeira's floral exports

MADEIRA

Madeira's benign weather has helped transform this rugged volcanic island into one vast, verdant garden—a botanical storehouse whose natural splendors and stunning vistas have been enjoyed by travelers since it was first discovered in the 15th century.

■ Looming out of the sea, the cliffs at Porto Moniz are protected by reefs and black lava rocks.

Madeira is one of Portugal's most intriguing outposts. Set in the eastern Atlantic, it lies closer to Morocco than to Portugal, and this southerly latitude gives it a warm subtropical climate, which helps make the island a popular year-round vacation destination. The tip of a submerged mountain chain, it is part of an archipelago, also called Madeira, which comprises Porto Santo, the Ilhas Desertas, and the Ilhas Selvagens. Madeira is the largest island, with an area of 286 square miles (740 sq km) and a population of around 260,000.

Porto Santo was the first island discovered in the archipelago by Portuguese explorers. In 1418, João Gonçalves Zarco and Tristão Vaz Teixeira, leading an expedition to explore the West African coast, sought shelter on this tiny landmass when they were blown off course. They returned two years later and found the main island, which they christened Ilha Madeira (Wooded Island) because of its thick forest cover. The forests were set alight to clear land for settlement, and the resultant ash and underlying volcanic soil proved fertile ground for the grapevines and sugarcanes that were introduced. Slaves were imported to terrace the steep hillsides and dig an extensive network of irrigation canals—the famous *levadas.* The capital, Funchal, soon developed into a port of call for transatlantic ships.

During the 17th century, Madeira abandoned sugar in favor of winemaking, establishing the basis for a trade that still flourishes today. The unique characteristics of Madeiran wine result from a long, hot maturing process. This was discovered by accident when it was found that barrels of wine sent as ballast on long sea voyages in the tropics were actually improved by the journey.

The island's mild climate attracted an increasing number of wealthy visitors in the 19th century—particularly well-to-do British citizens, who enjoyed stopping here on the way to and from their colonies. Funchal's famous Reid's hotel opened in 1891 to cater to this growing market. British visitors also introduced the crafts of embroidery and making cane furniture.

Madeira Today

Tourism is still Madeira's economic mainstay. The island is famous for its wonderful walking alongside the levadas that crisscross the lush hills. More energetic pursuits, such as scuba diving, rappelling, and canyoneering, are also popular. If one thing is lacking, it is a beach, but that is provided across the waves on Porto Santo.

NOT TO BE MISSED:

Dazzling displays of flowers at the Mercado dos Lavradores 223

Strolling in the Jardim Botânico 223

Looking over the edge at Cabo Girão 224

Driving the northern corniche 225

The amazing views from Boca da Encumeada 225

The toboggan ride in Monte 226

Walking the *levadas* in Madeira 229

An abundance of fruits and vegetables combines with fresh fish for a memorable cuisine, and a calendar of festivals ensures a lively cultural scene. Nearly two-thirds of this island, with its dramatic mountain scenery and colorful flora, is protected as a nature reserve. ■

FUNCHAL

The island capital has a glorious setting, sprawling across a wide amphitheater of mountains and hillsides with the glittering, boat-studded bay below. Often shrouded in clouds, the hills protect the city from the northeasterly winds, making it the warmest location on the island.

■ The Jardim Botânico includes a three-room Natural History Museum.

Funchal

221 B2

Visitor Information

Avenida Arriaga 16

291 211 902

visitmadeira.pt

Home to about one-third of Madeira's inhabitants, Funchal was named for the wild fennel (funcho) early settlers found here. Today it is sometimes dubbed "little Lisbon" for its elegant architecture, lively cafés, and smart shops. Luxuriant vegetation perfumes its winding streets. The old town fronts the harbor and marina, while the modern extension— home to most hotels—lies due west along the seafront. Despite being hit by destructive fires in 2016, Funchal and its inhabitants are resilient, and it is business as usual in the island's capital.

Start your visit at the main square, the **Praça do Município,** with its distinctive black-and-white patterned stone pavement. Note the **Câmara Municipal** (Town Hall), a gracious 18th-century mansion originally built for the count of Carvalhal, and, on the south side of the square, the former bishop's palace with its lovely arcaded gallery. The latter now houses the **Museu de Arte Sacra** (tel 291 228 900, masf.pt, closed Sun., €). Look for the beautiful processional cross donated to Funchal's Cathedral by Manuel I. On the second floor, Portugal's best collection of 15th- and 16th-century Flemish paintings hangs beside Portuguese artwork, including Jan Provost's serene "St. Mary Magdalene."

On the north side of the square is the 17th-century **Igreja** do Colégio, built by the Jesuits. Heading south from the praça brings you to Funchal's imposing Sé (Cathedral), completed in 1514. Except for the azulejo-faced belfry, the exterior is fairly austere, but the interior features an intricately carved, ivory-inlaid, wooden ceiling and flamboyant choir stalls. Funchal's main street, Avenida Arriaga, runs west from the Sé toward a seafront park, the Jardim de Santa Catarina, passing the Palácio de São Lourenço, an 18th-century fortress still used by the military.

Opposite the fortress is the tourist office and Blandy's Wine Lodge, also known as Adegas de São Francisco (Av. Arriaga 28, 291 228 978, blandyswinelodge.com, closed Sun., €€). Originally a Franciscan monastery, it now houses the offices of this big wine company. They offer the island's most atmospheric wine tour, concluding with a tasting of Madeira's famously sweet nectar. West of this central zone, Madeira Film Experience

(Rua Conselheiro José Silvestre, tel 291 222 748, madeirafilmexperience.com, €), offers a 30-minute audiovisual tour through 600 years of Madeira history.

In the Vila Velha (Old Town), take time to explore the cobbled streets lined with restaurants, cafés, fado bars, and craft shops. A highlight is the vast Mercado dos Lavradores (Largo dos Lavradores, closed Sat. p.m.–Sun.), a market where locals sell a colorful cornucopia of island produce. Close by is the terminal for the Teleférico (cable car) to the hill town of Monte (see p. 226).

No visit would be complete without a trip to the lovely Jardim Botânico (Quinta do Bom Sucesso, Caminho do Meio, tel 291 211 200, sra.pt/jarbot, €). Bountiful native vegetation grows here in terraces overlooking the valley, and exotics such as orchids, lilies, and birds-of-paradise bloom in the gardens. In the month of July, the city comes alive with an animated Jazz Festival. ∎

Madeira Wine

The island of Madeira has been producing world-famous wine for hundreds of years. In the 16th century, sailors headed to the New World took aboard barrels of local wine; as the wine traveled into tropical climates, it was heated in the hold of the ship and its taste greatly improved. By the 18th century, following the example of the port shippers, young wines were fortified with brandy to stabilize them and wine producers began to cut costs and heat the wines in their own cellars; a process still used today and known as estufagem.

There are four types of Madeira, named after the white grapes used in their production. The driest is Sercial, made from grapes grown above 2,600 feet (800 m); it is best served chilled as an aperitif. The white Verdelho, grown at 1,300 to 2,000 feet (400–600 m), produces a medium-dry, tawny wine best served with meat dishes. Bual is a rich and nutty, medium-sweet wine made from grapes grown on terraces below 1,300 feet (400 m); it is particularly good with cheeses and dessert. Finally, Malmsey, grown in sunny vineyards below 1,300 feet (400 m), produces a sweet, full-bodied wine, served as a digestive.

WESTERN MADEIRA

The breathtaking western coastline of Madeira sports villages clinging to the steep shoreline, with cultivated terracing tumbling down to the sea. Inland, more panoramic vistas await.

Heading west from Funchal, the first stop on the coastal highway is **Câmara de Lobos,** a quaint fishing village famed for its brightly painted boats. The fishermen catch *espada* (scabbard fish), a Madeiran specialty dish. These fishes rise from the depths at night to feed, so the boats head out in the evening.

Just past Câmara de Lobos is one of the island's most impressive sights: the magnificent **Cabo Girão.** The second highest sea cliff in Europe (beaten only by one in Norway), Cabo Girão plunges a dizzying 1,900 feet (580 m) to the sea below. Incredibly, terraced vineyards are carved into the vertiginous cliff face—further evidence of Madeira's industrious farmers. The more daring can head out onto the glass-bottomed skywalk.

Another popular stopping point is the seaside resort of **Ribeira Brava,** 20 twisty miles (32 km) west of Funchal. Lying at the entrance to a steep-sided valley, its name (Wild River) derives from the torrential flows pouring off the mountains in the winter months. The sizable town features a 15th-century parish church, a fishing harbor, and the informative **Museu Etnográfico da Madeira** *(Rua de São Francisco 24, tel 291 952 598, closed Sun.–Mon., €),* exploring the essentials of Madeiran life over the centuries: fishing, weaving, and winemaking.

The sunniest spot on the south coast is said to be the **Ponta do Sol,** 2.5 miles (4 km) west of Ribeira Brava. This "headland of the sun" is an unspoiled village straddling a deep ravine, with cobbled streets leading up toward

A vertigo-inspiring view from the towering cliff face of Cabo Girão looks east toward Funchal.

an unusual church. A sunset stroll along the harborfront is de rigueur.

Madeira's westernmost point, **Ponta do Pargo,** is famed for its sea views: There are thousands of miles of Atlantic Ocean between you and the east coast of North America. Just as Câmara de Lobos is known for its espada fishing, Ponta do Pargo is renowned for its catches of *pargo,* or dolphinfish (no relation to dolphins).

Rounding the Northernmost Point

A short distance from the island's westernmost tip is its northernmost point—**Porto Moniz.** A series of large rock pools here attract weary day-trippers to soak their aching limbs while contemplating the ocean spray breaking over the northern shoreline. Cafés, restaurants, and a hotel cater to more prosaic visitor needs. Porto Moniz has one of the only protected harbors on the north coast and was once an important whaling center. Today, the cetaceans are being sighted again and there are many organized whale-watching outings.

The **northern corniche** linking Porto Moniz to São Vicente, 12 miles (19 km) to the east, ranks as one of the most spectacular coastal roads in Europe: Clinging to the cliff edge with breathtaking views, this marvel of engineering took 16 years to complete. It can only be driven east to west; west-to-east traffic passes through numerous tunnels and ducks beneath several waterfalls (handy for a free car wash, according to

locals). **São Vicente,** a spruced-up agricultural crossroads with plenty of facilities for travelers, is the most substantial town on the north coast. The pedestrianized center, with cobbled streets, houses decorated with flowers, and cafés, is pleasant to stroll. If you feel more adventurous, head just south of town to the **Grutas de São Vicente,** an intriguing cave system with a short guided tour of volcanic tunnels, or lava tubes, featuring lava cakes and volcanic stalactites.

Connecting São Vicente to Ribeira Brava on the south coast, Route 104 passes over the stupendous **Boca da Encumeada,** a popular viewing point with panoramas north to São Vicente and down to the Serra de Água valley

---

INSIDER TIP:

Wear plastic sandals or some other footwear in the natural seawater pools at Porto Moniz. The volcanic rock underfoot can be rough on your feet.

—JANE SUNDERLAND
National Geographic contributor

---

in the south. Try to arrive at the 3,304-foot (1,007 m) pass in the morning; clouds tend to obscure the view as the day progresses. For vertigo sufferers, a tunnel dives underneath the pass. The Levada do Norte, a 38-mile-long (60 km) channel that irrigates the valley below, passes under the road. ∎

Western Madeira
🅰 221 A2–B2
Visitor Information
✉ Vila do Porto Moniz
☎ 291 853 075

✉ Forte de São Bento Ribeira Brava
☎ 291 951 675

Grutas de São Vicente
🅰 221 B2
✉ Sítio do Pé do Passo, São Vicente
☎ 291 842 404
💲 €€

grutasecentro dovulcanismo saovicente.com

EASTERN MADEIRA

Eastern Madeira offers rich pickings, from the eccentric toboggan ride of Monte to out-standing botanical gardens and the attractive fishing towns of Caniçal and Machico.

Spring wildflowers carpet rolling meadows near Camacha.

Eastern Madeira

🗺 221 B2–C2

Visitor Information

✉ Forte Nossa Senhora do Amparo, Machico

☎ 291 962 289

🕐 Closed Sat p.m.–Sun.

Teleférico da Madeira

✉ Caminho das Babosas 8, Monte

☎ 291 780 280

💲 €€€

madeiracablecar.com

Monte & Around

High above the northeastern outskirts of Funchal, the village of **Monte** is a perennial favorite for excursions from the city. During the 19th century it was fashionable to descend from Monte to Funchal by **toboggan.** This system is still used today, with tourists riding two abreast in a sled steered back to the Funchal's suburbs by two men, running and riding alongside. Alternatively, the more high-tech cable car, the **Teleférico da Madeira,** runs between Funchal's Vila Velha and Monte.

Thriving at the cool elevation of 1,970 feet (600 m), lush vegeta-tion surrounds Monte. The strik-ing sight of the church of **Nossa**

Senhora do Monte, with its twin towers and gray-basalt detailing on a white facade, rises from a hillock in the town center. Every August 15 (Assumption), pilgrims crawl up 74 steps to reach this church. Inside is the iron tomb of Charles I, Austria's last emperor, who lived in the Quinta do Monte hotel during his exile, in 1921, and died the following year. Within walking distance from here are two lovely gardens: the **Jardim do Monte,** with luxuriant ferns and flowering plants, and the **Jardim Tropical Monte Palace,** which covers 17 acres (7 ha) with statu-ary, ponds, bridges, Asian-style gar-dens, and typical subtropical flora.

The famous **Quinta do Pal-heiro** (also known as Blandy's

Gardens) lies just 5 miles (8 km) east of Funchal. Tended by successive generations of the Blandy family, the estate boasts botanical riches from all over the world and is considered to be the most beautiful on the island, displaying more than 3,000 species.

Machico & Beyond

The largest town in eastern Madeira is **Machico,** where discoverer João Gonçalves Zarco first stepped ashore in 1420; a river divides the old town from the fishermen's quarter. In the main square, an attractive 15th-century church boasts a lateral doorway presented by Manuel I. Here, too, is a statue of Zarco's fellow navigator, Tristão Vaz Teixeira, who became Machico's governor. East of the square, the **Capela dos Milagres** (Chapel of the Miracles) is the focus of a major festival every October. This event celebrates the rescue of the chapel's crucifix after the original chapel was washed out to sea by floods in 1803.

Just north of Machico, the tiny port of **Caniçal** was the center of

the island's whaling industry until the trade was banned in 1981. The whalers used small open boats and handheld harpoons to hunt their prey; the **Museu da Baleia** *(Rua Garcia Moniz 1, tel 291 961 858, museudabaleia. org, closed Mon., €€€)* documents their exploits. This whaling museum also outlines conservation efforts in progress, including the creation of a 77,220-square-mile (200,000 sq km) marine mammal sanctuary around the archipelago. Caniçal now has the island's biggest tuna-fishing fleet; the brightly colored boats are berthed on the beach.

Beyond Caniçal the landscapes take on a wild, desolate quality as the road dwindles to a potholed

Camacha Wicker

Not far from Quinta do Palheiro, reached by following Route 102 northward, the village of Camacha excels at wickerwork. The canes come from pollarded willows, which grow abundantly in the island's damp, humid valleys. Madeira's best selection of wickerwork can be seen at Camacha's **Café Relógio** *(Largo Conselheiro Aires de Ornelas 12, tel 291 922 777, caferelogio.com),* on the south side of the town square.

track at the easternmost tip of the island. At **Prainha** you will find Madeira's only sandy beach, signposted down steps from the road, and very crowded on hot summer days. From the parking lot at the end of the road, a footpath leads across the **Ponta de São Lourenço,** a rugged promontory with dramatic sea views across to the Ilhas Desertas. ∎

**Jardim Tropical
Monte Palace**

✉ Caminho do Monte 174, Monte

☎ 291 780 800

💲 €€€

montepalace.com

Quinta do Palheiro

🗺 221 B2

✉ Caminho da Quinta do Palheiro 32, Monte

☎ 291 793 044

🕐 Closed holidays

💲 €€€

palheirogardens.com

MADEIRA'S VEGETATION

The "pearl of the Atlantic" boasts two outstanding aspects: the first, a 1,500-mile-long (2,500 km) network of *levadas* (irrigation canals), and the second, luscious subtropical vegetation. Visitors can walk for miles on paths beside the levadas to reach remote and otherwise inaccessible areas. En route, as microclimates change, a seemingly miraculous world of hothouse plants and spectacular blooms is revealed—thriving in the wild.

■ Hikers enjoy the wild shrubs, laurel, and heather of Madeira's mountainous ridge near Rabaçal.

Every hillside and roadside of Madeira is a mass of technicolor flowers, dominated by large-scale geraniums, hydrangeas, scarlet and pink hibiscus, mauve blue agapanthus, creamy arum lilies, torchlike red hot pokers *(Kniphofia uvaria),* and deep crimson or orange bougainvilleas. All are backed up by flowering trees such as purple jacaranda, creamy yellow magnolia, giant pink camellia, and golden yellow mimosa. Perhaps the most spectacular blooms are the brilliant orange flowers of the tulip tree—or flame of the forest *(Spathodea campanulata)*—brought to Madeira by Capt. James Cook

in the 18th century. Madeira's most famous endemic plant is the dragon tree *(Dracaena draco),* shared with the Canary Islands and Cape Verde Islands. It now rarely grows in the wild, but can be found in gardens and parks. Like Africa's baobab, it looks as if it has been planted upside down; the straight trunk ends in a tangled mass of branches and stems. Barbary figs are encroaching along the nonirrigated areas of the warmer south coast, while countless fleshy succulents and flowering aloes opt to grow on rocky outcrops.

Such density and variety is hard to better—except when it comes to the cultivated varieties of cut flowers grown for export: Numerous orchid varieties, anthuriums, and spiky *Strelitzias* (birds-of-paradise) are foremost. Madeira's botanical gardens abound in imported species, offering yet another dazzling visual feast.

Ecological Variety

Levada walking (see sidebar below) is popular because the channels are easy to find and follow, and the gentle sound track of trickling water is only interrupted by the birdcalls or rustles of undergrowth courtesy of the lizards, typical island reptiles. One of the most striking features of the landscape is its tendency to suddenly change, offering walkers an electrifying experience of emerging from a damp and misty pine forest into a brilliantly sunny, verdant valley, where banana palms nestle at the base.

Madeira's steep elevations have endowed it with three distinct vegetation zones: Subtropical plants flourish at sea level up to about 1,000 feet (330 m); a more temperate, Mediterranean zone nurtures grapevines, cereals, citrus fruits, mangoes, and apples up to about 2,500 feet (750 m); and ancient forest blankets elevations above the 2,500-foot (750 m) mark. Dating back some 20 million years to the

Even in urban Funchal, the island's exotic blooms are never far away.

Tertiary era, this type of forest once covered much of southern Europe, but it was later destroyed by glaciation. Madeira is one of the last places where its species—sesame, tree laurel, mahogany, til *(Oreodaphne jetens),* and even ironwood—still grow in their original habitat. The laurel forests (supplying bay leaves) around Faial, Portela, and Queimadas are among the last pockets of woods that escaped being burned down by Madeira's first settlers; they now stand protected as nature reserves.

EXPERIENCE: Walk the *Levadas*

Immerse yourself in Madeira's stunning landscape by walking alongside the *levadas* that crisscross the island. These irrigation canals, which date back as far as the 16th century, stretch some 1,500 miles (2,500 km). They take their name from the Portuguese word *levar,* which means "to carry." They funnel water from the wet northern highlands to the drier south, where it is used to irrigate banana plantations, vineyards, orchards, and vegetable gardens. Some 870 miles (1,500 km) of the levadas have adjacent, well-maintained paths, allowing walkers to easily follow the gentle contours of the hills.

You can easily set off on your own (the Funchal tourist office has a leaflet of recommended walks, but better yet is Paddy Dillon's book *Walking in Madeira,* which you should bring with you), but you'll gain a greater appreciation of Madeira's flora and history on a guided walk. **Madeira Happy Tours** *(Estrada Monumental 284A, Hotel Monumental Lido, Shop 15, São Martinho, Funchal, tel 291 768 426, madeirahappytours.com, €€€€€)* offers full- and half-day levada walks with qualified mountain guides. Vertigo sufferers should mention their condition as some levadas, though safe, are somewhat precipitous.

PORTO SANTO & OTHER ISLANDS

In stark contrast to Madeira, Porto Santo is quite flat and mostly arid: Very little grows here, and most of the 5,000 inhabitants depend on a steady stream of summer tourists for income.

■ Incongruous electric lighting lines the jetty at Porto Santo—miles and miles from anywhere.

Porto Santo

🅰 221 D3

Visitor Information

✉ Centro de Artesanato, Avenida Dr. Manuel Gregório Pestana Junior

☎ 291 985 244

🕐 Closed Sun.

Casa Colombo— Museu do Porto Santo

✉ Travessa da Sacristia 2–4, Vila Baleira

☎ 291 983 405

🕐 Closed Sat.– Mon.

💲 €

museucolombo -portosanto.com

There is just one reason for visiting Porto Santo: Its glorious beach that sweeps 5 miles (8 km) along the south coast. Twenty-three miles (37 km) northeast of Madeira, it is reached by catamaran or plane.

The capital, **Vila Baleira,** was once home to the Genoese explorer Christopher Columbus, who came as a buyer for Lisbon sugar merchants in the 1470s. He later married Dona Filipa Moniz, the daughter of Porto Santo's governor. Their house is now the **Casa Colombo—Museu do Porto Santo,** where books, maps, and charts document the explorer's life. Dona Filipa died in childbirth and legend has it that while grieving, staring out to sea, Columbus became convinced that the

vegetation washing ashore came from another continent; he was thus inspired to make his Atlantic crossing in 1492. From the main square, palm-fringed Rua Infante D. Henrique leads to the famous beach. En route you will pass a drinking fountain, one of many on the island that flows with local mineral water, which is bottled and sold on Madeira. Reportedly even the beach sand has healing properties.

Nineteen miles (30 km) to the southeast of Madeira, the three **Ilhas Desertas** (Empty Islands) form a protected reserve, principally to nurture the nearly extinct monk seal. The most southerly outposts of Portuguese territory are the remote **Ilhas Selvagens** (Wild Islands), some 150 miles (240 km) away, also with protected status. ■

TRAVELWISE

Two-wheel transport in Lisbon

TRAVELWISE

PLANNING YOUR TRIP

When to Go

Mainland Portugal enjoys an attractive climate with long hot summers lasting roughly from May to September, and pleasantly mild winters, making it a safe-bet destination for much of the year.

In the north, mountainous areas do see snow, and a basic ski station functions in the Serra da Estrela from January to March. The region of Trás-os-Montes experiences the harshest winters, with high rainfall in December and January. In neighboring Minho, including Porto, the pattern is similar though less extreme. Summers are hot and sunny, although of course there are occasional showery days.

At the opposite end of the country, Algarve temperatures seldom fall below 50°F (10°C); limited rain falls mainly in December, January, and March, but it otherwise offers a very mild year-round climate. Come summer, temperatures soar to well over 86°F (30°C); July and August are peak family holiday time on the beaches, so you may wish to avoid those months. Inland in the Alentejo, temperatures are hotter, often topping 104°F (40°C).

Lisbon and the country's low-lying center fall between these extremes, coolest in January and February and with the highest rainfall from November to January. Temperatures rarely drop below 46°F (8°C) and in summer they hover around 86°F (30°C). As there is always a breeze from the Atlantic and the Tejo River, midsummers are usually quite comfortable.

The entire Atlantic coast offers a breezy summer climate, though the beaches get crowded and the crashing (and chilly) surf is not great for swimming. The sea here does not really warm up until July, unlike the protected coves of the Algarve where the brave swim even in spring.

The in-between seasons of spring and fall are the optimum time to visit to avoid domestic tourists and benefit from lower hotel rates. Spring (Apr.–May) especially is a wonderful period—wildflowers are in bloom and the countryside is seductively green. Early fall (Sep.–Oct.) is also enticing, with warm sunny days and russet vineyards.

Meanwhile, offshore in the Atlantic, Madeira is quite temperate and is a popular winter destination for northern Europeans.

Festivals

Portugal's calendar is peppered with festivals, large and small, religious and secular, so whenever you travel you are bound to find one of them.

In winter Carnaval explodes across the country in February. The liveliest carnival is in Loulé and Torres Vedras, where floats are heavy on political satire. Funchal, the capital of Madeira, also hosts an extravagant Brazilian-style parade.

Spring sees Easter Week, with some spectacular festivities and torchlit processions. The most memorable Easter celebrations take place at Óbidos, lasting two weeks, at Braga, and at Ourem. It is best to book hotels well in advance if you plan to attend any festivities in either city. Spring also sees Coimbra's large student population enjoying days of revelry and excess in May before their final exams.

Many local festivals occur during the summer months (June–Aug.). The Minho region has the most colorful traditional costumes. The bullfighting season lasts from Easter to October; though bullfights are now not so frequent, the best place to try is in the Ribatejo, in or around Santarém, where the bulls are actually bred.

Autumn (late Sep.) is the time for grape harvest festivals, held over most of the country—inquire at local tourist offices for precise dates.

What to Take

Portuguese stores stock the same goods and necessities as any other Western city. Clothing depends very much on where you are going and at what time of year, but usually follows a European style of informal chic, unless you're hiking in the hills. You only need to dress up a bit at top restaurants in Lisbon, Porto, or at luxury hotels and *pousadas*. It's always optimal to try to dress in layers. Portuguese clothes are reasonably priced, so if necessary you can always buy extras.

Take enough prescribed medication to cover your stay, although Portuguese pharmacies are well stocked with nonprescription drugs and the pharmacists are very helpful and many speak English. Most common forms of contraception are available, but may be hard to find in more remote areas. If you wear glasses, take a copy of your prescription in case you lose them.

Photographers will have no problem in finding batteries, digital peripherals, and printers in camera stores, although these are almost certainly cheaper in the United States. Video accessories are available in the large towns but take your own charger and transformer. You should also bring digital cards with you, as small towns are not necessarily well stocked.

Birders should bring their binoculars, as they, too, are expensive in Portugal.

Insurance

No vaccinations are necessary to enter Portugal. The country has a healthy climate and the seafood is generally fresh and carefully prepared, so you are unlikely to have any stomach problems. However, do make sure that you have reliable travel insurance for medical treatment, repatriation, and baggage and/or money loss, and make a note of the pertinent telephone numbers to call while abroad. If anything happens, keep all receipts for expenses, as you will need them to make a claim. Anything stolen should be reported to a police station where a signed statement will be given to you for insurance purposes.

Entry Formalities

Citizens of the United States and Canada do not need a visa for stays of up to 90 days, likewise for Australians and New Zealanders. European Union nationals are allowed to travel with just an ID card. As of January 2021, UK citizens will be required to have a passport that is less than 10 years old and is valid for at least 6 months. Regulations regarding UK citizens traveling to the EU are still being defined and modified. Updates are promptly posted on the website *www.gov.uk*. Portuguese police are empowered to make identity spot checks so keep your documents on you (in a safe place) all the time.

Customs formalities are the same as in all European Union countries. If a non-EU citizen, you may bring into Portugal 1 liter of spirits or 2 liters of liquor (not exceeding 22% vol) plus 2 liters of still wine, 200 cigarettes, and 50 milliliters of perfume—but all of these goods are cheaper in Portugal. All narcotics and illegal drugs are banned and customs officers are very alert, so beware.

HOW TO GET TO PORTUGAL

By Plane

Portugal's flagship airline is **TAP** (Air Portugal, *flytap.com*). It offers direct flights from the U.S. departing from Newark, New York, San Francisco, and Boston, and from Canada departing from Montreal. Flights on major American airlines have at least one stopover. Indirect flights such as those by **British Airways** *(britishairways.com)* offer a wider range of departure cities in the United States and can be cheaper.

Budget airlines **Easyjet** *(easyjet. com)* and **Ryanair** *(ryanair.com)* fly to Lisbon, Porto, and Faro from the UK and many European cities. Easyjet also flies to Funchal-Madeira and to the Azores.

Airports

Portugal's international airports *(ana.pt)* are located in Lisbon, Porto, Faro, and Funchal (Madeira).

Lisbon city center is only 4.5 miles (7 km) from the airport and trains leave from the red-line metro station approximately every 10 minutes (change at Alameda for the center). Buses (**Aerobus 1 & 2**) leave every 20 minutes, taking 20 to 30 minutes to Cais do Sodré or Sete Rios. The main downtown departure point for buses is Praça dos Restauradores, opposite Rossio station. In Porto, the purple E line of the metro goes to the center from the airport, 6 miles (11 km) away; it's about a 30-minute ride. At Faro, an airport bus outside the terminal takes you to the city center in about 20 minutes. Local buses Nos. 14 and 16 also run the 6 miles (11 km) to and from the airport. Madeira's airport at Funchal is a nerve-racking affair on a rocky outcrop quite a distance from the town center: Airport buses (local transport or shuttles) take 45 minutes and run approximately every hour.

Taxis are available at all airports; expect to pay extra for luggage. In Lisbon buy a prepaid voucher from the Turismo de Lisboa counter.

By Boat

There are no scheduled ferries to Portugal, but many cruise ships stop at Lisbon and many more at Madeira.

By Bus

Long-distance buses from Europe are now cushy affairs with air-conditioning, reclining seats, and onboard toilets. However, the proliferation of budget airlines has reduced their viability. In a short time, **Flixbus** *(global.flixbus. com)* has become the continent's lead company for ground travel and if you reserve far enough in advance, you can find tickets at great prices.

By Car

There are numerous entry points into Portugal from neighboring Spain and rented cars can generally be taken over the border without any extra cost or paperwork. Do check, however, with the rental agency you are using. As the Schengen agreement makes passports between European countries obsolete, border posts are unmanned.

By Train

Trains into Portugal from Spain follow two routes. The state-owned company **Comboios de Portugal** *(cp.pt)* offers daily connections between Porto and Vigo on the Celta train (approximately 2 hours and 20 minutes). Night service between Lisbon and Madrid aboard the Lusitânia Comboio Hotel departs 9:25 p.m. and arrives 8:40 a.m.; there is a restaurant on board and you can choose between economy seats and couchettes.

GETTING AROUND
In Lisbon

Lisbon has an excellent public transport system. The fast expanding subway system, **Metro-politano** (metrolisboa.pt), has four lines, 56 stations, and connections (correspondencia) with main and suburban railways and ferries across the Tejo River. Entrances at street level are marked with large red signs with a white M, and trains run from 6:30 a.m. to 1 a.m.

To travel you will need a Viva Viagem Card (€0.50), which is then loaded with a single ticket fare (€1.50) or a day ticket (€6.40), valid on metro and bus. Alternatively, the Lisboa Card (lisboacard.org) is an excellent value, giving free travel on bus, metro, tram, and Lisbon's unique lifts as well as free admission to 26 museums and monuments (including Sintra) and discounts to various other tours and river cruises. Valid for 24, 48, or 72 hours with reductions for children under 11, it makes sense if you are trying to cover a lot in a short time. It is sold at all Turismo de Lisboa offices and at Carris kiosks. **Carris** (tel 213 500 115, carris.pt) operates all Lisbon public transport except the metro.

Lisbon's most popular form of transport for visitors is the tram, a quaint visual feature of this hilly city. The No. 28 is the classic visitors' route that trundles up from the Baixa to the Alfama, and No. 12 takes you from Praça da Figueira through the Alfama. For Belém, pick up the modern No. 15 tram from Praça do Comercio. Be very careful about your pockets and bags, however, as pickpockets are common.

Suburban trains will whisk you on day trips out of town to Sintra (from Rossio station), to Estoril and Cascais (from Cais do Sodré), or to Setúbal and farther south from the spectacular station of Oriente.

Taxis are plentiful and can be hailed in the street. They run on meters and are reasonably priced. A tip of 10 percent is appreciated. To order a taxi, call **Radio Taxis de Lisboa** (tel 218 119 000 or 219 362 113). Alternatively, Uber now functions in both Lisbon and Porto (uberportugal.pt).

By Air

Throughout the country there are a number of small airports with limited facilities. It is possible to fly from the international airports to many of these smaller ones with the domestic airline Sevenair (tel 214 489 949 or 937 205 444, fly.sevenair.com). However, given Portugal's inspiring landscapes, it is a far better option to travel by car, train, or bus.

By Bus

Private bus routes crisscross the country, can be faster than trains, and are particularly useful for more remote areas. The most comfortable and fastest are expressos (tel 707 223 3444, rede-expressos.pt), closely followed by rápidos, but you should avoid the ultraslow carreiras. Timetables change with the seasons and school holidays so it is advisable to get information directly from the bus station.

By Car

Portugal's road network has greatly expanded and improved over the last few years, but the drivers have not! Portugal ranks first in the European Union for road fatalities. That being said, you can get around very safely if you remain extra alert to unexpected maneuvers by other drivers and to unannounced turnoffs. The other problem is the shortage of road signs, so make sure you have a good map and navigator. One-way systems through labyrinthine towns can also present frustrations; it is generally advisable to park in a town center and walk rather than attempt to explore by car.

The new six-lane highways (auto-estradas) are all toll roads (portagem). IP (itinerário principal) roads are direct routes, but sometimes only have three lanes and alternating passing lanes in each direction. At the bottom end of the scale, minor country roads are the most scenic and quiet—the only hazards being tractors, carts, or animals. One of Portugal's greatest pleasures is getting off the beaten track into remote villages, and having a car is the only way to do this.

Drive on the right and give priority to traffic coming from the right. Seat belts are obligatory in both front and back seats and children under 12 must sit in the back. There are strict penalties for driving under the influence, with imprisonment for more than 0.12 percent alcohol in your blood. On highways, dipped headlights in daylight are compulsory. Police will impose instant fines for traffic offenses such as speeding, parking, or lack of seat belts.

Speed limits are 75 miles per hour (120 kph) on toll highways, 62 miles per hour (100 kph) on IP and IC (secondary principal) roads, and 53 miles per hour (90 kph) on national roads. In towns the limit is 30 miles per hour (50 kph).

Car rental through **Hertz, Avis, National, Budget,** and **Europcar** is easy to arrange in your own country by phone or Internet. Most of these companies have counters at the airports of Lisbon, Porto, and Faro alongside local outfits and rates are reasonable, particularly out of season. You must be older than 21 years old (though some agencies require a minimum age of 23 or even 25) and have had a license for at least a year. An international driving license is not necessary. Rental rates usually include mileage and CDW (collision damage waiver), with optional daily surcharges for personal or passenger insurance. The rental company will give you details of breakdown services and what to do in case of an accident.

Fuel, whether unleaded *(sem chumbo)* or diesel *(gasóleo)*, is easily available with little difference in prices between vendors. International credit cards are accepted at most gas stations, but be aware that in small rural places ATM machines may be less frequently available.

By Ferry

Ferries cross the Tejo River in Lisbon from Belém, Cais do Sodré, and Terreiro do Paço (Praça do Comercio). You can also try a private river cruise with **Cruzeiros Tejo** *(tel 213 461 586, cruzeirostejo. pt)*, or **Tagus Cruises** *(tel 925 610 034, taguscruises.com)*. Porto is the starting point for numerous boat trips and cruises along the Douro River beginning at the Cais de Ribeira. Several companies offer tours: **PortoTours** *(tel 223 393 472 or 939 552 340, portotours .com)* has a wide range, from a boat tour of the bridges to an upriver trip to Pinhão; **Portowellcome** *(tel 223 747 320 or 916 986 257, portowellcome.com)*, in Vila Nova de Gaia, organizes similar boat trips.

By Train

There is a vast range of comfort in the Portuguese train network, from fast Alfa Pendular to the cattle-train style of the *regionais*. The quickest and most punctual Alfa Pendular (some only first class) cover north–south routes between Lisbon and Porto (via Coimbra) and Lisbon–Algarve (Faro). Next down come *directos intercidades*, reasonably fast local trains with first- and second-class sections. *Regionais* cover the rural routes, stopping at every stop along the way. Timetables and fare information are available from **Comboios de Portugal** *(tel 707 210 220, cp.pt)*, where seat bookings on fast trains should be made. Special tourist tickets are available in Porto and Lisbon, as well as the Algarve.

Portugal also offers quaint narrow-gauge railways in the Douro Valley.

PRACTICAL ADVICE
Communications

The word *correio* denotes a post office or services. First-class inland mail is *correio azul*. To mail packages, go to the counter marked *encomendas*. Most post offices have telephone booths with operators as well as fax services (Corfax), and in some cases Internet services. Also available at post offices is EMS, an express service. Post offices are normally open 8:30 a.m. to 6:30 p.m., Monday through Friday. In bigger towns they may also open on Saturday morning, while they may close at lunchtime in small towns.

Public telephones take coins, phone cards *(cartão telefónico)*, or credit cards. Phone cards can be bought at post offices and newsdealers. Phone numbers prefixed with 800 *(linha verde—green line)* are toll free and those with 808 charge local rates throughout the country.

International code for Portugal: + 351
Directory inquiries: 118
Emergency: 112

Internet

Internet cafés and wireless areas are readily available and you will have little trouble getting online in Lisbon and Porto. Even in smaller places public access is increasingly available in cafés and local shopping malls. Tourist offices sometimes offer free Internet as do some municipalities elsewhere.

You may want to purchase a local SIM card, particularly if you will be traveling in Portugal for more than a week. Prices are reasonable.

Conversions

1 kilo = 2.2 pounds
1 liter = 0.2642 U.S. gallon
1 kilometer = 0.62 mile
1 meter = 1.093 yards
1 centimeter = 0.39 inch

Women's Clothing

U.S.	8 10 12 14 16 18
Europe	36 38 40 42 44 46

Men's Clothing

U.S.	36 38 40 42 44 46
Europe	46 48 50 52 54 56

Women's Shoes

U.S.	6–6.5 7–7.5 8–8.5 9–9.5
Europe	38 39 40–41 42

Men's Shoes

U.S.	8 8.5 9.5 10.5 11.5 12
Europe	41 42 43 44 45 46

Electricity

Voltage is 220V or 225AC. Plugs have two round pins. American appliances will need an adaptor and a transformer.

Etiquette & Local Customs

The Portuguese are relaxed and self-confident, particularly the younger generation. Although formality and politeness are still very important to the Portuguese, much of their lifestyle is comparable to any Western country. Although many Portuguese speak English, French, or both, they will appreciate your effort if you learn a few greetings in Portuguese. Their age-old enmity with Spain means that the Spanish language is less welcome, although it is understood. Above all, the Portuguese are extremely helpful; you will never be at a loss for assistance.

Holidays

Regional festivals and saints' days are celebrated locally but the main public holidays are the following:

January 1 (New Year's Day)
February (Shrove Tuesday)
March/April (Good Friday)
April 25 (1974 Revolution Day)
May 1 (Labor Day)
Early June (Corpus Cristi)
June 10 (Portugal and Camões Day)
August 15 (Assumption)
October 5 (Republic Day)
November 1 (All Saints' Day)
December 1 (Restoration of Independence)
December 8 (Immaculate Conception)
December 25 (Christmas)

Media

There are four main daily newspapers, either Lisbon- or Porto-based, and two weeklies, in Portuguese. A weekly English-language news-paper, the *Portugal News (theportugalnews.com)* contains useful local information as well as a round up of Portuguese news stories. English and American newspapers can be found in the main towns of Lisbon, Porto, Coimbra, and Funchal, as well as more widely in the Algarve.

Most hotels have satellite TV bringing international channels to your bedroom. The country's channels are in Portuguese, with the exception of movies, usually broadcast in their original languages.

Money Matters

The currency in Portugal is the euro, like most other European countries. Exchange counters can be found at airports, otherwise most banks change foreign currency—although rates and charges vary considerably. ATMs are widespread and accept all major international cards. Large hotels will exchange currency but generally at lower rates.

A sales tax known as IVA (VAT) in Portugal is at present 23 percent. Persons from outside the European Union, when visiting for fewer than 180 days, can reclaim this tax by requesting the form "Isenção de IVA" and presenting it to customs when leaving Portugal.

Opening Times

Banks are open from Monday to Friday, 8:30 a.m. to 3 p.m., except on public holidays.

Shopping hours are 9:30/10 a.m. to 7 p.m. Monday to Friday, but in smaller towns most close for lunch 12:30/1 p.m. to 2:30 p.m. Saturday opening is 9 a.m. to 1 p.m., however, this is now changing and many reopen in the afternoon. Shopping centers are open 10 a.m. to 12 a.m. all week except possibly for the Christmas and Easter Day holidays.

Many museums are closed on Mondays, and some on Sunday afternoons as well. Attractions in smaller towns may close for lunch. For all sights, check ahead if you are planning a visit on a holiday.

Places of Worship

Catholic churches are found throughout Portugal, but it is rare to find facilities for other denominations, except in the Algarve and on Madeira. When visiting churches, be sensitive to local worshippers, dress conservatively, and keep your voices low.

Time Differences

Portugal runs on GMT (Greenwich Mean Time), so it is one hour behind Spain, the same as the United Kingdom, and five hours ahead of Eastern Standard Time. Between the end of March and end of October, it operates on GMT plus one hour.

Tipping

When tipping at restaurants, the Portuguese tend to leave approximately 5 percent. A foreign tourist is generally expected to leave 10 percent, though there is no law stating what you should leave. When tipping, bear in mind that one euro does not go very far and good service helps to make the meal.

Travelers With Disabilities

The needs of the disabled are addressed with reserved parking spaces in public areas and special toilets at airports, stations, and entertainment venues. In Lisbon there is a dial-a-ride disabled bus service *(tel 213 613 141).* For full information, visit *portugal acessivel.pt.*

In the United States, the best source of information for the blind is the **American Foundation for the Blind** *(tel 212 502 7600 in the U.S., afb.org).* Numerous tour operators are specialized in trips for people with various types of disabilities, including **Accessible Journeys** *(accessiblejourneys.com),* which operates from the U.S., and **Disabled Holidays** *(disabledholidays .com)* in the U.K., which also offers accessible vacations focused on adventure and sport.

Visitor Information

The Portuguese National Tourist Office has some useful tourist literature, but it is, above all, their large network of offices throughout the country that are to be commended. Bi- or trilingual staff in even the smallest towns will talk you through whatever you want to see and comment intelligently on recent changes.

Portuguese National Tourist Office
866 2nd Ave., 8th fl., New York
Tel 646 723 0213
info.usa@turismodeportugal.pt
visitportugal.com

EMERGENCIES
Crime & Police
Portugal is a generally safe, law-abiding country and the greatest crimes are petty thefts and pick-pocketing, mainly in the touristic areas of the cities. Drivers should not leave belongings visible inside the car: Lock everything up in the trunk.

By calling 112 from anywhere in Portugal you will be connected to fire, police, and ambulance services. Every fire brigade also maintains one or more ambulances for emergencies. Security in cities and towns is handled by the Polícia de Segurança Pública (PSP), in rural areas by the Guarda Nacional Republicana (GNR), and the traffic by the GNR's Brigada de Trânsito. On motorways and several major roads there are SOS phone boxes for help in accidents or breakdowns.

Embassies & Consulates
U.S. Embassy
Avenida das Forças Armadas, Lisbon
Tel 217 273 300 or 210 942 000
(after hours/emergency dial either telephone number and press 0 to speak to embassy official)
pt.usembassy.gov

Canadian Embassy
Avenida da Liberdade 196–200
3rd fl., Lisbon
Tel 213 164 600
lsbon.consular@international.gc.ca
travel.gc.ca

Canadian Consulate
Rua Frei Lourenço de Santa Maria 1, Faro
Tel 289 803 757

British Embassy & Consulate (Lisbon)
Rua de São Bernardo 33, Lisbon
Tel 213 924 000
(in case of emergency, also Tel 213 924 000)

www.gov.uk/world/organisations/british-embassy-lisbon

British Vice Consulate (Algarve)
Edifício A Fábrica, Avenida Guanaré, Portimão
Tel 282 490 750

Health
Pharmacists can give advice on simple health problems and suggest treatment. They are also allowed to sell many medicines without a doctor's prescription. A green cross on a white background denotes a pharmacy. A red cross on a white background denotes a Red Cross station. In most towns there are Emergency Treatment Centers (SAP), providing medical assistance 24 hours a day.
Ambulance, tel 112
Poisons unit, tel 217 950 143

Lost Property
In Lisbon, lost property is centralized at the police station in Praça Cidade Salazar *(tel 218 535 403)*. In the case of theft, you will need to make a police report at any station for insurance purposes.

What to Do in Case of a Car Accident
In the case of a minor accident, fill out a *Constat Amiable* (European Accident Statement), which is an exchange of basic information with the other driver. One of these forms should be included in your rental documents. In the case of a serious accident, dial 112.

FURTHER READING
The number one Portuguese author is undoubtedly the poet Fernando Pessoa, whose post-humous international best seller *Book of Disquiet* revolves around his melancholic ruminations in Lisbon, although its underlying sense of tragedy is perhaps not the most uplifting for vacations.

Luís Vaz de Camões's 16th-century classic, *The Lusiads*, is Portugal's national epic in the style of Homer's *Odyssey*; it relates Vasco da Gama's sea voyage to India.

In contemporary literature, António Lobo Antunes's novels should be read for a lucid perspective with a strong psychological bent. Some are harrowing indictments of society; all are deep, including *The Inquisitor's Manual* (which re-creates Salazar's regime and its iniquities).

José Cardoso Pires's exciting thriller *Ballad of Dog's Beach* is, on the surface, a detective story, yet it reveals the underside of the Salazar regime and its secret police.

José Saramago is considered the doyen of Portuguese literature, and his books vary considerably in their approach. His personal travel guide, *A Journey to Portugal*, is an insightful read while traveling. Saramago's best seller *Baltasar and Blimuda* gives a surrealistic reflection of life in 18th-century Portugal during the building of the Mafra palace. Saramago was awarded the Nobel Prize for literature in 1998.

Miguel Torga's books *The Creation Days One and Two* and *Tales from the Mountain* (banned under the Salazar regime) should be read by anyone traveling in the Trás-os-Montes area, where they are set.

Marion Kaplan's book, *The Portuguese: The Land and Its People* (rev. ed., 2006), somewhat overambitiously tries to cover everything under the sun, but gives great insight into the Portuguese way of life and recent history.

Jean Andersen's *Food of Portugal* (1994), although older, remains a standard for information on regional food, wine, markets, restaurants, and, of course, recipes.

Barbara Segall's illustrated book *The Garden Lover's Guide to Spain and Portugal* (1999) will inspire you to discover Portugal's beautiful private and public gardens.

HOTELS & RESTAURANTS

Finding comfortable and interesting places to sleep and eat can make all the difference in your visit. Portugal offers a wide range of hotel and restaurant selections in all price categories and styles—there's something for every taste.

HOTELS

Portuguese hotel classification is a minefield defying all logic, but luckily moves are afoot to simplify the system. Taxes are included in the rates unless stated otherwise. (Breakfast is generally included, but should be confirmed when booking.) There are, however, huge rate variations from season to season. April through September sees the highest rates, peaking in August, while November through February has the lowest.

You can rely on the 38 state-owned but privately managed *pousadas* (inns) for upscale comfort and atmosphere. These converted palaces, monasteries, and castles (*pousada charme, histórica,* or *histórica design*) or relatively modern hotels in exceptional locations (*pousada natureza*) offer individualized decors, excellent service, and reliable restaurants serving regional cuisine. If you intend to visit several, consider the Pousadas Passport discount program. For more information, contact **Pousadas de Portugal** (*tel 808 252 252, pousadas.pt*).

Private hotels range from luxurious palaces to basic accommodations. In between, *estalagens* (country inns) and *albergarias* (city or town inns), are generally very acceptable, but some can be frayed at the edges. The smaller scale *residencial* (denoted by an R) and *pensão* (P) can be an excellent value and are generally well maintained.

In recent years an almost countless number of trendy hostels have opened up, primarily in the larger cities. Some are cheap and basic, others offer quirky and often very comfortable lodging. For booking, visit hostelworld.com. At the bottom of the scale are rooms in restaurants or private houses, which can also be perfectly acceptable.

State-monitored, privately owned guesthouses fall into further categories: *turismo de habitação* (TH), in houses of architectural interest, *turismo rural* (TR), and *agro-turismo* (AT), the latter two offering rural and farmhouse accommodations respectively. These establishments provide good opportunities to meet local people and to experience Portuguese home life and generosity. Breakfasts can be epicurean feasts with home-baked pastries, local cheeses and sausages, freshly squeezed orange juice, and strong coffee or tea. Some places will also provide dinner for a modest charge.

Many of these establishments are available through **Solares de Portugal** (*Praça da República, 4990 Ponte de Lima, tel 258 931 750, solaresdeportugal.pt),* an association offering self-catering cottages or guest rooms in some superb manor houses and country estates.

For an excellent choice of private accommodation in manor houses and guesthouses, as well as well-vetted hotels, all of which can be reserved on its website, contact **Manor Houses of Portugal** (*tel 258 835 065, manorhouses.com*).

RESTAURANTS

Each region of Portugal has a plethora of restaurants that range from the lowly *tasca* (tavern) or *cervejaria* (beerhouse with simple food) to a *restaurante* (more upscale, offering a choice of dishes), a *marisqueira* (specializing in fish and shellfish), or a *churrasqueira* (featuring spit-roasted or grilled foods). Appearances can sometimes be deceiving: You may see smart businessmen lunching in a somewhat scruffy *tasca*—they are drawn by the quality of the food, the price, and the friendliness of the owners, not the decor. Cafés and some restaurants often serve a lunchtime *prato do dia* (dish of the day), which is generally homemade and a good value.

Depending on location and style, Portuguese restaurant prices are very reasonable compared with other European countries and servings can be gigantic. It may be possible to order a half portion—*meia dose*—particularly at lunch at more traditional, casual places.

A law passed in 2007 prohibited smoking in public places. Bars and restaurants are now nonsmoking, though some proprietors allow smoking in covered outdoor areas.

Hours of Eating

Generally speaking, lunch is eaten between 12:30 and 2:30 p.m.; dinner between 8 and 10 p.m. (sometimes later in large towns). If you wish to dine at one of the upscale city restaurants, you should make a reservation.

How to Order

At the table in most places, you'll be served bread, butter, olives, and assorted appetizers. These are not free; you can refuse them with a smile—though unless very elaborate they do not add much to the bill. And you may regret sending them back: It may take a while for your food to be prepared—always a good sign of freshness.

Vegetarians are not well catered to beyond soups and omelets. It may be necessary to special request vegetable side dishes. Fish dishes are plentiful throughout Portugal.

Drinks

The Portuguese grapes produce some excellent, little-known wines—reds, whites, and rosés—and the *vinho da casa* (house wine) can generally be relied upon to be an excellent choice.

In the north, enjoy the refreshing young *vinho verde* (white or red), with its low alcohol content. Portuguese beer, a strong lager, comes in three brands: Sagres, Crystal, and Super Bock. Mineral water *(agua mineral)* is always available either com gas (carbonated) or sem gas (still).

After eating (although rarely done by locals), you may wish to sample one of Portugal's famous fortified wines, like port or Madeira.

Check & Tip

A conta (the check) may be slow in coming, and is sometimes known to contain the odd error, so best to give it a quick look.

The Portuguese leave small tips—barely 5 percent—but if you like the service and food you should leave more.

Credit Cards

Many hotels and restaurants accept major credit cards. If the credit card icon is shown, then American Express, Master-Card, and Visa are all accepted. Those that accept some or none are noted.

ORGANIZATION

Hotels and restaurants are listed first by chapter area and town, then by price category, then in alphabetical order with hotels listed first.

Hotel restaurants of note have been boldfaced in the hotel entries and indicated by a restaurant icon beneath the hotel icon (if they're unusually special, they are treated in a separate entry within the restaurant section).

▶ LISBON

🏨 BAIRRO ALTO HOTEL
€€€€€
PRAÇA LUIS DE CAMÕES 2
TEL 213 408 288
bairroaltohotel.com
Situated on the Praça de Camões, between the Chiado and Bairro Alto districts, this elegant boutique hotel is well situated for exploring the city. It offers well-appointed rooms with a sophisticated decor in muted tones and classic, wood-paneled bathrooms. Its rooftop terrace enjoys outstanding views.
🛏 55 🅿 ⬆ 😊 🎯
📶 Free 🔒

🏨 POUSADA DE LISBOA
€€€€€
PRAÇA DO COMÉRCIO,
BAIXA
TEL 210 407 640
pousadas.pt
For consistently high standards, not to mention the prime location, check into one of the latest Pestana hotels to open in the capital. The well soundproofed rooms look out over the Praça do Comércio and the river Tejo beyond. Rooms are of a good size for a European capital, decorated in a minimal style with luxury bathrooms.
🛏 90 ⬆ 🏊 🎯 📶 Free 🔒

🏨 MY STORY HOTEL ROSSIO
€€€
PRAÇA D. PEDRO IV 59,
BAIXA
TEL 213 400 380
mystoryhotels.com
Perfectly located in the central Rossio square and set over four floors, this is one of Lisbon's new wave of fashionable establishments catering to the design-conscious on a mid-range budget.
🛏 46 ⬆ 😊 📶 Free 🔒

PRICES

HOTELS
An indication of the cost of a double room in the high season is given by € signs.

€€€€€	Over €250
€€€€	€200–€250
€€€	€150–€200
€€	€80–€150
€	Under €80

RESTAURANTS
An indication of the cost of a three-course meal without drinks is given by € signs.

€€€€€	Over €65
€€€€	€40–€65
€€€	€28–€40
€€	€15–€28
€	Under €15

🏨 AS JANELAS VERDES
€€
RUA DAS JANELAS VERDES 47
TEL 213 968 143
asjanelasverdes.com
Plush and ornate, this 18th-century mansion is now a boutique hotel. Well situated between Lapa and the docks in an area of embassies, this longtime favorite is close to the Museu Nacional de Arte Antiga. The top-floor library and terrace make relaxing escapes. Room sizes vary, and some offer views over the Tejo River.
🛏 29 🅿 ⬆ 😊 😊
📶 Free 🔒

🏨 STAY INN LISBON HOSTEL
€€
RUA LUZ SORIANO 19
TEL 213 425 149
stay-inn-lisbon-hostel.lisbon.
hotels-pt.net
Hostels in Lisbon are booming and offer exceptional value

🔆 Air-conditioning 🏊 Indoor Pool 🏊 Outdoor Pool 🎯 Health Club 📶 Wi-Fi 🔒 Credit Cards

with several consistently in the top-10 international hostel charts (hostelworld.com). In addition to dorm accommodation, many of these "design hostels" offer simple but tastefully decorated private rooms with ensuite facilities.

[1] 2 private suites, 4 private rooms, plus dorms 🛜 Free 🗑 All major cards

SOMETHING SPECIAL

🏨 YORK HOUSE
🍴 €€
RUA DAS JANELAS VERDES 32
TEL 213 962 435
yorkhouselisboa.com
Arguably one of Lisbon's most attractive hotels, this establishment—partly converted from a 17th-century convent—maintains its position in the upper echelons of style. Terraced patios and ivy-clad walls introduce a dramatic interior of vaulted corridors painted in deep oxblood and Prussian blue, yet the rooms have been given a discreet contemporary makeover. Graham Greene and John le Carré stayed here. The restaurant (€€€) serves seasonal cuisine with top wines.

[1] 32 P 🗑 🗑 🛜 Free 🗑

🍴 BELCANTO
€€€€€
LARGO DE SÃO CARLOS 10,
BAIRRO ALTO
TEL 213 420 607
belcanto.pt
One of the few restaurants in the country to boast two Michelin stars, Belcanto is the flagship restaurant of Portuguese chef José Avillez, who takes diners on a gastronomic and sensory journey where, as he likes to say, "each dish tells a story and stirs the emotions of those willing to try it." Reservations essential.
🕐 Closed Sun.–Mon.
🗑 🗑 🗑

SOMETHING SPECIAL

🍴 100 MANEIRAS
€€€€–€€€€€
RUA DO TEIXEIRA 39,
BAIRRO ALTO
TEL 910 918 181
100maneiras.com
This fashionable Bairro Alto restaurant only offers a ten-course, fixed-price tasting menu from a kitchen headed up by the highly acclaimed, Sarajevo born, Ljubomir Stanisic. His highly creative dishes fuse traditional Portuguese ingredients with French sophistication; for the complete experience, splash out on the accompanying wine-tasting menu. Alternatively, try the 100 Maneiras Bistro (Largo da Trindade 9), open until 2 a.m.
🕐 Closed L 🗑 🗑 🗑

🍴 ALMA
€€€€
RUA ANCHIETA 15, CHIADO
TEL 213 470 650
almalisboa.pt
In 2015, chef-of-the-moment Henrique Sá Pessoa reopened his restaurant Alma, in the Chiado, within the stone-arched, former warehouse of Livraria Bertrand (one of the oldest bookstores in Europe). His innovative creations are influenced by traditional Portuguese cuisine and by his personal travels, particularly to the far east. The work of the chef and his staff has been rewarded with two Michelin stars. Reservations required.
🕐 Closed Mon. 🗑 🗑 🗑

🍴 MINI BAR TEATRO
€€€€
RUA ANTÓNIO MARIA
CARDOSO 58, CHIADO
TEL 211 305 393
minibar.pt
One of chef Avillez's five Lisbon restaurants, this is a top pick if Belcanto is out of reach. The ambience is informal, yet dramatic, a nod

to the theater next door; the cocktails are prepared to perfection (arguably the best pisco sour this side of the Andes); and the tasting menu is 10 courses of tapa-sized sensory overload. Reservations advised.
🕐 Closed L 🗑 🗑 🗑

🍴 CLUB DE FADO
€€€
RUA SÃO JOÃO DA PRAÇA 86–94
TEL 218 852 704
club-de-fado.com
Tucked in the lower part of the Alfama, this bar/restaurant is geared to nightly fado sessions. Eat and drink traditional fare until 2 a.m. while listening to some of the capital's top voices. Be sure to note the Moorish arch integrated into the bare stone walls.
🕐 Closed L 🗑 🗑

🍴 CHAPITÔ À MESA
€€–€€€
RUA COSTA DO CASTELO 7
TEL 218 875 077
chapito.org
Just down from the castle, this young and cheerful tapas bar is part of the Chapito circus school cooperative. The attractive terrace is a good spot for a salad or grilled lamb on warm evenings; a smarter upstairs restaurant (with views) serves international cuisine. Live music most evenings.
🗑

🍴 MARTINHO DA ARCADA
€€–€€€
PRAÇA DO COMÉRCIO 3
TEL 218 879 259
In this elegant antique café, founded in 1782, you can breathe in the history of the literature and writers of this grand country. Pessoa stopped by often on his way home from work and events were held with José Saramago and the Brazilian author Jorge Amado. Get a seat at

---

a table outside, under the portico, order a cup of coffee or a snack, and savor your surroundings.

🖭 🗝

🍽 PALÁCIO CHIADO
€€–€€€
RUA DO ALECRIM 70,
CHIADO
TEL 210 101 184
palaciochiado.pt
For something a little different, try Lisbon's food court in a palace. Built in 1781, this elegant building reopened in 2016—its frescoes, elaborate cornices, and stained-glass windows carefully restored—its glorious salons now home to seven fine-dining experiences. Start on the ground floor with a drink and an appetizer before heading to the more sumptuous (and more expensive) rooms on the top floor.

🖭 🖭 🗝

🍽 BONJARDIM
€€
TRAVESSA DE SANTO ANTÃO
7–11
TEL 213 427 424 OR 213 424 389
Tourists flock to this Lisbon classic; a simple, no frills eatery with its several dining rooms and terraces. Try the typical Portuguese piri-piri chicken, served with generous portions of fries and tomato salad.

🕒 Closed Mon. 🖭 🗝

🍽 HIMCHULI
€€
RUA DO SACRAMENTO
A ALCANTARA 48
TEL 213 901 722
restaurantehimchuli.com
A total change from local venues, this Nepalese restaurant in Lapa has a very smart yet intimate setting. Friendly staff serve vegetarian specialties as well as rich meat dishes such as lamb with spinach.

🕒 Closed Sun. L 🖭 🗝

🍽 TIME OUT MARKET
€–€€
MERCADO DA RIBEIRA,
AVENIDA 24 DE JULHO
TEL 213 951 274
timeoutmarket.com
Part traditional food market, part gastro-food hall, come to pick up produce and deli items or explore at the approximately 50 food stalls next door, each representing well-established and highly regarded Lisbon restaurants and food outlets.

🍽 BREAD 4 YOU
€
RUA DOS SAPATEIROS 4, BAIXA
TEL 211 394 632
In the heart of the Baixa, this popular café is a fantastic place to stop off any time of the day, whether for fresh artisan breads and pastries or tapas and light meals. Prices are low and the owners friendly.

🗝 Cash only

🍽 CAFÉ A BRASILEIRA
€
RUA GARRETT 120
TEL 213 469 541
Part of a venerable old chain, this café has strong literary associations. Poet Fernando Pessoa, whose bronze statue sits outside, used to frequent this showpiece of wood paneling and ornate details. The café serves delectable pastries and coffee, although service can be offhand.

🖭 🗝

▶ ## PORTO E NORTE

AMARANTE

🏨 CASA DA CALÇADA
🍽 €€€€
LARGO DO PAÇO 6
TEL 255 410 830
casadacalcada.com
Ask for a river-facing room in this superb, ochre-painted, boutique hotel opposite the church. Rooms are spacious

and comfortably furnished; especially luxurious are the large marble-clad bathrooms. The staff are friendly and attentive. Don't miss the Michelin-starred **Largo do Paço** restaurant.

🛏 30 🅿 🖭 🌊 🛜 Free 🗝

🍽 CONFEITARIA DA PONTE
€
RUA 31 DE JANEIRO
TEL 255 432 034
Supplying the Amarante people with fluffy pão de ló (light eggy sponge cake) since 1930, this establishment, overlooking the river near the old bridge, is an obligatory stop for your morning coffee or an afternoon tea. In addition, there is a huge selection of typical doces conventuais (sweet, egg-based delicacies) to sample.

🖭 🗝 Cash only

BRAGA

🏨 HOTEL BRACARA AUGUSTA
€€
AVENIDA CENTRAL 134
TEL 253 206 260
bracaraaugusta.com
Centrally located downtown, offering exceptionally friendly service and superb value. Rooms are simple but clean and comfortably furnished and the breakfast is generous.

🛏 18 🅿 🖭
🛜 Free 🗝

🏨 HOTEL DO PARQUE
€€
LARGO DO SANTUÁRIO DO
BOM JESUS
TEL 255 603 470
hoteisbomjesus.pt
High on the hilltop above Braga, next to the church of Bom Jesus do Monte, are the Hotel do Parque and its sister hotels, **Hotel do Elevador** and **Hotel do Templo.** All three offer the same standard of

service and amenities, though the rooms at the Elevador can claim the most spectacular views and the Parque benefits from a quieter setting backed by the park.

🛏 49 🅿 🔃 🚭 📶 Free 🚭

🏨 HOTEL RESIDENTIAL DONA SOFIA
€

LARGO DE SÃO JOÃO DO SOUTO 131
TEL 253 263 160 OR 253 271 854
hoteldonasofia.com
Well located on an attractive square in central Braga within minutes of the sights. Rooms are bright and comfortable; a good, budget-friendly stopover.

🛏 34 🅿 🔃 🚭 📶 Free 🚭

🍴 COZINHA DA SÉ
€€

RUA D. FREI CAETANO BRANDÃO 95
TEL 253 277 343
cozinhadase.com
Arguably Braga's best restaurant, located around the corner from the Cathedral, its traditional, northern granite interior reflects the northern cuisine, served in generous portions. Pork with chestnuts and apple puree or the local Barrosã beef are good choices.

🕐 Closed Sun. D & Mon.
🚭 🚭

🍴 RESTAURANTE PANORAMICO
€€

HOTEL DO ELEVADOR BOM JESUS DO MONTE
TEL 253 603 400
This is the perfect spot to watch the sunset from high above Braga. Book a table by the window and indulge in the local cuisine, whether octopus or kid goat with rice, both preceded by classic cabbage soup. Helpful service and good wines will complete the evening.

🅿 🚭 🚭

🍴 A BRASILEIRA
€

LARGO BARÃO DE SÃO MARTINHO 17
TEL 253 262 104
Step into the past at one of Braga's oldest cafés, its interior retaining all its original architectural features. This city icon first began selling coffee in 1907; drinks and light snacks are served throughout the day.

🚭 🚭 Cash only

BRAGANÇA

🏨🍴 POUSADA BRAGANÇA
€€€

ESTRADA DO TURISMO
TEL 273 331 493
pousadas.pt
One of the more modern *pousadas* from the 1970s, offering efficiency and comfort. It lies just outside the city center of Bragança, across the Fervença River, and enjoys superb views over the valley to the distant mountains. All rooms have balconies and nice views.

🛏 28 🅿 🔃 🚭 🚭 🏊 📶 Free 🚭

🏨 A LAGOSTA PERDIDA
€€

RUA DO CIMO 4
ALDEIA DE MONTESINHO
TEL 273 919 031 OR 933 125 106
lagostaperdida.com
A great base for those wanting to explore the countryside around Bragança by car or on foot, this family-run guesthouse provides spacious, clean rooms with rustic features and modern bathrooms. Renovated to a high standard, the property has a heated pool and attractive landscaped patios. Standard prices include breakfast and a three-course dinner with wine.

🛏 6 🅿 🚭 🏊 📶 Free in public areas 🚭

PRICES

HOTELS
An indication of the cost of a double room in the high season is given by € signs.

€€€€€	Over €250
€€€€	€200–€250
€€€	€150–€200
€€	€80–€150
€	Under €80

RESTAURANTS
An indication of the cost of a three-course meal without drinks is given by € signs.

€€€€€	Over €65
€€€€	€40–€65
€€€	€28–€40
€€	€15–€28
€	Under €15

🏨 HOTEL TULIPA
€

RUA DR. FRANCISCO FELGUEIRAS 8–10
TEL 273 331 675
tulipaturismo.com
This friendly, well-maintained and well-managed hotel is right in the town center, and ideal for those traveling on a budget. The clean, simply furnished rooms have all the essentials.

🛏 29 🔃 🚭 📶 Free 🚭

SOMETHING SPECIAL

🍴 SOLAR BRAGANÇANO
€€

PRAÇA DA SÉ 34
TEL 273 323 875
Located in an 18th-century mansion, this gem of a restaurant seems to step back in time with chandeliers, heavy linen tablecloths, and classical music. Feast on game and regional dishes such as rabbit, pheasant with chestnut, partridge with grapes, wild boar,

or venison; fish is on offer, too. Wines are local, *vinho verde* or Barca Velha from the Douro. The owners ensure that everyone is happy. There is a garden for warmer days.

⊡ Closed Mon. 🔡 🝏

CHAVES

SOMETHING SPECIAL

🏨 FORTE DE SÃO
🍴 FRANCISCO
€€

RUA TERREIRO DA CAVALARIA
TEL 276 333 700
fortesaofrancisco.com

An unusual place converted from a former convent inside the walls of a fort. Patios are filled with antiques, architectural features, and paintings. Rooms are classically tasteful, but interest lies in the spacious public areas, including a huge pool with views. The restaurant serves seasonal Trás-os-Montes specialities such as chestnut soup, veal and chorizo, and Chaves smoked ham.

🛏 58 🅿 🝏 🝏 🝏 🝏
🝏 Free 🝏

DOURO VALLEY

🏨 VINTAGE HOUSE
€€€€

RUA ANTÓNIO MANUEL SARAIVA, PINHÃO
TEL 254 730 230 or 220 133 137
vintagehousehotel.com

This hotel occupies a breathtaking site in Pinhão, on the banks of the Douro River. Generous public areas are decorated in traditional Portuguese fashion and chintz prevails in the bedrooms, all of which overlook the river. Excellent amenities make it popular with boat cruises from Porto.

🛏 43 🅿 🝏 🝏 🝏 🝏
🝏 Free in public areas 🝏

🏨 CASA DOS VISCONDES
DA VARZEA
€€€

VARZEA DE ABRUNHAIS, LAMEGO
TEL 254 690 020 or 967 606 385
hotelruralviscondes varzea.com

This well-appointed rural hotel sits in a lovely vineyard setting. The owner has virtually rebuilt her family manor house and added lavish and antique furnishings, making your stay feel slightly akin to staying with an aristocratic friend. In addition to the pool, horseback riding and tennis are available.

🛏 29 🅿 🝏 🝏 🝏 Free in public area 🝏

GUIMARÃES

SOMETHING SPECIAL

🏨 HOTEL DA OLIVEIRA
🍴 €€

RUA DE SANTA MARIA
TEL 253 514 157
hoteldaoliveira.com

Smack in the middle of the monuments, this hotel retains the ambience of its former manor house status. Creaky wooden floors and whitewashed walls contrast delightfully with contemporary furnishings. Reserve a room on the top floor, as evening carousing in the square below can be noisy. The excellent restaurant serves regional specialities and has tables outside.

🛏 16 🝏 🝏 🝏 🝏 Free 🝏

🍴 SÃO GIÃO
€€€€

AVENIDA COMENDADOR JOAQUIM DE ALMEIDA FREITAS 56, MOREIRA DE CÓNEGOS
TEL 253 561 853 OR 253 141 086
restaurantesaogiao.pai.pt

For something sophisticated, head 20 minutes south of Guimarães to the village of Moreira de Cónegos. Considered to be one of the best

restaurants in the region, São Gião's elegant dining room looks out over vineyards; its food is traditional yet refined and its wine list is extensive.

⊡ Closed Sun. D & Mon 🔡 🝏

PENEDA-GERÊS

🍴 ESPIGUEIRO DE SOAJO
€–€€

SOAJO, ARCOS DE VALDEVEZ
TEL 258 576 136

The perfect place to stop for a well-deserved break from the national park's tortuous roads. Sit inside the rustic restaurant or in its garden to sample such local specialties as chicken and rice, *bacalhau* (salted cod), or roast kid. The owner speaks fluent English.

🅿 ⊡ Closed Sun. D & Mon., also Nov. 🝏

PORTO

SOMETHING SPECIAL

🏨 INTERCONTINENTAL
🍴 PORTO–PALACIO DAS
CARDOSAS
€€€€

PRAÇA DA LIBERDADE 25
TEL 220 035 600
ihg.com

This luxurious, five-star hotel sits on Porto's main square within a converted 18th-century palace and within walking distance of the city's main attractions. Guest rooms are beautifully furnished, marble bathrooms are packed with fluffy towels, and many rooms have views over the square. Staff are friendly and knowledgeable.

🛏 121 🅿 🝏 🝏 🝏 🝏
🝏 Free 🝏

🏨 PESTANA VINTAGE
🍴 PORTO HOTEL
€€€€

PRAÇA DA RIBEIRA 1
TEL 223 402 300

pestanaporto.com
The setting is hard to beat as this top hotel stands directly opposite the port lodges on the main quay of the Douro River. Built into a section of medieval wall and occupying houses dating from the 16th to 18th centuries, it still manages to maintain an intimate feel. Most rooms overlook the river.

🛏 48 🅿 🔄 Ⓢ 🔄 📶 Free 🚭

🏨 HOTEL EUROSTARS DAS ARTES
€€
RUA DO ROSÁRIO 160–164
TEL 222 071 250
eurostarsdasartes.com
A short walk or tram ride from the city center, this hotel offers a great base for those wishing to escape the bustle of downtown. Easily recognized by its period blue-tile facade, its interior is modern with all the expected amenities of a four-star hotel. Don't miss the excellent buffet breakfast. If you have a car, book a place in the underground parking lot.

🛏 89 🅿 🔄 🔄 📶 Free 🚭

🏨 CATS HOSTEL PORTO
🍴 €
RUA DO CATIVO 26–28
TEL 220 043 030
catshostels.com/porto
In recent years, as in Lisbon, Porto has seen a wave of design hostels open their doors to the more discerning budget traveler. In addition to dorm beds, many offer private rooms with ensuite bathroom facilities and family rooms, as well as self-catering facilities. The hostel is centrally located with a pleasant roof bar terrace.

🛏 16 🔄 Ⓢ 📶 Free 🚭

🍴 PEDRO LEMOS
€€€€€
RUA PADRE LUIS CABRAL 974
TEL 220 115 986
pedrolemos.net

Inside this Foz town house, Michelin-starred chef Pedro Lemos takes seasonal ingredients and traditional recipes and transforms them into works of art. Do not expect huge portions, but do expect exceptional quality and creativity. The tasting menu is a good option and there is an extensive list of Portugal's best wines, available by the glass.

🪑 44 🕒 Closed Sun. & Mon. Ⓢ 🚭

🍴 CANTINHO DO AVILLEZ
€€€
RUA MOUZINHO DA SILVEIRA 166
TEL 223 227 879
cantinhodoavillez.pt
One of star-chef José Avillez's seven restaurants this, like its Lisbon counterpart (Rua dos Duques de Bragança 7, Chiado, tel 211 992 369), produces simple, well-executed dishes rooted in Portuguese tradition. Service is friendly and well informed.

Ⓢ 🔄 🚭

🍴 O PAPARICO
€€€
RUA DE COSTA CABRAL 2343
TEL 225 400 548
opaparico.com
The best way to get to this discreet restaurant is by taxi, as it is a 10- to 15-minute drive from the center and quite hard to find, with no sign. Knock to get in, and you'll be rewarded with a true Portuguese dining experience. English-speaking proprietor Sergio is enthusiastic in presenting traditional dishes made with quality ingredients and a great selection of affordable wines.

🕒 Closed L & Sun.–Mon. 🔄 🚭

🍴 FLOW
€€–€€€
RUA DA CONCEIÇÃO 63
TEL 222 054 016
A restaurant that's very elegant, very chic, and very good. Its modern style has traditional

touches and great attention to detail is evident in all of its dishes. If you're looking for a romantic evening and the opportunity to enjoy Mediterranean fusion specialties, this is the place to be.

🕒 Closed Mon. L & Sun. 🔄 🚭

🍴 DAMA PÉ DE CABRA
€
PASSEIO DE SÃO LÁZARO 5
TEL 223 196 776
Deli-café offering fresh snacks at great prices throughout the day. Sit out on the terrace to watch the world go by.

🕒 Closed Sun.–Mon. & Tues.–Thurs. D 🔄
🚭 Cash only

🍴 MERCADO DO BOM SUCESSO
€
PRAÇA DO BOM SUCESSO 132
TEL 226 056 610
mercadobomsucesso.com
To sample some of the best the city has to offer, all under one roof, head to the Bom Sucesso market, south of the Boavista roundabout. Built in the 1940s, the building is home both to traditional market vendors selling fresh produce from across the region, and now a fashionable, urban food hall where some of the city's most renowned restaurants have set up stalls.

🕒 Produce market closed Sun.

🍴 PEDRO DOS FRANGOS
€
RUA BONJARDIM 223
TEL 222 008 522
Portuguese fast food at its best. There are other options but most come for the excellent no-frills *frango* (chicken) and fries with optional hot *piri-piri* sauce. An icy-cold *imperial* (draught beer) goes well with it.

🔄 🚭

VIANA DO CASTELO

CASA MELO ALVIM
€€€
AVENIDA CONDE DA
CARREIRA 28
TEL 258 808 200
casameloalvim.com
This palatial boutique hotel makes a stylish base for exploring the northern Minho. Each room is furnished in a different period style, integrating modern fittings; bathrooms are in marble and polished granite. The restaurant serves new Portuguese cuisine as well as traditional fare. A courtyard garden adds to the charms.
🛈 20 🅿 🚻 🅢 🛜 Free 🅢

QUINTA DA BOUÇA D'ARQUES
€€€
RUA ABREU TEIXEIRA 333,
VILA DE PUNHE
TEL 968 044 992
boucadarques.com
A 20-minute drive south of Viana do Castelo, and 10 minutes from the Atlantic beaches, this beautiful quinta makes the perfect base for exploring the region. The owners have ingeniously married centuries-old architecture with chic lines of glass and steel to create this tranquil haven.
🛈 7 self-catering cottages 🅿 🅢 🏊 🛜 Free 🅢 Cash only

TASQUINHA DA LINDA
€€€
DOCA DAS MARÉS A-10
TEL 258 847 900
tasquinhadalinda.com
For the freshest of seafood head toward the fishermen's quarter near the docks and the fort. Tasquinha da Linda is frequented by locals and visitors alike thanks to its quality and good service. The latest catch is always on display and once selected, comes grilled with potatoes and vegetables.

When in season, try the highly prized and rather pricey percebes (goose barnacles).
⊕ Closed Sun. 🅢 🅢 🅢

O CAMELO
€€
RUA DE SANTA MARTA 119,
SANTA MARTA DE PORTUZELO
TEL 258 839 090
camelorestaurantes.com
For the best in Minho fare, drive 10 minutes east of Viana, along the road N202, to this local landmark. If visiting at lunchtime, sit outside under the vines and enjoy delicious, tapas-style starters, succulent roast meats, and mouthwatering desserts, perfectly accompanied by a glass of fresh vinho verde.
🅿 ⊕ Closed Mon. 🅢 🅢

LIZ CAFFE BAR
€
RUA GAGO COUTINHO 17
TEL 963 062 529
As their slogan implies, this establishment serves primarily "tapas and toast." The tapas include platters of cheeses, quince jam, and regional sausages; the toasts are hearty slabs of local bread topped with cured hams, cheese, tomato, and more. Try to accompany this with a carafe of sangria, a cold beer, or a house cocktail.
⊕ Closed L & Sun.–Mon. 🅢 🅢

▶ CENTRO

AVEIRO

AVEIRO PALACE HOTEL
€€
RUA DE VIANA DO CASTELO 4
TEL 234 421 885
hotelaveiropalace.com
Located opposite the bridge over Aveiro's central canal in the heart of town with classically furnished rooms and a

large TV lounge. Noisier front rooms have double-glazed windows. Good value and friendly.
🛈 48 🚻 🅢 🛜 Free 🅢

HOTEL MOLICEIRO
€€
RUA BARBOSA DE MAGALHÃES 15–17
TEL 234 377 400
hotelmoliceiro.pt
Centrally located and overlooking Aveiro's main canal, this independently owned, modern hotel with abundant artworks welcomes with a glass of port wine and ovos moles (local pastry), served upon arrival.
🛈 49 🚻 🅢 🛜 Free 🅢

CASA DE CHÁ MUSEU DE ARTE NOVA
€
CASA MAJOR PESSOA, RUA DR. BARBOSA MAGALHÃES 9
TEL 234 406 485 OR 916 842 029
Located on the ground floor of its outstanding art nouveau building, the Museu de Arte Nova's tearoom, with both indoor and patio seating and a range of teas, coffees, and local cakes, is the perfect place to take a break. In the evening the teapots are exchanged for cocktail shakers and the venue becomes a lively bar, often with live music at the weekends. Caipirinhas are the drink of choice.
⊕ Closed Mon. 🅢 🅢

COIMBRA

PALACE HOTEL DO BUÇACO
€€€
MATA DO BUÇACO
TEL 231 937 970
almeidahotels.pt
This classic fairy-tale hotel sits in the wonderful Buçaco forest. Built in 1885 in neo-Manueline style, it has since 1917 been a luxury hotel with all the expected

trimmings—marble, antiques, azulejos, tapestries, chandeliers—with service to match.
(i) 64 P ⊖ ⊗ 📶 Free in public areas ⊗

🏨🍴 PALÁCIO DA LOUSÃ BOUTIQUE HOTEL
€€€
RUA VISCONDESSA DO ESPINHAL
TEL 239 990 800
palaciodalousa.com
With a new and modern wing, this village manor house is full of charm, about 14 miles (23 km) southeast of Coimbra. Antiques and contemporary styles mix well, and many original baroque features remain. Views over the mountains from the bar, restaurant, and pool.
(i) 46 P ⊖ 🛏 📶 Free in public areas ⊗

SOMETHING SPECIAL

🏨🍴 QUINTA DAS LAGRIMAS
€€€
RUA ANTÓNIO AUGUSTO GONÇALVES
TEL 239 802 380
quintadaslagrimas.pt
Fully renovated in 2016, this historic manor house on the Mondego River is an absolute gem. It features romantic botanical gardens, a designer spa, two restaurants (one fusion and the other award-winning gourmet), indoor and outdoor pools, and a golf course. The elegant salons and supposed aristocratic ghosts create a refined atmosphere.
(i) 54 P ⊖ ⊗ 🛏 🎾 📶 Free in public areas ⊗

🏨 HOTEL ASTÓRIA
€€
AVENIDA EMÍDIO NAVARRA 21
TEL 239 853 020
astoria-coimbra.com
Centrally located by the river, this art deco hotel is one of Coimbra's landmarks., a 1919 flat-iron building with a good standard of rooms and service.
(i) 62 ⊖ ⊗ 📶 Free in public areas ⊗

🍴 RESTAURANTE DOM PEDRO
€€€
AVENIDA EMÍDIO NAVARRO 58
TEL 239 829 108
Steps lead down to this traditional, somewhat touristy restaurant, where tiled walls, a fireplace, and copper pans give a timeless appeal. Specialties include roast kid and lamb, but there is plenty of seafood, too.
⊗ ⊗

🍴 DUX PETISCOS E VINHOS
€€
RUA DOS COMBATENTES DA GRANDE GUERRA 102
TEL 239 402 818
duxrestaurante.com
Describing itself as an "urban taverna," Dux takes regional specialities and gives them a modern twist, a welcome break from the delicious, yet often heavy, traditional fare. Dishes such as smoked mountain sausage with caramelized pear are served on wooden boards or wrapped in brown paper. Extensive and complete wine list.
⊗ ⊗

🍴 NOTES BAR & KITCHEN
€€
RUA DR. MANUEL RODRIGUES 17
TEL 239 151 726
This tapas bar 10 minutes north of Coimbra's center is worth the walk. Among others, try the *ameijoas à bulhão pato* (clams with coriander and garlic broth) or the black açorda with clams. Good selection of artisan beers, and quality wines by the glass.
(🕐) Closed Sun.–Mon.
⊗ ⊗

🍴 CAFÉ SANTA CRUZ
€
PRAÇA 8 DE MAIO
TEL 239 833 617
cafesantacruz.com
Open since 1923, Coimbra's classiest café is found inside a wing of the Santa Cruz monastery. The palatial vaulted hall and wooden features give it character, while outside tables have a great view of the square. Drinks, coffee, and snacks served until midnight.
⊗ Cash only

🍴 ZÉ MANEL DOS OSSOS
€
BECO DO FORNO 12
TEL 239 823 790
Arrive early at this popular, rustic *tasca* (eatery) tucked behind the Hotel Astória; it doesn't take reservations. Tables are cramped but the food is honest, portions generous, and prices cheap. Soups and roast meats recommended.
(🕐) Closed Sun. ⊗ Cash only

GUARDA

🏨 SOLAR DE ALARCÃO
€€
RUA D. MIGUEL DE ALARCÃO 25
TEL 271 214 392
solardealarcao.pt
The rooms in this unusual 17th-century family guesthouse opposite Guarda's Cathedral feature dark wood and a general surfeit of furnishings. Garden, pergola, game room, and café also on hand.
(i) 3 P 📶 Free in public areas ⊗ Cash only

SERRA DA ESTRELA

SOMETHING SPECIAL

🏨🍴 POUSADA DO CONVENTO DE BELMONTE
€€€€
SERRA DA ESPERANÇA, BELMONTE
TEL 275 910 300

pousadas.pt
Perched on the far end of Belmonte's outcrop, this stylishly converted medieval monastery is a real dream. When you can see them through the clouds, the mountain views are hard to beat. Granite is omnipresent, but the rooms and public spaces have subtle modern touches. Excellent restaurant serves regional cuisine.

[] 24 🅿 🚫 💺 ♨
🛜 Free 🚫

VISEU

🏨 HOTEL GRÃO VASCO
€€
RUA GASPAR BARREIROS 1
TEL 232 423 511
hotelgraovasco.pt
Classic in style, with a sense of grandeur despite its relative youth, this hotel is perfectly located by the old quarter in leafy gardens. Facilities are excellent, for the price, with spacious rooms comfortably appointed, some with balconies.

[] 109 🅿 🚫 🚫 ♨
🛜 Free 🚫

SOMETHING SPECIAL

🍴 CORTIÇO
€€
RUA AUGUSTO HILÁRIO 47
TEL 232 416 127
restaurantecortico.com
It's worth the trip to eat here. Two restaurants on both sides of a narrow cobbled street serve mouthwatering regional fare in a rustic setting; hams hang from the ceiling, yet tablecloths are embroidered white linen. Try the three-day-old rabbit bean stew or, better still, the divine duck rice baked with *chouriço* sausage and bacon. Excellent wines accompany the hearty dishes, and the service is warm, yet professional.

🕒 Closed Mon. 🚫 🚫

▶ LISBOA E REGIÃO

BATALHA

🏨 CASA DO OUTEIRO
€€
ESTRADA DE FÁTIMA 15
TEL 244 765 806
casadoouteiro.com
Recently upgraded from guesthouse to hotel, this modern house sits opposite Batalha's monastery. Good facilities and prices for immaculate white rooms, some with balconies and monastery views. Note: The nearby highway can be noisy.

🅿 🚫 ♨ 🛜 Free 🚫

🍴 SOPAS & C.
€
TRAVESSA ALVARO SAMPAIO 1
This small, simple restaurant is unpretentious and inexpensive. Why should you go there? With an excellent location, behind the monastery, the cuisine is light and very good. Serving Portuguese specialties, along with excellent steak, you can also find delectable vegetarian dishes.

🚫 🚫

CALDAS DA RAINHA

🍴 ADEGA DO ALBERTINO
€€
RUA JÚLIO SOUSA 7
TEL 262 835 152
adegadoalbertino.pt
Checkered tablecloths, tiled floors, and a multitude of rustic objects suspended from the rafters make this a welcoming restaurant. Specialties include *bacalhau* (salted cod), shrimp rice, and entrecôte steak served with an unusual wine, honey, and almond sauce.

🅿 🕒 Closed Sun. D & Mon.
🚫 🚫

CASCAIS

SOMETHING SPECIAL

🏨 FAROL DESIGN HOTEL
🍴 €€€€€
AVENIDA REI HUMBERTO II
DE ITALIA 7
TEL 214 823 490
farol.com.pt
Right beside the lighthouse at the western end of Cascais, this hotel is part century-old mansion, part sleek glass box jutting out over the waves. Rooms have balconies or glazed walls; all have hydromassage tubs. Hip interiors styled by different Portuguese designers impress in scarlet, black, and white. The funky bar and adjoining restaurant, **The Mix and Sushi Design** (€€€), prepare sushi as well as Mediterranean fusion dishes.

[] 34 🅿 🚫 🚫 ♨ 🛜
Free 🚫

🏨 FORTALEZA DO
🍴 GUINCHO
€€€€
ESTRADA DO GUINCHO
TEL 214 870 491
fortalezadoguincho.pt
This mock medieval fortress built in 1956 occupies a prime position at the end of the lovely and otherwise wild beach, Praia da Guincho. The rooms are ornately decorated. The Michelin-starred French restaurant's panoramic windows overlook the waves, and the central patio is just the place for a relaxing drink.

🅿 🚫 🚫 ♨
🛜 Free 🚫

🏨 PESTANA CIDADELA
🍴 CASCAIS
€€€€
FORTALEZA DA CIDADELA,
AVENIDA D. CARLOS I
TEL 214 814 300
pestana.com
Set within the 16th-century Cidadela fortress, this hotel offers every state-of-the-art

comfort in airy rooms, some with spectacular views over the sea and bay area. Several terraces and an indoor pool that opens out in warmer months enjoy the sea breeze.

🛏 126 🔁 🚭 🏊

📶 Free 🚭

🏨 CASA DA PERGOLA
€€

AVENIDA VALBOM 13
TEL 214 840 040
pergolahouse.pt

A turn-of-the-20th-century mansion cascading in bougainvilleas and decorated in traditional Portuguese style. Lots of character and a friendly staff make this guesthouse shine in keeping with Cascais's aristocratic past. A large living room can be used by guests and the pretty front garden has plenty of sitting areas.

🛏 10 🚭 📶 Free 🚭

🍴 CAFÉ GALERIA HOUSE OF WONDERS
€€

LARGO DA MISERICÓRDIA 53
TEL 911 702 428

With a delightful roof terrace for warmer days and a cozy ground-floor dining room with a blazing log burner for chillier evenings, this café serves homemade vegetarian dishes, mezze platters, fresh juices, and tasty cakes. It also acts as a gallery for local artists.

🚭 🚭

🍴 MERCADO DA VILA
€–€€

RUA PADRE MOISÉS DA SILVA
TEL 911 702 428

As is the trend, Cascais's municipal market now, in addition to the traditional stalls, has several trendy eateries and juice bars, some under cover, others in the central courtyard. Try **Marisco na Praça** (tel 214 822 130) for seafood and **Páteo do Petisco** (tel 218 002 663) for tapas.

🍴 POLVO VADIO
€

RUA AFONSO SANCHES 47
TEL 214 830 968 OR 912 799 519

As its name suggests, this rustic little eatery specializes in polvo (octopus), fresh from the ocean off Cascais. Served grilled, fried, or baked, it is especially good stewed with rice (arroz de polvo). Don't miss craft beers from nearby Estoril.

🕐 Closed Tues. 🚭
🚭 Cash only

🍴 SOMOS UM REGALO
€

AVENIDA VASCO DA GAMA 36
TEL 214 865 487

With its recognizable chimney, this popular restaurant offers some of the best grilled chicken in the area; for the real deal, order with piri-piri.

🕐 Closed Wed. 🚭
🚭 Cash only

LEIRIA

🍴 RESTAURANTE O MANEL
€€

RUA DR CORREIA MATEUS 50
TEL 244 832 132

This old-fashioned classic, popular with local business people at lunch, has an open fireplace at the back used to barbecue fresh fish—in particular sea bass—priced by the kilo. Bacalhau (salted cod) is another house specialty and there is a good wine list.

🕐 Closed Sun. 🚭 🚭

ÓBIDOS

🏨 HOTEL REAL D'ÓBIDOS
€€€€

RUA DOM JOÃO DE ORNELAS
TEL 262 955 090
hotelrealdobidos.com

Medieval themes run riot in this hotel just outside the castle walls. Men in velvet tunics, tights, and pointy

shoes proffer your room key on a heavy chain, while armor rattles in the corridor. Each room shows its own different, always medieval, style. The pool has fabulous views toward the castle and the surrounding countryside.

🛏 18 🔁 🚭 🏊 📶 Free 🚭

🏨🍴 POUSADA DE ÓBIDOS
€€€€

PAÇO REAL
TEL 210 407 630
pousadas.pt

Portugal's first castle converted into a pousada, in 1951, this unique place is a real eyrie, reached by steep steps. As well as rooms within the castle, there are also rooms set in adjoining village houses. The restaurant offers superb views.

🛏 18 🅿 🚭 🔁 📶 Free 🚭

🏨 CASA DE S. THIAGO DO CASTELO
€€

LARGO DE S. THIAGO
TEL 262 959 587
casas-sthiago.com

This pretty little corner guesthouse nestles under a cascade of bougainvilleas on the main street inside the castle walls. Cozy rooms are arranged around a sitting room and breakfast patio.

🛏 8 📶 Free 🚭

🍴 A NOVA CASA DE RAMIRO
€€€

RUA PORTA DO VALE
TEL 967 265 945

Attractively decorated in warm colors with large stone urns and archways, the Casa de Ramiro is an excellent address for a romantic dinner. It has won local gastronomic awards for specialties such as arroz de pato (duck rice), cabrito assado (roast kid), and bife com pimenta (pepper steak).

🕐 Closed Sun. & Mon. L
🚭 🚭

PENICHE

🏨 CASA DO CASTELO
€€

ESTRADA NACIONAL 114 NO. 16,
ATOUGUIA DA BALEIA
TEL 262 750 647
casacastelo.com
These picturesque 17th-century buildings originated in a Moorish castle. In season, oranges from the beautiful shady garden are squeezed into your breakfast juice. Rooms are decorated with good taste. It is located only about 4 miles (6.5 km) from Peniche, and Óbidos lies a short distance in the opposite direction. There is a minimum three-night stay.

🛏 8 🅿 📶 Free in public areas 🔕 Cash only

🏨 ME PENICHE
🍴 €€

AVENIDA MON. MANUEL
BASTOS
TEL 262 780 500
mh-hotels.pt
This huge five-story modern hotel, among the best at Peniche, overlooks a pool and gardens beside Praia da Consolaçao, a beach just south of town. All rooms have balconies.

🛏 90 🅿 🔄 ❄ 🏊 ≋ 📶 Free 🔕

🍴 ESTELAS
€€

RUA ARQUITECTO PAULINO
MONTEZ 21
TEL 965 030 770
Peniche's best seafood restaurant consistently wins local gastronomic awards. Easily located on the street that runs inland from the tourist office. Anyone tiring of lobster or fish stew should try the juicy Tournedos steak accompanied by one of the excellent local wines.

🅿 ❄ 🔕

🍴 MARISQUEIRA MIRANDUM
€€

RUA DOS HEROIS DO ULTRAMAR
TEL 963 270 017
Not much to look at from the outside, and set back from the shore in a rather run-down part of town, Marisqueira Mirandum serves some of the best seafood in the area, including clams, crab, lobster, and fish grilled to perfection. The fish selection will be limited to what was available from the local fishermen that day. It is also popular among locals, so book ahead.

🕐 Closed Wed. & Thurs. L ❄ 🔕

🍴 RESTAURANTE A SARDINHA
€€

RUA VASCO DA GAMA 81
TEL 262 781 820
restauranteasardinha.com
In addition to sardines (when in season), A Sardinha is renowned for its excellent fish stew (caldeirada de peixe) and rice with mixed seafood or monkfish (arroz de marisco or arroz de tamboril). Meat lovers should try the highly prized porco preto (pork from free-range Alentejo black pigs). Portions are big—leave some room for the delicious desserts.

❄ 🔕

SANTARÉM

SOMETHING SPECIAL

🏨 CASA DA ALCÁÇOVA
€€€

LARGO DA ALCÁÇOVA 3,
PORTAS DO SOL
TEL 243 304 030 OR 936 080 100
alcacova.com
Guarded by the citadel ramparts, this 18th-century manor house offers imaginatively but classically decorated rooms (each different in style and furniture) with great views of

the river and plains. Original artworks adorn the walls, the bathrooms have Jacuzzis, and the furnishings are of high quality; you will more than likely sleep in a four-poster bed. A minimum stay of two nights is requested.

🛏 8 🅿 🔄 ❄ 📶 Free in public areas 🔕

🏨 CORINTHIA SANTARÉM HOTEL
€€

AVENIDA MADRE ANDALUZ
TEL 243 330 800
santaremhotel.net
A large modern hotel with predictable facilities geared to business travelers. Rooms have good views over the Tejo River and the city.

🛏 105 🅿 🔄 ❄ 🏊 ≋ 🎾 📶 Free 🔕

SÃO MARTINHO DO PORTO

🏨 QUINTA DA VIDA SERENA
€€

RUA PRINCIPAL 115,
MACALHONA, ALFEIZERÃO
TEL 262 989 287
quinta-serena.com
This guesthouse, surrounded by nature, a few-minutes drive outside São Martinho do Porto, has farm animals, organic fruit trees, vineyards, and complete quiet. The kind management offers both self-catering apartments and studios, plus an outdoor plunge-pool and private beach for swimming in the river Dão.

🛏 4 🅿 🏊 ≋ 📶 Free in public areas 🔕

SESIMBRA

🍴 MARISQUEIRA O RODINHAS
€€–€€€

RUA MARQUÊS DE POMBAL 25
TEL 212 231 557
marisqueiraorodinhas.pt

Simple, with no frills, this traditional Portuguese restaurant offers quality food and prompt and efficient service. Opt for the seafood platter or the grilled prawns or, for something a little unusual, try the house specialty *chocos fritos* (fried cuttle fish). Arrive early or book in advance.

🕐 Closed Wed. 🚭

🍴 O CANHÃO
€€

RUA DA FORTALEZA 13
TEL 212 231 442 OR 969 188 786
restauranteocanhao.pt
Just behind the fortress, this welcoming seafood restaurant serves regional classics such as fish stew and *cataplana*. The interior has partly tiled walls and a traditional style plus a few tables for outside dining.

🚬 🚭

SETÚBAL

🏨 HOTEL DO SADO
🍴 BUSINESS & NATURE
€€

RUA IRENE LISBOA 1
TEL 265 542 800
hoteldosado.com
Renovated to a high standard, this 18th-century manor house with its additional modern wings offers comfortable accommodation with fine views over the Sado estuary. Claiming to be Portugal's first allergy-friendly hotel, it provides specially prepared rooms for guests with respiratory problems and its restaurant caters for a variety of food allergies and intolerances.

🛏 66 🅿 ⬍ 🚭 📶 Free 🚬

🍴 COPA D'OURO II
€€

AVENIDA LUISA TODI 530
TEL 265 232 942
Traditional and professional, this well-established seafood restaurant is a favorite with the locals. Now on the main bayside road, with a big

glass-sided dining room, the menu features the morning's catch, from red mullet to sea bass.

🕐 Closed Tues. 🚬 🚭

🍴 PEROLA DA MOURISCA
€€

RUA DA BAIA DO SADO 9
TEL 265 793 689
A few minutes drive west of Setúbal, this restaurant is popular among locals in the know for serving some of the best seafood in the region (meat lovers are also well catered for). Staff are efficient and friendly.

🕐 Closed Tues. 🚬 🚭

SINTRA

SOMETHING SPECIAL

🏨 TIVOLI PALÁCIO DE
🍴 SETEAIS
€€€€

RUA BARBAROSA DU BOCAGE 8
TEL 219 233 200
tivolihotels.com
This magical 18th-century palace with extensive gardens is a 10-minute walk from central Sintra. The interiors of the numerous salons and guest rooms are stunning, spacious, and decorated in fittingly regal style. Guests are cosseted with a choice between a pool with valley views, tennis courts, or a long drink at the terrace bar.

🛏 30 🅿 ⬍ 🚭 〰
📶 Free 🚬

🏨 LAWRENCE'S
🍴 HOTEL
€€€

RUA CONSIGLIÉRI PEDROSO 38–40
TEL 219 105 500
lawrenceshotel.com
This privately owned boutique hotel trades on its age and brief association with Lord Byron. Rooms are cozy, and quite small, but the hotel is

quaint with enjoyable patios and terraces. Centrally located with views, it also has a gourmet restaurant (€€€€).

🛏 17 🅿 ⬍ 📶 Free 🚬

🏨 SINTRA BLISS HOUSE
€€

RUA DR. ALFREDO COSTA 15–17
TEL 219 244 541
sintrablisshouse.com
Situated in the center of Sintra, near the train station, Bliss House offers designer interiors and, in warmer months, breakfast in the leafy garden.

🛏 17 🚭 📶 Free 🚬

🍴 CAFÉ SAUDADE
€

AVENIDA MIGUEL BOMBARDA 6
TEL 212 428 804
A three-minute walk from the train station, this café serves homemade snacks and light meals into the early evening. Its popular fixed breakfast and brunch menus offer good

value; afternoon tea offers scones and other homemade pastries.

🅰 🅢

🍴 NAU PALATINA
€

CALÇADA DE SÃO PEDRO 18
TEL 219 240 962
This cozy little eatery serves a variety of delicious tapas, either in individual portions on a slab of bread or in dishes to share. The attentive staff are happy to talk you through the menu of cured meats, regional cheeses, wild prawns, and more—and don't miss desserts! Arrive early or book in advance.

⊕ Closed L & Sun.–Mon.
🅰 🅢 Cash only

TOMAR

🏨 HOTEL DOS
🍴 TEMPLÁRIOS
€€

LARGO CÂNDIDO DOS REIS 1
TEL 239 310 100
hoteldostemplarios.pt
Pleasantly located, this efficient large-scale hotel's grandiose lobby is something straight out of Bollywood. All the rooms are well laid out, most of them with generous balconies and both river and castle views.

🛏 176 🅿 🅢 🅢 🅢 🅰 🅣
🅰 Free 🅢

🏨 THOMAR STORY
GUEST HOUSE
€

RUA DE JOÃO CARLOS EVERARD 53
TEL 249 327 268 OR 925 936 273
thomarstory.pt
Its location within a historic 19th-century building in the heart of the old town makes this an ideal base for exploring the town on foot. Decor is modest but clean and modern, with some rooms equipped with their own kitchenette.

🛏 12 🅢 🅢 🅰 Free 🅢

🍴 CAFÉ PARAISO
€

RUA SERPA PINTO 127
TEL 249 312 997
This unexpected art deco jewel in an otherwise resolutely medieval town opened in 1911 and is still in the same family. It's a rare relic of the days when Portugal's intellectuals and artists would meet over coffee. Don't miss your turn sitting beneath whirring ceiling fans in this grandiose mirror-and-marble setting.

🅢 Cash only

▶ ALENTEJO

BEJA

🏨 POUSADA CONVENTO
🍴 DE BEJA–SÃO
FRANCISCO
€€€€

LARGO D. NUNO ÁLVARES PEREIRA
TEL 284 313 580
pousadas.pt
This impressive, rambling *pousada*, a Franciscan convent back in the 13th century, stands in the heart of the old town, though the one-way streets make access tricky. The massive proportions are decorated firmly in the classical style. Guests can enjoy the tennis court, pool, and billiards room.

🛏 35 🅿 🅢 🅢 🅢 🅰
🅰 Free 🅢

🍴 DOM DINIS
€€

RUA DOM DINIS 11
TEL 965 337 578
Typical Alentejano fare. Fish and seafood are on the menu, but the grilled meats—lamb or pork—are the best bet; all with generous sides of vegetables.

⊕ Closed Tues. D & Wed.
🅢 🅢

ESTREMOZ

🏨 POUSADA CASTELO
🍴 ESTREMOZ–RAINHA
SANTA ISABEL
€€€

LARGO D. DINIS
TEL 268 332 075
pousadas.pt
This castle-palace has a seven-century-long story of deaths, murder, and explosions—with Vasco da Gama, star-struck Crown Prince Pedro, and his grandmother, saintly Queen Isabel (for whom the palace was built), all thrown in at different moments. This *pousada* is one of the best, with vast, palatial proportions, antiques, character, comfort, gardens, pool, and stupendous views. You'll feel like a Liliputian in the enormous restaurant.

🛏 29 🅿 🅢 🅢 🅢 🅰
🅰 Free 🅢

🍴 CAFÉ ALENTEJANO
€€

ROSSIO MARQUÊS DE POMBAL 13–15
TEL 268 322 834
There's plenty of atmosphere at this venerable café, a favorite with the local old men. A marble staircase leads to an excellent little restaurant serving Alentejano bread soup (*açorda*), lamb and chickpea stew, and pig's feet. Comfortable en suite guest rooms (€) are also available.

🅢 🅢

ÉVORA

🏨 CONVENTO DO
ESPINHEIRO
€€€€

ESTRADA DOS CANAVIAIS, APARTADO 594
TEL 266 788 200
conventodoespinheiro.com
This luxury hotel stands in a rural setting a few miles

northeast of Évora. Once a 15th-century convent, the hotel offers slick service, extensive landscaped gardens, a gourmet restaurant, and luxury.

🛏 93 🅿 ⬛ ⬛ ⬛ ⬛ ⬛
⬛ 🛜 Free ⬛

SOMETHING SPECIAL

🏨 POUSADA CONVENTO 🍴 DE ÉVORA
€€€€
LARGO DO CONDE DE VILA FLOR
TEL 266 730 070
pousadas.pt
This superb converted convent is part of Évora's main historic cluster. Tiled floors, stone steps, a cloister garden, and tasteful antiques contribute to the atmosphere. The downside is the size of the "cell" rooms; try the main suite where a sitting room has painted walls and ceiling. The restaurant (€€€€), overlooking the cloister, has excellent regional dishes and, unusually, caters to vegetarians.

🛏 33 🅿 ⬛ ⬛ ⬛ 🛜 Free ⬛

🏨 EVORA OLIVE HOTEL
€€€–€€€€
RUA DE EBORIM 18
TEL 266 760 050
evora.luxhotels.pt
This hotel inside the city walls is modern and offers every comfort. The very cordial staff will make you feel pampered.

🅿 ⬛ ⬛ ⬛ 🛜 Free in public areas ⬛

🏨 ALBERGARIA DO CALVÁRIO
€€
TRAVESSA DOS LAGARES 3
TEL 266 745 930
adcevora.com
Located inside the old city gates, the warm staff at this charming inn serve a great breakfast. Enjoy a leisurely coffee in the lovely courtyard.

🛏 22 ⬛ 🛜 Free ⬛

🍴 O FIALHO
€€€
TRAVESSA DOS MASCARENHAS 16
TEL 266 703 079
In the same family for three generations, O Fialho has been serving traditional Alentejo food since 1945. Located in the historic center of the city, this restaurant is known across the region and beyond for its use of quality prime ingredients sourced locally. It also boasts an excellent wine cellar. Reservations advised.

🕐 Closed Mon. ⬛ ⬛

SOMETHING SPECIAL

🍴 A CHOUPANA
€€
RUA DOS MERCADORES 16–20
TEL 266 704 427
Locals queue for lunch here—the food is delicious and amazingly good value. The cozy interior has two sections, a dining room and a long bar; turnover is fast, but there is no pressure. Specialties include Alentejano pork and roast lamb with onion, garlic, and white wine; in winter they feature game dishes. Portions are gigantic; consider ordering the half portion—*meia dose*.

🕐 Closed Sun. ⬛ ⬛

ÉVORAMONTE

🍴 CAFE RESTAURANTE O EMIGRANTE
€
TRAVESSA DO MONTINHO
TEL 268 950 053
This excellent little restaurant is inexpensive and comfortable. It has indoor and outdoor seating, meticulous service, and offers appetizing traditional cuisine. The restaurant is open every day from morning until evening, and here you can savor what many consider the best Alentejo pork in the area.

⬛ ⬛

MONSARAZ

🍴 XAREZ RESAURANTE BAR
€€
RUA DE SANTIAGO 33
TEL 266 557 052
Near the castle, this friendly, popular small-scale restaurant in rural style has alfresco eating on a stone-paved terrace overlooking the plains. Daily specials include Alentejo tapas, such as asparagus with egg and bread crumbs *(migas)*.

🕐 Closed Thurs. ⬛ ⬛

PORTALEGRE

🏨 POUSADA MOSTEIRO 🍴 DO CRATO
€€€€
MOSTEIRO DA FLOR DA ROSA, CRATO
TEL 245 997 210/1
pousadas.pt
Yet another surprising *pousada*, hidden away in an imposing monastery complete with nesting storks in the hamlet of Flor da Rosa. West of Portalegre near Crato, the pousada is in the center of a rural region. The decor is ultracontemporary and imaginative. Nearby is the Alter do Chão stud farm, famed for Lusitanian horses.

🛏 24 🅿 ⬛ ⬛ ⬛ ⬛
🛜 Free ⬛

🏨 ROSSIO HOTEL
€€
RUA 31 DE JANEIRO 6
TEL 245 082 218 OR 910 265 268
rossiohotel.com
Conveniently located on the edge of the old town, the Rossio is an environmentally friendly hotel, including solar panels, LED lighting, rainwater recycling, and more. Guest rooms are well equipped with spacious bathrooms. Head to the rooftop terrace for views of the Serra de São Mamede.

🛏 18 🅿 ⬛ ⬛ ⬛ ⬛
🛜 Free ⬛

🍽 TOMBA LOBOS

€€€€

RUA 19 DE JUNHO 2

TEL 245 906 111

On the eastern side of town (off the N246-2), this is Portalegre's most sophisticated dining option. Chef José Júlio Vintém varies the menu daily, depending on what is at the local market, creating innovative dishes with unusual combinations. Don't miss the quality Alentejo wines.

🕐 Closed Sun. D & Mon.

🌀 🅰

🍽 RESTAURANTE SOLAR DO FORCADO

€€

RUA CÂNDIDO DOS REIS 14

TEL 245 330 866

If not averse to the framed bullfighting photos that grace the walls, O Forcado offers some of the best traditional cooking in town and some amazing regional wines. Housed in a former coach house, it is slightly more sophisticated than the competition. Dishes here are plated with care and service is very attentive.

🕐 Closed Sat. L & Sun. 🌀 🅰

SANTIAGO DO CACÉM

🏨 HERDADE DO FREIXIAL

€€

ESTRADA DE SÃO LUIS, VILA NOVA DE MILFONTES

TEL 283 998 556 OR 963 697 680

herdadedofreixial.com

Check in here for a rural retreat from which to explore the Alentejo coast. With spectacular views overlooking the river Mira, choose between self-catering accommodation or guest suites. The infinity pool (with poolside bar) and Jacuzzi offer plenty of opportunity for relaxation.

ℹ️ 8 🅿 🌀 🈂 🛜 Free 🅰

SERPA

🏨 CASA DA MURALHA

€€

RUA DAS PORTAS DE BEJA 43

TEL 284 543 150

casadamuralha.com

This very unusual private guesthouse is built into the walls of Serpa, with aqueduct arches looming overhead. Large, tasteful rooms with Alentejano painted furniture all open onto a lovely courtyard of orange trees. (The oranges will become your breakfast marmalade.) Access from outside the walls is from Rua dos Arcos.

ℹ️ 4 🌀 🛜 Free 🅰

🍽 RESTAURANTE O ALENTEJANO

€€

PRAÇA DA REPÚBLICA 6

TEL 284 544 335

This restaurant, popular with locals, sits above a café on Serpa's main square. Lofty vaulted ceilings lend style, and the wine list is impressive. Tasty Alentejano fare includes a delicious *ensopada de borrega* (lamb stew), pork with clams, and *bacalhau* (cod).

🍽 48 🕐 Closed Sun. D & Mon. 🌀 🅰

SERRA DE SÃO MAMEDE

🏨🍽 POUSADA DE MARVÃO SANTA MARIA

€€€

RUA 24 DE JANEIRO 7

TEL 245 993 201

pousadas.pt

Friendly and small in scale, two adjoining houses have been converted into this cozy, fairly simple *pousada*. Rooms are cheerful and some have great views over the countryside, as does the restaurant.

ℹ️ 31 🌀 🌀 🌀 🛜 Free 🅰

🏨🍽 HOTEL CASTELO DE VIDE

€

AVENIDA DA EUROPA, CASTELO DE VIDE

TEL 245 908 210

This small modern hotel on the edge of town offers good value rooms with balconies overlooking the hills. Though a little worn, rooms are well furnished and immaculate; cuisine is satisfactory.

ℹ️ 53 🅿 🌀 🌀 🌀 🈂 🛜 Free 🅰

VILA VIÇOSA

SOMETHING SPECIAL

🏨🍽 POUSADA CONVENTO VILA VIÇOSA

€€€

CONVENTO DAS CHAGAS

TEL 268 980 742

pousadas.pt

Located next to the royal palace in this elegant town, this *pousada*, built within a handsome Renaissance convent, maintains the cloister, oratories, and frescoed niches balanced by contemporary elements and a garden. White marble is rampant. Guest rooms have secluded balconies and public areas are generously staffed.

ℹ️ 39 🅿 🌀 🌀 🌀 🈂 🅰

▶ ALGARVE

ALBUFEIRA

🏨🍽 PINE CLIFFS RESORT

€€€€€

PRAIA DA FALESIA

TEL 289 500 300

pinecliffs.com

Commanding a prime clifftop spot and designed in spacious Moorish style, Pine Cliffs offers excellent service and facilities. A glass elevator transports you down to a fabulous beach, while up among the pines await three pools, a nine-hole

---

golf course, a tennis academy, and a children's village.

[i] 215 [P] 🔄 🔄 🔄 🔄 🔄
🔄 📶 Free 🚭

🏨 VILA JOYA
🍴 €€€€€
PRAIA DE GALÉ
TEL 289 591 795
vilajoya.com
This delicious two-star Michelin restaurant is part of a small luxury hotel, so book your table ahead. The evening five-course meal may include such specials as lobster with citrus fruit.

➕ 45 [P] [C] Closed one month Nov.–Mar. (dates vary)
🚭 🔄

COSTA VICENTINA

🍴 PONT'A PÉ
€
LARGO DA LIBERDADE 12, ALJEZUR
TEL 282 998 104
pontape.pt
This great little restaurant sits just inland from Portugal's wildest coast. A table inside the rural interior or outside by the footbridge makes a perfect spot to indulge in grilled meats, fresh shellfish, fish, and delicious homemade desserts. Occasionally live music is hosted.

[C] Closed Sun. 🚭 🔄

FARO

🏨 POUSADA PALÁCIO
🍴 DE ESTOI
€€€€
RUA SÃO JOSÉ, ESTOI
8005-465 FARO
TEL 210 407 620
pousadas.pt
Set within the restored 18th-century palace of the Count of Cadaval, 7 miles (11 km) north of Faro, this pousada retains all its former rococo splendor. Public rooms are a riot of ornate stucco, chandeliers, and mirrors; a modern wing

houses the more minimalist bedrooms.

[i] 63 🔄 🔄 🔄 🔄 🔄 🔄
📶 Free 🔄

LOULÉ

🍴 MONTE DA EIRA
€€€
MONTE DA EIRA, EN396, CLAREANES
TEL 289 438 129
restaurantemontedaeira.com
A few minutes into the hills above Loulé, a traditional farm building has been converted into this charming family-run restaurant. Traditional Portuguese food includes marinated shoulder of Iberian pork and casserole of wild boar with chestnuts and herbs.

[C] Closed Sun. D & Mon.
[P] 🚭 🔄

MONCHIQUE

🍴 A CHARRETTE
€€
RUA DOUTOR SAMORA GIL 30
TEL 282 912 142
After exploring the Algarve interior, head to this welcoming rustic establishment for hearty, traditional, mountain cuisine such as farinheira (sausage made with corn-flour and paprica) or pork with chestnuts.

[C] Closed Wed. 🚭 🔄

OLHÃO

🏨 PEDRAS VERDES
€€
SITIO DA BOAVISTA-CP 658 T, QUELFES
TEL 963 364 252
pedrasverdes.com
An exceptionally stylish guesthouse located just outside Olhão. The rooms in the whitewashed house are bright and colorful with imaginative ethnomodern designer touches. Verandas with views and dinner (€€) on request.

[i] 6 [P] 🔄 🔄 📶 Free 🔄

🍴 TASCA O GALO
€€
RUA DE A GAZETA DE OLHÃO 7
TEL 964 709 746
Situated in a narrow pedestrian street back from the main waterfront, its tables set either in the alley or in the snug interior. In addition to all the regular fish and meat dishes there are, more unusually, several vegetarian options.

[C] Closed L & Sun. 🚭 🔄

SAGRES

🏨 POUSADA DE SAGRES–
🍴 INFANTE
€€€
PONTA DA ATALAIA
TEL 282 620 240
pousadas.pt
In splendid isolation, this cliff-side pousada draws its theme from Henry the Navigator, with maps and globes omnipresent. Comfortable rooms are enlivened with vividly colored accessories, but their best asset is the view from the balcony: far-reaching vistas of Atlantic waves.

[i] 51 [P] 🔄 🔄 🔄 🔄
📶 Free 🔄

🍴 RETIRO DO PESCADOR
€
RUA DOS MURTÓRIOS
TEL 282 624 438
"If it comes from the sea, it can come to the table," is the philosophy behind this no-frills, great-value eatery. The cataplana de amêijoas (clam stew) is the house specialty, but there are plenty of options from the large coal-fired grill.

[C] Closed Sun. D & Mon.
🚭 🔄 Cash only

SILVES

🍴 RUI MARISQUERIA
€€
RUA COMENDADOR
VILARINHO 23–27
TEL 282 442 682

It's one of the Algarve region's most famous seafood restaurants. This place packs people in with its vast selection of fresh shellfish, grilled fish, seafood rice, and special *cataplana*.

🕐 Closed Tues. 🅱 🅰

🍴 CAFÉ INGLÊS
€

ESCADA DO CASTELO
TEL 282 442 585

Pizzas, fresh juices, homemade soups, and desserts are served on the sunny terrace or inside the brightly painted rooms. Live music on weekends, in season.

🍴 60 🕐 Closed Mon. 🅱 🅰

TAVIRA

🏨 POUSADA DE TAVIRA
🍴 CONVENTO DA GRAÇA
€€€€€

RUA D. PAIO PERES CORREIA
TEL 210 407 680
pousadas.pt

Well located, only a short walk from the center of the town, this restored 16th-century monastery provides comfortable, spacious rooms plus an outdoor pool and pleasant gardens.

🛏 36 🅿 🔄 🅱 🏊
🕐 Free 🅰

🍴 ZECA DA BICA
€

RUA ALMIRANTE CANDIDO DOS REIS 22
TEL 281 323 843

Whether you find a table outside in the picturesque alleyway or inside this traditional but a bit atypical restaurant, you'll feel at home at the Zeca da Bica. The personnel may seem a bit rough but they always have a smile for you, and the dishes that come out of the kitchen are the quintessence of genuine Portuguese cuisine.

🕐 Closed Wed. 🅱
🅰 Cash only

VILA DO BISPO

🏨 HOTEL MIRA SAGRES
€€

RUA 1° DE MAIO 3
TEL 282 639 160
hotelmirasagres.com

Located at the entrance to the town, this hotel, once an old pension and now restored, will surprise you with the simplicity of its décor and its relaxing atmosphere, together with a number of comforts such as a spa, a gym, and a pool. It's great for a visit to the city or as a starting point for a trip to the beach.

🛏 21 🅿 🔄 🅱 🏊 🏊 🕐 🕐 🅰

🍴 RIBEIRA DO POÇO
€€

RUA RIBEIRA DO POÇO 11
TEL 282 639 075
ribeiradopoco.com

This family-run restaurant, a former hay barn, serves all kinds of fresh fish and seafood, including *lapas* (limpets) and the highly prized *percebes* (goose barnacles). Finish with fig cheese and a shot of medronho, the local fruit brandy.

🕐 Closed Mon. & Jan. 🅱 🅰

▶ MADEIRA

FUNCHAL

🏨 BELMOND REID'S
🍴 PALACE
€€€€€

ESTRADA MONUMENTAL 139
TEL 291 717 171
belmond.com

For more than a century this palatial clifftop hotel has welcomed royalty, heads of state, and celebrities; some guests still don black tie for dinner. Stroll through the delightful lush gardens or luxuriate in the spa. The wicker furniture suits the dowager character.

🛏 163 🅿 🔄 🅱 🅱 🏊
🕐 Free 🅰

🏨 HOTEL THE
🍴 CLIFF BAY
€€€

ESTRADA MONUMENTAL 147,
SÃO MARTINHO
TEL 308 804 221
portobay.com

This exquisite high-quality hotel is located in a splendid position, just outside the city center, and offers beautiful views of both the city and the Atlantic Ocean. You will be pampered with an infinity of services and small delightful comforts that include private access to the beach, the wellness center, the pools, the whirlpool baths, and the specialties served at the hotel's restaurants and bars. You may never want to go home.

🅿 🔄 🅱 🅱 🏊 🏊 🕐 🕐 🅰

🏨 QUINTA DA PENHA DE
FRANÇA
€€

RUA IMPERATRIZ DONA AMÉLIA
TEL 291 204 650
penhafranca.com

Nestled in a lush garden a 15-minute stroll from downtown, this family-run hotel breathes old-time Madeira. Ask for a room in the atmospheric old house rather than in the modern wing.

🛏 109 🅿 🔄 🅱 🏊
🕐 Free in public areas 🅰

🍴 RESTAURANTE DO
FORTE
€€€

RUA PORTÃO SÃO TIAGO
TEL 291 215 580 OR 919 581 326
forte.restaurant

Service here is attentive and the food beautifully presented, with à la carte as well as a fixed three-course menu with drinks included, offering good value. At lunchtime, weather permitting, you can sit out by the battlements looking over the ocean.

🅱 🅰

🅱 Air-conditioning 🅱 Indoor Pool 🏊 Outdoor Pool 🕐 Health Club 🕐 Wi-Fi 🅰 Credit Cards

SHOPPING

Portugal's shopping offerings range from regional food and drink specialties, such as goat and sheep cheese or vintage port wine, to an imaginative and varied range of traditional handicrafts. Nearly every small town has a handful of specialty stores selling local products, while Lisbon is, of course, the mecca for more up-to-date designs in every field. Outside the capital, you will see some local crafts at weekly markets, but better-quality goods are sold in the specialty shops.

Throughout Portugal, craftspeople excel at making household linen and towels: In the northern Minho area you will find fantastic quality, delicately embroidered or otherwise (Amarante and Viana do Castelo are good sources). People in the know look for cotton bedspreads and lace from Guimarães and the much prized *colchas* (silk-embroidered bedspreads) of Castelo Branco—these are real investments, as they take months to make. Close rivals are the stunning appliqué bedspreads made in Nisa, in the Alentejo.

Lace is big business from the seaside resort of Peniche as far as Madeira and the Azores, as lacemaking is the traditional occupation of seamen's wives during their husbands' absences. The Serra da Estrela mountains are known for beautiful woolen blankets in subtle, natural tones and countless sheepskin products.

To the south, the Alentejo produces handwoven shawls, and blankets and, at Arraiolos, woolembroidered rugs made with techniques going back to the Middle Ages. And Portalegre is home to Portugal's tapestry industry. Another major Alentejo handicraft is woodwork, from painted furniture (Évora and Nisa) to colorful children's toys. Cork products are typical, too, in a wide variety of wares. Tourist offices have lists of workshops that can be visited, making shopping far more interesting.

Farther south still, the Algarve is where to find wickerwork, copper, and brassware.

Portugal is above all a country of potters, whether making traditional

forms of *barro* (basic terra-cotta), biscuit-ware porcelain, colorful glazed tableware, or cutting-edge designer objects. Although ceramics are not the easiest items to carry home, large outlets can arrange to ship them abroad. Head into the center to Caldas da Rainha to find Portugal's most whimsical range of ceramics, above all majolica tableware in vegetable or animal forms by Bordallo Pinheiro. Contemporary designs have been developed here, too. Coimbra is another town with a strong ceramics tradition; here you can pick up quality glazed ceramics decorated with fine floral patterns, traditionally in blue.

Outside Aveiro is the factory for a national institution: Vista Alegre porcelain. It has been produced here since 1824, but you can find the exquisite, pricey ceramic in shops all over the country. More unusual and localized is the black pottery from Bisalhães, near Vila Real, and Viseu. In the Alentejo, Estremoz specializes in charming pottery figurines and unglazed terra-cotta, and Santiago do Cacém in tiles.

If you're interested in glassware, we suggest you head to Marinha Grande, just north of Caldas da Rainha (outlets in Porto and Lisbon). Designs range from the traditional to ultramodern.

For clothing, Portugal is a great place to buy good value leather accessories. The sharpest designs are found in Lisbon. Look, too, for old-fashioned haberdashery and ironmongers' shops, both of which stock unusual and seemingly outdated items. Upscale jewelry shops, found in all large towns, sell traditional gold and silver filigree

designs (produced near Porto) or, alternatively, imaginative and stylish contemporary designs.

Aim to catch at least one street market. The vast Thursday market at Barcelos, near Braga, is Portugal's largest market for handicrafts.

■ LISBON

Arcadia, Rua de Belém 53–55, Chiado, Belém, tel 213 621 897, *arcadia.pt.* Delicious artisan chocolates made to traditional recipes and using only natural ingredients. In the same family since 1933.

Artesanato do Tejo, Rua do Arsenal 15, tel 210 312 810. Part of the Lisbon Tourism complex. A good selection of regional handicrafts.

A Vida Portuguesa, Rua Anchieta 11, Bairro Alto, tel 213 465 073, *avidaportuguesa.com.* Top quality, traditional, and retro Portuguese products make for original gifts, with four stores across the city.

Caza das Vellas Loreto, Rua do Loreto 53, Bairro Alto, tel 213 425 387, *cazavellasloreto.com.pt.* Every conceivable type of candle for sale in an 18th-century store.

Colombo Shopping Center, Avenida Lusiada, *colombo.pt.* One of the largest shopping malls in Iberia; it has around 420 stores that are open until midnight daily.

Confeitaria Nacional, Praça da Figueira 18B, tel 213 424 470, *confeitarianacional.com.* All types of confectionery set in tempting rows in wooden cabinets in the original ornate 1820s store.

Conserveira de Lisboa, Rua dos Bacalhoeiros 34, tel 218 864 009, *conserveiradelisboa.pt.* East of Praça do Comércio, this small shop sells traditional canned goods tied in brown paper and string.

Deposito da Marinha Grande, Rua de São Bento 234–236, tel 213 963 234, *dmg.com.pt.* It is impossible not to buy something at this outlet for Portugal's best glassmakers.

El Corte Inglés, Avenida António Augusto de Aguiar 31, tel 213 711 700, *elcorteingles.pt.* A useful branch of the Spanish department store stocks fashionwear, gourmet food, and household goods.

Isabel Lopes da Silva, Rua da Escola Politécnica 67, tel 213 425 032, *isabellopesdasilva.com.* Rare objects and jewelry from the 1920s through 1950s.

Leitão & Irmão Joalheiros, Largo do Chiado 16–17, tel 213 257 870, *leitao-irmao.com.* Producing high-quality jewelry and filigree for royalty and others since the 18th century.

Luvaria Ulisses, Rua do Carmo 87, Chiado, tel 213 420 295, *luvariaulisses.com.* Superlative kid gloves in wonderful hues and designs—unbeatable chic offerings.

Pelcor, Pátio do Tijolo 16, Príncipe Real, tel 218 864 205, *pelcor .pt.* Contemporary designs and top craftsmanship producing high-end fashion accessories from cork.

Santos Oficios, Rua da Madalena 87, tel 218 872 031, *santosoficios -artesanato.pt.* Wide selection of folk art from all over Portugal displayed in a restored stable, not far from the Cathedral.

Vista Alegre, Largo do Chiado 20–23, tel 213 461 401, *visaalegre. com.* The flagship showroom for Portugal's superb manufacturer of fine porcelain.

PORTO E NORTE

A Oficina, Rua da Rainha 126, Guimarães, tel 253 515 250, *aoficina.pt.* Municipal outlet for fine linens and other quality crafts.

A Pérola do Bolhão, Rua Formosa 279, Porto, tel 222 004 009. For more than 100 years, historic grocers selling great array of cured meats and cheeses.

A Vida Portuguesa, Rua Galeria de Paris 20, Porto, tel 220 022 105, *avidaportuguesa.com.* Housed in a former 19th-century textiles shop, sells classic Portuguese products in retro packaging and local Claus Porto soaps.

Arcadia, Rua do Almada 63, Porto, tel 222 001 518, *arcadia. pt.* Best chocolate in town, 100 percent all natural; in business since 1933.

Armazém, Rua de Miragaia 93, Porto, tel 222 011 702 or 918 511 959. Armazém (meaning warehouse) has maintained its original features while being transformed into a hip and fashionable cultural hub, with design and vintage shops, tapas bars, and art galleries.

Casa Ferreira da Cunha, Largo do Toural 38–39, Guimarães, tel 253 412 223, *ferreiradacunha.net.* Carry home an ornate iron doorknocker—it will be unique!

Chocolateria Delícia, Avenida Alberto Sampaio 10, Viseu, tel 232 431 950. Fine artisan chocolates made on the premises for all to see.

Deposito da Marinha Grande, Rua do Bonjardim 133, Porto, tel 222 030 752, *dmg.com.pt.* Glassware in every shape and form: carafes, vases, glasses, bowls.

Garrafeira do Carmo, Rua do Carmo 17, Porto, tel 222 003 285, *garrafeiracarmo.com.* An exhaustive range of national wines, including rare port wine vintages.

Livraria Lello & Irmão, Rua das Carmelitas 144, Porto, tel 222 002 037, *livrarialello.pt.* Neo-Gothic, palatial bookstore with ornate wood paneling and sweeping stairs; a Porto landmark.

Mercado de Barcelos, Largo Campo da Republica, Barcelos. Held in the main square every Thursday, this market is a sprawling affair selling clothing, shoes, local handicrafts, ceramics, and delicious local delicacies.

Oficina do Ouro, Sobradelo da Goma, Póvoa de Lanhoso, tel 253 943 945, *oficinadoouro.com.* Tour the gold filigree workshop (€) then visit the store at this traditional Minho jewelry center 20 miutes east of Braga.

Ourivesaria Freitas, Rua Sacadura Cabral 16, Viana do Castelo, tel 258 801 230, *ourivesariafreitas. com.* Selling quality filigree and traditional Portuguese jewelry since 1920.

CENTRO

Casa dos Linhos, Rua Visconde da Luz 103–105, Coimbra, tel 239 822 465, *casadoslinhos.pai.pt.* Good selection of household linen with traditional and modern designs.

Celeiro dos Sonhos, Avenida Capitão Silva Pereira 161, Viseu, tel 965 405 206. Good choice of regional products such as cheeses, mountain honey, and Dão wines.

Coisas e Sabores, Praça 8 de Maio 16–17, Coimbra, tel 239 824 869, *coisasesabores.com*. Quality gourmet food and gift shop selling cheeses, fine olive oils, wine, and traditional ceramic pieces.

Fábrica Vista Alegre, Ílhavo, tel 234 320 600, *vistaalegre.com*. Visit the factory, museum, and outlet store at these world-class porcelain works south of Aveiro.

■ LISBOA E REGIÃO

Chapelaria e Sapataria Liz, Rua Barão de Viamonte14 A (Rua Direita), Leiria, tel 244 823 244. Founded in 1928 and located in the center of the old town, this old-world establishment specializes in quality head- and footwear.

Made in Alcobaça, Praça 25 de Abril 64, Alcobaça, tel 262 585 402. Small craft shop selling bags, aprons, and decorative items made from the traditional all-cotton Chita de Alcobaça fabric.

Piriquita, Rua das Padarias 1–18, Sintra, tel 219 230 626, *piriquita. pt*. Do not leave Sintra without trying the local queijadas. The best are to be found at Periquita, serving since 1862.

■ ALENTEJO

A Chapelaria, Rua da República 7–9, Évora. Come here for every conceivable type of hat.

A Roda da Fortuna, Praça 10 de Maio 10, Évora, tel 266 752 619. Regional crafts including jewelry, ceramic, and cork items, many with a contemporary design element.

Aldeia da Terra, Quinta das Canas Verdes, Estrada das Hortas 202, Arraiolos. Quirky ceramic

model village with shop, 2 km from the center of town.

Ameixas de Elvas, Pastelaria Cantarinha, Rua da Cadeia 41A, Elvas, tel 268 624 241. One of the many places to pick up the famous Elvas plums (greengages).

Arabe, Rua Jorge Raposo 25, Beja, tel 961 276 559 or 968 718 872. A wide choice of local artisans' wares, ranging from ceramics to embroidery, wicker, and copper.

Fábrica de Tapetes Hortense, Rua Alexandre Herculano 22, Arraiolos, tel 266 043 082. One of many shops in town selling the world-famous Arraiolos carpets.

Loja Coisas de Monsaraz, Largo do Castelo 2, Requengos de Monsaraz, tel 266 557 484. Rustic village shop selling colorful pottery in traditional Alentejo designs.

Mizette, Rua do Celeiro, Monsaraz, tel 266 502 179. The most authentic shop in this touristy village, offering beautiful locally made handwoven wool blankets, scarves, and mats.

Mont'Sobro, Rua 5 de Outubro, Évora, tel 266 704 609. *montsobro. com*. In a town full of cork-item shops Mont'Sobro is in a league of its own with tasteful, quality jewelry, watches, and bags.

O Cesto, Rua 5 de Outubro 77, Évora, tel 266 703 344, *ocesto artesanato.com*. Wide selection of cork goods, ceramics, and painted wood items.

■ ALGARVE

Artesanato (craft) shops along the main N125 road abound with gift items, especially pottery.

About Wine, Rua Horta Machado 20, Faro, tel 965 006 735, *about wine.pt*. Extensive selection of fine wines and port, with bar area and organized tastings.

Casa das Portas, Rua 5 Outubro 1–3, Tavira, tel 281 328 772, *casa dasportas.com*. Offering choice of top-quality and original souvenirs at top prices.

Mar d'Estorias, Rua Silva Lopes 30, Lagos, tel 282 792 165, *mardestorias.com*. Innovative new venue incorporating a gift shop, art gallery, bar and bistro, and rooftop terrace with amazing views over the town and water.

■ MADEIRA

Artur de Barros e Sousa, Rua dos Ferreiros 109, Funchal, tel 291 220 622. A quaint and atmospheric family wine lodge beside several more commercial outlets.

Café Relógio, Largo Conselheiro Aires de Ornelas 12, Camacha, tel 291 922 777, *caferelogio.com*. Camacha is the center of the island's wickerwork trade and Café Relógio has been in production since 1896. Come here for every conceivable wicker item, as well as other traditional crafts.

Patricio e Gouveia, Rua do Visconde de Anadia 34, Funchal, tel 291 222 723, *patriciogouveia.pt*. One of Madeira's biggest and best embroidery outlets, with high-quality clothes and table linens.

São Francisco Wine Lodge, Avenida Arriaga 28, Funchal, tel 291 228 978, *blandyswinelodge.com*. The widest choice of Madeira wines, including vintage versions.

ENTERTAINMENT

The hottest nightlife and cultural life is in Lisbon: Pick up the monthly listings magazine *Follow Me Lisboa* at the tourist office, as new venues are always opening. Lisbon's nightlife is closely followed by that of Porto, while Coimbra boasts fun, young venues. Most discos and clubs close on Sunday nights and/or Mondays. Outside the big cities, Portugal's entertainment concentrates on the summer months, when seaside nightclubs open their doors to throngs of visitors, particularly in the Algarve.

LISBON

Adega do Ribatejo, Rua do Diario de Noticias 23, Bairro Alto, tel 213 468 343. Attractive tiled interior with a relaxed crowd listening to fado serenades at dinner.

Casa de Linhares, Beco dos Armazens do Linho 1, tel 218 239 6600 or 910 188 118, *casadelinhares.com.* Atmospheric fado restaurant and bar at the base of the Alfama.

Cinco Lounge, Rua Ruben A. Leitão 17A, Príncipe Real, tel 213 424 033 or 914 668 242, *cinco lounge.com.* Arguably the best cocktail bar in Lisbon.

Docas de Alcântara, Doca de Santo Amaro, Alcântara. Former warehouses overlooking the marina, now home to many bars and restaurants.

Park, Calcada do Combro 58, tel 215 914 011. With no signs, this bar on the roof of a Bairro Alto carpark is tricky to find. Amazing views make it memorable.

Pensão Amor, Rua do Alecrim 19, tel 213 143 399, *pensaoamor.pt.* Former well-known city brothel, Pensão Amor retains its air of decadence with intimate lounges and attentive staff.

Portas Largas, Rua da Atalaia 105, Bairro Alto, tel 213 466 379. Attracting a primarily gay crowd, this bar is at the top of the hill.

Red Frog Speakeasy, Rua do Salitre 5A, tel 215 831 120, *redfrog.pt.*

Inspired by the American Prohibition era, with a nod to 1950s and 1960s tropical influences.

Senhor Vinho, Rua do Meio, Lapa 18, tel 213 972 681, *srvinho.com.* More restaurant than club, an elegant setting to listen to nightly fado singers. Excellent wine list.

PORTO

Casa da Musica, Avenida da Boavista 604–610, Porto, tel 220 120 220, *casadamusica.com.* Wide variety of musical events.

Hot Five Jazz & Blues Club, Largo Actor Dias 51, tel 934 328 583. Top musicians play live jazz and blues in a friendly atmosphere.

The Wall, Rua Cândido dos Reis 90, tel 936 916 301. Cool and contemporary bar attracting Porto's hip crowd.

Vinologia, Rua de São João 28–30, tel 910 404 435, *vinologia. pt.* More than 200 port wines available to taste, aided by a knowledgeable staff.

Zenith Lounge, Rua de Serralves 124, Hotel HF Ipanema Park, tel 913 879 404. Great city views from this 17th-floor rooftop bar. Good music, cocktails, and pool complete the package. *(May–Sep.)*

COIMBRA

À Capella, Rua Corpo de Deus, Largo da Vitória, tel 239 833 985, *acapella.com.pt.* This former 14th-century chapel offers a superb setting for live fado shows.

Bar Diligência, Rua Nova 30, tel 239 827 667. One of the oldest fado venues where fado is sung in its Coimbra version.

Garden Bar, Rua Sá de Miranda, tel 239 041 648. Best place in town for a gin and tonic.

ALGARVE

Note: Out of season *(Oct.–May)*, most Algarve nightspots operate limited opening hours; some are only open July–Aug.

Caniço, Aldeamento da Prainha, Praia dos Três Irmãos, Alvor, tel 282 458503, *canicorestaurante.com.* Picture-perfect bar and restaurant nestled into the cliff edge serving cocktails late into the night.

Casino Vilamoura, Praça Casino Vilamoura, Quarteira, tel 289 310 000, *casinovilamoura.solverde.pt.* Gaming machines and tables as well as nightly shows.

Le Club Santa Eulalia, Praia de Santa Eulalia, Albufeira, tel 289 598 000. Bar areas, lounge, dance floor, and a restaurant with veranda overlooking the sea *(Open Fri.–Sat. in Aug.).*

No Solo Água, Marina de Portimão, tel 282 498 180, *nosolo agua.com.* Beach club with occasional live music.

Stevie Ray's Blues Jazz Bar, 9 Rua Sra. da Graça, Lagos, tel 914 923 883. *stevie-rays.com.* Live jazz and blues attracting a slightly older crowd *(Fri.–Sat.).*

ACTIVITIES

From hiking or rock climbing in the Serra de Peneda-Gerês to scuba diving, windsurfing, surfing, canoeing, tennis, and golf, Portugal has something for everyone in the way of physical activities.

Sport Federations

The following organizations are good sources of information on all things related to their sport in Portugal.

Federação Equestre Portuguesa (horseback riding)
Avenida Manuel da Maia 26, 1000-201 Lisbon, tel 218 478 774, *fep.pt*

Federação Portuguesa de Actividades Subaquaticas (scuba diving)
Rua do Alto Lagoal 21A, 2760-003 Caxias, tel 211 910 868, *fpas.pt*

Federação Portuguesa de Canoagem (canoeing)
Rua Manuel Pinto de Lima s/n, Oliveira do Douro, 4430-750 Vila Nova de Gaia, tel 225 432 237, *fpcanoagem.pt*

Federação Portuguesa de Ciclismo (cycling)
Rua de Campolide 237, 1070-030 Lisbon, tel 213 802 140, *uvp-fpc.pt*

Federação Portuguesa de Golfe (golf)
Rua Santa Teresa do Menino 948, Algés, tel 214 123 780, *fpg.pt*

Federação Portuguesa de Surf (surfing)
Avenida Marginal, Edificio Narciso, 2775-604 Praia de Carcavelos, tel 219 228 914, *surfingportugal.com*

Federação Portuguesa de Ténis (tennis)
Rua Actor Chaby Pinheiro 7A, 2795-060 Linda-a-Velha, tel 214 151 356, *tenis.pt*

Federação Portuguesa de Vela (sailing)
Doca de Belém, 1300-038 Lisbon, tel 213 658 500, *fpvela.pt*

Golf

There are some 70 golf courses in mainland Portugal, with the majority in the Algarve (see pp. 212–213). An informative website for this area is *algarvegolf.net;* for all of Portugal try *portugalgolf.pt*. The Lisbon area is well served by the coastal resorts, from Estoril north to Quinta da Marinha (Guincho), and there are more courses south of the Tejo River. Although less concentrated, northern Portugal has its share of courses, and Madeira has three. Here is a selected listing:

Lisbon Area

Clube de Golf do Montado,
Algeruz, 2950 Palmela, tel 265 708 150, *montadoresort.com*
18 holes, par 72
6,961 yards/6,366 m
Architect: Duarte Sottomayor
Surrounded by vineyards and cork tree groves.

Golf do Estoril,
Avenida da República, 2765 Estoril, tel 214 680 054, *clubegolfestoril.com*
18 holes, par 69
5,728 yards/5,238 m
Architect: Mackenzie Ross
There's also a nine-hole course.

Lisbon Sports Club, Casal de Carregueira, 2605-213 Belas, tel 214 310 077, *lisbonclub.com*
18 holes, par 69
5,772 yards/5,278 m
Architect: Hawtree & Sons
One of Portugal's oldest golf courses.

Oitavos Dunes, Quinta da Marinha, Casa do Quinta 25, 2750-004 Cascais, tel 214 860 020, *oitavosdunes.com*
18 holes, par 71
6,893 yards/6,303 m
Architect: Arthur Hills
Links-type holes in woodland with views of the ocean. Considered to be one of the best courses in Portugal.

Penha Longa Clube de Golf,
Caesar Park, Penha Longa, Estrada da Lagoa Azul, Linhó, 2710 Sintra, tel 219 249 031, *penhalonga.com/golf*
18 holes, par 72
6,878 yards/6,290 m
Architect: Robert Trent Jones II
Host of the 1994–95 Portuguese Open Championships. Also has a nine-hole course on property.

Quinta da Beloura, Rua das Sesmarias No. 3, Quinta da Beloura, 2710-692 Sintra, tel 219 106 350, *pestanagolf.com*
18 holes, par 72
5,986 yards/5,474 m
Architect: Rocky Roquemore
One of the more recent courses on the Estoril coast, with views of the Sintra mountains range.

Quinta do Perú Golf Course,
Alameda da Serra 2, 2975-666 Quinta do Conde, tel 212 134 320, *orizontegolf.com*
18 holes, par 72
6,601 yards/6,036 m
Architect: Rocky Roquemore
The Arrábida mountain range acts as a backdrop to this course south of the Tejo River.

Troia Golf, Troia Resort, Troia 7570-789 Carvalhal, tel 265 494 112, *troiaresort.pt*

18 holes, par 72
6,930 yards/6,337 m
Architect: Robert Trent Jones
It is thought to be one of the
most difficult layouts in the
country.

Algarve

Golf Santo Antonio, Vale do
Poço, Budens, 8650-060 Vila do
Bispo, tel 282 690 054, *saresorts.
com*
18 holes, par 72
6,041 yards/5,524 m
Dramatic, rugged course, a
contrast with the usual parkland
layouts of the Algarve.

Monte Rei, Monte Rei Golf &
Country Club, Sesmarias, 8901-
907 Vila Nova de Cacela, tel 281
950 960, *monte-rei.com*
18 holes, par 72
7,182 yards/6,567 m
Architect: Jack Nicklaus
Set in the rolling foothills of the
eastern Algarve with views of
the Atlantic.

Oceanico Old Course, 8126-507
Vilamoura, tel 289 310 333,
oceanicogolf.com
18 holes, par 73
6,754 yards/6,176 m
Architect: Frank Pennink, remodeled by Martin Hawtree
One of Oceanico's seven courses
in the Algarve.

**Pine Cliffs Golf and Country
Club,** Sheraton Algarve at Pine
Cliffs Resort, 8200-912 Albufeira,
tel 289 500 113, *pinecliffs.com*
9 holes, par 32
2,541 yards/2,324 m
Part of the Sheraton Pine Cliffs
Hotel.

Quinta do Lago Norte, Socie-
dade do Golfe da Quinta do Lago,
8135–024 Almancil, tel 289 390
705, *quintadolago.com*
Three 18-hole courses,
all par 72

Not only the Algarve's first golf
course, but also one of the country's largest golf clubs.

San Lorenzo Golf Club, Quinta
do Lago, 8135 Almancil, tel 289
396 522
18 holes, par 72
6,821 yards/6,238 m
Architect: Joseph Lee
This 2,000-acre (809 ha) Quinta
do Lago estate is surrounded by
pine woods and lakes.

Northern & Central Portugal

Amarante Golf Club, Quinta da
Deveza, Fregim, 4600-593 Amarante, tel 255 446 060,
golfedeamarante.com
18 holes, par 68
5,561 yards/5,085 m
Architect: Jorge Santana da Silva

Estela Golf, Lugar Rio Alto, Estela,
4570-242 Póvoa de Varzim,
tel 252 601 567, *estelagolf.pt*
18 holes, par 72
6,890 yards/6,300 m
Architect: Duarte Sottomayor

Golf de Montebelo, 3510-643
Farminhão, Viseu, tel 232 856
464, *golfemontebelo.pt*
18 holes, par 72
6,903 yards/6,312 m
Architects: Mark Stilwell and
Malcolm Kenyon
Mountainous course with excellent views over Serra da Estrela
and Serra do Caramulo.

Praia del Rey, Avenida D. Afonso
Henriques, Vale de Janelas, 2510-
451 Óbidos, tel 262 905 005,
praia-del-rey.com
18 holes, par 73
7,072 yards/6,467 m
Architect: Cabell B. Robinson

Quinta da Barca Golf Course,
Quinta da Barca, Gemeses 4740-
476 Esposende, tel 253 966 723,
golfebarca.com

9 holes, par 31
2,200 yards/2,012 m
Architect: Jorge Santana de Silva

Madeira

Palheiro Golf, Rua do Balancal
29, 9060-414 Funchal, tel 291 790
125, *palheirogolf.com*
18 holes, par 72
6,655 yards/6,086 m
Architect: Cabell B. Robinson

Guided Activities

Algarve Birdwatching, tel 912
824 053, *algarvebirdman.com*
Expert guide Simon Wates
offers well-informed and well-
organized bird-watching trips
across the region.

Turaventur, Caminho Municipal
1182-2, Senhor dos Aflitos, Évora,
tel 266 743 134 or 966 758 940,
turaventur.com
Dynamic Alentejo adventure
tourism company organizing
guided treks, mountain biking,
and kayaking.

Walkin'Sagres, Aldeamento de S.
Vicente, Bl. A-1o C, 8650 Sagres,
tel 925 545 515, *walkinsagres.com*
Informative family hikes with
enthusiastic guide Ana Carla
through the Parque Natural
Sudoeste Alentejano e Costa
Vicentina.

Horseback Riding

Portugal has a special feeling for
horses and is the home of the
Lusitano breed. This agile, hot-
blooded horse has been bred in
the Ribatejo region for hundreds
of years and is a mixture of the
Arab and English Thoroughbred.
Visitors will find stables easily, in particular in the Algarve,
Alentejo, and Ribatejo. A full
list of riding stables in Portugal
can be found at *cavalonet.com*
(*horsesinportugal.com* is the English
version).

Albufeira Riding Centre, CP The Stables 151H, Vale Navio, Albufeira, tel 961 269 526, *albufeiraridingcentre.com*
Offers a range of activities including lessons and treks of 30 minutes to a full day.

Centro Hípico Quinta da Marinha, Quinta da Marinha Casa 25, 2750-004 Cascais, tel 214 860 006, *quintadamarinhahipico.com*

Ecotura, Lugar do Queimadelo Castro Laboreiro, Melgaço (Peneda-Gerês National Park), tel 967 442 217, *ecotura.com*
An introduction to the small Portuguese Garrano horse, which lives wild in the Peneda-Gerês National Park, and horseback riding for the whole family.

Escola Portuguesa de Arte Equestre, Palácio Nacional de Queluz, tel 219 237 300, *parques desintra.pt, artesquestre.pt*
This is the sharpest show of Portuguese dressage every Saturday at 11 a.m., May through Oct.

Morgado Lusitano, Quinta da Portela, Cabeço da Rosa—EN 116, 2615-365 Alverca do Ribatejo, tel 219 936 520, *morgadolusitano.pt*

Classical dressage on superb stallions near Lisbon.

Solar do Espírito Santo, Rua do Espírito Santo 25/27, Azinhaga do Ribatejo, Golegã, tel 249 957 252 or 919 343 391, *solarespiritosanto.com*
Horseback riding trips, courses, and equestrian vacations at a luxury estate in the heartland of the Lusitanian horse.

Tiffany's Riding Centre, Vale Grifo, 1677 E. Almádena, 8600-102 Luz, Lagos, Algarve, tel 282 697 395, *teamtiffanys.com*
Riding center for beginners to advanced, a couple hours to a full day.

Tennis

Tennis is the third most played sport in Portugal. The center of this sport is the Estoril Tennis Club, where the annual Open Clay Court Tournament is held. Other important centers can be found in Porto, Coimbra, Évora, and the Algarve. Some clubs offer special packages that include accommodations and coaching. Courts range from all-weather artificial grass to American clay.

Water Sports

Along the Atlantic coast, the obvious sports are windsurfing, sailing, surfing (see p. 141 for more surf schools), and scuba diving. Water temperatures range from 61° to 71°F (16°–22°C); wet suits are advisable. Portugal is recognized as the best place in Europe for surfing; Guincho beach (near Cascais) is the most challenging thanks to its considerable undertow. Other popular places are Aveiro farther north and the Algarve's Costa Vicentina.

Algarve Watersport, *algarvewatersport.com.*
Camps, lessons, and equipment rental for surfing, kitesurfing, and windsurfing in western Algarve.

Carcavelos Surf School, Windsurfcafé, Praia de Carcavelos, Carcavelos, tel 962 850 497 or 966 131 203, *carcavelossurfschool.com.*
Surf lessons and equipment for all levels.

Haliotis, Casal Ponte 2525-376 Atouguia da Baleia, Peniche, tel 262 781 160 or 913 054 926, *haliotis.pt*
Scuba diving around Peniche and the Berlengas.

LANGUAGE GUIDE

The Portuguese themselves are the first to admit that they have a fiendish language, so they will make every attempt to speak yours. As a Romance language based on Latin, Portuguese shares common roots with Spanish, French, and Italian, but all similarity stops there. Pronunciation is the big stumbling block, so be ready to mouth "sh" and "ow" sounds every other word. Masculine and feminine subjects and words have agreements: The most obvious that you will encounter is the word for "thank you": *obrigado* (for a man) and *obrigada* (for a woman).

English is widely spoken in tourist areas, in hotels, upscale restaurants, and in pharmacies. In more remote places, among older generations, French is often the only foreign language spoken. Spanish is understood but few people feel like using it as their rivalry goes back for centuries.

Basic Words & Phrases

yes/no	*sim/não*
please	*faz favor*
thank you	*obrigado/a*
You're welcome	*De nada*
good morning	*bom dia*
hi	*olá*
good afternoon	*boa tarde*
goodbye/bye	*adeus/tchao*
See you	*Até logo*
Excuse me/sorry	*Desculpe*
How are you?	*Como está?*
very well, thank you	
	muito bem, obrigado/a
My name is	*Chamo me*
I'm from the USA	
	Sou dos Estados Unidos
Do you speak English?	*Fala inglês?*

Getting Around

Where is?	*Onde está?*
Where are?	*Onde estão?*
When?	*Quando?*
Turn left	*Vire à esquerda*
Turn right	*Vire à direita*
straight on	*sempre emifrente*
opposite	*em frente*
traffic lights	*semáforo*
train station	*estação ferroviária*
metro station	*estação de metro*
market	*mercado*
Do you have?	*Tem?*
a single room	*um quarto individual*
a double room	*um quarto de casal*
a twin-bed room	*um quarto duplo*
with bathroom	*com casa de banho*
Can I see the room?	
	Posso ver o quarto?

Time

What time?	*A que horas?*
leave/arrive	*parte/chega*
morning	*manhã*
afternoon	*tarde*
When do you open/close?	
	Quando abrem/fecham?
yesterday	*ontem*
today	*hoje*
tomorrow	*amanhã*
now	*agora*
later	*mais tarde*
Monday	*segunda feira*
Tuesday	*terça feira*
Wednesday	*quarta feira*
Thursday	*quinta feira*
Friday	*sexta feira*
Saturday	*sábado*
Sunday	*domingo*

Shopping

Do you sell?	*Vendem?*
How much is it?	*Quanto custa?*
Can I look at it?	*Posso ver?*
open/closed	*aberto/ encerrado*
Do you take credit cards?	
	Aceitam cartões de crédito?
I'll take this	*Levo isto*

Numbers

1	*um*
2	*dois*
3	*tres*
4	*quatro*
5	*cinco*
6	*seis*
7	*sete*
8	*oito*
9	*nove*
10	*dez*
11	*onze*
12	*doze*
13	*treze*
14	*catorze*
15	*quinze*
16	*dezasseis*
17	*dezassete*
18	*dezoito*
19	*dezanove*
20	*vinte*
30	*trinta*
40	*quarenta*
100	*cem*
1,000	*mil*

Menu Reader

I'd like	*Queria*
breakfast	*pequeno almoço*
lunch	*almoço*
dinner	*jantar*
the check please	*a conta se faz favor*
daily special	*prato do dia*
half portion	*meia dose*
spoon	*colher*
fork	*garfo*
knife	*faca*

Food Basics

açucar	sugar
azeite	olive oil
azeitonas	olives
limão	lemon
manteiga	butter
pão	bread
pimenta	pepper
piri-piri	chili sauce
queijo	cheese
sal	salt
vinagre	vinegar

Cooking Methods

assado	roast
bem passado	well cooked
cozido	boiled
estufado	stewed/steamed
frito	fried
grelhado	grilled
mal passado	rare
no carvão	barbecued
no espeto	on the spit
no forno	baked/in the oven

Peixe e Mariscos/ Fish & Seafood

arroz de marisco	seafood rice
arroz de polvo	octopus rice
atum	tuna
bacalhau	salted cod
caldeirada de peixe	fish stew
camarões	shrimps
cataplana	shellfish and ham cooked in a sealed pan
chocos	cuttlefish
espadarte	swordfish
gambas	prawns
lagosta	lobster
lampreia	lampreys (baby eels)
linguado	sole
lulas	squid
pargo	sea bream
robalo	sea bass
rodovalho	halibut
salmão	salmon
salmonete	red mullet
sardinhas	sardines
truta	trout

Carne e Aves/ Meat & Poultry

bife	steak (not necessarily beef)
borrego	lamb
cabrito	kid goat
carne assada	roast beef
chouriço	spicy smoked sausage
churrasco	spit-roasted pork
coelho	rabbit
costeleta	cutlet/chop
cozido	meat & vegetable stew
entrecosto	rump steak
feijoada	bean stew with rice and meats
fiambre	cooked ham
fígado	liver
frango	chicken
leitão assado	roast suckling pig
lombo	pork fillet
pato	duck
porco	pork
salsicha	sausage
tripas	tripe
vaca	beef
vitela	veal

Legumes/Vegetables

alface	lettuce
alho	garlic
batatas	potatoes
cebola	onion
cenoura	carrot
cogumelos	mushrooms
ervilhas	green peas
espargos	asparagus
espinafres	spinach
favas	broad beans
feijão	dried beans
lentilhas	lentils
pepino	cucumber
pimentos	peppers
salada/mista	salad/mixed
tomate	tomato

Ovos/Eggs

cozido	hard boiled
escalfado	poached
estrelado	fried
mexido	scrambled
omelete	omelet
quente	boiled

Fruitas/Fruit

alperces	apricots
ameixas	plums
amendoas	almonds
ananas	pineapple
bananas	bananas
figos	figs
framboesas	raspberries
laranjas	oranges
limões	lemons
maças	apples
meloa	melon
morangos	strawberries
pessegos	peaches
uvas	grapes

INDEX 265

INDEX

Bold page numbers indicate
illustrations.
CAPS indicates thematic categories.

A

Abrantes 153
Activities 260–262
Adrão 107
Afife 102
Afonso, Jorge 41
Afonso, José 42
Afonso Henriques, King of Portugal
20, 22–23, 52, 53, 94, 95, 97, 117,
133, 138
Afonso II, King of Portugal 183
Afonso III, King of Portugal 23
Afonso IV, King of Portugal 121
Afonso V, King of Portugal 24, 149
Afonso VI, King of Portugal 160
Alandroal 192
Albufeira **204,** 205, 254
Albuquerque, Afonso de 24
Alcácer do Sal 11, 196
Alcobaça 9, 16, 22–23, 36, 70, 121,
145, 145–147, **146–147**
Aldeia da Venda 193
Alentejo 11, 17, 173–198
Alentejo's Coast **196,** 196–197, 256
Beja, Serpa, and Moura 36, **194,**
194–195, 251, 253
climate 17
Estremoz 11, **184,** 184–185,
251, 256
Évora and around 11, **176,** 176–
181, **178, 181,** 251–252
Guadiana Valley **192,** 192–193
hotels and restaurants 251–253
megaliths 17, 20, **20–21**
Portalegre and Serra de São
Mamede **188,** 188–191,
252–253
shopping 256, 258
surfing 141
Vila Viçosa and Borba **186,**
186–187, 192, 253–254
Algar Seco 205
Algarve 199–218
activities 261
Cabo de São Vicente 215, **216,**
216–217
Castro Marim 151
climate 17
Costa Vicentina 17, 218, **218,** 254
entertainment 259
Faro and Coastal Algarve 202–
205, **204,** 254
golf **212,** 212–213
hotels and restaurants 253–255
Inland Algarve 206–211, **207, 211**
Lagos **2–3,** 214, **214,** 216
Sagres 141, 215, **215,** 254–255
shopping 258
touradas (bullfights) 17
Aljezur 218

Almancil 207, **207,** 208
Almeida 127
Alqueva, Lago **192,** 193
Alte 209
Alter do Chão 11, 190
Alvito 11
Amarante 10, 18, 89, **89,** 241, 256
Amoreira 218
Anta de Pêra do Moço 126
Antunes, António Lobo 45, 237
Aqueduto dos Pegões 152
Architecture 34–40
Arcos de Valdevez 106
Arraiolos 256
Arrifana 141, 218
Arruda, Diogo de 36, 64–65, 152, 181
Arruda, Francisco de 37, 64–65, 177
Arruda, Miguel de 38
Arruda dos Vinhos 155
Arts 34–46
Aveiro **16,** 114–115, 245, 256
Azenhas do Mar 169
Azulejos (painted tiles) **12, 22,** 34, **70,**
70–71, **71,** 72, **111, 155, 207**

B

Bacalhau (cod) 25, 32, 33
Badoca Safari Park 197
Ballooning 190
Balsemão 87–88
Barcelos **73,** 110
Barra 115
Barragem da Idanha 131
Basílica, Mafra 156–157
Batalha 9, 16, 36–37, **37,** 38, **135,**
143, 143–144, 247
Beja 36, 194, **194,** 251
Belhoa 193
Beliche 215, 217
Belmonte 134
Berlengas 142
Bicycling 180
Bird-watching 209, 261
Bisalhães 256
Boca da Encumeada 225
Bom Jesus do Monte 98, **99**
Bombarral 155
Borba 187
Bordalo Pinheiro, Columbano 41
Bordalo Pinheiro, Rafael 41, 148
Braga 18, 21, 39, **96,** 96–98, 241–242
Bragança **108,** 108–109, 242–243
Buarcos 134
Buçaco 121
Bullfights (*touradas*) 17, 18
Burgau 216

C

Cabo Carvoeiro 142
Cabo da Roca 166, **166**
Cabo de São Vicente 215, **216,** 216–217
Cabo Espichel 170
Cabo Girão 224, **224**
Cabo Sardão **196,** 197

Cabral, Pedro Álvares 24, 134, 154
Caetano, Marcelo 31
Caldas da Rainha 148, **148,** 247, 256
Caldas de Manteigas 10, 129
Caldas de Monchique 211, **211**
Camacha **226,** 227
Câmara de Lobos 224
Caminha 102
Camões, Luís Vaz de 44, 61, 237
Caniçal 227
Car accidents 237
Carcavelos 141
Carminho (fado singer) 42, 58, 59
Carmona, Óscar 30
Carnaval 18, 208
Carr, William (later Viscount
Beresford) 29
Carrapateira 218
Carrasqueira 172
Carrilho da Graça, João Luís 40
Carthaginians 20
Carvoeiro 205
Casa Colombo–Museu do Porto
Santo, Vila Baleira 230
Casa da Música, Porto 81
Casa das Histórias–Paula Rego,
Cascais 167
Casa Museu Bissaya Barreto, Coimbra
120
Casa-Museu Dr. Anastácio Gonçalves,
Lisbon 68
Cascais 17, 166–167, 247–248
Castelo Branco 130–131
Castelo de Vide 11, 191
Castro Marim 151
Celorico da Beira 129
Celts 20, 34
Centro 16–17, 111–134
Aveiro and environs **16, 114,**
114–115, 245, 256
Castelo Branco and around **130,**
130–131
Coimbra and around 9, 16, 34,
58, **112, 116,** 116–121, **119,**
120, 245–246, 256, 259
Conímbriga 122, **122**
Guarda 125, **125,** 246
hotels and restaurants 245–247
Serra da Estrela 10, **128,** 128–
129, 246–247
Serra da Marofa **126,** 126–127
shopping 257–258
Viseu 10, **111,** 123–124, **124,**
247, 256
Chanterene, Nicolas de 38, 61, 97,
119–120, 125, 161
Chaves 110, 243
CHURCHES
etiquette 236
Basílica, Mafra 156–157
Ermida de Nossa Senhora dos
Remédios, Lisbon 55
Igreja da Graça, Santarém 154

ILLUSTRATIONS CREDITS

All photographs by Tino Soriano unless otherwise noted below:

National Geographic
TRAVELER
Portugal
FOURTH EDITION

Since 1888, the National Geographic Society has funded more than 14,000 research, exploration, and preservation projects around the world. National Geographic Partners distributes a portion of the funds it receives from your purchase to National Geographic Society to support programs including the conservation of animals and their habitats.

National Geographic Partners, LLC
1145 17th Street NW
Washington, DC 20036-4688 USA

Get closer to National Geographic explorers and photographers, and connect with our global community. Join us today at nationalgeographic.com/join

For rights or permissions inquiries, please contact National Geographic Books
Subsidiary Rights: bookrights@natgeo.com

Artwork by Maltings Partnership, Derby, England (pp. 62–63 & 146–147).

NATIONAL GEOGRAPHIC and Yellow Border Design are trademarks of the National Geographic Society, used under license.

Fourth edition edited by White Star s.r.l.
Licensee of National Geographic Partners, LLC.
Iceigeo, Milan (Alice Avanzi, Cynthia Anne Koeppe, Max Rankenburg)

The information in this book has been carefully checked and to the best of our knowledge is accurate. However, details are subject to change, and the publisher cannot be responsible for such changes, or for errors or omissions. Assessments of sites, hotels, and restaurants are based on the author's subjective opinions, which do not necessarily reflect the publisher's opinion.

ISBN: 978-88-544-1709-0

Printed by
Rotolito S.p.A. - Seggiano di Pioltello (MI) - Italy

NATIONAL GEOGRAPHIC TRAVELER
THE BEST GUIDES BY YOUR SIDE

M

IRELAND

PERU

VIETNAM

AVA
and

N

NAL
GRAPHIC

hic Partners, LLC